the
LINUX
KERNEL
book

the
LINUX
KERNEL
book

Rémy Card
Éric Dumas
Franck Mével

Translated by
Chris Skrimshire

JOHN WILEY & SONS
Chichester · New York · Weinheim · Brisbane · Singapore · Toronto

Translation from the French language edition of *Programmation Linux 2.0* by Rémy Card, Éric Dumas and Franck Mével © 1997 Éditions Eyrolles, Paris, France

English language edition published in 1998 by John Wiley & Sons Ltd,

Baffins Lane, Chichester,
West Sussex PO19 1UD, England

National   01243 779777
International (+44) 1243 779777
e-mail (for orders and customer service enquiries):
cs-books@wiley.co.uk
Visit our Home Page on http://www.wiley.co.uk
or http://www.wiley.com

Reprinted December 1998

Other Wiley Editorial Offices

John Wiley & Sons, Inc., 605 Third Avenue,
New York, NY 10158-0012, USA

WILEY-VCH Verlag GmbH, Pappelallee 3,
D-69469 Weinheim, Germany

Jacaranda Wiley Ltd, 33 Park Road, Milton,
Queensland 4064, Australia

John Wiley & Sons (Asia) Pte Ltd, 2 Clementi Loop #02-01,
Jin Xing Distripark, Singapore 129809

John Wiley & Sons (Canada) Ltd, 22 Worcester Road,
Rexdale, Ontario M9W 1L1, Canada

British Library Cataloging in Publication Data

A catalogue record for this book is available from the British Library

ISBN 0 471 98141 9

Produced from Camera Ready Copy supplied by Chris Skrimshire.
Printed and bound in Great Britain by Bookcraft (Bath) Ltd, Midsomer Norton, Somerset.
This book is printed on acid-free paper responsibly manufactured from sustainable forestry, in which at least two trees are planted for each one used for paper production.

Contents

Foreword

Hi Dear Reader,

The book you have in your hand will hopefully help you understand the Linux operating system kernel better, and you can delve into the strange and wonderful world of systems programming. Because it really *is* a strange and wonderful world, full of subtle details ranging from how to control the physical hardware to how to manage multiple different users at the same time with limited resources.

After more than five years, I certainly still enjoy working on the Linux kernel, and hope that others will find it as fascinating as I have.

Linus Torvalds
University of Helsinki
12/9/1996

Preface

Over the last few years the Linux operating system has become adopted more and more in industrial and academic environments. This Unix clone, whose power and stability allow it to stand alongside other commercial operating systems, possesses certain particular features which make it very interesting. Furthermore, the free dissemination of Linux source code on the Internet has widely contributed to the popularisation of Linux, and this makes it an ideal subject to study.

LAYOUT OF THE BOOK

This book attempts to present the different facets of Linux 2.0 from the standpoint of the developer, and to analyse its kernel, which forms the centre of the operating system. The book not only covers the Unix programming system, but also explains the internal working of the kernel.

The book comprises 13 chapters which cover most system aspects, with the exception of the management of network protocols, which would require a separate volume to itself.

The first three chapters contain introductory material:

- The first deals with the origins of the Linux system functionality, and contains a list of references.
- The second briefly surveys the different components of operating systems, and Linux in particular. It explains the ideas of kernel mode and user mode, and gives details of the system call mechanism. It also contains a description of the organisation of kernel sources, and some references are given to the configuration of basic Linux tools.
- The third chapter describes the development tools available for Linux, and introduces the ideas of system programming.

The following chapters describe the Linux system in detail, each one describing the system interface associated with the concept presented, and then describing the implementation of this concept in the Linux kernel.

- Chapters 4 and 5 deal with process and signal management.
- Chapter 6 deals with file management. The implementation description covers virtual file systems and gives two examples of file systems: Ext2, and /proc.
- Chapter 7 covers input and output to peripherals and analyses in particular the printer driver and the disk memory manager.

- Chapter 7 covers input and output to peripherals and analyses in particular the printer driver and the disk memory manager.
- Chapter 8 presents an important concept in current systems, the management of virtual memory.
- Chapter 9 is concerned with management of terminals.
- Chapters 10 and 11 describe communications between processes, pipelines and IPC system V.
- The two final chapters deal with the dynamic loading of modules into the kernel, and useful system administration functions.

Finally, four appendices describe the use of Linux development tools (C compiler, debugger, *make,* and library management tools).

Each chapter is split into several sections: the first of these presents the concepts in question, as well as the system calls involved, whilst the following sections give details of the kernel functions, by describing the data structures used and the internal Linux function.

This format allows the reader to proceed from the general concepts through to the implementation detail, and the book can thus be followed in sequential manner by chapters, but also in other ways according to requirements, time or inclination.

The material is illustrated by programme examples (written in C), diagrams and tables, providing a clear and comprehensive presentation. A list of references on operating systems and existing technical documentation on Linux is provided at the end of the book.

The book comes with a CD-ROM containing a copy of Red Hat Linux 5.0 together with kernel documentation and source programmes. This material is described in the following section.

INTENDED READERSHIP

This book is aimed at system developers, whether they be students, computer professionals or information technology researchers, and it can be used as support material in systems courses, as a programming development aid, or to assist kernel development. The structure of the book makes it accessible to a varied readership: the beginner may make an initial pass through it by just reading the first parts of the chapters, whilst the experienced 'hacker' (system programmer) may concentrate more on the internal kernel operations.

It should be noted that a knowledge of the C language and its standard library is required in order to follow the book. In addition, the reader should be familiar with general concepts of operating systems, and of Unix in particular, in order to understand the examples and the internal kernel operations.

Because these sections are the most demanding, it is recommended that the kernel source code is studied at the same time.

CONVENTIONS USED

All system calls presented in a chapter are listed at the beginning of the chapter:

System calls described

call1, call2, ...

Tables are used in order to simplify the description of structures and linkages presented. Tables are also used to list errors associated with system calls, for lists of constants and for instruction macros.

Standard forms of the standard C library functions and the different system calls presented are all shown in an **arial bold 8pt** font. The arial bold font is also used for the names of types, structures and functions.

System call names, library functions, and commands are given in italics, and program statements and code examples use a teletype font.

THANKS

The writing of this book would not have been possible without the work of numerous people.

We thank all of the Linux developers, especially the foremost among these, Linus Torvalds. Without them, the operating system would not have seen the light of day.

We thank Benjamin Bayart for his invaluable assistance in the layout of the original French edition (LaTex), and we particularly wish to thank the people who agreed to carry out the unrewarding process of re-reading the document and who greatly participated in improving the contents through their numerous suggestions and constructive criticisms: Eric Commelin, Pierre David, Pierre Ficheux, Thomas Quinot, Pierre-Guillaume Raverdy, and Stéphan Voisin.

Finally, we record our thanks to Julien Simon who contributed greatly to the design and structuring of the book.

It is to be expected that a book such as this might contain errors and inaccuracies. We invite all readers to send us the comments, suggestions and corrections by e-mail to:- **livre-linux@Linux.EU.Org**.

Rémy Card (Remy.Card@linux.org)
Éric Dumas (dumas@Linux.EU.Org)
Franck Mével (mevel@Linux.EU.Org)

Linux version 2.2

FOREWORD

The original French edition of this book was published at the end of 1996, and the Spanish edition in October 1997. However, Linux has not stood still, and kernel development has continued since then. At the time of the French publication, the latest stable version was 2.0.26. Today, version 2.0.33 is available but the development series (2.1) is at version 2.1.73 (December 1997). It is understood that the next 'stable' version will be 2.2 (but it could be 3.0 - it isn't clear), and this is expected to appear in a few months time (according to information available at the time of this first English publication).

This short chapter briefly covers the major kernel enhancements since the version 2.0.26, and those anticipated in the next stable version.

NEW ENHANCEMENTS TO THE KERNEL

Support for binaries

In Linux 2.1, the kernel can only be compiled as ELF (Executable and Linking Format), although the old a.out binary format. A new kernel option (**BINFMT_MISC**) has been added, allowing wrapper-driven binary formats to be plugged into the kernel.

File systems

The old file system EXT has been removed, and the file systems ROM and Coda have been added. A new filesystem feature (autofs) which allows filesystems to be mounted automatically has also been added.
[WWW site http://www.coda.cs.cmu.edu contains details about the Coda file system].

New files have been added to the /proc directory, including /proc/swap, which contains partitions and files used in swapping. The whole buffer cache and dcache system has been re-written, and NFS has been reshaped.

Memory Management System

There is a new memory management design, and the kernel no longer uses x86 segmentation to access user mode.

Loadable modules

The whole system of loadable modules has been re-written. Now, `register_symtab` is no longer necessary, and this function is carried out automatically.

Several new drivers have been added, including IPv6, IDE, SCSI, network drivers, and various peripheral devices. However, as the book concentrates on internal functioning of the kernel as well as the external (library) part, driver and network aspects are not covered in detail.

DEVELOPER INTERFACE

The developer interface for system calls has not really changed. The major enhancement is the new libc library , called GNU libc, and the first 'stable' release to use this is Red Hat Linux 5.0 (see the CD-ROM enclosed with this book or visit http://www.redhat.com). A few new system calls have been added (for example, `poll`).

The aim of the new library is to be usable with any platform running Linux (Intel, Sparc, Alpha, Mips, …). More details are to be found in the 'Glibc2-HOWTO'. The use of this new library should make source code more portable between operating systems. The GNU-libc includes some external libraries, for example the *pthread* library. This will allow the developer to create applications using Posix threads.

Information contained in the current edition concerning C development, system calls, and library functions, which is generally contained in the first part of each chapter, should in most cases be valid even for future kernel implementations.

KERNEL INTERNALS

This edition is aimed primarily at users working with the 2.0 kernel. Newer kernels (2.1, 2.2) incorporate several modifications, principally in the file system, and memory and process management. Specific elements, including dcache entry and loadable modules, have been re-written from scratch.

The sections in the present edition which analyse internal structures and internal functions will not be completely correct with respect to the new forthcoming Linux versions. However, this is almost inevitable given the speed of change of Linux. Users who have followed changes to the kernel should be able to ascertain which elements have changed. Specific information on these changes is to be found at the website http://www.linuxhq.com.

CD-ROM contents

The CD-ROM supplied with this book was created in February 1998. This CD-ROM conforms to ISO 9660, however it also makes use of Microsoft specifications.

The Microsoft CD-ROM recording specifications, known as 'Joliet' are an extension to ISO 9660, and allow filenames of up to 64 Unicode characters. This Joliet CD-ROM actually contains two file systems: the first complying with ISO 9660 to ensure full compatibility with all other systems; the second, currently only readable by Windows 95.

This CD-ROM contains:

The Red Hat Linux 5.0 (Hurricane) distribution, which includes the source code and the x386 architecture.

DIRECTORY STRUCTURE OF THE CD-ROM

Directory	Details
Doc	Various FAQs and HOWTOs
Dosutils	MS/DOS Utilities
Images	Installation utilities
Misc	Source files, install trees
Redhat	Distribution version for the x86 architecture
SRPMS	Source programs forming part of the distribution

Files	
Copying	Copyright Information
Readme	README File
RPM-PGP-	PGP Signature for packages from Red Hat

Installation is carried out after creating *boot* floppy disks. These may be created from the images by the *rawrite* command (available in the directory *dosutils*) in MS/DOS or by the *dd* command in Unix.

Once the *boot* disk has been created, it simply needs to be inserted in the drive and the machine re-started. This will then launch the installation.

1

Linux: Introduction

Linux, Linux, Linux, ... where did this name come from? Before tackling the minutiae of this operating system and its kernel, a brief look at its history and conception are called for. Indeed the story of Linux is particularly original in the field of operating systems. In presenting this account, the kernel functionality is revealed and a list of references given.

The story of Linux began in Finland in 1991 when a certain Linus B. Torvalds *(torvalds@transmeta.com)*, then a student at the university of Helsinki, bought himself a PC equipped with a 386 processor in order to study how it worked. Since MS/DOS did not fully exploit the properties of the 386 (in *protected* mode for example), Linus used another commercial operating system: *Minix*, developed mainly by Andrew Tanenbaum. The Minix system was miniature Unix system.

Driven by the limitations of the system, Linus started to re-write certain parts of the software in order to add functionality, and features. He then broadcast his results freely by means of the Internet under the title of Linux, a contraction of Linus and Unix. And so Linux was born! The first version of Linux, called version 0.01, was sent out in August 1991.

This first version was what may be thought of as embryonic. There was not even an official announcement. The first official version was published on October 5th 1991 (version 0.02). It allowed a few GNU programs to be run, such as **bash, gcc** etc, ... but not much else. These first versions were very limited (Linux 0.01 could only run under Minix!). However, the fact that the source codes were widely disseminated helped the system to develop quickly. Over the years, the number of developers has continued to grow. Right at the beginning, just a few enthusiasts noticed the system and became interested. Today, Linux is developed by dozens of people scattered all over the world, who for the most part have never met each other[1].

The role played by the World Wide Web is important because it facilitated a rapid expansion of the system. Indeed, one can imagine a developer installing Linux on his machine and finding an bug, fixing it and sending a source file to Linus. A few days later (sometimes even a few minutes later) the upgraded kernel can be broadcast on the Net.

Although the first versions of Linux were relatively unstable (how many times must the system have had to be re-booted!), the first version claimed to be stable (1.0) was made public in around March 1994. The version number associated with the kernel has a particular meaning because it is linked to the development cycle. In fact the evolution of Linux has proceed by a succession of two phases:

- A development phase: here the kernel is not reliable and the process is to add functionality to it, to optimise it and to try new ideas. This phase gives rise to odd-numbered version numbers, such as 1.1, 1.3, etc. This is the time when the maximum amount of work is done on the kernel.
- A stabilisation phase: where the aim is to produce as stable a kernel as possible. In this case, only minor adjustments and modifications are made. The version numbers of so-called stable kernels are even, such as 1.0, 1.2, and more recently, 2.0.

Nowadays, Linux is entirely a Unix system. It is stable, but continues to evolve. Not only is it found controlling the latest peripheral devices on the market (flash memory, optical disks, etc.) but its performance is also comparable to certain commercial Unix systems, and is even superior on certain points. Finally, if Linux has for a long time remained confined to university environments (often because of access to the Internet, which only universities have the facilities for), it is now starting to become adopted in industrial firms. Indeed, its power and flexibility, and the fact that it is free, means that it is beginning to interest a growing number of companies.

At the present time, the latest stable version is version 2.0, and it is this version that is covered in this book.

1.2
DESCRIPTION OF LINUX
AND ITS FUNCTIONALITY

Linux was originally conceived as a freely distributed Unix clone operating on PCs equipped with 386, 486 or more advanced processors. Although it was originally developed for the x86 architecture, it can now operate on other platforms such as

---

1 Approximately 80 people contributed to version 1.0, but there are more than 190 developers registered as working on version 2.0.

Alpha, Sparc, certain 68000 platforms such as Atari and Amiga, certain MIPS machines, and Power PCs.

Linux is a Unix implementation conforming to POSIX (Portable Operating System Interface) specifications, but is equipped with certain extensions proper to Unix System V and BSD. This makes it very easy to transport code from applications written for other Unix systems.

POSIX concerns documents produced by the IEEE and standardised by ANSI and the ISO. The aim of POSIX is to provide a portable source code. Linux 2.0 conforms to the POSIX.1 standard as well as supporting some other calls defined in POSIX.4 (see [Lewine, 1991], and [Gallmeister, 1995]).

Linux code is entirely original, and is not in any way proprietary. The source programs are distributed freely under the GPL licence, which is the general public licence GNU.

The Linux operating system functions are numerous and they exploit the capability of modern Unix systems in the following ways:

- multi-process, multi-processors: more than one program can be executed at a time, whether using one or several processors,
- multiple platforms: (see above),
- multi-user: as with all Unix systems, Linux allows several users to work on the same machine at the same time,
- supports inter-process communication (Pipes, IPC, Sockets),
- manages different control messages,
- terminal management conforming to the POSIX standard. Linux also supports pseudo-terminals as well as process control,
- supports a wide range of peripheral devices such as sound cards, graphics interfaces, networks, SCSI, etc.
- buffer cache: a memory area reserved to buffer inputs and outputs from different processes,
- demand paging memory management: a page is not loaded unless it is needed in memory,
- dynamic and shared libraries: dynamic libraries are only loaded when they are needed and their code is shared if several applications are using them,
- file systems which can equally well manage Linux file partitions used by filesystems such as Ext2 as partitions having other formats (MS-DOS, ISO9660 etc.),
- support of TCP/IP and other network protocols.

Above all, Linux is a complete and powerful Unix system, and can easily be implemented. In addition, its widespread public use is helping it to evolve rapidly. Finally, set up procedures enabling straightforward installation of the system have made it popular among users.

1.3
MANY THANKS
INTERNET!

Linux has become as popular as it has thanks to the fact that its source codes have been freely distributed without charge on the global Internet. Indeed, the net has wiped out distances between developers, and e-mail has allowed them to rapidly and readily discuss their work between them. Ftp sites have also been of great help in spreading source codes and development tools.

At the present time, Linux developers tend to use Usenet news groups as well as electronic mail. Thus there are now many e-mail distribution lists dealing with quite a wide range of topics in the Linux development arena.

There are several of the lists of developers which are open to all. It is therefore easy to discuss problems encountered, but also enhancements that can be made, and new functions to add to the kernel, and so on. Some of the relevant e-mail addresses are given in section 4.

1.4
REFERENCES

There follows a non-exhaustive list of references and links that users and developers may freely consult: they contain rich sources of information on numerous documents.

Reference Books

An extensive list of references can be found at the back of the book, of which the vast majority are still current. However, three works in particular should be cited:

- the work by Beck (Beck et al. 1996) detailing the internal functioning of the kernel, though for version 1.2 of Linux,
- Welsh and Kaufman (1995) is the reference work for new users and for system administrators using Linux,
- finally, Kirch (1995) may be cited as the reference book dealing with network configuration and installation aspects of Linux.

Usenet forums

- **comp.os.linux.advocacy**: advantages of Linux compared to other operating systems
- **comp.os.linux.announce**: bulletin board for the Linux community (moderated newsgroup)
- **comp.os.linux.answers**: distribution of information documents such as FAQ, How to's etc. (moderated group)
- **comp.os.linux.development.apps**: writing and porting of applications under Linux

- **comp.os.linux.development.system** : kernel development
- **comp.os.linux.hardware** : compatibility and management of peripherals
- **comp.os.linux.networking** : Linux and the network
- **comp.os.linux.setup** : installation and system administration
- **comp.os.linux.x**: X Windows under Linux
- **comp.os.linux.misc**: topics not covered in other groups.

Electronic mail lists

Several mailing lists exist covering Linux topics. Their proliferation does not allow a complete list to be given, but the main ones are as follows:

- **linux-kernel@vger.rutgers.edu**: intended for developers,
- **linux-scsi@vger.rutgers.edu**: concentrating on problems and development of SCSI controllers,
- **linux-gcc@vger.rutgers.edu**: concerning standard C libraries as well as gcc,
- **linux-security@tarsier.cv.nrao.edu**: dealing with security problems,
- **linux-alert@tarsier.cv.nrao.edu**: distribution list of warning messages.

FTP sites

All the tools necessary for effective Linux operation are found on two main sites:

- **sunsite.unc.edu:/pub/Linux**
- **tsx-11.mit.edu:/pub/linux**

Download of kernels can be made from the following sites:

- **ftp.cs.helsinki.fi:/pub/Software/Linux/Kernel**
- **ftp.funet.fi:/pub/Linux/PEOPLE/Linus**
- **ftp.kernel.org**

However, numerous mirror sites of the above exist almost anywhere. The French main one of these is : **ftp.ibp.fr:/pub/linux.**

Websites

As Linux was evolved and grown, the number of websites specialising in it has increased continuously. The following list gives some of the main sites from which a wealth of information can be gained, and from which numerous further websites can be reached:

- **http://src.doc.ic.ac.uk**
- **http://www.linuxhq.com**

- http://goshawk.mcc.ac.uk/ManLUG
- http://www.linux.org
- http://www.cs.Helsinki.FI/linux/

Two further (French) sites gather together all the relevant Linux documentation in English and in French:

- http://www.freenix.fr/linux
- http://www.loria.fr/linux

Download sites

Linux is the operating system kernel. Its installation onto a machine (and the necessary recompilation of all the tools) is not straightforward. For this reason, a number of 'ready to go' versions have been distributed. They can be found on any respectable ftp server, and are readily available in other media such as CD-ROM at very economic prices. For information, the following list gives some of the most common ftp sites.

- Red Hat: ftp://ftp.redhat.com/pub/redhat/
- Slackware: ftp.cdrom.com:/pub/Linux/slackware
- Debian: ftp.debian.org:/debian
- Jurix: susix.jura.uni-sb.de:/pub/linux

These download files are found on the central Linux sites, as well as on the numerous mirror sites mentioned above.

2

General overview

This chapter presents the general characteristics of Unix systems, and of Linux in particular. It cannot repeated often enough that Linux is above all a Unix system, and therefore inherits all the characteristics of such an operating system.

Of course when one is familiar with the role played by an application, or software, the term *operating system* has a certain vagueness. In fact, it is too often used incorrectly, although it is in fact an essential pillar of all systems. This chapter will set out the role of the operating system, together with its structure and modes of functioning. Finally, going into greater detail, the concepts of *kernel* and the *user* are discussed.

'Operating System' is a generic term which in fact describes several families of systems:

- Single task systems: only one program may be run at a time, and therefore only one person may work on a machine at one time. However, the process may make use of the whole of the resources and power of the machine.
- Multi-task systems: several processes can be executed in parallel. Operating time is cut up into small intervals and each process is executed during these short periods. In order that these processes are not impaired, a complex prioritisation and scheduling algorithm is put in place to ensure an optimum sharing between the processes is achieved. These systems may be multi-user as well as multi-processor.

The first Unix versions available to the general public were multi-tasking and multi-user systems. But today, information technology has advanced to the point where many Unix systems are capable to also exploit multi-processor machines as well.

Although the first versions of Linux only supported single-processor PCs, version 2.0 of Linux supports the control of multi-processor machines.

2.2 THE ROLE OF THE OPERATING SYSTEM

Unix differs from other operating systems in that it was developed in the high level C language, rather than assembly language. The use of a high level language has allowed the porting of the system to several different machine types. The same applies to Linux. It is therefore of fundamental importance that application scripts may be compiled in a transparent (or nearly transparent) manner whatever the machine type and peripheral used.

In fact, the issues of porting of Linux onto another machine boil down to adapting that part of the code which is machine-specific. Architecture-independent modules may be re-used as they are.

2.2.1 Virtual Machine

The operating system gives the user, and the programs he uses, what amounts to a virtual machine within the real one. The virtual machine operates on the physical machine which contains the low level programming interface, and provides the high-level abstractions as well as a more advanced programming and user interface.

With the first operating systems in the 1950s, programmers needed to be familiar with the physical interface to the machine and to be able to program it directly. Modern systems provide a higher level interface, and translate high level requests into low level commands at the physical level.

Operating systems are thus interfaces between applications and the machine, as shown in figure 2.1. This is why all physical processes (access to external or internal peripherals, memory access etc.) are delegated to the operating system. This encapsulation of the physical layer, and its diversity, frees developers from the complexity of managing all the existing peripherals. The operating system takes care of all this.

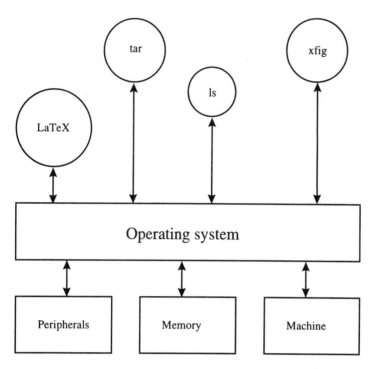

FIGURE 2.1   Context of applications and the machine.

This function also avoids exposing to the user the limitations of particular machines. If the system is available on several machine architectures, the user and programming interfaces will be the same on all of them.

For example, when the developer wants to read the contents of a file, he carries out the same operation whether the file is on tape, hard disk or CD-ROM, or other medium. The programmed code is the same, however the kernel carries out different operations according to which peripheral the file is contained in. It is easier to open a file and to read the contents than to physically read the bytes by creating a physical address composed of numbers for the disk, sector and read/write head.

2.2.2   Sharing the processor

One of the main characteristics of Unix systems is that it operates in *multi-tasking* mode, that is it can run several programs (*processes*) at the same time.

To achieve this, the system implements a scheduling system, which is described in chapter 4, section 4.1.8, and which connects each of these processes in turn to the processor. If there is only a single processor, only a single program can be executed at a time. But by cycling the processes rapidly, machine users have the impression that the processes are being carried out in parallel. The control of multi-tasking must be very sophisticated not to penalise any one process or user, and this constitutes one of the key mechanisms of the system.

2.2.3 Memory management

The system has to control the physical memory of the computer. In fact, in a multi-user and multi-tasking computer, the operating system must implement very rigorous control of memory. Because physical memory is typically insufficient, the system uses part of the disk as auxiliary memory (*swap* area).

The operating system must be capable of efficiently controlling memory in order to meet the demands of the different processes as quickly as possible. In addition, it must ensure that the zones of memory allocated to different processes are protected so as to prevent unauthorised modifications.

Memory management is covered in greater depth in chapter 8.

2.2.4 Resource management

In general, the operating system is charged with managing the available computer resources, of which the processor and the memory are particular instances.

This function provides processes with an interface allowing resources (such as disks, printers, etc.) to be shared. It implements a protection system which allows users and system administrators to protect access to their data.

The system keeps a list of resources available and in use, which allows it to attribute them to processes which have a need for them. At any given moment the system is aware of which processes are using machine resources and can thus detect conflicts of access.

2.2.5 Communication hub of the machine

One of the operating system jobs is to manage different events arising from either the physical layer (interrupts), or from applications (system calls). These events are important, and the system must deal with them, and if necessary send them to the processes concerned.

But if the operating system must be able to respond to events, it must also be able to put several processes in communication with each other. In this way, these processes will be able to communicate with each other, exchange data, synchronise with each other, etc. Unix provides developers with several mechanisms ranging from signals to IPC, and including pipes and *sockets*[1].

---

[1] *Sockets* are not covered in this book.

This is why the kernel is the communication hub of the machine. When two processes exchange data, it is as a result of the operating system invoking sophisticated mechanisms, as well as specific resources.

The operating system as it has been described is composed of several different elements. Unix and Linux in particular, being rather important systems, have been designed in a modular fashion so that different constituent parts can be distinguished.

The advantage of this structure, apart from the fact that it can be easily studied, is that it facilitates modification. The addition of certain elements such as system calls, control of peripherals and others is quite simple and does not necessitate the system structure to be rethought. This is why Unix, although it was conceived at the end of the 1960s, has evolved and still exists today.

The different elements of the Unix system kernel are the following:

- system calls: implementation of operations which should be run in kernel mode,
- filing system: inputs/outputs on peripherals,
- buffer cache: sophisticated buffer for inputs and outputs,
- management of peripherals: management at the level of disks, various i/o devices, printers, etc.
- network management: communication network protocols,
- machine interface: machine code interface (normally assembly code) for low-level access to physical resources of the machine,
- kernel:
  - process management (creation, copying, deletion, etc.)
  - scheduler,
  - messages,
  - loadable modules (loading of certain parts of the kernel on demand),
  - memory management (control of physical memory and virtual memory).

Figure 2.2 shows the structure of the Unix operating system together with the interactions between its constituent parts. This scheme has been somewhat adapted for Linux and varies slightly from the traditional structure which can be found in [Bach, 1993].

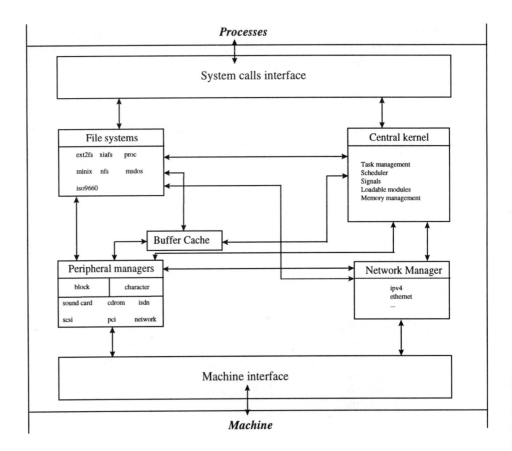

Figure 2.2   System structure.

The layout in figure 2.2 shows the boundary which exists between the machine and applications. With Unix, there is no way of directly accessing physical memory in the machine, or accessing the video card, or any other device. Furthermore, the partitioning of the kernel into distinct entities facilitates its development and implementation.

Finally, to make use of the functionalities provided by the operating system, Unix provides processes with a communication interface known as 'system calls'.

2.4
KERNEL MODE, *USER* MODE

2.4.1 Principle

A process in the Unix system consists of two levels of execution: *kernel* mode, and *user* mode.

The kernel mode is a privileged mode, in which no restriction is imposed on the kernel of the system. The kernel may use all the instructions of the processor, manipulate the whole of the memory, and talk directly to the peripheral controllers.

The user mode is the normal execution mode for a process. In this mode, the process has no privileges: certain instructions are forbidden to it, it is only allowed access to zones allocated to it, and it cannot interact with the physical machine. In user mode, a process carries out operations in its own environment, without interfering with other processes, and may be interrupted at any moment. This does not upset the progress of a process.

2.4.2 System Calls

A process which is executed in user mode cannot directly access the machine resources, for which it must use *system calls*. A system call is a request transmitted from the process to the kernel. The latter deals with the request in kernel mode, without any restrictions, and sends the result to the process, which continues executing.

Under Unix, the system call invokes a trap: the process executes an instruction in the processor, which switches it to kernel mode. It next executes a function linked to the system call which it carried out, and then switches back to user mode to continue its execution. In this way, it is the process itself which deals with its system call, by executing a kernel function. This function is assumed to be reliable, and can therefore be executed in privileged mode, in contrast to the program run by the process in user mode.

3

Development with Linux

This chapter presents the different development tools and techniques used under Linux. Indeed, though Linux is the kernel of the operating system, it is accompanied by a whole suite of development tools. The key characteristic of these products is that they are free, and available by remote downloading from most ftp sites around the world, as well as the operating system itself.

In this chapter, the layout of kernel source codes is detailed, and some ideas on system programming are also introduced.

3.1.1 Introduction

The letters GNU are the initials of the phrase Gnu's Not Unix. The Gnu[1] is a species of buffalo which lives in southern Africa.

GNU arose from a large project initiated by Richard Stallman (known as RMS) in 1983. At the time this project was announced RMS was the author of a powerful text editor – *emacs*. After he took up a position in the artificial intelligence laboratory in MIT, he decided to start up a vast project aiming at creating an operating system whose source code would be freely distributed. However, the GNU project quickly became diverted towards creating all the tools which would be needed by such a system, from a compiler to a text editor.

---

1 Several programs have taken their names from various animals: yak, bison, etc.

However, Linux is not GNU and they should not be confused: Linux is the operating system, and some of its development tools come from the GNU project. These tools are all distributed with a particular user licence: the GPL, or GNU Public Licence, which has become known as an instance of *CopyLeft*[2]. This licence allows the source codes to be distributed freely, and modified etc.

It should be pointed out that the operating system that RMS was aiming at was not Linux. The GNU kernel is still under development and is known under the name **Hurd**[3].

3.1.2 GNU tools

3.1.2.1 Introduction

The range of tools for GNU is considerable, and extends from compilers (*gcc, gnat, ...*) to universal text editors (*emacs*) and includes graph editors(*gnuplot*) and games (*gnuchess ...*). GNU products can be found covering most of the field, whether for the developer or the user. These tools are usually of good quality and are quite powerful, and furthermore are included in the majority of the various Linux distributions, often being distributed with the source codes.

These tools are widely distributed on the various ftp sites[4]. Thanks to this broadcast of the source programs, they have been corrected, improved and optimised in step with the different versions. To keep up to date with this evolution, all that is necessary is to subscribe to the Usenet news group **gnu.announce** which acts as a bulletin board for these changes.

One tool in particular has marked out Linux: the compiler *gcc*.

3.1.2.2 gcc

As with all Unix operating systems, Linux is implemented in the language C. It has therefore been necessary from the beginning of its development to have a C compiler available. The program *gcc* (derived from GNU C compiler) was the first C compiler to provide code generation for Linux. *gcc* is considered to be one of the most elegant of existing GNU products. The reader is referred in particular to the document by Barlow [Barlow, 1996], which gives details of Linux and *gcc*. The *gcc* compiler is generally considered to be one of the most powerful compilers. As well as being efficient in terms of speed, the code generated, and its optimisation, it also supports all the C programming standards, whether ANSI, the so-called K&R[5] form, or other extensions of the C language. For further details on the

---

[2] To distinguish it from *Copyright*!

[3] See WWW site **http://www.gnu.ai.mit.edu/** for more information.

[4] The reader is referred to the main GNU site : **prep.ai.mit.edu**

[5] Kernighan and Ritchie.

different forms of the C language, the reader is referred to [Kernighan and Ritchie, 1992].

gcc is also a C++ compiler, which supports virtually all of the features of the latest version (3.0) defined by Margaret Ellis and Bjarne Stroustrup [Ellis and Stroustrup, 1990]. For example, it supports templates, exceptions, multiple inheritance, etc.

Finally, *gcc* enables compilation in a rather special language: *Objective C*. This is an object oriented language which is still relatively little used.

3.2
DEVELOPMENT TOOLS

For a developer, the compiler, the link editor, and the debugger are vital. The compiler indicates whether there are syntax errors in the code, and the link editor resolves the different symbols.

Nevertheless, successful compiling of a program never guarantees that it will work! This is where the debugger comes into its own, by running relevant applications step by step.

3.2.1 The different phases of compilation

The compilation phase which begins with C code, and which produces executable code, is in fact the result of a number of actions. It is not within the scope of this book to describe in detail precisely what happens with respect to the syntactical, lexical and semantic analyses. There are specialist works in this domain (for example [Aho et al., 1991], which gives detail of compiler operation. Therefore, only the operation of the tools available to the developer is described here.

The course of a compilation is in fact a series of multiple stages, as can be seen from figure 3.1. These are:

- The C code is sent through a pre-processor which sets up header files, as well as replacing the different macro-instructions that have been defined. The *cpp* program is responsible for this operation.

- The compilation of the code is carried out in order to generate assembly code. The compiler not only does the conversion, but it also carries out a significant number of optimisations. This operation is carried out by the *cc1* program.

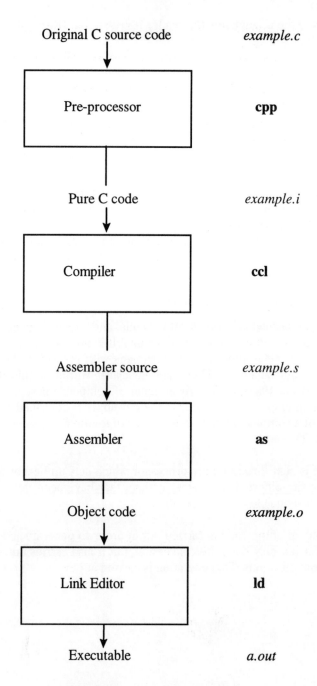

FIGURE 3.1:   Stages of compilation.

- The assembly operation carried out by the program *as* consists of generating the associated file object.
- Then, the final operation consists of generating the executable code of the program. This requires the grouping of all the file objects and the editing of the links. This complex operation is carried out by the program *ld*.

Appendix A gives the different stages in the compilation of a C program.

3.2.2 gcc

The *gcc* command links the different phases of the compilation of a program. This requires a program launcher to execute the different stages (pre-processor, compilation, assembly and link editing) whilst transmitting to the programs the options input by the programmer.

The option **-v** enables the different programs performed by *gcc* to be visualised:

```
gandalf# gcc -v exemple.c
Reading specs from /usr/lib/gcc-lib/i486-linux/2.7.2/specs
gcc version 2.7.2

/usr/lib/gcc-lib/i486-linux/2.7.2/cpp -lang-c -v -undef -D_ _GNUC_ _=2
-D_ _GNUC_MINOR_ _=7 -D_ _ELF_ _ _-Dunix -Di386 -Dlinux -D_ _ELF_ _-D_ _unix_ _
-D_ _i386_ _ -D_ _linux_ _ -D_ _unix -D_ _i386 -D_ _linuc -Asysten(unix)
-Asystem(posix) -Acpu(i386) -Amachine(i386) -D_ _i486_ _ exemple.c
/tmp/cca01212.i
GNU CPP version 2.7.2 (i386 Linux/ELF)
#include "à" search starts here:
#include <à> search starts here:
 /usr/local/include
 /usr/i486-linux/include
 /usr/lib/gcc-lib/i486-linux/2.7.2/include
 /usr/include
End of search list.

/usr/lib/gcc-lib/i486-linux/2.7.2/cc1 /tmp cca01212.i -quiet -dumpbase
exemple.c -version -o /tmp/cca01212.s
GNU C version 2.7.2 (i386 Linux/ELF) compiled by GNU C version 2.7.2.

/usr/i486-linux/bin/as -V -Qy -o /tmp cca01212.o /tmp cca01212.s
GNU assembler version 960228 (i486-linux(, using BFD version 2.6.0.12
/usr/i486-linux/bin/ld -m elf_i386 -dynamic-linker /lib/ld-linux.so.1
/usr/lib/crt1.o /usr/lib/crti.o /usr/lib/crtbegin.o
-L/usr/lib/gcc-lib/i486-linux/2.7.2 -L/usr/i486-linux/lib /tmp/ccao1212.o
-lgcc -lc -lgcc /usr/lib/crtend.o /usr/lib/crtn.o
```

Apart from the different default options (such as **_linux_**) it should be noted that the version numbers of the different tools are mentioned, which makes it convenient when the machine environment needs to be made known by the administrator. As indicated in the first line following the call to **gcc -v**, in the above code example, the compiler gathers the options by default in the file */usr/lib/gcc-lib/i486-linux/2.7.2/specs*. The access path is variable according to the compiler version and the installation configuration loaded. In certain cases, it may be of interest to modify certain options, or to add in others, for example in order to optimise the compiler to its processor.

The following is a list of some of the options which may be passed directly to *gcc*.

- **-M**:   stop after the pre-processor stage.
- **-S**:   stop after generating the assembly code.
- **-c**:   stop after generating the object code.
- **-g**:   insert symbols to assist debugging.
- **-destname:**   name of the file generated.
- **-DMACRO:**   defines the macro-instruction.
- **-DMACRO=value**: defines the macro-instruction and gives it a value.
- **-IDIRECTORY**: the list to which *cpp* must go to find the header files.
- **-LDIRECTORY**: the list to which *lp* must go to find the libraries.
- **-library**: includes the library at the time that the links are edited.
- **-pipe**: links the different compilation options without using temporary files. This option speeds up compilation, but at the expense of using more memory.
- **On**:   optimisation level (0 -> 3).

The number of *gcc* options is enormous. The reader is referred either to the relevant section in the manual or [Stallman, 1995] for more details.

3.2.3 Debugger

Not all successfully compiled programs work, and it is for this reason that one of the most utilised tools is the debugger program. Several debuggers exist under Unix. Under Linux, *gdb* is most often used.

In order to be able to debug a program, it needs to have been compiled using the option **-g**. In fact, the debugger requires certain information about the program which is not included in the normal compilation. As a result, the code generated can be larger. The scope of *gdb* is vast, and an example of its use is provided in Appendix B. The reader is referred to [Stallman and Support, 1994] for more information.

3.2.4   strace

The *strace* command enables system calls to be followed by a program. It indicates the primitives called, together with their parameters (by translating certain values.

into symbolic constants), and the code returned. An example of this code is given below.

```
mmap(0, 4096, READ |WRITE, PRIVATE, 4294967295, 0) = 0x400006000
SYS_125(0x8048000, 0x7ce, 0x7, 0x8048000, 0x8048084 = 0
stat ("/etc/ld.so.cache", {dev 3 2 ino 14351 mode 0100644 nlink 1 uid 0
gid 0 size 3154 ...}) = 0
open("/etc/ld.so.cache", RDONLY) = 3
mmap(0, 3154, READ< SHARED, 3, 0) = 0x400007000
close(3) = 0
open("/usr/lib/libc.so.5.3.9", RDONLY) = û1 (No such file or directory
open("/lib/libc.so.5.3.9", RDONLY) = 3
read(3,  "\7fELF\1\1\1\0\0\0\0\0\0\0\0\0\3\0\3\0\1\0\0\0\f0\3\1\04\0\0\0"
...4096) = 4096
mmap(0, 724992, , PRIVATE, 4294967295, 0) = 0x400008000
mmap(0x400008000, 492382, READ |EXEC, PRIVATE |FIXED, 3, 0) = 0x400008000
mmap(0x400081000, 20304, READ |WRITE, PRIVATE |FIXED, 3, 0x78000) =
0x400081000
mmap(0x400086000, 204856, READ |WRITE, PRIVATE |FIXED, 4294967295, 0) =
0x400086000
close(3) = 0
SYS_125(0x40008000, 0x7853e, 0x7, 0x40008000, 0x7853e) = 0
munmap(0x40007000, , 3154, ) = 0
SYS_125(0x8048000, 0x7ce, 0x5, 0x8048000, 0x7ce) = 0
SYS_125(0x40008000, 0x7853e, 0x5, 0x40008000, 0x7853e) = 0
scno out of range: 136
indir(Bogus syscall: 1073774592) = 0
brk(0x8049918) = 0x8049918
brk(0x804a000) = 0x804a000
fstat1, {dev 0 0 ino 35430 mode 010600 nlink 1 uid 501 gid 100
size 0 à}) = 0
mmap(0, 4096, READ |WRITE, PRIVATE, 4294967295, 0) = 0x400007000
write(1, "Cha\eene initial : exemple \n Cha" .., 68 Chaɛne initiale :
exemple Chaɛne dupliquθe: exemple -> exemple ) = 68
exit(1074283076) = ?
```

In the above example, the program starts by loading itself, then looks for the dynamic C library. After failing in this, (the C library is not located in */usr/lib/*), the libc (C library), located in */lib* is loaded.

Different calls to *mmap* and to *mprotect* (SYS_125) perform different loadings of the program and of the library. The two *brk* calls correspond to memory allocations set up within the program.

Finally, the calls to *fstat* and *write* give rise to writing to the standard output of the result of the operation. The program terminates, like all programs, by a call to *exit*.

3.2.5 make

3.2.5.1 Outline

The *make* tool facilitates compilation of program drafts and is a standard tool which is installed in all Unix systems. This program allows an intelligent compilation of programs to be made, according to the modified files which actually need to be re-compiled. However, the syntax of *Makefile* is rather tedious to write because it adheres to the rules of re-writing. A view of the capabilities of this tool are given in Appendix C. For more details, the reader should consult the *make* manual, or documentation in the GNU version [Stallman and McGrath, 1995].

3.3
FORMAT OF
EXECUTABLES

Linux supports two formats for executable programs. The first binary format that was used by Linux was the format called **a.out**. However, since this format is rather impractical for implementing dynamic libraries, the binary format now used is the **ELF** format.

3.3.1 a.out: the original!

The **a.out** format (Assembler.OUTput) was the format for libraries and executables used in the first versions of Unix in general, and by Linux in particular.

Several variants of this format exist (e.g. ZMAGIC, QMAGIC, etc.). QMAGIC is a format which somewhat resembles the old **a.out** binaries (also known as ZMAGIC), but which leaves a blank first page in the program. This allows non-affected addresses in the range 0–4096 (such as **NULL**) to be more easily retrieved.

Old fashioned link editors only handle the ZMAGIC format, whilst more recent ones manage both. The two types are, in any case, supported by the kernel.

To find out if a program is in the **a.out** format, all that is needed is to use the *file* command:

```
gandalf# file /usr/local/bin/kermit
/usr/local/bin/kermit: Linux/i386 demand-paged executable (ZMAGIC)
```

If the string Linux/i386 appears, then the binary specified is in the **a.out** format. It also means that it is a binary in the **ZMAGIC** format.

The format of **a.out**-type binaries is implemented in the file *fs/binfmt_aout.c*. However, the support of this format is only maintained for historic reasons, and its details will not be discussed here.

3.3.2 ELF

3.3.2.1 *Welcome to the world of ELF*

The new binary format used by Linux is the ELF[6] format. ELF is an abbreviation of **E**xecutable and **L**inking **F**ormat. The format was initially created and developed by USL (**U**nix **S**ystem **L**aboratories), and is used by SVR-4 and Solaris 2.x type systems.

Given that ELF is much more flexible than the **a.out** format, Linux developers decided to migrate towards this format in 1994. The method of effecting this migration is described by Barlow and Dumas [Barlow, 1995], [Dumas, 1996].

3.3.2.2 *The ELF format*

ELF has become widely known and used (on several Unix systems) because of its ease of manipulation. This usability derives from its structure. The ELF format is completely described in [TIS 1993].

The ELF format enables three types of file to be generated;

- re-locatable file (object file),
- executable file,
- shared file (libraries).

In each case, the file format is the same, as illustrated in figure 3.2.

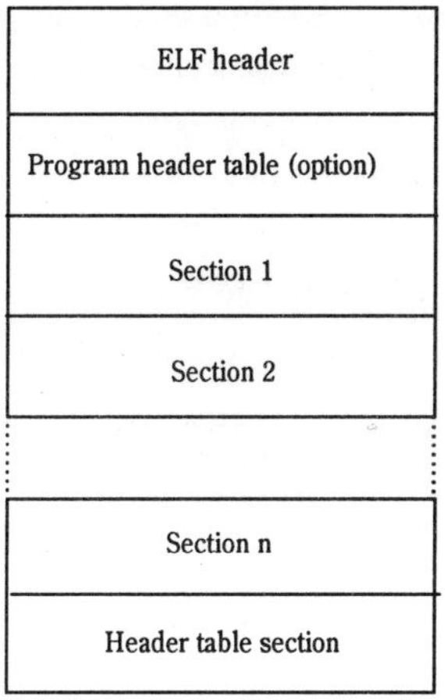

ELF header
Program header table (option)
Section 1
Section 2
⋮
Section n
Header table section

FIGURE 3.2:   The ELF format: structure.

---

[6] No, ELF is nothing to do with Tolkien and the *Lord of the Rings*, even if certain characteristics do appear strange, weird or magical. And there is no 'Gandalfery' lurking behind it.

The file header of an ELF file incorporates the description of the file organisation. This is the only element which has a fixed position within the ELF file format: other sections may be placed anywhere within the file. It is quite possible to directly access this data.

The file header **<elf.h>**[7] contains the declaration of an ELF file header. This is the **Elf32_Ehdr** structure.

type	*field*	*description*
unsigned char[EI_NIDENT]	e_ident	Magic number of the file, along with certain information
Elf32_Half	e_type	File type
Elf32_Half	e_machine	File architecture
Elf32_Word	e_version	Version of the file format
Elf32_Addr	e_entry	Virtual address of the point of entry of the program
Elf32_Off	e_phoff	Search offset to find the program header table
Elf32_Off	e_shoff	Search offset to find the section header table
Elf32_Word	e_flags	Particular processor options
Elf32_Half	e_ehsize	Header size in bytes
Elf32_Half	e_phentsize	Size of an entry into the header table of the program
Elf32_Half	e_phnum	Number of entries in the entry table of the program
Elf32_Half	e_shentsize	Size of a section header
Elf32_Half	e_shnum	Number of entries in the section table
Elf32_Half	e_shstrndx	Section table index

The identification field, although simply composed of a table of bytes, is very important, and can be broken down in the following way:

type	*field*	*description*
EI_MAG_0,EI_MAG_1,EI_MAG_2, I_MAG_3	Magic number	Composed of 4 bytes: 0x7f E L F. This magic number is actually made up of four macro-definitions: **ELFMAG0, ELFMAG1, ELFMAG2,** and **ELFMAG3.**
EI_CLASS	File class	ELF being a portable format, the file words can be of 32-bit or 64-bit format. This byte can have the values **ELFCLASSNONE** (invalid), **ELFCLASS32,** and **ELFCLASS64.**

---

[7] In fact, it is the file **<linux/elf.h>** which contains the data.

Continuation of the description of the identification field		
type	*field*	*description*
EI_DATA	Encoding type	Determines whether this has a small or large trailer environment. Can have values **ELFDATANONE** (invalid), **ELFDATA2LSB** and **ELFDATA2MSB**.
EI_VERSION	Header version	Must be **EV_CURRENT**
EI_PAD	Mark	Marks the beginning of unused bytes and which are allocated for future extensions.

The different sections of the file can be accessed from this file header. Their number and position are entirely variable according to the compiler which generated the code, the options specified when the object file is created, or simply from the language in which the source was written.

However, manually inspecting a binary **ELF** file turns out to be a complex and obscure task. A library aids access to the information in an **ELF** file, by providing analysis functions. To make use of these, it is necessary to include the file <libshelf.h> and to add the option -lelf when the links are edited.

**3.4
LIBRARIES**

3.4.1 Library functionality

Libraries constitute a simple means of gathering several object files together. Two types of library are found:

- Static: during link editing, the library code is integrated with the executable code;
- dynamic: the library code is loaded when the program is executed.

Dynamic libraries economise on disk space, but especially on memory because a dynamic memory is only loaded once, and the code can be shared between all the applications which need it. Finally, when a dynamic library is opened, it is unnecessary to re-compile the applications which use it. A dynamic library which is commonly used is the C library. All applications (with a few exceptions) are dynamically linked with the C library. The program *ldd* makes known the lists of libraries linked to an application.

```
gandalf# ldd /usr/X386/bin/xv
        libXext.so.6 => /usr/X11/lib/libXext.so.6.0
        libX11.so.6 => /usr/X11/lib/libX11.so.6.0
        libm.so.5 => /lib/libm.so.5.0.5
        libc.so.5 => /lib/libc.so.5.3.9
```

3.4.2 Use of libraries

The use of a library is very simple: when linking the program, it is only necessary to specify the library. For example:

```
gandalf# gcc -o demo_complex main.c -L/usr/local/complex -lcomplete -lm
gandalf# ldd demo_complex
        libm.so.5 => /lib/libm.so.5.0.5
        libc.so.5 => /lib/libc.so.5.3.9
```

The above result corresponds to a case of a library created statically rather than dynamically. Appendix D contains details of management tools for libraries.

3.5
ORGANISATION OF KERNEL SOURCE PROGRAMS

3.5.1 Kernel

Linux kernel source programs are normally installed in the directory */usr/src/linux.*

They are organised in a hierarchical manner, as can seen in figure 3.3.

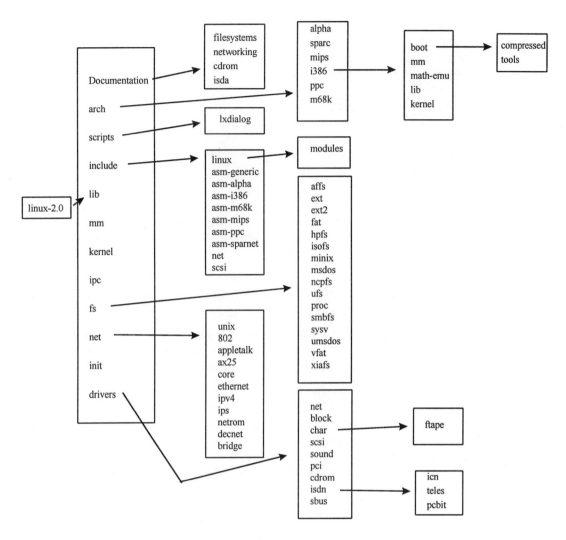

FIGURE 3.3   Tree structure of source files.

Each directory or sub-directory is dedicated to certain kernel functionalities:

- *Documentation:* a number of documentation files concerning the configuration of certain kernel functions,
- *include*: all the header files necessary for the kernel and the compilation of applications,
- *fs:* filing systems,
- *init:* the *main.c* of Linux,

- *ipc*: management of inter-process communications conforming to the System V standard,
- *mm*: memory management,
- *kernel:* main system calls,
- *lib*: various modules,
- *drivers*: device managers,
- *net*: network protocols,
- *arch*: platform-dependent code,
- *scripts*: scripts used for the configuration and the generation of the kernel.

3.5.2 Header files

The header files used by the C pre-processor (such as **<stdio.h>**, for example) are situated in the directory /usr/include. They define the library interfaces used by the programs compiled. These header files are linked to the C library, which is distributed independently of the kernel.

The Linux kernel also has access to header files which are used when it is compiled. These files are situated in the directory */usr/src/linux/include*. Two sub-directories in particular are to be found there:

- *linux*: this directory contains the architecture-independent declarations,
- *asm*: this directory contains the architecture-dependent declarations: this refers to the link to another directory (*asm-i386* for the x86 architecture for example).

Two symbolic links generally allow access to these files from the */usr/include* directory. It is thus possible to include in a program header files defining the constants of the types utilised by the kernel using the notations **<asm/file.h>** and **<linux/file.h>**. It should, however, be noted that inclusion of these files is not advised. It is preferable to include standard C library files, since they are designed for this purpose. These header files are responsible for bringing the definitions from the kernel.

In the following chapters, a description of the Linux system calls introduces standard header files, which an be found on any Unix system. Certain definitions of constants and types are carried out in the kernel header files, but the latter are not described in detail in the first parts of the chapters for reasons concerning portability.

On the other hand, kernel header files are described when various parts of the kernel are explained.

3.6
KERNEL OPERATION
3.6.1 System calls

As explained in chapter 2, section 2.4.1, a process is normally run in user mode and must change to kernel mode in order to execute system calls.

3.6.1.1 *Implementation of a system call*

A system call is characterised and identified by a name and a unique number. This number can be found in the file **<asr/unistd.h>**. For example, the system call *open* has the number 5. The name is defined in the assembler file *arch/i386/kernel/entry.S*[8], and is called **sys_open**.

The C library provides functions for executing system calls, and the functions carry the names of the system calls. To execute a system call, all that is thus necessary is to call the corresponding function.

In kernel source programs, system calls are of the following standard form:

```
asmlinkage int sys_namecall(argument list)
{
        /* System call code */
}
```

The number of arguments must be between 0 and 5. The key-word **asmlinkage** is a macro instruction defined in the file **<linux/linkage.h>**:

```
#ifdef __cplusplus
#define asmlinkage extern "C"
#else
#define asmlinkage
#endif
```

When a process executes a system call, it calls the corresponding function of the C library. This function processes the parameters and passes the process to the kernel mode.

For the x386 architecture, the transfer to the kernel mode is achieved in the following way:

- the system call parameters are placed in certain processor registers:
- a trap is invoked by invoking the 0x80 software interrupt;
- this trap invokes the transfer to kernel mode: the process executes the system call function **system_call** defined in the source file *arch/i386/kernel/entry.S*;
- this function uses the system call number (transmitted to the **eax** register) as an index in the table **sys_call_table**, which contains the system call addresses, and calls the kernel function corresponding to the system call;
- when this function is returned, **system_call** is returned to the caller; and this return passes the process back into user mode.

---

[8] Although this file is located in the subdirectory dedicated to the x86 architecture, equivalent files exist for other architectures.

3.6.1.2 *Creation of a system call*

In order to fully understand the functioning of a system call, one may be created. The system call to be created consists of taking three arguments, doing a multiplication on the first two of them, and placing the result in the third.

First, it is necessary to 'declare' the system call, and therefore to assign it a number. Version 2.0 of Linux contains 164 system calls. The system call *show_mult* therefore has the number 164 (whilst the first system call, *setup*, is numbered 0). In order to declare the new call to be created, the following must be added to the file include/*asm/unistd.h*:

```
/* Kernel system calls */
#define __NR_sched_get_priority_min   160
#define __NR_sched_r_get_interval     161
#define __NR_nanosleep                162
#define __NR_mremap                   163


/* System calls added */
#define __NR_show_mult                164
```

Then, in the file *arch/i386/kernel/entry.S*[9]:

```
/* Kernel system calls */
.long SYMBOL_NAME(sys_sched_get_priority_min) /* 160 */
.long SYMBOL_NAME(sys_sched_rr_get_interval)
.long SYMBOL_NAME(sys_nanosleep)
.long SYMBOL_NAME(sys_mremap)


/*Initial value of number of calls */
/* .space (NR_syscalls-163)*4 */


/* System name added */
.long SYMBOL_NAME(sys_show_mult)
.space (NR_sysalls-164)*4
```

At this stage, all the links which allow system calls to be made are in place, and all that remains is to implement it. The system call code can be integrated with the kernel file kernel /sys.c which collects together a number of system calls. The code that must be added is the following:

```
asmlinkage int sys_show_mult(int x, int y, int *res)
{
        int error
```

---

[9] Or in the file *entry.S* of the architecture.

```
    int compute

    /* Checking the validity of the variable res */
    error = verify_area(VERIFY_WRITE, res, sizeof(*res));
    if (error)
            return error;

    /* calculation of the value */
    compute = x*y:

    /* copy into the user memory zone for the result */
    put_user(compute, res);

    printk("Value computed : %d x %d = %d \n", x, y, compute);

    /* Call terminated */
    return 0;
}
```

Once the kernel has been recompiled and the machine rebooted, it is possible to test the system call that has been implemented. In order to utilise this system call, it is necessary to declare a function which runs it. Indeed, this function does not exist in the C library, and it is necessary to declare it explicitly. Several macro instructions facilitating the definition of this type of function are declared in the header file **<syscall.h>**. When the system call accepts three parameters, the macro instruction **_syscall3** must be used.

———————— showmult.c ————————————————————————

```
#include <stdio.h>
#include <stdlib.h>
#include <linux/unistd.h>

_syscall3 (int, show_mult, int, x, int, y, int *, resul);

main ()
{
    int ret = 0;

    show_mult (2, 5, &ret);
    printf ("Result %d %d = %d \n", 2, 5, ret);
}
```
————————————————————————— showmult.c ————————

The macro instruction **_syscall3** is expanded by the pre-processor and provides the following code:

```
int  show_mult (  int   x , int   y , int *   resul )
{
      long _ _res;
      _ _asm_ _ _ _volatile ("int $0x80"
             : "=a" (_ _res)
             "0" (164),
             "b" ((long) ( x )),
             "c" ((long) ( y )),
             "d" ((long) ( resul )));
      if (_ _res>=0)
             return ( int ) _ _res;
      errno=-_ _res;
      return û1;
} ;
```

The function **show_mult** is generated by **_syscall3**. It initialises the processor registers (the system call number is placed in the register **eax**, and the parameters are placed in the registers **ebx ecx**, and **edx**.), then it launches the **0x80** interrupt. When returning from this interrupt, that is returning to the system call, the return value is tested. If it is positive or null, it is returned to the caller, otherwise the value contains the error code returned; it is then kept in the global variable **errno** and a value of −1 is returned.

3.6.1.3 Return codes
Errors can be detected by the kernel when a system call is executed. In this case, an error code is returned to the calling process.

Generally, the value −1 is returned in the event of error. This value indicates unambiguously that an error has occurred. In order for the calling process to determine the cause of the error, the C library provides a global variable called **errno**. This variable is flagged up after each system call causing an error, and it contains a code indicating the cause of the error. It is not flagged after a successful system call. In addition, it is necessary to test the return code of each system call and to only use the value of **errno** when there is a problem.

The header file **<errno.h>** defines the numerous constants which represent the possible errors. In the following chapters, detailed lists of the error codes which may be returned are given when the relevant system calls are introduced.

The C library also provides the following two constants:

```
extern int _sys_nerr;
extern char *_sys_errlist[];
```

The variable **_sys_nerr** contains the number of error codes implemented. Table - **_sys_errlist** contains the strings of characters describing all these errors. The error message corresponding to the most recent error detected can thus be obtained from **_sys_errlist[errno]**

In addition, two functions are provided by the C library:

```
#include <stdio.h>
#include <errno.h>

void perror (const char *s);

har *strerror (int errnum);
```

The function *perror* puts an error message in the error output of the calling process. This message contains the string specified by the parameter **s** and the error message corresponding to the value of **errno**. The function *strerror* returns the string of characters corresponding to the error whose code is specified by the parameter **errnum**.

3.6.2 Utility functions

The kernel contains several utility functions which it is now necessary to introduce. Although the functions are described in later chapters, we need to know how they work in order to understand the description of the internal functions.

3.6.3 Manipulation of address space

The address space for a process in kernel mode is different from the address space in user mode. It is thus not possible to directly access the data whose address has been passed as a parameter to a system call.

Linux provides several functions for accessing this data:

```
int verify_area (int type, const void *addr, unsigned long size);

void put_user (unsigned long value, void *addr);
unsigned long get_user (void *addr);

void memcpy_tofs (void *to, const void *from, unsigned long size);
void memcpy_fromfs (void *to, const void *from, unsigned long size);
```

The function **verify_area** checks that the address supplied (parameter **addr**) is valid. The parameter **size** represents the number of bytes for the zone, and **type** specifies the type of check carried out. This parameter can take the value VERIFY_READ to check that the memory zone may be read, or VERIFY_WRITE to check that the zone may be written to.

The function **put_user** writes the value specified by the parameter **value** in the address space of the calling process, in the address specified by the parameter **addr**. The function **get_user** returns the value located in the address passed in the parameter **addr**, in the address space of the calling process.

The function **memcpy_tofs** copies the data from the kernel address space to the address space of the calling process. The parameter **to** contains the address in the address space of the process, and **from** contains the address in the address space of the kernel. **size** specifies the number of bytes to be copied. The function **memcpy_fromfs** copies the data from the address space of the calling process to the kernel address space.

These functions are described in detail in chapter 8, section 6.5.

3.6.3.1 *Memory allocation and release*
Several functions for dynamically allocating and dis-allocating memory are provided for internal needs in the kernel.

```
void *kmalloc (unsigned int size, int priority);
void kfree (void *addr);

void *vmalloc (unsigned long size);
void vfree (void *addr);
```

The function **kmalloc** allocates a memory zone whose size is specified by the parameter **size**. It returns the address of the allocated zone. If there is a problem the value **NULL** is returned. The parameter **priority** specifies the type of allocation:

constant	meaning
GFP_BUFFER	Memory allocation for the buffer cache
GFP_ATOMIC	Memory allocation for an interruption manager
GFP_USER	Memory allocation for a user-mode process
GFP_KERNEL	Memory allocation for the kernel
GFP_NFS	Memory allocation for NFS filesystem support

The function **kfree** releases the memory zone whose address is passed in the parameter **addr**. This address corresponds to the value returned by **kmalloc**.

The functions **vmalloc** and **vfree** also implement the memory allocation and release operations. They are more flexible than **kmalloc** and **kfree**.

These functions are described in detail in chapter 8, section 8.5.3.

4

Processes

System calls described

4.1
BASIC CONCEPTS

4.1.1 The idea of process

In general terms, a process can be considered to be a program being run. The latter progresses in a sequential manner: at any given time a single instruction is carried out within the process.

However, a process is more than merely the program being executed. It is also characterised by the current activity, represented by the value of the program counter and the values in the processor registers. It also includes a stack, containing temporary data, and a segment of data containing global variables.

A program is not a process of itself: it is a passive entity (an executable file residing on disk), whilst a process is an active entity with a program counter specifying the next instruction to be carried out, as well as the total associated resources.

4.1.2 Process states

During the course of execution, processes change state. The state of a process is defined by its current activity. The different possible states of a process are the following:

- in execution: the process is being executed by the processor,
- ready: the process could be executed, but another process is currently being executed,
- suspended: the process is waiting for a resource, for example it is waiting for input/output to finish,
- stopped: the process has been suspended by an external process,
- zombie: the process has finished execution, but it is still referenced in the system.

The changes of state of a process are represented in the state diagram shown in figure 4.1.

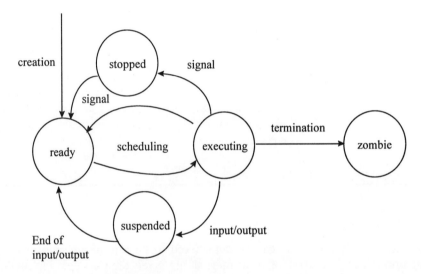

Figure 4.1:   State diagram of a process.

4.1.3 Attributes of a process

During execution, a process is characterised by several attributes maintained by the system:

- its state,
- its identification (unique number),
- the values of the registers, including the program counter,
- the user identity under whose name the process is executing,
- the information used by the kernel to establish the schedule of the processes (priority, ...),
- information concerning the address space of the process (segments for the code, data, stack),

- information concerning the inputs/outputs carried out by the process (descriptions of open files, current directory, ...),
- compatibility information summarising resources used by the process.

4.1.4 Process identifiers

Several user and group identifiers are assigned to a process:

- identification of the real user: this is the identifier of the user who started up the process,
- identification of the effective user: this is the identifier which is used by the system for access control; it can be different from the real user, especially in the case of programs with the *setuid* bit set,
- identification of the real group: this is the identifier of the primary group of the user who started the process,
- identification of the effective group: this is the identifier which is used by the system for access control: it can be different from the real group, especially in the case of programs with the *setgid* bit set,
- a list of group identifiers: any user can belong to several groups simultaneously, and the kernel keeps a list of groups associated with each process in order to carry out access control. Under Linux, a process can possess up to 32 groups.

Linux also maintains two other identifiers: the saved *uid* and the saved *gid*. When a process modifies its effective user or group identifier by calling up the primitives *setreuid* and *setregid*, the kernel authorises the modification in the following cases:

- the process possesses superuser privileges,
- the process specifies the same value for the new identifier,
- the new identifier is the same as the saved identifier.

These saved identifiers are particularly useful for a process executing a program including the *setuid* or *setgid* bits respectively set. That is, the process possessing respectively different real and effective user and/or group identifiers. Such a process may use the primitives *setuid* and *setgid* to change the effective user and/or group, and the *setreuid*, and *setregid*, to swap between its real or effective user and or group identifiers.

4.1.5 Process creation

The creation of a new process is achieved by duplicating the current process: the system call *fork* enables a process to make a copy of itself which is the same except for the process identifier. The original process which duplicates itself is called the parent process and the copy created is called the child process.

When Linux starts up, it creates process number 1 which runs a program *init* which is responsible for initialising the system. This process itself creates other processes to carry out different functions, which can themselves create other processes. This results in a hierarchy of related processes.

Figure 4.2 shows a typical process hierarchy, displayed by the command *pstree*.

```
init(1) auto
|- (agetty, 9700)
|- (agetty, 9699)
|- (agetty, 9698)
|- (agetty, 71)
|- cron(26)
|- innd(63) -p4 -i0 -c360
|      '-overchan(72)
|- (kflushd,2)
|- (kswapd,3)
|- selection(40) -t msc -c 1 -p m
|- syslogd(36)
|- (tcsh, 9701)
|     '-(startx, 9724)
|        '-(xinit, 9725)
|             |-X(9726)       :0
|              '-fvwm(9728)
|                   |-FvwmPager(9735) 9 4 /home/card/.fvwmrc 0 8 0 2
|          |-GoodStuff  (9733) 7 4   /home/card/.fvwmrc 0 8
|          |-(xclock, 9734)
|          |-xterm(9731) -geometry 80x50+20+50
|          |     '-tcsh(9737)
|          |-xterm(9732) -geometry 80x20+530+70
|          |     '-tcsh(9736)
|                        '-bash(10771)
|-update(9)
|-xterm(10311)
|    '-tcsh(10316)
|-xterm(10321)
|    '-tcsh(10328)
|-xterm(10325)
|    '-tcsh(10330)
|        '-vi(30664) . ./Processus/ConceptsBase.tex
|        '-tcsh(30716) -c pstree -a -c -p
|                    '-pstree(30720) -a -c -p
```

Figure 4.2:   Typical hierarchy of a process.

```
|-xterm(17889)
|    '-tcsh(17893)
|            |-make(30696)
|            |      '-latex(30715) Livre.tex
|            '-xdvi(28449) Livre
|         '-gs(28531) -sDEVICE-x11 -dNOPAUSE -q -
|-xterm(10788)
|    '-tcsh(10791)
-xterm(10790)
   '-tcsh(10792)
```

Figure 4.2 (continued): Typical hierarchy of a process.

4.1.6 Process Groups

Linux maintains groups of processes. A process group is a collection of several processes. All processes belong to a group and any descendant processes belong to the same group by default. A process may decide to create a new group and becomes the head (*leader*) of that group in so doing. A group is identified by its group number, which is equal to that of the group *leader*.

This concept of groups allows messages to be sent to all the processes which are members of the same group (see chapter 5, section 2.1), in order to implement *job control*. The command interpreters (*bash, csh, ksh, etc.*) use these groups to allow the user to suspend execution of a process and to continue it, in the foreground or in the background.

Process groups are also used in the management of terminals (see chapter 9, section 9.2.6).

4.1.7 Sessions

A session is a collection of one or more groups of processes. Each session is assigned to a single control terminal. This control terminal is either a peripheral device or a pseudo-device (when there is a network connection to a distant terminal). When a process creates a new session:

- it becomes the process *leader*,
- a new group of processes is created and the calling process becomes its *leader*,
- the calling process has no control terminal.

A session is identified by its number, which is equal to the number of its process *leader*.

Generally, a new session is created by the program *login* when a user is connected. All processes subsequently become members of the same session. In the case of linked commands (for example by pipes), the command interpreter (*shell*) creates new process groups to implement job control.

4.1.8 Multi-programming

At any given moment, there is only one process being executed[1]. This process is called the current process. The system keeps a list of processes that are ready for execution and periodically proceeds to scheduling.

Each process has a time 'quantum' attributed to it. Linux selects a process to run and leaves it to execute in this quantum period. When the quantum time period is used up, the system puts the process in the 'ready' state and goes to another process which it executes in another time quantum. The time quantum is very short, and users have the impression that processes are all executing simultaneously, even if only one is actually executing at a time. The processes are said to be executing in pseudo-parallel.

4.2
BASIC SYSTEM CALLS

4.2.1 Creation of processes

The current process can create a child process by using the system call *fork*. His primitive causes the current process to be duplicated. It is of the following form:

```
#include <unistd.h>

pid_t fork (void);
```

When *fork* is called, the current process is duplicated: a copy which conforms to the original, except in its identifier, and that of its parent, is created. When *fork* is returned, two processes, the parent and child, execute the same code.

The primitive *fork* returns the value 0 to the child process, and it returns the identifier of the created process to the parent process. It is therefore vital to test the returned value in order to distinguish the code which should be executed by the parent process from that which should be executed by the child process. In the case of failure, *fork* returns a value –1, and the variable **errno** can take the following values.

---

[1] At least, on a single-processor computer.

error	meaning
EAGAIN	The maximum number of processes for the current user, or in the system, has been reached
ENOMEM	The kernel has not been able to allocate enough memory to create another process

The following program uses the system call *fork* to create a child process:

──────── CreerProcessus.c ──────────────────────

```
#include <errno.h>
#include <stdio.h>
#include <unistd.h>


void main(void)
{
        pid_t pid

    pid = fork ();
    if (pid == -1)
            perror ("fork");
    else if (pid == 0)
            printf ("I am the child : pid = %d\n", pid);
    else
            printf ("I am the parent : pid = %d\n", pid);


}
```
────────────────────────────── CreerProcessus.c ────────

4.2.2 Termination of current process

The current process terminates automatically when it finishes executing the function **main,** by using the instruction **return**. It also has system calls which allow it to explicitly stop execution:

```
#include <unistd.h>

void _exit (int status);

#include <stdlib.h>

void exit (int status);
```

The primitives *_exit* and *exit* cause the current process to stop. The parameter **status** specifies a return code, in the range 0 to 255, to communicate to the parent process. By convention, a process should return a value of 0 in the case of a normal termination, and a non-zero value in the case of termination following an error.

Before terminating the process, *exit* executes the functions finally recorded by calling library functions *atexit* and *on_exit*.

If the current process includes child processes, the latter are attached the program *init*, a process whose pid is 1. The signal **SIGCHLD** is sent to the parent process to warn it that one of its child processes has terminated.

4.2.3   Waiting for the termination of a child process

A process may wait for the termination of a child process by using the primitives *wait* and *waitpid*. Their syntax is the following:

```
#include <sys/types.h>
#include <sys/wait.h>

pid_t wait (int *status);

pid_t waitpid (pid_t pid, int *status, int options);
```

The primitive *wait* suspends execution of the current process until a child process has terminated. If a child process has already terminated, *wait* returns the result immediately. The primitive *waitpid* suspends execution of the current process until the child process specified by the parameter **pid** terminates. If a child process corresponding to **pid** has already terminated, *waitpid* returns the result immediately.

The result of *waitpid* depends on the value of the parameter **pid**:

- if **pid** is positive, it specifies the number of the child process to expect;
- if **pid** is null, it specifies any child process whose process group number is equal to that of the calling process;
- if **pid** is equal to −1, it specifies waiting for the termination of the first child process; in this case, *waitpid* has the same semantics as *wait*.
- if **pid** is less than −1, it specifies any child process whose process group number is equal to the absolute value of the **pid** number.

Two constants, which are declared in **<sys/wait.h>** , can be used to initialise the parameter **options** order to modify the behaviour of *waitpid*:

constant	meaning
WNOHANG	Causes an immediate return if no child process has terminated
WUNTRACED	Causes the child whose state is changing to be taken into consideration, that is, the child process whose state has changed from ready to suspended

These two primitives return the number of the child process which has finished, or the value –1 in the case of a fault. The status of the child process is returned in the variable whose address is passed by the parameter **statusp**.

This status is interpreted by means of the macro instructions defined in the header file **<sys/wait.h>**:

macro-instruction	meaning
WIFEXITED	Non-null if the child process is terminated by a call to _exit or exit
WEXITSTATUS	Return code sent by the child process when it terminates
WIFSIGNALED	Non-null if the child process is interrupted by the reception of a signal
WTERMSIG	Number of the signal having given rise to the termination of the child process
WIFSTOPPED	Non-null if the child process changes from the ready state to the suspended state
WSTOPSIG	Number of the signal having given rise to suspension of the child process

Two other system calls, which provide compatibility with BSD Unix systems, are also implemented by Linux.

```
#define _USE_BSD

#include <sys/types.h>
#include <sys/resource.h>
#include <sys/wait.h>

pid_t wait3 (int *status, int options, struct rusage *rusage);

pid_t wait4 (pid_t pid, int *status, int options, struct rusage *rusage);
```

These calls are quite similar to *wait* and *waitpid*. They accept an additional parameter, rusage, which points to a variable in which compatibility information on terminated processes is stored.

The rusage structure, defined in the header file **<sys/resource.h>**, contains the following fields:

type	field	description
struct timeval	ru_utime	Processor time used up by the process in user mode
struct timeval	ru_stime	Processor time used up by the process in kernel mode
long	ru_maxrss	Maximum size of the address space of the process residing in memory, expressed in kbytes
long	ru_ixrss	Number of kilobytes of process address space shared with other processes
long	ru_idrss	Number of kilobytes of the process data segment not shared with other processes
long	ru_isrss	Number of kilobytes of the segment of the process stack
long	ru_minflt	Number of page defaults caused by the process, which have been resolved without invoking an input/output
long	ru_majflt	Number of page defaults caused by the process, which have been resolved by invoking an input/output
long	ru_nswap	Number of times where the process has been deleted from memory to be relocated in secondary memory
long	ru_inblock	Number of times that the process has carried out a data read for a process
long	ru_oublock	Number of times that the process has carried out a data write for a process
long	msgsnd	Number of message sent by the process
long	msgrcv	Number of message received by the process
long	ru_nsignals	Number of signals received by the process
long	ru_nvcsw	Number of times that the process has voluntarily broken off from the processor (generally to await the arrival of an event, such as the end of an input/output)
long	ru_nivcsw	Number of times that the process has voluntarily broken off from the processor because it has used up its time slot or because a higher priority process was in the ready state

The structure of timeval, which is used to define the fields ru_utime and ru_stime, is as follows:

type	field	description
long	tv_sec	Seconds
long	tv_usec	Microseconds

The function *wait3* corresponds to the system call *wait4*, to which the value of –1 is passed for the parameter **pid**.

In the event of a problem arising from using these primitives, the variable **errno** can take the following values:

constant	meaning
ECHILD	The process specified by **pid** does not exist
EFAULT	**statusp** or **rusage** contains an invalid address
EINTR	The system call was interrupted by reception of a signal
EPERM	The calling process does not have privileges and the effective user identifier is not equal to that specified by **pid**

4.2.4 Reading attributes of the current process

Several system calls enable a process to retrieve its characteristic attributes:

```
#include <unistd.h>

pid_t getpid (void);

pid_t getppid (void);

uid_t getuid (void);

uid_t geteuid (void);

gid_t getgid (void);

gid_t getegid (void);

int getgroups (int size, gid_t list[]);
```

getpid returns the unique identifier of the current process, *getppid* returns the unique identifier of the parent of the current process.

getuid returns the identifier of the real user of the current process, *geteuid* returns the identifier of the effective user of the current process.

getgid returns the identifier of the real group process, *getegid* returns the identifier of the effective group of the current process.

Finally, *getgroups* allows a list of groups associated with the current process to be called up. The identifiers of these groups are returned in the parameter list. *Getgroups* returns the total number of groups associated with the current process.

4.2.5 Modification of attributes

A process may, in certain circumstances, modify its attributes. Linux provides several system calls for this purpose:

```
#include <unistd.h>

int setuid (uid_t uid);

int setreuid (uid_t ruid, uid_t euid);

int seteuid (uid_t euid);

int setgid (gid_t gid);

int setregid (gid_t rgid, gid_t egid);

int setegid (gid_t egid);

#define __USE_BSD
#include <grp.h>

int setgroups (size_t size, const gid_t *list);
```

The call *setuid* lets a process modify its effective user identifier. The process should have privileges[2], or the new identifier should either be equal to the old one or to the saved user identifier. In the case of a process enjoying privileges, the real user identifier and the saved user identifier are both modified in the same way, which means that a process possessing superuser privileges which modifies its user identifier using *setuid* cannot later restore its privileges. The identifiers of the real and effective current process may be modified using *setreuid*, and are

---

[2] That is, it should possess superuser permissions.

represented by the parameters **ruid** and **euid**. If the value –1 is used, the corresponding identifier is not modified.

The call *setgid* allows a process to modify its effective group identifier. The process should be privileged, or the new identifier should be equal to the old one, or to the saved group identifier. In the case where the process is privileged, the real group identifier and the saved group identifier are modified in the same way.

The group identifiers of the real and effective current process may be modified using *setregid*, and are represented by the parameters **rgid** and **egid**. If the value –1 is used, the corresponding identifier is not modified. A non-privileged process may invert these two identifiers. The call *setegid* corresponds to a call on *setregid* where the parameter **rgid** has the value of –1.

The system call **setgroups** enables the group identifiers associated with the current process to be changed. The parameter **list** specifies the groups to be set, with the size of the table being indicated by the parameter **size**.

In addition to these system calls, Linux also offers two specialised primitives relating to the control of access to files:

```
int setfsuid (uid_t fsuid);
```

```
int setfsgid (gid_t fsgid);
```

The primitive *setfsuid* modifies the user identifier used by the kernel in the control of access to files.

The primitive *setfsgid* modifies the group identifier used by the kernel in the control of access to files.

These two system calls are not commonly called by a 'classic' process. Indeed, by default, the kernel uses effective user and group identifiers for controlling access to files, which is consistent with classic semantics for controlling file access. These primitives are, however, available to allow servers to access files by using permissions of particular users and groups, when acting on a request on account of these users. The NFS server for example utilises these two primitives to modify its permissions at each request to access files.

All these system calls return the value 0 in the event of a successful transaction, and the value –1 in the case of a problem being encountered. The variable **errno** can take the value **EPERM**, which indicates that the process does not have the necessary privileges to modify its identifiers.

4.2.6 Compatibility information

The system call *getrusage* enables a process to find out what resources it has used. Its syntax is as follows:

```
#include <sys/time.h>
#include <sys/resource.h>
```

```
#include <unistd.h>

int getrusage (int who, struct rusage *rusage);
```

The parameter **who** specifies which process the operation should be applied to: it can take the value **RUSAGE_SELF** to obtain the resources used by the current process, or **RUSAGE_CHILDREN** to obtain the resources consumed by the child processes. The result is a conveyed in a variable pointed to by the parameter **rusage** (see section 4.2.3 for a definition of the structure of **rusage**). In the event of a successful transaction, the value 0 is returned, and –1 in the case of failure being encountered, *getrusage* returns a value –1, and the variable **errno** may take the value **EFAULT**, which indicates that the parameter **rusage** contains an invalid address.

Linux also provides a primitive *times* which allows a process to find out how much processor time it has used up. Its syntax is as follows:

```
#include <sys/times.h>

clock_t times (struct tms *buf);
```

The parameter **buf** specifies the address of a variable in which the result will be conveyed. The structure of **tms**, defined in the header file **<sys/times.h>**, contains the following fields:

type	field	description
time_t	tms_utime	Processor time used by the process in user-mode expressed in seconds
time_t	tms_stime	Processor time used by the process in kernel-mode expressed in seconds
time_t	tms_cutime	Processor time used by the child process in user-mode expressed in seconds
time_t	tms_cstime	Processor time used by the child process in kernel-mode expressed in seconds

times returns the number of clock cycles elapsed since the system was started up. If the parameter **buf** contains an invalid address, a value of –1 is returned and the variable **errno** takes the default value **EFAULT**.

4.2.7 Limits

A process may set limits on the resources that it consumes. Generally, these limits are set up when logging on to the system, and are inherited by the processes that are created, but a process may modify them by using the following system calls:

```
#include <sys/time.h>
#include <sys/resource.h>
#include <unistd.h>

int setrlimit (int resource, const struct rlimit *rlim);

int getrlimit (int resource, struct rlimit *rlim);
```

The primitive *setrlimit* allows a limit to be set. The parameter **resource** indicates the resource to be limited, and the limit is specified by the parameter **rlim**. If successful, the parameter 0 is returned, if not, *setrlimit* returns the value –1.

The structure of **rlimit**, defined in the file **<sys/resource.h>**, contains the following fields:

type	*field*	*description*
int	**rlim_cur**	Soft limit
int	**rlim_max**	Absolute limit

A non-privileged process can increase its soft limit, which may not exceed the absolute limit: it may equally reduce its absolute limit, but only a privileged process may increase the absolute limit.

The system call *getrlimit* allows a process to find out the limit assigned to a resource. If successful, the parameter 0 is returned, if not, *setrlimit* returns the value –1.

For these two system calls, the constants representing different resource are defined in the header file **<sys.resource.h>** :

constant	*meaning*
RLIMIT_CPU	Processor time, expressed in milliseconds
RLIMIT_FSIZE	Maximum file size, expressed in bytes
RLIMIT_DATA	Maximum size of data segment ,expressed in bytes
RLIMIT_STACK	Maximum size of stack segment, expressed in bytes
RLIMIT_CORE	Maximum size of core file to be created in the event of a fatal program error, expressed in bytes
RLIMIT_RSS	Maximum size of data resident in central memory, expressed in bytes
RLIMIT_NPROC	Maximum number of processes per user
RLIMIT_NOFILE	Maximum size of open files
RLIMIT_MEMLOCK	Maximum size of data locked in central memory, expressed in bytes
RLIMIT_AS	Maximum size of address space, expressed in bytes

In the event of failures using these primitives, the variable **errno** may take on the following values:

error	*meaning*
EFAULT	**rlim** contains an invalid address
EINVAL	**resource** contains an invalid value
EPERM	The process does not have sufficient privileges allowing it increase its absolute limit

4.2.8 Groups of processes

Linux provides several system calls enabling groups of processes to be managed:

```
#include <unistd.h>

int setpgid (pid_t pid, pid_t pgid);

pid_t getpgid (pid_t pid);

int setpgrp (void);

pid_t getpgrp (void);
```

The primitive *setpgid* modifies the group associated with the process specified by the parameter **pid**, and the parameter **pgid** specifies the number of the group. If **pid** is null, the modification applies to the current process, and if **pgid** is null, the number of the current process is used as the number of the group.

The system call *getpgid* returns the number of the group to which the process specified by the parameter **pid** belongs. If **pid** is null, the number of the group of the current process is returned. The system call *getpgrp* returns the group number of the current process.

The function *setgrp* modifies the group number of the current process and corresponds to the call **setpgid (0, 0)**.

In the event of failures using these primitives, the variable **errno** may take on the following values:

error	meaning
EINVAL	**pgid** contains a negative value
EPERM	The process is not authorised to modify the group to which the process specified by **pid** belongs
ESRCH	The process specified by **pid** does not exist

4.2.9 Sessions

Two system calls allow process sessions to be manipulated:

```
pid_t setsid (void);
```

```
pid_t getsid (pid_t pid);
```

The system call *setsid* creates a new session. The current process must not be a *leader* of the process group. When this call is made, the current process is at the same time the *leader* of a new session and the *leader* of a new process group, and no terminal is associated with it. The number of the current process is used as the identifier of the new session and the new process group, and this identifier is returned by *setsid*. In the event of a problem, the value –1 is returned and the variable **errno** takes the value **EPERM**, which means that the current process is already a process group *leader*.

The association of a control terminal to a session is established automatically when the process *leader* of the session enables a peripheral terminal or a pseudo-terminal that is not already associated.

The primitive *getsid* returns the session number of the process specified by **pid**. If **pid** is null, the session number of the current process is returned. In the event of a problem, the value –1 is returned and the variable **errno** takes the value **ESRCH**, which means that the process specified by the parameter **pid** does not exist.

4.2.10 Program execution

A new process, created by calling the primitive *fork,* is a copy based on its parent process, and therefore runs the same program. A system call allows a process to run a new program:

```
#include <unistd.h>

int execve (const char *filename, const char *argv [],   const char
*envp[]) ;
```

The primitive *execve* triggers the execution of a new program. **pathname** specifies the name of the file to be executed, which must be a binary program or a file of commands beginning with the line **#!interpreter_name**. The parameter **argv** indicates the program arguments to execute: each element of the table **argv** should point to a string of characters representing an argument. The first element of the table should contain the name of the program, the elements following this should contain the arguments, and the final element should contain the value **NULL**. The parameter **envp** specifies the variables in the program environment. Each of the elements should contain the address of a character string of the form **name_of _variable=value**, and the final element of the table should contain the value **NULL**. The system call *execve* triggers the overwriting of segments of code, data and stack. By those of the specified program. If the process is successful, there is therefore no return, since the calling process then runs a new program. If a problem occurs, *execve* returns a value –1, and the variable **errno** can take the following values:

error	meaning
E2BIG	The list of arguments or of environment variables is too large
EACCES	The process does not have runtime access to the file specified by **pathname**
EFAULT	**pathname** contains an invalid address
ENAMETOOLONG	**pathname** specifies a filename which is too long
ENOENT	**pathname** refers to an non-existent filename
ELOOP	A symbolic link continuous loop has been encountered
ENOEXE	The file specified by **pathname** is not an executable program
ENOMEM	The available memory is too small to run the program
ENOTDIR	One of the components of **pathname**, used as a directory name, is not a directory
EPERM	The filesystem containing the file specified by **pathname** has been mounted with options barring running of programs

Several library functions, offering alternatives to *execve*, are also provided by Linux:

```
#include <unistd.h>

int execl (const char *path, const char *arg, à);

int execle (const char *path, const char *arg, à);
char *const envp[];

int execlp (const char *file, const char *arg, à);

int execv (const char *path, char *const argv[]);

int execvp (const char *file, char *const argv[]);
```

For all these functions, the parameter pathname specifies the program to be run. The parameter argv of *execv* and *execvp* indicate the parameters to pass to the program, in the same way as for *execve*. The parameter envp indicates the environment variables to be passed to the program. Finally, for the functions *execl*, *execle* and *execlp*, the program arguments are stated by explicit parameters: arg should contain the address of a character string representing the name of the program, and should be followed by a list of pointers containing the argument addresses, and the last parameter on the list should be the value NULL.

The two functions *execlp* and *execvp* treat pathname as a simple command, in contrast to other functions and to *execve*: the search route associated with the current process (environment variable PATH) is used to search for the executable program specified.

4.3
ADVANCED CONCEPTS

4.3.1 Scheduling

The scheduler is the kernel function which decides which process should be executed by the processor: the scheduler scans the list of processes in the 'ready' state, and uses several criteria to choose which process to execute.

The Linux scheduler has three different scheduling policies: one for 'normal' processes, and two for 'real time' processes.

Each process has an associated process type, a fixed priority, and a variable priority. The process type can be:

- SCHED_FIFO, for a unalterable 'real time' process,
- SCHED_RR, for an alterable 'real time' process,
- SCHED_OTHER, for a 'classical' process.

The scheduler policy depends on the type of processes in the 'ready' list:

- When a process of the type **SCHED_FIFO** becomes ready, it is executed immediately. The scheduler nominates the process with the highest priority and executes it. This process is not normally pre-emptible, that is, it has the processor resource, and the system will not interrupt its execution except in three situations:

  1. Another process of the type **SCHED_FIFO** having a higher priority becomes ready, and is then executed,
  2. The process becomes suspended whilst waiting for an event, such as an input or output,
  3. The process voluntarily gives up the processor following a call to the primitive *sched_yield*. The process then passes to the 'ready' state, and other processes are executed.

- When a process of the type **SCHED_RR** becomes ready, it is executed immediately. Its behaviour is thus similar to **SCHED_FIFO**, with one exception: when the process is executed, a time slot is attributed to it. When this time period has elapsed, processes of the types **SCHED_FIFO** or **SCHED_RR** and having an equal or higher priority to the current process, may be selected and executed.

Process of the type **SCHED_OTHER** can only be executed when no 'real time' processes in the ready state exist. The process to be executed is then selected after considering the dynamic priorities. The dynamic priority of a process is decided partly the level specified by the user using system calls *nice* and *setpriority*, and partly by a factor calculated by the system. The priority of all processes which take several clock cycles to execute diminishes during execution and it may become of lower priority than processes which are not executing and whose priority is not modified.

A more complete definition of these different scheduling policies can be found in [Gallmeister, 1995].

4.3.2 Personalities

In order to allow programs coming from other operating systems to be run, Linux supports the idea of 'personality'. Each process is assigned to an execution domain. This domain specifies the way in which system calls are carried out, and the way in which messages are processed.

A 'personality' defines how the following are dealt with:

- system calls: Linux uses software interrupts to change into kernel mode, whilst other Unix systems use an inter-segment jump,
- message numbers specified by processes: when a process specifies a message number, for example in calling the primitives *sigaction* or *kill*, the message number is converted by means of a look-up table,

- numbers of messages sent to processes: when a message is to be sent to a process, the message number is converted by means of a look-up table.

By default, processes use the native Linux execution domain, which specifies that system calls are carried out by software interrupts, and message numbers are not converted. An emulation system can, however, use different execution domains in order to run binary programs belonging to other operating systems.

4.3.3 Cloning

With Linux, as with Unix, processes have different address spaces, and they need to use specialised communication channels such as pipes (see chapter 10) or System V IPC (see chapter 11), in order to exchange data. However, Linux has an extension which enables process 'clones' to be created. A clone process is created, using the primitive *clone*, by duplicating its parent process. But, unlike classical processes, it may share its context with its parent.

Depending on the options enabled when *clone* is called, the sharing affects one or several parts of its context:

- the address space: the two processes share the same segment of code and data. Any modification of one is visible to the other,
- filesystem control information: the processes share the same root and current directories. If one of these directories is modified by a process (by the primitives *chdir* or *chroot*), the modification acts also on the other,
- open file descriptors: the two processes share the same open file descriptors. If one of the processes closes a file, the other can no longer access it,
- Message managers: the two processes share the same table of called functions when a message is received. Any modification by one of the processes, using the primitive *sigaction* for example, brings about a change in the message processing regime for the other process,
- process identifier: the two processes can have the same number.

In the extreme case of two processes having the maximum number of common attributes, they remain uniquely distinguished by their processor register values and by their stack segments.

The ability to clone processes brings, amongst other things, the possibility of implementing servers in which several threads may be executing. These operations may simply share data, without making use of the inter-process communication mechanisms.

4.4
COMPLEMENTARY SYSTEM CALLS

4.4.1 Changing 'personality'

Linux allows the personality of a process to be modified in order to enable a program belonging to another operating system to be run. This possibility is made use of by emulators, for example the emulator iBCS2, which runs binary programs intended for the Unix SCO or System V Release 4 systems.

The system call *personality* allows a process to modify its execution domain in order that Linux can emulate the behaviour of another operating system. It is not included in the standard C library, and must therefore be declared specifically:

```
#include <syscall.h>

_syscall1 (int, personality, int, pers);
```

This declaration corresponds to the following format:

```
int personality (int pers);
```

The parameter **pers** specifies the operating system to be emulated. In the event of a successful transaction, the former personality is returned by *personality*. In the event of an error, the value –1, is returned, and the variable **errno** takes the value **EINVAL,** which indicates that the parameter **pers** contains a invalid value.

The Linux header **file <linux/personality.h>** defines several constants specifying the operating systems to be emulated:

constant	meaning
PER_LINUX	Linux, that is, not an emulation
PER_SVR4	System V, release 4
PER_SVR3	System V, release 3
PER_SCOSVR3	SCO Unix version 3.2
PER_WISE386	UNIX System V/386 Release 3.2.1
PER_ISCR4	Interactive Unix
PER_BSD	BSD Unix
PER_XENIX	Xenix

4.4.2 Schedule modification

Several system calls allow the policy and scheduling parameters associated with a process to be modified:

```
#include <sched.h>

int sched_setscheduler (pid_t pid, int policy, const struct sched_param
*param);

int sched_setscheduler (pid_t pid);

int sched_setparam (pid_t pid, const struct sched_param *param);

int sched_getparam (pid_t pid, const struct sched_param *param);
```

The system call *sched_scheduler* enables the policy and scheduling parameters associated with a process to be modified, and the parameter **pid** specifies the process upon which it should act. It can be zero to indicate the current process. The parameter **policy** specifies the scheduling policy to apply to the process, and should have one of the values **SCHED_FIFO**, **SCHED_RR**, or **SCHED_OTHER**. The parameter **param** specifies the scheduling parameters to be used. The primitive *sched_getscheduler* enables the scheduling policy associated with a process characterised by **pid** to be established, or the current process if **pid** is zero.

The system call *sched_setparam* enables the scheduling parameters associated with a process to be modified. The parameter **pid** specifies the process upon which it should act. It can be zero to indicate the current process. The parameter **param** specifies the scheduling parameters to be used. The primitive *sched_getparam* enables the scheduling parameters associated with a process characterised by **pid** to be established, or the current process if **pid** is zero. These parameters are passed n the parameter **param**.

Linux 2.0 only enables the static priority associated with a process to be modified. The structure of **sched_param**, defined in the header file **<sched.h>**, only contains one field, **sched_priority**:

type	*field*	*description*
int	sched_priority	Static priority associated with process

In the event of a fault, these primitives return a value of −1 and the variable **errno** can take the following values:

error	meaning
EFAULT	**param** contains an invalid address
EINVAL	**policy** or the variable pointed to by **param** contains an invalid value
EPERM	The process does not possess the necessary privileges to modify its scheduling parameters
ESRCH	The process specified by **pid** does not exist

The primitives *sched_get_priority-min* and *sched_get_priority_max* allow the minimum and maximum static priorities associated with a scheduling policy to be determined. Their syntax is as follows:

```
#include <sched.h>


int sched_get_priority_min (int policy);


int sched_get_priority_max (int policy);
```

The primitive *sched_rr_get_interval* allows the time quantum attributed to a process of type **SCHED_RR** to be determined. Its syntax is as follows:

```
#include <sched.h>


int sched_rr_get_interval (pid_t pid, struct timespec *interval);
```

The parameter **pid** specifies the process, and it can be null to indicate the current process. The process in question must be of the type **SCHED_RR**, and the parameter **interval** should contain the address of a variable in which the time slot assigned to the specified process will be stored. If successful, the value 0 is returned, if not *sched_rr_get_interval* returns the value –1 and the variable **errno** may take the following values:

error	meaning
EFAULT	**interval** contains an invalid address
ESRCH	The process specified by the parameter **pid** does not exist

The structure of **timespec** includes the following fields:

type	field	description
long	**tv_sec**	Number of seconds
long	**tv_nsec**	Number of nanoseconds

The primitive *sched-yield* enables the current process to relinquish the processor. Its syntax is as follows:

```
#include <sched.h>

int sched_yield (void);
```

When this primitive is executed, the current process is placed at the end of the list of processes marked 'ready', and the scheduler is executed. If other processes which are ready exist in the system, there is therefore a change of current process.

4.4.3 Process priorities

Linux provides several system calls enabling process priorities to be altered:

```
#include <unistd.h>

int nice (int inc);

#include <sys/resource.h>

int setpriority (int which, int who, int prio);

int getpriority (int which, int who);
```

The primitive *nice* enables the dynamic priority of the current process to be modified, and the parameter **inc** is added to the current priority. Only a privileged process may specify a negative value in order to increase its priority. If successful, the value 0 is returned, if not *nice* returns the value –1, and the variable **errno** takes the value **EPERM**, which indicates that the calling process does not have enough privileges to increase its priority.

The system call *setpriority* modifies the priority of a process, a group of processes, or all the processes of a user. The parameter **which** may take the values **PRIO_PROCESS, PRIO_PGRP, or PRIO_USER**. The parameter **who** specifies a process number, a process group number, or a user number, according to the value of **which**. The parameter **prio** indicates the priority to be ranked. Only a privileged process can give one or more other processes a higher priority. The primitive *setpriority* returns a value of 0 in the event of a successful transaction and –1 in the event of a fault.

The system call *getpriority* finds out the priority of a process, a group of processes, or all the processes of a user. The parameters **which** and **who** have the same meaning as for *setpriority*. The value returned is the highest priority attributed to the specified processes. In so far as *getpriority* can return a value of –1 without that indicating an error, it is necessary to reset the variable **errno** to 0 and to check its value after the system call return.

In the event of failure with these primitives, the variable **errno** can take the following values:

error	*meaning*
EACCES	The calling process does not possess the necessary privileges to increase the priority of other processes
EINVAL	**which** contains an invalid value
EPERM	The current process does not have the same real and effective user identifiers as the process(s) specified by **who**
ESRCH	No process corresponds to the combination specified by **which** and **who**

4.4.4 Control of the execution of a process

The system call *ptrace* allows a process to control execution of another process. Its syntax is as follows:

```
#include <sys/ptrace>

int ptrace (long request, pid_t pid, long addr, long data);
```

The parameter **request** specifies the operation to carry out on the process whose number is passed in the parameter **pid**. The meanings of the parameters **addr** and **data** depend on the value of **request**.

The operations that are available are defined in the header file **<sys/ptrace.h>**. The constants are as follows:

constant	meaning
PTRACE_TRACEME	The current process is indicating that it will be controlled by another process.
PTRACE_ATTACH	The current process is indicating that it will control the process identified by **pid**. The signal SIGSTOP is sent to the controlled process in order to suspend execution.
PTRACE_PEEKDATA	The contents of the word located at the address **addr**, in the data segment of the address space of the controlled process, is returned in the variable whose address is contained in **data**.
PTRACE_PEEKTEXT	The contents of the word located at the address **addr**, in the code segment of the address space of the controlled process is returned in the variable whose address is contained in **data**.
PTRACE_PEEKUSR	The contents of the word located at the address **addr**, in the **user** structure of the controlled process (see section 4.5.2) is returned in the variable whose address is contained in **data**.
PTRACE_POKEDATA	The value contained in **data** is written in the word located in the address **addr**, in the data segment of the address space of the controlled process.
PTRACE_POKETEXT	The value contained in **data** is written in the word located in the address **addr**, in the code segment of the address space of the controlled process.
PTRACE_POKEUSR	The value contained in **data** is written in the word located in the address **addr**, in the **user** structure of the controlled process.
PTRACE_SYSCALL	The execution of the controlled process is continued until the next system call is executed. The command strace uses this option in order to display the system calls executed by a process.
PTRACE_CONT	The execution of the controlled process is continued.
PTRACE_KILL	The execution of the controlled process is terminated.
PTRACE_SINGLESTEP	The execution of the controlled process is continued for a single machine instruction.
PTRACE_DETACH	The process is no longer controlled.

In the event of an error, *ptrace* returns to the value −1 and the variable **errno** may take the following values:

error	*meaning*
EFAULT	**addr** contains an invalid address
EIO	**request** or **data** contain an invalid value
EPERM	The calling process does not have the necessary privileges for controlling the process specified by **pid**, or the latter is already controlled
ESRCH	The process specified by **pid** does not exist

The debugger programs, such as *gdb*, use *ptrace* in order to run a program instruction by instruction, and to allow the user to visualise the program.

4.4.5 Cloning

The system call *clone* creates a 'clone' of the current process. Since this primitive is not included in the standard library it is necessary to declare it explicitly.

Before calling *clone*, a stack segment must be allocated[3], and the parameters of the function to be executed must be arranged in this memory zone. Following this, the processor registers must be initialised in the following manner (for an x86 processor):

- **eax** must contain the code for the call *clone*, represented by the constant __NR_clone;
- **eax** must contain a combination of constants introduced later;
- **eax** must contain the stack pointer for the child process.

The program *clone*.S mentioned below, and derived from a source file from the C library in the GNU scheme, carries out the call for the primitive *clone* in x86 assembly language. The standard form of the *clone* function is as follows:

```
int clone (int (*fn)(), void *child_stack, int flags, int nargs, ...);
```

The parameter **fn** is a pointer from the child process to the function to be executed, and the parameter **child_stack** is the pointer to the zone of memory allocated for the stack of the child process. The parameter **flags** defines methods for cloning, and finally, the parameter **nargs** defines the number of arguments to be passed to the function pointed to by **fn** and is followed by these arguments.

Several constants, defined in the header file **<linux/sched.h>**, stipulate the cloning protocols:

---

[3] By a call to the function *malloc* for example.

constant	meaning
CLONE_VM	The child process shares the address space with the parent process
CLONE_FS	The child process shares root and current directories with the parent process
CLONE_FILES	The child process shares the open file descriptors with the parent process
CLONE_SIGHAND	The child process shares signal managers with the parent process
CLONE_PID	The child process has the same number as the parent process

Furthermore, the message to be passed to the parent process when the child process has terminated may also be specified.

──────── Clone.S ────────────────────────────

```
#define __ASSEMBLY__

#include <linux/linkage.h>
#include <asm/errno.h>
#include <asm/unistd.h>

        .text
ENTRY(clone)
        /* Check of arguments */
        movl   $-EINVAL,%eax
        movl   4(%esp), %ecx /* the function pointer must not be null */
        testl  %ecx,%ecx
        jz     syscall_error
        movl   8(%esp),%ecx  /* the stack address must not be null */
        testl  %ecx,%ecx
        jz     syscall_error
        movl   16(%esp),%edx /* the number of arguments must be positive
*/
        testl  %edx,%edx
        js     syscall_error

        /* Allocation of stack space, and copy of arguments */
        movl   %edx,%eax
        negl   %eax
        lea    -4(%ecx,%eax,4),%eax
```

```
        jz     2f
1:      movl   16(%esp,%edx,4),%eax
        movl   %eax,0(%ecx,%edx,4)
        dec    %edx
        jnz    1b
2:
        /* Backup of function pointer: it will be removed `from the
           stack once clone has been called */
        movl   4(%esp),%eax
        movl   %eax,0(%ecx)

        /* Calling of clone */
        pushl  %ebx
        movl   16(%esp),%ebx
        movl   $__NR_clone,%eax
        int    %0x80
        popl   %ebx

        /* Check of return code */
        test   %eax,%eax
        jl     syscall_error
        jz     thread_start

        ret

syscall_error:
        /* Error, -1 returned */
        movl   $-1,%eax
        ret

thread_start:
        /* Code of the process clone */
        subl   %ebp,%ebp
        call   *%ebx              /* Function call */
        movl   $__NR_exit,%eax    / End of process */
        int    $0x80
```

——————————————————————— Clone.S ———————

The program *ExempleClone.c* is a simple (and not very powerful) example of the use of the function *clone*. It creates a child process which shares the address space, the file descriptors, and the message management with its parent process, and the child process modifies a variable and closes a file. The parent process declares the contents of the variable and checks to see if the file is still open.

─────────── ExempleClone.c ───────────

```
#include <signal.h>
#include <stdio.h>
#include <stdlib.h>
#include <fcntl.h>

#include <linux/sched.h>
#include <linux/unistd.h>

#define STACKSIZE 16384

/*
 *This function is similar to thr_create() from the pthreads library,
but less advanced */
 int start_clone (void (*fn) (void *), void *data)
{
    long retval;
    void *newstack;

    /*
    *Allocation of the stack for the new process
     */
    newstack = (void **) malloc (STACKSIZE);
    if (!newstack)
            return -1;

    /*
     *Stack Initialisation
    */
    newstack = (void *) (STACKSIZE + (char *) newstack);

    /*
     *Clone creation
    */
    retval = clone (fn, newstack, CLONE_VM | CLONE_FS | CLONE_FILES
                | CLONE_SIGHAND | SIGHLD,
                  1, data);
    if (retval < 0) {
```

```
                        errno = -retval;
                        retval = -1;
            }
        return retval;
    }


int show_same_vm;

void cloned_process_starts_here (void *data)
{
    printf ("child:\t got argument %d as fd\n", (int) data);
    show_same_vm = 5;
    printf ("child:\t vm = %d\n", show_same_vm);
    close ((int) data);
}

int main (void)
{
            int fd,
                pid;

            fd = open ("/dev/null", O_RDONLY);
            if (fd < 0) {
                    perror ("/dev/null");
                    exit (1);
            }
            printf ("mother:\t fd = %d\n", fd);

            show_same_vm = 10;
            printf ("mother:\t vm = %d\n", show_same_vm);

            pid =   start_clone (cloned_process_starts_here, (void *)
fd);
            if (pid <0) {
                    perror ("start_clone");
                    exit (1);
            }
            sleep (1);
            printf ("mother:\t vm = %d\n", show_same_vm);
            if (write (fd, "c", 1) <0)
                    printf   ("mother:\t   child   closed   our   file
descriptor\n");
            exit (0);
    }
```

_____ ExempleClone.c _____

Execution of the program results in the following statement:

```
mother: fd = 3
mother: vm = 10
child:  got argument 3 as fd
child:  vm = 5
mother: vm = 5
mother: child closed our file descriptor
```

It should be noted that *clone* is a very low level system call, and is without doubt rather tedious to use directly. A library of *threads* utilising *clone* is currently being developed by Xavier Leroy and is available at URL
http://pauillac.inria.fr/~xleroy/linuxthreads/.

4.5
GENERAL INTRODUCTION
TO IMPLEMENTATION

4.5.1 Table of processes

4.5.1.1 Process descriptors
Each process is referenced by a descriptor which contains the process attributes together with the information enabling the process to be managed.

The structure **process_struct** defined in the file **<linux/sched.h>**, characterises a process. It contains the following fields:

type	field	description
volatile long	**state**	State of a process
long	**counter**	Number of clock cycles during which the child is authorised to run
long	**priority**	process priority
unsigned long	**signal**	Signals waiting (see chapter 5, section 5.5.1)
unsigned long	**blocked**	Signals masked (see chapter 5, section 5.5.1)
unsigned long	**flags**	see page 73
int	**errno**	Error code set by system calls
long [8]	**debugreg**	Copy of hardware set up registers

Continuation of the definition of the structure **task_structure**		
type	*field*	*description*
struct exec_domain *	exec_domain	Process execution domain
struct linux_binfmt *	binfmt	Pointer to the operations linked to the format of the program run by the child
struct task _struct *	next_ task	Pointer to the following process in the list
struct task _struct *	prev_ task	Pointer to the previous process in the list
struct task _struct *	next_run	Pointer to the next child in the list of children which are ready
struct task _struct *	prev_task	Pointer to the previous process in the list
unsigned long	saved_kernel_stack	Stack pointer used in kernel mode
unsigned long	kernel_stack_page	Address of the memory page containing the stack used in kernel mode
int	exit_code	Return code to transmit to the parent process: the least significant 8 bits (bits 0 to 7) contain the number of the signal which caused the process to terminate, or the following 8 bits (bits 8 to 15) contain the return code provided by the process when the primitive _exit is called
int	exit_signal	Signal number to be transmitted to the parent process when it terminates
unsigned long	personality	Personality associated with a process
int:1	dumpable	Boolean expression indicating whether a file core should be created in the event of a fatal error
int:1	did_exec	Boolean indicating whether a process has used execve to run a program

Continuation of the definition of the structure **task_structure**		
type	*field*	*description*
int	pid	Process number
int	pgrp	Number of the group containing the process
int	session	Number of the session containing the process
int	leader	Boolean expression indicating whether a process is the leader of the session
int [NGROUPS]	groups	Groups associated with a process
struct process_struct *	p_opptr	Pointer to the original parent process descriptor
struct process_struct *	p_pptr	Pointer to the parent process descriptor
struct process_struct *	p_cptr	Pointer to the descriptor of the most recently created child process
struct process_struct *	p_ysptr	Pointer to the following 'brother' process, which has been created by the same parent process
struct process_struct *	p_osptr	Pointer to the previous 'brother' process
struct wait_queue *	wait_chldexit	Variable used in waiting for the child process to terminate
unsigned short	uid	Real user identifier assigned to the process
unsigned short	euid	Effective user identifier assigned to the process
unsigned short	suid	Saved user identifier assigned to the process
unsigned short	fsuid	User identifier assigned to the process for controlling access to the files
unsigned short	gid	Real group identifier assigned to the process
unsigned short	egid	Effective group identifier assigned to the process
unsigned short	sgid	Saved group identifier assigned to the process

Continuation of the definition of the structure **task_structure**		
type	*field*	*description*
unsigned short	fsgid	Group identifier assigned to the process for controlling access to the files
unsigned long	timeout	Max. wait during which the process must be suspended
unsigned long	policy	Scheduling policy associated with the process
unsigned long	rt_priority	Static priority assigned to the process
long	utime	Processor time used in user mode
long	stime	Processor time used up in kernel mode
long	cutime	Processor time used up by the processes in user mode
long	cstime	Processor time used up in kernel mode
long	start_time	Creation date of the process
unsigned long	min_flt	Number of memory traps processed for the process without loading a page
unsigned long	maj_flt	Number of memory traps processed for the process while loading one page from disk
unsigned long	nswap	Number of process pages saved in the *swap* zone
unsigned long	cmin_flt	Number of memory traps processed by the child process without loading a page
unsigned long	cmaj_flt	Number of memory traps processed for child process while loading one
unsigned long	cnswap	Number of child process pages saved in the swap zone
int:1	swappable	Boolean indicating whether the process can be returned to secondary memory
unsigned long	swap_cnt	Number of memory pages to erase

continuation of the definition of the structure of **task_struct**		
type	*field*	*description*
unsigned short	**used_math**	Boolean expression indicating whether the process has used the maths co-processor
char [16]	**comm**	Name of the program run by the process
int	**link_count**	Number of symbolic links scanned during the Resolution of the filename (see chapter 6)
struct tty_struct *	**tty**	Pointer to the descriptor of the terminal assigned to the process (see chapter 9)
struct sem_undo *	**semundo**	Pointer to a list of System V semaphores (see chapter 11)
struct sem_queue *	**semsleeping**	Pointer to the System V semaphore wait queue in which the process is suspended (see chapter 11)
struct desc_struct *	**ldt**	Pointer to the descriptor of the segment table local to this process. This table is used and modified by the emulator Wine
struct thread_struct	**tss**	Value of processor register s
struct fs_struct *	**fs**	Checking information used when accessing files (see chapter 6)
struct files_struct *	**files**	Pointer to the file descriptors opened by the process. (see chapter 6)
struct mm_struct *	**mm**	Control information used for memory management (see chapter 8)
struct signal_struct *	**sig**	Pointer to the action descriptors assigned to the signals (see chapter 5, section 5.5.1)
int	**processor**	Processor identifier on which the process is run
int	**last_processor**	Identifier of the most recent processor on which the process was run

The status of the process (the **state** field) can be expressed using several constants:

constant	meaning
PROCESS_RUNNING	The process is in the ready state or execution is in progress
PROCESS_INTERRUPTIBLE	The process is suspended but may be awoken by a signal
PROCESS_UNINTERRUPTIBLE	The process is suspended and may not be woken by a signal
PROCESS_ZOMBIE	The process has finished running
PROCESS_STOPPED	The process has been suspended by the user

Several constants are also defined in the field **flags**:

constant	meaning
PF_PTRACED	The process is controlled by another one
PF_TRACESYS	The process is controlled by another one and it should be run until the next system call
PF_FORKNOEXEC	The process is has not executed the system call execve in order to run another program
PF_SUPERPRIV	The process has used superuser privileges
PF_DUMPCORE	The process has terminated by producing a file core
PF_SIGNALED	The process has been terminated by the arrival of a signal
PF_STARTING	The process is being created
PF_EXITING	The process is finishing
PF_USEDFPU	The process used the maths co-processor during its last time interval (this state is used by code-managers in multi-processors)

4.5.1.2 Organisation of the table of processes

The process descriptors are dynamically allocated by the kernal by calling the function **kmalloc** and the table **task**, defined in the source file *kernel/sched.c* contains the pointers to the descriptors of processes in execution on each processor. A macro instruction, called **current**, refers to the address of the descriptor of the current process on a processor.

The variable **init_process** contains the descriptor of the first process created when the system starts up. After start up, the process only executes if no other process is ready, and its descriptor serves to reference the beginning of the table of processes.

The process descriptors are organised in the form of a doubly linked list, by means of the fields **next_process** and **prev_process**. The descriptors of processes that are ready or in execution are put in another doubly linked list by means of fields **next_run** and **prev_run**.

The fields **p_opptr**, **p_pptr**, **p_cptr**, **p_ysptr**, and **p_osptr** are used to manage relationships between processes. When a process duplicates itself by calling the primitive *fork* the following occur:

- the pointers **p_opptr**, and **p_pptr** of the descriptor of the child process contain the address of the parent process;
- the pointer **p_osptr** of the descriptor of the child process takes on the value of the pointer **p_cptr** of the descriptor of the parent process;
- the pointer **p_ysptr** of the descriptor of the child process is initialised with the value zero;
- the pointer **p_ysptr** of the most recent 'brother' process (referenced by the pointer **p_cptr** of the descriptor of the parent process) contains the address of the descriptor of the new child process;
- the pointer **p_cptr** of the descriptor of the parent process contains the address of the descriptor of the child process.

Figure 4.3 represents the pointers for the case of a processor P having created three successive child processes F1, F2, and F3.

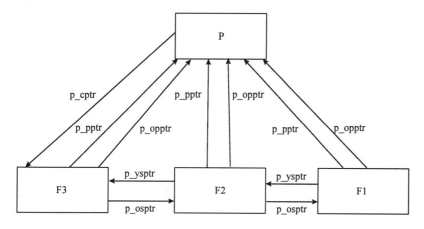

Figure 4.3: Relationships between process descriptors.

4.5.1.3 *Processes table management*

Several macro instructions, which enable process descriptor lists to be managed are defined in the file **<linux/sched.h>**:

macro-instruction	*meaning*
REMOVE_LINKS	This macro-instruction deletes a descriptor from all lists that it appears on
SET_LINKS	This macro-instruction inserts a descriptor in all lists: it updates the descriptor pointers before putting it in the list of its 'siblings'
for_each_process	This macro-instruction enables all the process descriptors to be searched, by having their parameters varied

4.5.2 Processor registers

The context of a process includes the contents of the processor registers. In the event of a change of context, or when a system primitive is called, these registers are saved in memory by the kernel. The structure **pt_regs**, defined in the header file **<asm/ptrace.h>**, contains the following fields for the x86 architecture:

type	*field*	*description*
long	**ebx**	Value in the register **ebx**
long	**ecx**	Value in the register **ecx**
long	**edx**	Value in the register **edx**
long	**esi**	Value in the register **esi**
long	**edi**	Value in the register **edi**
long	**ebp**	Value in the register **ebp**
long	**eax**	Value in the register **eax** to be restored when returning to the system call
unsigned short	**es**	Value in the register **es**
unsigned short	**fs**	Value in the register **fs**
unsigned short	**gs**	Value in the register **gs**
long	**orig_eax**	Value in the register **eax** when the system call is made (**eax** contains the number of the primitive to be executed)
long	**eip**	Value in the register **eip** (sequence number counter)
unsigned short	**cs**	Value in the segment register **cs** (code segment descriptor)
long	**eflags**	Value of processor flags
long	**esp**	Value in the register **esp** (stack pointer)
unsigned short	**ss**	Value in the register **ss** (stack segment descriptor)

The structure **user,** defined in the header file **<asm/user.h>,** is used by the kernel when a file *core* needs to be created: this structure is placed at the beginning of the file in order that a debugger may find the process context when it is terminated. The system call *trace* also utilises this structure when enabling a process to read and modify its contents.

The fields contained in the structure **user** are as follows:

type	*field*	*description*
struct pt_regs	**regs**	Values of processor registers
int	**u_fpvalid**	Boolean indicating whether the process uses the maths co-processor
struct user_i387_struct	**i387**	Values of the maths co-processor registers
unsigned long int	**u_tsize**	Size of data segment, expressed in memory pages
unsigned long int	**u_dsize**	Size of code segment, expressed in memory pages
unsigned long int	**u_ssize**	Size of stack segment, expressed in memory pages
unsigned long	**start_code**	Virtual address of the start of the code segment
unsigned long	**start_stack**	Virtual address of the start of the stack
long int	**signal**	Number of the signal which caused the process to terminate
int	**reserved**	Unused
struct pt_regs *	**u_ar0**	Address of the value of registers in the structure **user** (used by gdb)
struct user_i387_struct *	**u_fpstate**	Address of the value of the co-processor in the structure **user** (used by gdb)
unsigned long	**magic**	Value of processor flags
char[32]	**u_comm**	Name of the program run by the process
int[8]	**u_debugreg**	Value of hardware setup registers

4.5.3 Process synchronisation

4.5.3.1 *Principle*

At any given moment, only one process can be executing in kernel mode. Although physical and software interrupts may be able to intervene in this process, Linux does not instigate scheduling if the current active process is in kernel mode. A process which is executing in kernel mode may, however, bring about a change of current process by suspending its execution. This voluntary suspension is normally due to waiting for an event to occur, such as an input/output, or the termination of a child process.

Linux provides two tools allowing two processes to synchronise themselves in kernel mode: wait queues and semaphores. The corresponding structures are defined in the header file <linux/wait>.

4.5.3.2 *Wait queues*

A wait queue is a linked and circular list of descriptors. Each descriptor contains the address of a process descriptor as well as a pointer to the next element in the queue. The structure **wait_queue** characterises items in the wait queue:

type	field	description
struct process_struct *	**process**	Pointer to the descriptor of the waiting process
struct wait_queue *	**next**	Pointer to the next element in the queue

4.5.3.3 *Semaphores*

Semaphores constitute a general synchronisation mechanism between processes. They are not really a means of communication, but rather a process synchronisation device.

In computing, and particularly in the case of operating systems, a semaphore is utilised to control access to a resource.

The semaphore, and its associated operations were defined in 1965 by E.W. Dijkstra [Dijkstra 1965]. A semaphore is composed of an integer value (counter) and two operations, as described below:

- P (from the Dutch *proberen*, to test): this operation is used when a process needs to enter a critical section. The operation is performed in the following two stages:

1. check the value of the semaphore counter which controls the resource;
2. if this value is positive, the process may make use of the resource. It decrements the counter value by 1 to indicate that it is using one unit of resource;
3. if the value is zero, the process pauses until the value becomes positive again. When the process is reactivated, it returns to stage 1.

- V (from the Dutch *verhogen*, to increment): this operation is symmetrical with the preceding one, and is used when a process leaves the critical section. The value of the semaphore counter is incremented by 1, and the paused processes are reactivated.

The operations P and V must be carried out in priority mode, that is, they must not be interrupted.

The operations P and V are frequently also referred to as **down** and **up**.

Semaphores are used in computer systems principally to solve two problems:

- **mutual exclusion**: processes must be prevented from accessing the same resource at the same time. In fact, if this were to happen, the resource may go into an indeterminate state;
- **the problem of producers and consumers**: this concerns permission for two processes to co-operate: one producing the information that the other one requires. The semaphore is used to flag to the consumer that the data is ready.

These problems are resolved by binary semaphores, but the semaphore counter may take other positive values. This is the case when several units of one resource are available; the counter then takes the value of the number of units which are simultaneously accessible.

In Linux, the **semaphore** structure, defined in the file **<asm/semaphore.h>**, contains the following fields:

type	field	description
int	count	Semaphore counter
int	waiting	Number of waiting processes
struct wait_queue *	wait	List of processes waiting for the semaphore

4.5.4 *Timers*

Linux manages a list of *timers* to enable processes to be put on hold for a specified delay. These *timers* are organised in the form of a doubly linked circular list.

Timers to be activated in the near future are put at the head of the list, and those to be activated later are put at the end of the list.

The structure of **timer_list**, defined in the file **<linux/timer.h>**, defines the format of elements in the list.

type	field	description
struct timer_list *	next	Pointer to the next element in the list
struct timer_list *	prev	Pointer to the previous element in the list
unsigned long	expires	Expiry date of the timer
unsigned long	data	Parameter to be transmitted to the associated function
void (*) (unsigned long)	function	Address of the function to call when the timer expires

The variable **timer_head**, defined in the source file *kernel/sched.c*, contains the address of the first element in the list.

The expiry date (field **expires**) is expressed in terms of the number of clock cycles since the start-up of the system. The global variable **jiffies** is maintained by the kernel (its value is incremented at each clock interrupt) and always contains the number of clock cycles elapsed since the start.

4.5.5 Execution domains

The kernel maintains the supported execution domains. For this, a singly linked list of descriptors is kept.

The structure **exec_domain**, defined in the file **<linux/personality.h>**, describes the elements in this list:

type	field	description
const char *	name	Domain name
lcall7_func	handler	Address of the function to call if the process performs a system call via an intra-segment jump in the segment number 7 (call method used by System V and BSD Unix)
unsigned char	pers_low	Code of the personality associated with the domain
unsigned char	pers_high	Code of the personality associated with the domain

continuation of the definition of the structure of **exec_domain**		
type	*field*	*description*
unsigned long *	**signal_invmap**	Mapping table enabling signal numbers sent to the calling process to be converted
long *	**use_count**	Number of processes using this domain
struct exec_domain *	**next**	Pointer to the next domain in the list

The variable **exec_domains**, defined in the source file *kernel/exec_domain.c*, contains the address of the first element in the list. When the system boots up, the list contains just one element, called **default_exec_domain**, which defines the Linux personality.

4.5.6 Formats of executable files

Linux supports several executable program formats, in particular the binaries **a.out** and **ELF**. Each format has associated with it several functions for manipulating executable programs.

The structure **linux_binfmt** defined in the header file **<linux/binfmts.h>**, contains pointers to the necessary functions:

- **int (*load_binary)(struct linux_binprm *binprm, struct pt_regs *regs)**
  This function is called to load the executable program in memory when the system call *execve* is executed. The first parameter specifies the program to be run, as well as its context and the second parameter indicates the values to be set in registers.

- **int (*load_shlib)(int fd)**
  This function is called to load a shared library in memory. The parameter **fd** specifies the descriptor of input/outputs associated with the file containing the shared library.

- **int (*core_dump)(long signr, struct pt_regs *regs)**
  This function is called to create the file *core*. The parameter **signr** indicates the number of the message leading to termination of the message, and **regs** specifies the context of the process at the time the message is received.

The function for loading an executable, **load_binary**, uses its first parameter to establish the context of the process. The structure **linux_binprm**, defined in the file **<linux/binfmts.h>**, is used for this purpose and contains the following fields:

type	field	description
char[128]	buf	First 128 bytes of the executable file
unsigned	page	Addresses of pages containing the arguments
long[MAX_ARG_PAGES]	sh_bang	Boolean expression indicating whether a line of the form **#!interpreter** has already been interpreted
struct inode *	inode	Descriptor of the file inode to be executed
int	e_uid	Effective user identifier
int	e_gid	Effective group identifier
int	argc	Number of arguments
int	envc	Number of environment variables
char *	filename	Filename to be executed
unsigned long	loader	Field used only in the Alpha architecture
int	dont_iput	Boolean expression indicating whether the function **iput** should be called to free the inode descriptor

4.6
DETAILED DESCRIPTION OF IMPLEMENTATION

4.6.1 Internal functions

4.6.1.1 Process synchronisation
The file *kernel/sched.c* contains the service functions facilitating process synchronisation in kernel mode. These functions are used in all parts of the kernel when a process needs to be suspended whilst waiting for an event, or when it needs to be 'woken up'.

The function **add_to_runqueue** inserts a process descriptor into the list of processes that are ready. The function **del_from_runqueue** enables a descriptor to be removed from this list. A process descriptor may be placed at the end of a list by the function **move_last_runqueue**.

The function **wake_up_process** wakes up a suspended process: it marks it status as **PROCESS_RUNNING** and inserts it in the list of ready processes.

The wait queues are manipulated by the functions **__add_wait_queue**, and **__remove_wait_queue**, defined in the header file **<linux/sched.h>**. An element is added to the wait queue by **__add_wait_queue**, and is removed from this queue by **remove_wait_queue**. The functions **__add_wait_queue** and **__remove_wait_queue**, call **__add_wait_queue** and **__remove_wait_queue** respectively, having previously masked out all interrupts.

The function **wake_up** enables all processes that are waiting for an event in a wait queue to be woken up. It examines the queue and calls **wake_up_process** for each process whose status is **PROCESS_UNINTERRUPTIBLE** or **PROCESS_INTERRUPTIBLE**. A similar operation is carried out by the function **wake_up_interruptible**, but the latter only causes a wake-up if the process is in the **PROCESS_INTERRUPTIBLE** state. The function **__sleep_on** suspends the current process and puts it in a wait queue. It modifies the state of the process, records its descriptor in a file by calling **add_wait_queue**, then causes a change in the current process by calling the function **schedule**. When the process is woken up, the remainder of the function is executed, and the process descriptor is removed from the wait queue by a call to **remove_wait_queue** . The functions **interruptible_sleep_on** and **sleep_on** call **__sleep_on** and instruct it to set the status of the current process at **PROCESS_INTERRUPTIBLE** and **PROCESS_UNINTERRUPTIBLE** respectively.

The function **__down** enables the current process to be suspended whilst waiting for an event on a semaphore signal. The descriptor of the current process is added to the wait queue of the semaphore, its status is changed to **PROCESS_UNINTERRUPTIBLE**, then the semaphore counter is interrogated. As long as the counter is less than or equal to zero, the function **schedule** is called to change the current process, and the status of the current process is set to **PROCESS_UNINTERRUPTIBLE**. When the semaphore counter becomes positive, the status of the current process is set to **PROCESS_RUNNING**, and the process descriptor is removed from the semaphore wait queue by a call to **remove_wait_queue**.

The use of semaphores is carried out with the help of the functions **down** and **up**, defined in the header file **<asm/semaphore.h>**.

4.6.1.2 Scheduling
The process scheduler is implemented by the function **schedule**, situated in the source file *kernel/sched.c*.

The function **goodness** is used to select the process. It returns a value indicating at which point the process needs the processor. In the event of a process in execution on another processor, it returns a value of –1000 to indicate that the process should not be selected. In the case of a real-time process, the function returns the static priority of the process (field **rt.priority**) increased by 1000. In the case of a normal process, it returns the value of the field **counter**, which represents the number of clock cycles during which the process should be executed.

The function **schedule** implements the scheduler in its strict sense, starting by moving the current process to the end of the 'ready processes' list by calling the function **move_last_runqueue**, if this process has exhausted all it clock cycles.

If the process is in the state **PROCESS_INTERRUPTIBLE, schedule** checks if it has received an unmasked signal: if so, the status of the current process is again set to **PROCESS_RUNNING** in order to wake it up. An examination of the table of processes is then carried out: for each process the function **goodness** is called in order to determine whether the process should be chosen. At the end of this interrogation, the chosen process becomes the current process: the function **get_mmu_context** is called to restore the context memory of the process, and the change of context is triggered by a call to **switch_to**.

The criterion used by the scheduler is the value of the field **counter** of the process descriptor. This field contains the number of clock cycles during which the process should be executed. The field is modified by several functions:

- **update_process_times**: this function is called periodically by **timer_bh**, which is a member if the process queue **tq_timer**, activated by the interrupt clock manager. The field counter is decremented by **update_process_times**, which sets the variable **need_resched** to 1, if the current process has used up its time quantum.
- **schedule**: when the field **counter** is zero for all processes, the scheduler implements a loop on all descriptors in the process table in order to reinitialise the field **counter**. The field **priority** is then adopted as the base value.
- **add_to_runqueue**: this function, which adds a process to the list of processes that are ready, checks the field **counter**: if it is greater than that of the current process, the variable **need_resched** is set to 1, in order to trigger the change of current process.

4.6.1.3 Timers
The kernel, as an internal operation, implements *timers* in order to set up wait phases with given delays. Several management functions are defined in the source file *kernel/sched.c*.

The function **add_timer** adds a *timer* to the list: it scans the list of *timers* already recorded in order to insert its argument in such a way that the list remains sorted. In this way the first elements in the list are the first *timers* to be set off.

The function **del_timer** removes a *timer* from the list: it simply modifies the strings to delete it from the list.

The function **run_timer_list** is called by the process queue **tq_timer**. It scans the list of *timers* and execute each expired *timer*, that is those in which the field **expires** is less than or equal to the global variable **jiffies**, by calling the associated function (field **function**) with the specified parameter (field **data**). Each of the *timers* executed is removed from the list.

4.6.1.4 Wait delays
A process in kernel mode can suspend its execution by specifying a delay whilst waiting for an event. For this, the process uses the field **timeout** from its descriptor. It sets the delay to the desired value, expressed in clock cycles, changes its status

to **PROCESS_INTERRUPTIBLE**, then calls the function **schedule** to instigate a schedule as follows:

```
current->timeout = delay;
current->state =TASK_INTERRUPTIBLE;
schedule ();
```

When the process changes, **schedule** checks to see if the process field is non-null, that is, to see if the process has a specified wait delay. If this is the case, **schedule** activates a *timer*, by calling the functions **init_timer** and **add_timer**. This *timer* will call the function **process_timeout**, by passing it the process descriptor address as a parameter, after a specified delay.

The function **process_timeout**, when called, sets to zero the field **timeout** of the descriptor corresponding to the process, then wakes up the process by calling the function **wake_up_process**.

If the process is woken up before the expiry of the delay, by the arrival of the expected event, or the reception of a message, it resumes execution of the function **schedule** which suppresses the corresponding *timer* by calling **del_timer**.

4.6.2 Implementation of system calls

4.6.2.1 *Process creation*
The implementation of the system call *fork* is found in the source file *kernel/fork.c*. This file defines several global variables:

- **nr_processes**: the number of processes existing in the system;
- **nr_running**: the number of processes in the ready state existing in the system;
- **total_forks**: the total number of system calls *fork* executed since the start up of the system;
- **last_pid**: the number attributed to the last process created.

Several internal functions are also defined. The function **find_empty_process** looks for a spare space in the table **process**. It checks that the user executing the current process is authorised to create a new process, that is that the maximum number of processes has not been exceeded, and the user has not reached his own maximum number of processes. It then carries out a search loop looking for a free slot in the table **process** and returns its position index.

The function **get_pid** is called to establish a new process number. If the new process shares a process identifier with the parent process (by means of the option **CLONE_PIC** of the primitive *clone*), then this identifier is returned, if not, **get_pid** increments the value of **last_pid** and then carries out a search of the table **process** to check that that this number has not already been used as a process, group or session identifier. If the number is already in use, **last_pid** is again incremented and the search begins again.

The functions **dup_mapp** and **copy_mm** duplicate the address space of the current process. They are described in more detail in chapter 8, section 6.7.

The functions **copy_fs** and **copy_files** duplicate descriptors of files opened by the current process. They are described in more detail in chapter 6, section 6.3.10.

The function **copy_sighand** duplicates the message descriptors of the current process. It is described in more detail in chapter 5, section 5.1.1.

The function **copy_thread**, defined in the source file *arch/i386/kernel/process.c*, initialises that value of the processor registers which are assigned to the process created. It modifies the contents of the field **tss** of the process descriptor.

The function **do_fork** goes on to duplicate the current process when the primitives *clone* and *fork* are executed. It allocates a new process descriptor by calling **kmalloc**, allocates a page of memory for the kernel mode stack by calling **alloc_kernel_stack**, and then finds an entry in the process table by a call to **find_empty_process**. The descriptor of the new process is then initialised by copying the information characterising the current process, whose descriptor is pointed to by the variable current, and then by modifying the different attributes between the parent and child. The new descriptor is inserted in the process table, and the functions **copy_files**, **copy_fs**, **copy_sighand**, **copy_mm** and **copy_thread** are called to initialise the context of the process created. Finally, the number attributed to the new process is returned.

For the x86 architecture, the implementation of the primitives clone and fork is contained in the source file *arch/i386/kernel/process.c*. The functions **sys_fork** and **sys_clone** both call **do_fork**, providing them with different parameters.

It should be noted that **sys_fork** and **sys_clone** are called without parameters. However, they do have access to the processor register values when the call is made. These registers are saved in the stack by the macro instruction **SAVE_ALL** when the system call is activated (the function **system_call** is defined in the source file *arch/i386/kernel/entry.S)*, and **sys_fork** and **sys_clone** access the register values via a fictitious parameter **pt_regs**.

4.6.2.2 Process termination

The source file *kernel/exit.c* contains the system calls linked to the termination of a process: *exit* and *wait4*.

The function **notify_parent** warns a process of the termination of one of its children. It sends a message to the parent of the current process by a call to **send_sig**, using the field **exit_signal**, then it uses the function **wake_up_interruptible** to wake up the parent process if it is waiting for one of its children to terminate, that is, it has been placed on hold in the **wait_chldexit** queue by a call to the primitive *wait4*.

The functions **close_files**, **__exit_files**, and **__exit_fs** release the open file descriptors belonging to a process. This operation is described in more detail in chapter 6, section 6.3.10.

The function __exit_sighand releases the message management descriptors of a process. Its operation is described in more detail in chapter 5, section 5.5.11.

The function __exit_mm releases the descriptors of a process's memory zones. Its operation is described in more detail in chapter 8, section 8.6.7.

The function exit_notify is called when a process is terminated in order to flag this to the processes that are related to it. It first calls forget_original_parent, which scans the process table and modifies the process pointers p_opptr to make them point at the process *init* if they were pointing at the process being terminated. If the current process is *leader* of a group which includes the suspended processes (in the PROCESS_STOPPED state), the messages SIGHUP and SIGCONT are sent to the group process by calling the function kill_pg. The parent process is then warned by calling notify_parent. Finally, a search loop of child processes is carried out: each of these child processes is attached to the process *init*, and a message is sent to *init* by calling notify_parent if the child process is in the PROCESS_ZOMBIE state.

The function do_exit goes on to terminate the current process. It releases the descriptors assigned to the process by calling functions __exit_mm, __exit_files, __exit_fs, and __exit_sighand. It then sets the status of the current process to PROCESS_ZOMBIE, records the process return code, then calls exit_notify in order to warn the parent process of the termination of one of its children. Finally the function schedule is called in order to proceed to the scheduling.

The primitive *exit* is implemented by the function sys_exit. This function simply calls do_exit and passes to it the return code, supplied by the process and multiplied by 256. In this way, the return code is placed in bits 8 to 15 of the field exit_code of the current process descriptor.

The function sys_wait4 invokes a wait phase while the child process terminates. It first of all checks that its arguments are valid, then records the descriptor of the current process in the wait queue referenced by the field wait_chldexit. It then carries out a scan of the child processes relating to the current process, checking each one to see if it corresponds to the parameter pid. For each child process meeting the specified criteria at the system call, two cases are considered:

1. The child process is in the state PROCESS_STOPPED, WUNTRACED is included in the wait options, and the parent process has not yet been warned of its change of status.
2. The child process is in the state PROCESS_ZOMBIE.

At the end of this interrogation, if the current process has child processes none of which has finished execution, and if the wait options do not include WNOHANG, the current process is suspended whilst waiting for a child process to terminate by modifying its status to PROCESS_INTERRUPTIBLE, and by calling the function schedule to invoke a scheduling; then the processing starts up again when the current process is woken up by the termination of a child process.

If no child processes exist, the return code of the function is set to **ECHILD**. Finally, the current process is removed from the wait queue referenced by the field **wait_chldexit.**

Other system calls relating to awaiting the termination of the child process are implemented by calling *wait4*:

- **wait (&status)** corresponds to
- **wait4 (-1, &status, 0, NULL)·**
- **wait3 (&status, options, &rusage)** corresponds to
- **wait4 (-1, &status, options, &rusage)**
- **wait (pid, &status, options)** corresponds to
- **wait4 (pid, &status, options, NULL)**

4.6.2.3 *Establishing attributes*
The source file *kernel/sched.c* contains the system calls enabling the current process to establish its attributes: *getpid, getpid, getuid, getgid,* and *getegid.* The functions for processing these primitives are very simple since they simply consist of returning a descriptor field of the current process, pointed to by the variable **current.**

The system call *getgroups* is implemented in the source file *kernel/sys.c.* The function **sys_getgroups** checks the validity of its arguments, counts the number groups associated with the current process, and then copies them from the current process descriptor to the buffer memory provided by the calling function. The function then returns the number of groups.

4.6.2.4 *Modification of attributes*
The source file *kernel/sys.c* contains the implementation of system calls enabling the current process to modify its attributes: *setregid, setgid, setreuid, setuid, setfsuid, setfsgid,* and *setgroups.* The functions which implement these primitives are very simple: they check that the current process is authorised to modify its attributes, and change the values in the corresponding fields in the descriptor.

4.6.2.5 *Process and Session groups*
The system calls which manipulate the process and session groups are implemented in the source file *kernel/sys.c.*

The function **sys_getpgrp** returns the field **pgrp** of the descriptor of the current process, pointed to by the variable **current.** The function **sys_getpgid** carries out a scan of the descriptor of the process whose number is passed to it as a parameter, and returns the field **pgrp** of this descriptor. The function **get_sid** carries out a similar operation, but returns the field **session** of the descriptor found.

The function **sys_getpgid** implements the primitive *setpgid.* It carries out a scan of the process to be modified in the table **process.** Once the corresponding descriptor is found, it carries out a number of controls:

- if a process modifies the group of one of its child processes, the two processes must belong to the same session and the child process must not have used the primitive *execve* to run a new program, if it has, the process to be modified must be the current process;
- the process to be modified must not be the *leader* of a session;
- the group identifier to be set must be the identifier of the current process.

After these checks, the group to which the current process belongs is modified, by changing the value of the field **pgrp** in its descriptor.

The system call *setsid* is implemented by the function **sys_setsid**. This function first scans the table **process** to check that the current process is not a process group *leader*. Once this check has been made, the function modifies the identifiers of the process group of the session of the current process (fields **pgrp** and **session**), flags that the current process is session *leader* by setting the field **leader** to 1, dissociates the control terminal from the process by modifying the field **tty** and **tty_old_pgrp**, and returns the number of the session created.

4.6.2.6 Process control

The system call *ptrace* is implemented in the source file *arch/i386/kernel/ptrace.c*, for the x86 architecture, since this primitive is processor dependent.

The function **get_process** returns the descriptor of the process corresponding to the number of the specified process. **get_stack_long** returns a word situated in the kernel stack of the specifies process, and **put_stack_long** modifies the contents of a word in the kernel stack.

Several functions manipulate the process address space: **get_long, put_long, find_extend_vma, read_long** and **write_long**. These functions are described in more detail in chapter 8 in view of their interactions with memory management mechanisms.

The function **sys_ptrace** implements the system call *ptrace*. It first of all processes the request **PTRACE_TRACEME**: if the flag **PF_TRACED** is already set in the current process descriptor, the error **EPERM** is returned, if not the flag is set. After some validity checks, the request **PTRACE_ATTACH** is processed: if the process specified is already under control, the error **EPERM** is returned, if not the flag **PF_TRACED** is set in the field **flags** of its descriptor, the process is re-attached to its controlling process by modifying the pointer **p_pptr** and by using the macro instructions **REMOVE_LINKS** and **SET_LINKS**: finally, the message **SIGSTOP** is sent to the process by calling the function **send_sig**, in order to suspend process execution.

Before processing other requests, **sys_ptrace** carries out several checks: the specified process should be under control (the flag **PF_TRACED** of the field **flags** of its descriptor should be set), it should be in the state **PROCESS_STOPPED**, it should be re-attached to the current process (the pointer **p_pptr** should contain the address of the descriptor of the current process, contained in the variable **current**). After these checks, various requests are processed:

- **PTRACE_PEEKTEXT, PTRACE_PEEKDATA**: the specified word is read in the process address space by **read_long**, then returned to the calling process.
- **PTRACE_PEEKUSR**: the specified word is read in the structure **user** of the process by **get_stack_long**, then returned to the calling process.
- **PTRACE_POKETEXT, PTRACE_POKEDATA**: the specified word is written in the process address space by **write_long**.
- **PTRACE_POKEUSR**: the specified word is written in the structure **user** of the process by **put_stack_long**, then returned to the calling process.
- **PTRACE_SYSCALL, PTRACE_CONT**: the field flag of the descriptor the process is modified so as to set or delete the flag **PF_TRACESYS**, the process is woken up by a call to **wake_up_process**. Finally, the trace bit contained in the processor flags is set to zero.
- **PTRACE_KILL**: the process is woken up by a call to **wake_up_process**, then the field **exit_code** is set in order to indicate that the process should receive the message **SIGKILL**. Finally, the trace bit contained in the processor flags is set to zero.
- **PTRACE_SINGLESTEP, PTRACE_CONT**: the trace bit contained in the processor flags is set, then the process is woken up by a call to **wake_up_process**.
- **PTRACE_DETACH**: the field flag of the descriptor the process is modified so as to delete the flags **PF_TRACED** and **PF_TRACESYS**,and the process is woken up by a call to **wake_up_process**. The process is then reattached to its original parent, by modifying the pointer **p_pptr**, and by calling the macro instructions **REMOVE_LINKS** and **SET_LINKS**. Finally, the trace bit contained in the processor flags is set to zero.

5

Signals

System calls described

5.1
BASIC CONCEPTS

5.1.1 Introduction

Signal management is a mechanism that has existed since the first versions of Unix. It allows processes to react to events triggered by themselves, or by other processes. The mechanism can be incorporated into the management of software interrupts.

5.1.2 Definition of signals

Each signal corresponds to a particular event. A signal is represented in the system by a name of the form **SIGXXX**. The total number of signals existing in the system is marked by the constant **NSIG** defined in the header file **<signal.h>**. A signal may be generated in several ways, such as:

- The signal is the result of a particular physical circumstance. When a process writes to a non-allocated zone of memory, there is an invalid access to a page of memory, which raises a flag. This flag is recognised in the kernel, which generates a **SIGSEGV** signal which in turn is sent to the process at fault.

- It is the result of the terminal user typing **[CTRL-C]**. This generates the signal **SIGINT** for which the default action is to terminate the process in the session foreground.
- It is the result of the system call *kill* or of the command of the same name which allows a signal to be sent to a selected process (see section 2.1).
- It is the result of an event under the control of the kernel. For example, when an alarm times-out, the signal **SIGALRM** is sent out by the system to the process that requested it (see section 5.4.2.1).

Signals generated are not received in a synchronous manner by the process they are destined for, but are acknowledged by a process when the process changes from system mode to user mode. There can therefore by a significant delay between the sending and the reception of signal.

There are various actions a process may take upon receiving a signal, and three different defaults:

- ignore the signal;
- terminate the program;
- terminate the program and generate a file *core*.

In the latter case, the system creates an image of the process memory and saves it in a file called *core*. This file is used when the program is debugged by means of tools such as *gdb*.

The default action assigned to a signal may be modified by the receiving process. The process then uses an interception function currently known as *handler*.

There are two signals whose behaviour may not be modified. These are **SIGKILL** and **SIGSTOP**. This characteristic allows a super-user to interrupt or suspend any process.

Two signals do not correspond to any particular event: they are **SIGUSR1** and **SIGUSR2**. These are available for use by the programmer.

5.1.3 List of signals

This section presents a list of the different signals defined in Linux. The signals are classified according to the actions that they give rise to. For each signal, the tables describe their cause, and the default action that they trigger. In addition, an asterisk indicates that the signal conforms to POSIX.1. The numerical value of the signal is not listed because, for certain signals, this is dependent on the architecture that the system is installed on.

The first table shows signals for terminating or suspending processes.

signal	cause	default action
SIGHUP*	Termination of the session leader process or disconnection of a modem	Termination
SIGINT*	Sending of the interrupt character from the terminal **[CTRL-C]**	Termination
SIGQUIT*	Sending of the stop character from the terminal **[CTRL-\]**	Termination with *core*
SIGABRT*, **SIGIOT**	Abnormal termination (abort), hardware fault	Termination; Terminate
SIGKILL*	Irrevocable termination signal	Termination
SIGTERM*	Default signal sent out by the kill command	Termination

The next table contains signals triggered by a particular physical circumstance.

signal	cause	default action
SIGILL*	Illegal instruction	Termination
SIGTRAP	Breakpoint in a program (system call *ptrace*)	Termination with core
SIGBUS	Bus error	Termination
SIGFPE*	Arithmetic error	Termination
SIGSEGV*	Memory address invalid	Termination with core
SIGSTKFLT	Maths co-processor stack overflow (only in the Intel architecture)	Termination

The following signals are available for use by the programmer:

signal	cause	default action
SIGUSR1*	Defined by the programmer	Termination
SIGUSR2*	Defined by the programmer	Termination

The following signal may be generated by the system when a pipe is closed (see chapter 10):

signal	cause	default action
SIGPIPE*	Pipe without reader	Termination

Signals linked to the control of activity are special since they allow processes to be suspended or resumed.

signal	cause	default action
SIGCHLD*, SIGCLD	Termination of child process	None
SIGCONT*	Repetition in the foreground or background of the process	Resume execution if it is stopped
SIGSTOP*	Suspension of process	Suspension (non-changeable)
SIGSTP	Sending out of suspension character from the terminal [CTRL-Z]	Suspension
SIGTTIN*	Terminal read for a background process	Suspension
SIGTTOU	Writing to a terminal for a background process	Suspension

The following signals are linked to resources which are modifiable by the process (see chapter 4, section 4.2.7).

signal	cause	default action
SIGXCPU	CPU time limit exceeded	Termination
SIGXFSZ	File size limit exceeded	Termination

The following signals are linked to the management of alarms. They are generated after the process has used the system call *setitimer* or *alarm* in the case of SIGALRM (see sections 4.2.1 and 4.2.2).

signal	cause	default action
SIGALRM*	End of timer **ITIMER_REAL**	Termination
SIGVTALRM*	End of timer **ITIMER_VIRTUAL**	Termination
SIGPROF	End of timer **ITIMER_PROF**	Termination

The signals relating to the management of inputs and outputs are as follows:

signal	cause	default action
SIGWINCH	Change of window size (used by X11)	None
SIGIO, **SIGPOLL**	Data available for an input/output	Termination
SIGURG	Urgent data for sockets	None

An alert signal indicates a fault with the power supply to the system. This signal is obviously sent out when there is a backup power supply.

signal	cause	default action
SIGPWR, **SIGINFO**	Power fault	Termination

5.1.4 Display of signals

A table containing the character string assigned to each signal is defined in the file **<signal.h>**:

```
extern const char * const sys_siglist[];
```

This table is not used directly, but through the intermediary action of two functions from the C library: *strsignal* and *psignal*.

The standard form of these functions is as follows:

```
#include <string.h>
#include <signal.h>

char *strsignal (int sig);

void psignal (int sig, const char *s);
```

The first of these functions takes the numerical value of the signal as its parameter and sends back the associated character string, which is stored in **sys_siglist**.

The second function puts in the error output a message composed of the string specified by the parameter **s** and the message associated with the signal whose number is contained in **sig**. The principle of operation of the function is similar to that of *perror*.

5.2

BASIC SYSTEM CALLS

The semantics of system calls managing signals in Linux conforms to the POSIX standard. However, signal management in Unix systems existed well before the definition of a standard, and there are therefore a number of non-POSIX system calls defined. These system calls arose in both the classes of Unix systems; SystemV and BSD. In some cases they have the same name, but different semantics. By default, the semantics of System V are used, but the inclusion of a header file **<bsd/signal.h>** in place of **<signal.h>** at the point when the programs are compiled , and the later inclusion of the library **libbsd.a** at the point when the links are edited allows these to obey the semantics of BSD also.

In the description of system calls, the two semantics are presented when appropriate.

5.2.1 Sending a signal

The system call *kill* is used to send a signal to a process or a group of processes.

```
#include <signal.h>

int kill (pid_t pid, int sig);
```

The second argument of the call indicates the signal to be sent out. The first argument gives the identity of the receiving entity. Several circumstances are possible:

- if **pid** is positive, the signal **sig** is sent to the process identified by **pid**;
- if **pid** is null, the signal **sig** is sent to the processes of the process group of the sender;
- if **pid** is equal to –1, the signal **sig** is sent to all processes, except the first (the program *init*);
- if **pid** is less than –1, the signal **sig** is sent to the group of processes identified by **-pid**.

If the signal sent is null, the call does not generate a signal but checks that the receiving process exists[1].

---

[1] N.B. if the task is in the ZOMBIE state, it is considered to exist.

A process may send a signal to another process if its real or effective identifier is equal to the real or effective identifier of the other process.

If the call proceeds correctly, the value zero is sent, if an error is produced, –1 is sent and the variable **errno** contains one of the following values:

error	meaning
EINVAL	The signal specified is invalid
ESRCH	The target process or process group does not exist
EPERM	The value of the effective user identifier of the calling process is different from that of the target processes(s)

A process belonging to a super-user of course has permission to send a signal to all the other processes (except *init*[2]).

To send a signal to a group of processes, there is also the call *killpg*. It has the following form:

```
#include <signal.h>

int killpg (int pgrp, int sig);
```

The first argument of the call represents the group the signal is sent to. If its value is null, then the signal is sent to the processes in the group of the sending process. If not, then the operation is similar to that with *kill*.

There is also an ANSI-C function which allows a process to send itself a signal. This is the function *raise*. Its general form is the following:

```
#include <signal.h>

int raise (int sig);
```

This function is equivalent to kill(getpid(), sig). In the event of an error, a non-zero value is sent.

5.2.2 Signal handling

Processes which wish to change the default behaviour of a signal, divert to a different function.

The system call *signal* enables this process. Its standard form is as follows:

---

[2] In order to protect the system, no process may send a signal which would cause *init* to terminate.

```
#include <signal.h>

void (*signal (int signum, void (*handler) (int))) (int);
```

The first argument is the signal involved in the operation, and the second is a pointer to the signal handling function, or one of the two following constants; **SIG_IGN** to ignore the signal, **SIG_DFL** to reset the default behaviour. The handling parameter takes an integer value corresponding to the signal which activated it, and does not return any argument.

When a signal is received, the system interrupts the normal execution of a process in order to execute the signal handling function. It passes the value of the transmitted signal to this function.

The return value of the system call *signal* is a pointer to the signal handling function which is in place before the call, or the constant **SIG_ERR** if an error is produced. The following program describes the way the call *signal* is used.

——————— DerouteSIGUSR1.c ———————————————————

```
#include <signal.h>
#include <stdio.h>
#include <string.h>

void divert (int sig);

int  main ()
{
    if (signal (SIGUSR1, divert) == SIG_ERR) {
            perror ("signal not divertable");
            exit (1);
    }
    for (;;) ;

    return 0;
}

void divert (int sig)
{
    printf ("Signal received : %s\n", strsignal (sig));
}
```
———————————————————————————————— DerouteSIGUSR1.c ———

The signal **SIGUSR1** is diverted to the function **deroute**, and the shell command *kill* allows the program to be tested.

```
scylla (2)>./example1 &
[1] 4031
scylla (2)>kill -USR1 4031
scylla (2)>Signal received : User defined signal 1
```

When the program receives the signal **SIGUSR1**, it executes the function **deroute** in order to display the message on the screen. It then resumes its normal execution.

If the program receives the same signal again, it stops execution.

```
scylla (2)>kill -USR 4031
scylla (2)>
[1]  User signal 1            ./example1
scylla (2)>
```

When the diversion function executes, the system automatically re-installs the default handler. In this example, it terminates the program. To avoid this problem, the function **deroute** can be rewritten in the following manner;

```
void
divert (int sig)
{
        signal (SIGUSR1, divert);
        printf ("Signal received : %s\n", strsignal(sig));
}
```

This time, from the beginning of execution of the diversion function, the signal is reset. However, this method cannot work when the computer is heavily loaded. In this case it is possible that the process receives a second signal before diverting it, and therefore terminates execution.

Furthermore, during the execution of the diversion function, the process may receive other signals.

Section 4.1.3 describes a more reliable method for dealing with signals.

The semantics presented here conform to those of System V. The BSD semantics for this call differ slightly. By default, the default handler is not reinstalled after the signal is received. In this example, it therefore serves no purpose to use the call *signal* at the beginning of the function *handler*.

5.2.3 Waiting for the signal

A process may be put into a state awaiting the arrival of a signal by using the system call *pause*, of which the following is the standard form:

```
#include <unistd.h>

int pause (void);
```

This call suspends the calling process until the arrival of the signal in question. The return value of the call is always −1, and the variable **errno** contains the value **EINTR**.

The following program returns to the example of the previous section and adds the call *pause* into the infinite loop.

─────────── PauseSIGUSR1.c ─────────────────────────────────────

```
#include <signal.h>
#include <stdio.h>
#include <string.h>
#include <unistd.h>


void divert (int sig);

int main ()
{
    if (signal (SIGUSR1, divert) == SIG_ERR) {
            perror ("signal not divertable");
            exit (1);
    }
    for (;;)
            pause ();

    return 0;
}

void divert (int sig)
{
    printf ("Signal received : %s\n", strsignal (sig));
}
```

─────────────────────────────────────── PauseSIGUSR1.c ───────

This program therefore allows the wait to be circumvented by suspending the process.

The system call *pause* has one big disadvantage: it does not allow a particular signal to be waited for. The process will be woken up by any signal. Section 5.4.1

introduces another call allowing the expected signals to be defined, and for the others to be blocked.

5.3.1 Interruptible system calls

System calls, which depend typically on inputs or outputs, may be interrupted by the arrival of a signal, the system call is interrupted and the signal is processed. The resulting return value is generally –1, and the variable **errno** contains the value **EINTR**. In general, the system call is not re-executed, except when the program explicitly forces this. Section 4.1.3 describes a mechanism allowing the automatic re-execution of certain system calls.

5.3.2 Re-entrant functions

The arrival of a signal may give rise to errors in the course of a process if it is badly managed. Indeed, certain library functions manipulate static data and are not re-entrant. If these functions are called during the handling of a signal, the behaviour of a process may be altered. For example, the function *malloc* controls memory zones in the form of linked lists: if a signal arrives during a call to this function, and if the handler function also calls *malloc*, these lists are at risk of being in an intermediate state, and the process may then give rise to errors. It is therefore preferable to only use re-entrant functions in signal handlers.

5.3.3 Signal groups

It is possible to suspend or to block several signals simultaneously. The following section presents in detail the system calls facilitating these operations. In this case, the signals are managed in groups. A number of functions are defined for this purpose.

A number of prototypes are listed below:

```
#include <signal.h>

int sigemptyset (sigset_t *set);

int sigfillset (sigset_t *set);

int sigaddset (sigset_t *set, const int signum);

int sigdelset (sigset_t *set, const int signum);

int sigismember (const sigset_t *set, const int signum);
```

The first two functions initialise a group:

- the first creates an empty set/group;
- the second creates a group with all signals.

The two following functions add a signal to a group (**sigaddset**), remove it (**sigdelset**). Removing a signal enables a check to be made to see if it belongs to a set: it returns a 1 if the signal does belong to a set, and a 0 if not. **sigdelset** enables a signal to be checked to see if it belongs to a group.

The only way an error can be generated for the group of these functions is if an invalid signal is received. The return value then is –1, and the variable **errno** contains the value **EINVAL**.

5.4
COMPLEMENTARY SYSTEM CALLS

5.4.1　Advanced signal management

5.4.1.1　*Interruption of signal calls*

In order to control the behaviour of a program when it is interrupted by a signal, BSD systems provide the function *siginterrupt*, whose general form is as follows:

```
#include <signal.h>

int siginterrupt (int sig, int flag);
```

The function behaves as follows. If the value of the parameter **flag** is null, a system call will be re-submitted if it is interrupted by the signal **sig**.

If the value of the parameter flag is 1, and no data has been transferred, then a system call interrupted by the signal **sig** returns –1, and the variable **errno** contains the value **EINTR**.

If the value of the parameter **flag** is 1, and the data has been transferred, then a system call interrupted by the signal **sig** returns the amount of data transferred.

5.4.1.2　*Blocking of signals*

A process is able to control the arrival of different signals. It may delay their arrival by blocking them, and they are then said to be 'pending'. Each process has a group called a signal mask, which contains the list of blocked signals. This group may be modified by a system call *sigprocmask*. The form of this call is as follows:

```
#include <signal.h>

int sigprocmask (int how, const sigset_t *set, sigset_t *oldset);
```

The first mask indicates the manner in which the group of signals passed in the second argument should be processed. It takes one of the following values:

option	meaning
SIG_BLOCK	The blocked signals are the combined current group and the members of the group **set**.
SIG_UNBLOCK	The signals of the group **set** are removed from the list of blocked signals
SIG_SETMASK	The blocked signals are in the group **set**

The third argument of the call contains the group of signals defined before the call to *sigprocmask*.

The return value of the call is 0 if it is successful, and –1 if not. In this case the variable **errno** takes on one of the following values:

error	meaning
EINVAL	The value of how is incorrect
EFAULT	**set** or **oldset** contain an invalid address
EINTR	The system call has been interrupted

If the new signal mask un-blocks some of the pending signals, at least one of these will be delivered before the call *sigprocmask* is returned.

The process may ask the system for its list of pending signals by means of the system call *sigpending*, whose general form is as follows:

```
#include <signal.h>

int sigpending (sigset_t *set);
```

When the call is made, the parameter **set** contains the list of pending signals from the calling process.

The only possible source of error for this call occurs if the address or the parameter **set** is invalid. The variable **errno** then contains the value **EFAULT**.

Example
The following program varies the signal mask blocking the signal **SIGINT,** to check for its arrival and to un-block it.

——————— BloqueSignal.c ———————————————

```
#include <signal.h>
#include <stdio.h>
#include <string.h>
#include <unistd.h>
```

```
            void divert (int sig);

            int main ()
            {
                sigset_t mask,
                         pending;

                if (signal (SIGINT, divert) == SIG_ERR) {
                        perror ("signal SIGINT not divertable");
                        exit (1);
                }
                sigemptyset (&mask);
                sigaddset (&mask, SIGINT);
                if (sigprocmask (SIG_BLOCK, &mask, NULL) <0) {
                        perror ("SIG_BLOCK in sigprocmask");
                        exit (1);
                }
                sleep (5);

                if (sigpending (&pending) < 0 {
                        perror ("sigpending");
                        exit (1);
                }
                if (sigismember (pending, SIGINT))
                        printf ("Signal SIGINT pending\n");

                if (sigprocmask (SIG_UNBLOCK, &mask, NULL) <0) {
                        perror ("SIG_UNBLOCK in sigprocmask");
                        exit (1);
                }
                printf ("Signal SIGINT unblocked\n");

                return 0;
            }

            void divert (int sig)
            {
                printf ("Signal received : %s\n", strsignal (sig));
            }
```

———————————————————————————————— BloqueSignal.c ——————

The program is run, it receives the signal **SIGINT** following the keystrokes **[CTRL-C]**.

```
scylla (2)>./BloqueSignal
                              <- Type CTRL-C
Signal SIGINT pending
Signal received : Interrupt
Signal SIGINT unblocked
```

The signal **SIGINT** is first of all blocked, and appears in the list of pending signals. It is then processed at the point at which it is blocked.

A second transmission of this signal terminates the process because the default handler is automatically re-installed by default. In addition, if the process receives the signal **SIGINT** whilst it is blocked, just one instance of this signal will be accounted for.

There exist also four calls in BSD systems which control signal masks. These are *siggetmask, sigsetmask, sigmask,* and *sigblock.* They are rendered obsolete by the call *sigprocmask* and are in any case implemented in the form of library functions and use this call.

5.4.1.3 Diversion of signals

Section 2.2 showed that the system call *signal* had some limitations. These have to do with the control of process behaviour when a signal is received. The system call *sigaction*, introduced under the POSIX standard, also allows a signal to be diverted and these problems to be resolved. The standard form of this call is as follows:

```
#include <signal.h>

int sigaction (int signum, const struct sigaction *act, struct sigaction
*oldact);
```

The first parameter represents the signal to be diverted. The second and third parameters are respectively the new and original action to be taken when the signal arrives.

The definition of the structure **sigaction** is as follows:

type	*field*	*description*
void (*) (int)	**sa_handler**	Diversion function
sigset_t	**sa_mask**	Signal mask whilst the diversion function[3] is running
unsigned long	**sa_flags**	Options determining the response of the process to the arrival of the signal
void (*) (void)	**sa_restorer**	Unused, will contain the stack pointer for the diversion function (not yet implemented)

The possible options for the value of the field **sa_flags** are indicated in the following table:

option	*meaning*
SA_NOCLDSTOP	If the signal is **SIGCHLD**, do not receive the signal when the child process is suspended[4]
SA_ONESHOT, **SA_RESETHAND**	Re-install the default handler by default after the reception of the signal
SA_RESTART	Automatically re-launch the system call which was interrupted by the signal
SA_NOMASK, **SA_NODEFER**	Do not block reception of the signal while the diversion function is running

The errors possible for this call are as follows:

error	*meaning*
EINVAL	**sig** is an invalid signal; either **SIGKILL** or **SIGSTOP**
EFAULT	**act** or **oldact** contain an invalid address

If the second argument of sigaction contains the value **NULL**, the system call returns the current handler for the signal **sig**.

If the second and third arguments contain the value **NULL** the system call checks the validity of the signal (verifies that the signal exists for this machine).

5.4.1.4 *Waiting for signals*
The system call *pause* does not allow the process to wait for particular signals, the process is suspended until any signal arrives.

---

[3] By default, the diverted signal is automatically added to the signal mask.
[4] When one of the following signals is received: **SIGSTOP, SIGSTP, SIGTTIN, SIGTTOU**.

The POSIX standard puts this right with the system call *sigsuspend*. This call temporarily replaces the signal mask for the process by a wait mask and suspends the process until a signal not belonging to the waiting mask arrives. These two operations are accomplished in a discrete fashion.

The form of this call is as follows:

```
#include <signal.h>

int sigsuspend (const sigset_t *mask);
```

When this call is sent, the original signal mask for the process is reset.

A similar call exists in BSD systems. This is the call *sigpause*. Its implementation is realised in the C library by a simple call to *sigsuspend*.

5.4.2 Alarm management

5.4.2.1 *The system call* alarm
A process can request a system to send it a signal at a given time. For this, it uses the system call *alarm*. The form of this call is as follows:

```
#include <unistd.h>

long alarm (long seconds);
```

The parameter **seconds** represents the period after which the system sends the signal **SIGALRM** to the process. The return value of the system call represents the amount of time which remained before a previously requested alarm is set off. The new alarm cancels the old one. Calling *alarm* with a zero time period corresponds to the cancelling of the alarm.

This system call is generally used to control process delays. The following example illustrates the use of this call to limit the waiting time whilst capturing the data entered at the keyboard.

──────── TempoAlarm.c ────────────────────────

```
#include <stdio.h>
#include <signal.h>
#include <unistd.h>

void alarm_hdl (int sig);

int my_time

int main ()
```

```
    {
        signal (SIGALRM, alarm_hdl);
        while (1) {
                my_time = 8;
                printf ("Press 'Enter' or the program will stop");
                printf (" in 10 seconds\n");
                alarm (2);
                getchar ();
                alarm (0);
        }
    }

    void alarm_hdl(int sig)
    {
        signal (SIGALRM, alarm_hdl);
        alarm (2);
        if (my_time) {
                printf ("there are %d seconds remaining \n", my_time);
                my_time - = 2;
        } else {
                printf ("Too late, end of the program\n");
                exit (1);
        }
    }
```

———————————————————————————————— TempoAlarm.c ————

On execution, the following result is obtained:

```
bash$ ./TempoAlarm
Press 'Enter' or the program will stop in 10 seconds
There are 8 seconds remaining
There are 6 seconds remaining
                        <- Hit 'Enter'


Press 'Enter' or the program will stop in 10 seconds
There are 8 seconds remaining
There are 6 seconds remaining
There are 4 seconds remaining
There are 2 seconds remaining
Too late, the program has terminated
bash$
```

This program loops upon detecting that the [Enter] key has been pressed. The time remaining before the end of the program is displayed every two seconds. If the user presses the key within 10 seconds, the time counter is reset to zero and the loop restarts, if not the program terminates.

The time indicated when the alarm is set is the minimum time during which the process will process the signal. In fact, the process will only process the signal when the scheduler has given it access to the processor. There is therefore no maximum limit for processing the signal.

5.4.2.2 Finer time control

The system call described above is limited since it does not allow the automatic control of alarms. Time control is solely in relation to real time, whereas it could be of interest to control alarms relative to the timing of executing processes. BSD and system V systems have overcome these problems by introducing two new system calls which allow periodic alarms to be automatically controlled in different time reference frames. The system allows each process to control three periodic alarms with respect to three different time references. When one of the alarms expires, a signal is sent to the process and the alarm is reactivated.

The alarms are represented by three counters described in the following table:

option	meaning
ITIMER_REAL	Counter decremented in real time: when expired, the signal **SIGALRM** is sent to the process
ITIMER_VIRTUAL	Counter decremented when the process is executed: when expired, the signal **SIGVTALRM** is sent to the process
ITIMER_PROF	Counter decremented when the process is executed and when the system executes on behalf of the process: when expired, the signal **SIGPROF** is sent to the process

The form of these calls is as follows:

```
#include <sys/time.h>

int getitimer (int which, struct itimerval *value);

int setitimer (int which, const struct itimerval *value, struct
itimerval *ovalue);
```

They act respectively to receive or to post information relating to an alarm. The first parameter of the calls indicates which counter is involved. The second parameter points to a structure containing the value of the next alarm and the current value of the counter: each of these fields is described by the structure **timeval**, which is described in chapter 4, section 4.2.3.

The structure of **itimerval** is as follows:

type	*field*	*description*
struct timeval	**it_timeval**	Next alarm
struct timeval	**it_value**	Current counter value

The counter is decremented from **it_value** to zero; a signal is generated, then the field **it_value** is re-initialised to the value **it_interval**, and the count down starts again. The alarm is stopped if reaches zero, a value which is arrived at when **it_value** is set to zero, or when the counter runs out and when the value of **it_interval** is null.

In the event of an error, the system call returns –1 and the variable **errno** contains the following values:

option	*meaning*
EFAULT	**value** or **ovalue** contain an invalid address
EINVAL	The first parameter of the system call is not one of the values: **ITIMER_REAL, ITIMER_VIRTUAL** or **ITIMER_PROF**

The precision of alarms is linked to the precision of the system clock (currently 10ms). Alarms may therefore expire slightly after their real timepoints. The delivery of the signal will be carried out immediately if the process is active, or may be slightly delayed as a function of the load on the system.

In certain cases the load on the system is very important, since the generation and reception of the signal are separated in the system, it is possible that the periodic alarm **ITIMER_REAL** expires twice before the process has been able to register expiry once: a single signal is therefore generated and the process only takes one alarm into account.

The system call *alarm* utilises the counter **ITIMER_REAL**: it is therefore necessary to avoid using this system call together with the call *setitimer*.

In order to illustrate these system calls, the previous example is re-written with the call *setitimer*:

──────── TempoTimer.c ──────────────────────────────────

```
#include <stdio.h>
#include <signal.h>
#include <sys/time.h>
#include <unistd.h>

void alarm_hdl(int sig);

int my_time

int main ()
{

    struct itimerval my_alarm;
    my_alarm.it_interval.tv_sec = 2;
    my_alarm.it_interval.tv_usec = 0;

    signal (SIGALRM, alarm_hdl);
    while (1) {
            my_time = 8;
            printf ("press æEnterÆ or the program will exit");
            printf ("in 10 seconds\n");
            my_alarm.it_interval.tv_sec = 2;
            my_alarm.it_interval.tv_usec = 0;
            setitimer (ITIMER_REAL, & my_alarm, NULL);
            getchar ();
            my_alarm.it_interval.tv_sec = 2;
            my_alarm.it_interval.tv_usec = 0;
            setitimer (ITIMER_REAL, & my_alarm, NULL);
    }
}

void alarm_hdl (int sig)
{
   signal (SIGALRM, alarm_hdl);
   if (my_time) {
            printf ("you have %d seconds \n", my_time);
            temps -= 2;
   } else {
       printf ("Too late, end of the program\n");
       exit (1);
   }
}
```

──────────────────────────────────── TempoTimer.c   ────────

It is not worth repeating the alarm arising from reception of the signal at this point since it recurs.

5.4.3   The signal SIGCHLD

When a process terminates, it remains in the ZOMBIE state, until its parent process is made aware of its termination by one of the system calls *wait* or *wait4*. The parent process is warned of the termination of one of its children by the system, which sends it the signal SIGCHLD. The signal is nullified only when the parent process carries out one of the above system calls.

By default in Linux, the signal SIGCHLD is set to SIG_IGN and the system does not warn the parent of the termination of a child: the system is automatically made ware of the termination of the child and the latter disappears from the process table.

The recognition of the signal SIGCHLD is important in the writing of client-server applications. In general, a server master recognises the arrival of requests and sets up a slave-server, which replies to them. When the request is made, the slave-server terminates and server master checks that there have been no problems by reading its termination code. It is necessary to read the termination state, if not there is a risk of saturation of the process table by processes in the ZOMBIE state.

The following example shows a means of managing the signal SIGCHLD.

─────────── WaitChild.c ───────────────────────

```
#include <stdio.h>
#include <unistd.h>
#include <signal.h>
#include <sys/types.h>
#include <sys/wait.h>

void deroute (int sig);
{
    printf ("Termination of the child process %d\n", wait (NULL));
}

int                    main (void)
{
    struct sigaction action;
    int              i;

    action.sa_handler = deroute
    action.sa_flags = 0;
    action.sa_mask = 0;
```

```
     sigaction (SIGCHLD, &action, NULL);

     for (i = 0; i < 5; i++) {
               switch (fork (){
                  case 0;
                         sleep (1);
                         exit (0);
                         break;
                  default;
                         pause ();
                }
          }
          return 0;
}
```

——————————————————————— WaitChild.c ————————

The variable **action** is initialised with the diversion function, and the parent process creates a child and awaits the termination on five successive occasions. In a real situation, the arrival of a signal is not synchronised with the waiting process of the parent process, but intercepting **SIGCHLD** allows the termination state of the child to be captured.

5.5
GENERAL OVERVIEW OF IMPLEMENTATION

5.5.1 Data structures

Information about the management of signals for processes are stored in the structure **process_struct** already presented in chapter 4, section 4.5.1. The fields of this structure linked to the signals are the following:

- **signal**: signals in waiting, expressed in the form of a string of bits;
- **blocked**: masked signals, expressed in the form of a string of bits;
- **exit_signal**: number of the signal causing the termination of a process;
- **sig**: table containing the address of signal diversion functions.

The structure **signal_struct**, which defines the type of the field **sig**, is declared in the file **<linux/sched.h>**. It contains the following fields:

type	field	description
int	count	Counter used by the system call clone to track the number of processes pointing to the structure
struct sigaction[32]	action	Table of diversion functions

5.5.1.1 *Process creation and termination*

Processing of the signals is carried out at each process creation. Indeed, by default a process inherits actions defined from signals by its parent; it is therefore necessary to copy these actions from the parent to the child. This is the role of the function **copy_sigband**, which is defined in the source file *kernel/proc.c*. This function is called by the main function creating the process **do_fork** (see chapter 4, section 4.6.2). If it involves a call *fork*, the function allocates memory space to the new structure **signal_struct** and resets the field **sig** of the process descriptor with the address of this function. If, on the other hand, a call *clone* has been made with the option **CLONE_SIGHAND**, the new process shares the actions linked to the signals with its parent, and therefore only the field **sig->count** of the parent descriptor is incremented (this could correspond to the creation of a *thread* in the process).

At the termination of a process, an inverse process to the above should be applied. This is the role of the function **exit_sighand**, which is defined in the source file *kernel/exit.c*, and is called by the terminating function **do_exit** (see chapter 4, section 6.2.2). The function decrements the references counter of the field **sig** of the process descriptor, and if it becomes null (i.e. the current process is the latest active *thread* for this structure), the function de-allocates the memory space reserved for storing the actions arising from the signals.

This function is also called by **do_fork** when the creation process has not been able to complete.

5.5.1.2 *Transmission of signals*

The emission of signals is carried out in the kernel by the function **send_sig**, which verifies that the signal can be sent by checking that the emitting process is part of the right group. This function prepares the new selection mask in the case of special signals or for a particular process state. Finally, it calls the function **generate** which modifies the field **signal** of the structure **process_struct** of the target process and wakes it up, if it is in the sleeping, but interruptible, state.

A signal may also be sent out directly from the kernel to a process. This generally a sign that there is a problem, and the kernel then uses a function **force_sig**, which by-passes all the checks. This function removes the signal from the list of masked signals if it resides there, and resets the actions by default for the signals which are ignored in order to force the signal which is emitted to be received.

5.5.1.3 *Signal reception*

Reception of a signal and the processing associated with a process is carried out by the targeted process before the change is made from kernel mode to user mode, either on returning from a system call, or after the scheduler has passed it to the processor. This stage is accomplished by a routine written in assembly language. For the x86 architecture, this is the routine **ret_from_sys_call**, defined in the source file *arch/i386/kernel/entry.S* which checks whether there are signals to process and which calls the function do_signal, defined in the source file *arch/i386/kernel/signal.c* to ensure that the latter has been received. This function analyses the state of the process and the signal to be received in order to carry out an effective course of action:

- If the process is *traced* (option PF_TRACED in the field flags of the descriptor), it passes into the stopped state and its parent is warned by the function notify_parent.
- If the action is SIG_IGN and the signal is SIGCHLD, a call to the function sys_waitpid is carried out to bring about the deletion of the process from process table.
- If the action is SIG_DFL, either the function do_exit is called directly, or a file *core* is created by the function current->binfmt->core.dump then the function do_exit is called to terminate the process.

The function handle_signal is next invoked. This function checks whether the process was executing a system call or not. If it was, it may be necessary to re-execute it or to flag the interrupt. If it needs to be re-executed, the program counter of the process in user mode is used to point to the call code in the system call. If not, the error EINTR is returned.

handle_signal then calls setup_frame. This is the most sensitive function because it is the one which modifies the process stack in user mode in order to save the process context. This context is described by the structure sigcontext of the file <asm/sigcontext.h>. This structure contains the set of registers of the processor and the maths co-processor, the flag number of the system call in progress and the associated error code, as well as the signal mask. This context is put in the stack but at an earlier point, the function stacks the value of the signal converted by the process execution domain. In the case of binary Linux, the signal value is simply stacked, but for other emulations, it calls the field of exec_domain->signal_invmap[signr] to stack the converted value of the signal. After these modifications to the stack, the function stacks a system call which will be executed after the signal processing function in order to recover the stack data and to reinstate the saved signal mask (this call is *sigreturn* is described below). Finally, the function modifies the instruction register in user mode so that it can execute the diversion function.

The system call *sigreturn* is used solely by the previous function to clean the stack and to carry out the actions described above. In future versions of the kernel, this call will also serve to reinstate the original user stack if a stack change occurs during the processing of a signal.

5.6

5.6.1 Library functions

5.6.1.1 *Management of signal sets*

These functions are implemented in the C library, where a test is performed to check that the signals passed as parameters are valid, then the macros defined in the file **<signal.h>** are invoked. For example, the implementation of the function *sigaddset* defined in the file *libc/signal/sigaddset.c* is the following:

```
/* Add SIGNO to SET.  */
int
DEFUN(sigaddset, (set, signo), sigset, sigset_t *set AND int signo)
{
        if (set == NULL ||  signo <= 0  ||  signo >=NSIG)
        {
          errno = EINVAL;
          return -1;
        }

   return __ sigaddset (set, signo);
}
```

the macro instruction **sigaddset** is defined in the header file **<signal.h>** in the following way:

```
#define __sigmask(sig)   (1 << ((sig) - 1))
#define __sigaddset(set, sig)   ((*set) |= __sigmask (sig)),0
```

5.6.1.2 *The function* raise

This function is implemented in the source file *posix/raise.c* in the C library. It consists of a single call to *kill*.

5.6.2 System calls

5.6.2.1 *Blocking of signals*

The system call *sigprocmask* is implemented in the file *kernel/signal.c* in most architectures. Only the version for Alpha processors implements the call *sigprocmask* in a particular way so as to be compatible with the corresponding system call in OSF/1. For the latter architecture, the corresponding code is kept in the file *arch/alpha/kernel/signal.c*.

The function **sys_sigprocmask**, which corresponds to the call *sigprocmask,* modifies the field **blocked** of the structure **process_struct** of the current process according to the parameters of the system call. This function checks that the process is not trying to mask non-maskable signal by carrying out a binary *and* between the supplied mask and the constant **_BLOCKABLE**. The latter defines the set of maskable signals:

```
#define _BLOCKABLE (~(_S(SIGKILL) | _S(SIGSTOP)))
```

Depending on the modification desired, the set of signals is added to the mask **(SIG_BLOCK),** or deleted from the mask **(SIG_UNBLOCK),** or indeed becomes the mask itself **(SIG_SETMASK).** Finally, if the parameter **oset** is non-null, the function writes the original mask in the user space (function **put_user**) after checking that the parameter points to a valid memory zone in user space.

5.6.2.2 *Signal diversion*

The system call *sigaction* is implemented in the file *kernel/signal.c.*

The function **sys_sigaction** corresponds to the call *sigaction*. This function checks first of all that the signal to be modified is valid (it should fall within the range 1 to 32). Next the function finds the address of the structure **sigaction** corresponding to the signal by means of the field **sig** in the structure **process_struct** of the current process.

If the parameter action is non-nul, the function checks that the signals **SIGKILL** or **SIGSTOP**, whose behaviour cannot be modified, are not involved, reads the structure **sigaction** from the user memory space and puts it in the new variable **new_sa**. There, once more, a check is made to see that the address of the new diversion function is valid.

If the parameter **oldaction** is non-null, the function checks that it points to a valid memory zone for writing in user space, and puts there the contents of the **sigaction**, which have been recovered earlier, and which correspond to the signal before the call.

If there is a modification to be carried out, the structure **process_struct** is enabled with the new structure **sigaction**. The function **check_pending** is then called. This function checks to see if the action on the signal is **SIG_IGN** or **SIG_DFL** and in this case, it deletes the signal if it is being waited for. This operation is not possible if the signal is **SIGCONT**, **SIGCHLD** or **SIGWINCH** and if the action is **SIG_DFL**. In this case, the function **check_pending** does not modify the waiting signals.

The system call *signal* is not implemented by the function **sys_signal** which is part of the kernel resources but by a C library function. This library function is situated in the file *libc/sysdeps/linux/signal.c.* Indeed, the library function calls *sigaction* in building, based on the address of the diversion function passed as a parameter, a variable of the structure of **sigaction**. The field **sa_flags** of this variable takes the value **(SA_ONESHOT | SA_NOMASK | SA_INTERRUPT)** and **SA_RESTART**, in order to conform to the semantics of the call *signal*. When the call returns, the address of the diversion function is sent back to the process.

In the case where the constant **__USE_BSD_SIGNAL** is defined in the program compilation, it is the library function *__bsd_signal* which corresponds to the call *signal*. Its definition is in the file *libc/sysdeps/linux/__bsd_sig.c* in the library resources. This function is similar to the previous one, except for the flags, which are set to zero. If a call to *siginterrupt* destined for the signal has been carried out before the execution of the library function, then the flag **SA_INTERRUPT** is set.

5.6.2.3 Waiting signals

The system call *sigpending* is implemented by the function **sys_sigpending** which is in the file *kernel/signal.c*.

This function simply returns the result of the operation *and* between the field signal and the field blocked of the structure **process_struct**. This represents the list of blocked signals awaiting reception.

5.6.2.4 Process suspension whilst awaiting signals

The system call *sigsuspend* is implemented by a function which is dependent on the machine architecture. For x86 models, this function is **sys_sigsuspend** and it is located in the source file *arch/i386/kernel/signal.c*.

The function modifies the mask of blocked signals according to the received parameters and saves the former mask (the field **blocked** belonging to the process descriptor). The function next frees the processor (function **schedule**) and waits for the arrival of an event (state **PROCESS_INTERRUPTIBLE**). The function continues executing when a signal is sent to a process, then it calls the internal reception function: **do_signal**. If the signal is part of the mask for blocked signals, the function loops back to the point at which the processor is freed.

When a non-blocked signal arrives, the system call terminates and sends back the error **EINTR**.

5.6.2.5 Sending of signals

The functions corresponding to the sending out of signals are defined in the source file *kernel/exit.c*. Two internal functions are used directly by the function corresponding to the system call *kill*. These are **kill_pg** and **kill_proc**.

The first function transmits a signal to all processes having the group number passed as a parameter. For that, it calls the function **send_sig** described earlier for each of the processes. The processes are found by scanning the process list by means of the macro instruction **for_each_process**. The result returned is the number of processes to which the signal has been sent.

The second function sends out the signal to that number of processes in the parameter which is passed. It returns the result of the function **send_sig** after having found the process descriptor as before.

The system call *kill* is implemented by the function **sys_kill**. This function tests the value of the process identifier to find out if the signal should be sent to one or several processes:

- if this value is null, the function returns the result of the function **kill_pg**, with as parameter the number of the group to which the process carrying out the system call belongs.
- If this value is –1, the function **send_sig** is called by all the processes except the process number 1 (*init*) and the calling process itself. The result returned is either an error, or the number of processes having effectively received the signal.
- If the value is negative, the function **kill_pg** is called with the value which is the negative of the process identifier, and its result is returned.
- If not, the result of the call to the function **kill_proc** is returned.

The system call *killpg* is implemented in the C library function situated in the source file *posix/killpg.c*. This function uses the system call *kill* to send out a signal to the process group, passing as parameter the negative of the group number that it receives.

5.6.2.6 Alarm management

The internal control of the three alarms is different. **ITIMER_VIRTUAL** and **ITIMER_PROF** depend only on the process execution time, and they are therefore controlled when the process is executed. The scheduler enables the alarm counters when it hands the processor resource over to the process. This operation is carried out by the function **update_process_times** of the source file *kernel/sched.c*. The function first of all updates the fields **utime** and **stime** of the process descriptor with the help of the function **do_process_times**. Then the two counters are modified by the functions **do_it_virt** and **do_it_prof**, which use the fields **it_virt_value** and **it_prof_value** of the current process descriptor. If they time-out, the signals **SIGVTALRM** or **SIGPROF** are sent out by the function **send_sig**.

The alarm **ITIMER_REAL** should be modified without the process taking control of the processor. Itws counter can therefore not be generated in the same way. An internal *timer* (see chapter 4, section 4.6.1) is used. The counter is therefore enabled automatically and the signal is sent out by the function **it_real_fn** to which points, from the initialisation of the process, the field **real_timer->function** of its descriptor.

The system calls *setitimer* and *getitimer* are implemented by the kernel functions **sys_setitimer** and **sys_getitimer** which are defined in the source file *kernel/itimer.c*. These two functions, after having checked the validity of their parameters, call the functions **_setitimer** and **_getitimer**. Here again, the operations are simple for the two alarms which are dependent on the process execution time, since it is sufficient to read or to modify the process descriptor fields. On the other hand, for the real time alarm, it is necessary to remove the *timer* from the list (del_timer) in order to inspect it, and then to re-insert it (add_timer).

Two functions for converting the internal time of the machine to or from the real time in seconds are used by the preceding system calls: these are tvtojiffies and jiffiestotv.

The system call *alarm* is still located in the kernel although it is implemented as a library function in certain architectures. Indeed, *alarm* simply uses _setitimer after building a variable of the itimerval structure. The alarm used is ITIMER_REAL.

6

File systems

System calls described

access, bdflush, chdir, chmod, chown, chroot, close, closedir,
dup, dup2, exec, fchdir, fchmod, fchown, fcntl, fdatasync, flock,
fstat, fstatfs, fsync, ftruncate, getdents, ioctl, link, llseek, lseek,
lstat, mkdir, mount, open, opendir, quotactl, read, readdir,
readlink, rename, rmdir, select, stat, stafs, symlink, sync, sysfs,
truncate, umount, unlink, ustat, utime, utimes, write, writev

6.1
BASIC CONCEPTS

6.1.1 Organisation of files

Under Linux, as under any Unix system, files are organised in a tree-like structure. The top of the tree is represented by the root directory, indicated by "/", and each of the branches is a directory which can contain sub-directories (subordinate branches), or files (leaves). Each directory contains a catalogue of names, with each of the names indicating a file or a directory. Two particular entries exist in all directories: "." represents the directory itself, and ".." represents the parent directory.

Figure 6.1 shows a representation of a tree structure where the directories are represented by rectangles, and the files by circles.

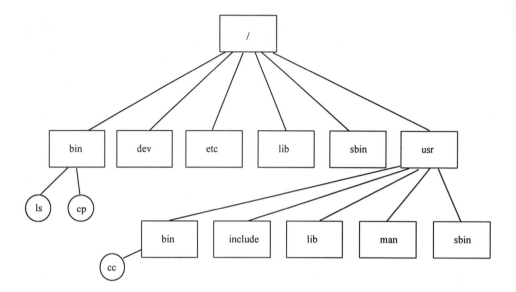

Figure 6.1:   Hierarchical organisation of files.

Each file or directory is characterised by an absolute name. This name cites all the directories to scan, starting with the root directory, in order to access an item, the directories being separated by the character "/". For example, the absolute name of the directory *include* in the figure is */usr/include/* and that of the file *cc* is */usr/bin/cc*.

The names of files may equally be expressed in a manner relative to a directory. Each process has a current directory that it can modify and which forms the base from which relative names can be resolved. For example, if the current directory is */usr*, the file */usr/bin/cc* can be represented by the relative name *bin/cc*, and the relative name of the file */bin/ls* is *../bin/ls*.

6.1.2 File types

Each file present in the tree structure is characterised by its type, and the type is used by the system in order to determine the use to which the file will be put. Linux defines the following types:

- directory: a directory is a catalogue of file names;
- normal file: such a file is designed to contain data belonging to users, whatever the format of the data (text files, source programs, executable programs, etc.);
- symbolic link: a symbolic link is a pointer to another file; when a link is the subject of an action, the file pointed to is accessed;

- special file: a special file is assigned to a device controller embedded in the kernel; when a file is accessed, the physical device associated to it is actually acted upon;
- named pipe: a named pipe is a communications channel which can be used by several processes in order to exchange data.

6.1.3 File linkages

Under Unix in general, it is possible to associate several names to the same file. This operation is called the creation of a file linkage. Once a link has been created, two different names can be used to access the same file. In practice, this implies that several entries in a directory, which may be different, are assigned the same link name. Any operation may be carried out by citing arbitrarily any link name.

The kernel maintains a count of the links assigned to each file. When a link is created, this number is incremented. When a link is deleted, by the command *rm*, the number is decremented. When the number becomes zero, that is when the last link corresponding to a file is deleted, the file contents are effectively deleted, and the space on the disk is made free.

The number of links may be displayed by the command *ls* -l (second field of each line):

```
bbj>ls -1
total 10
-rw-rùr--     1 card users   9940 Apr 22 15:23 a
bbj>ln a b
bbj>ls -1
total 20
-rw-rùr--     2 card users   9940 Apr 22 15:23 a
-rw-rùr--     2 card users   9940 Apr 22 15:23 b
bbj>rm a
bbj>ls -1
total 10
-rw-rùr--     1 card users   9940 Apr 22 15:23 b
```

There are several restrictions on the use of links:

- It is impossible to create links to directories. Indeed, the existence of links between directories would have the effect of turning the file tree structure into a graph which could contain cycles, and the kernel could go into an infinite loop in trying to resolve file names.
- It is impossible to create links between files residing on different filesystems. If */usr* and */home* are situated on different partitions or different disks, it is impossible to create links between these hierarchies.

In order to offset these restrictions, a new type of link has been introduced: this is the symbolic link. Whilst conventional links are additional names to a file, symbolic links are pointers to other files. They can point to any sort of file, even non-existent ones. In fact, a symbolic link is a special type of file whose contents specify the name of the target file:

```
bbj>ls -1
total 10
-rw-rùr--      1 card users   9940 Apr 22 15:31 a
bbj>ln -s a b
bbj>ls -1
total 10
-rw-rùr--      1 card users   9940 Apr 22 15:31 a
lrwxrwxrwx     1 card users   1 Apr 22 15:31 b -> a
bbj>rm a
bbj>ls -1
total 0
lrwxrwxrwx     1 card users   1 Apr 22 15:31 b -> a
bbj>cat b
cat: b: No such file or directory
```

6.1.4 File attributes

Each file has several attributes associated with it :

- its size in bytes;
- the user/owner identifier of the file, that is, the user who created the file;
- the group identifier of users who own the file;
- the number of links;
- the access permissions;
- the dates of access and modification.

The access permissions of a file are expressed according to a triplet: the permission of the user/owner, the permission of the owning group, and the permission of the rest of users. Each of these permissions is formed from a set of three permissions:

- the permission to read file data (r);
- the permission to write data to the file (w);
- the permission to execute the contents of a file (x).

For a directory, read access means that the contents of a file may be listed, write access means that entries in the directory may be added or deleted, and the right to execute means that the directory may be examined.

When a process accesses a file, Linux verifies that it is authorised to carry out the specified operation. To establish this, it compares the permissions requested by the operation with the permissions associated with the file.

In addition to these permissions, the access permission code contains three bits having a particular significance:

- the *setuid* bit: when an executable file having this bit set is started, it executes with the identifier of the user/owner of the file in force instead of the calling user;
- the *setgid* bit: when an executable file having this bit set is started, it executes with the identifier of group owning the file in force instead of the calling user group;
- the *sticky* bit: when a directory has this bit set, the files that it contains may only be deleted by their respective owners.

Three times are associated with each file:

- the date of the most recent access (*atime*), which is enabled at each access (reading or writing) to the file;
- the date of the last modification of the file contents (*mtime*), which is enabled at each writing of data to the file;
- the date of the last modification of the file (*ctime*), which is enabled at each modification of the state of the file. For example, the changing of access permissions of a file does not modify *mtime* because the contents have not changed, but it does cause the flagging of *ctime*.

6.1.5 Input and Output primitives

Linux provides two sorts of input and output functions:

- system calls:

  These primitives are carried out directly from the kernel. They enable files to be manipulated directly (creation, deletion, name change, etc.) as well as inputting and outputting un-typed data.
- The standard input/output library:

  This library provides a group of functions allowing 'high level' inputs and outputs to be achieved on files. In contrast to system calls, whose functionalities are powerful, but which are sometimes difficult to use, this library particularly allows data conversions during input and output, by means of functions of the type *printf* and *scanf*.

In this chapter, only system calls for manipulating files and 'high level' functions which are part of the C language definition will be described in detailed.

6.1.6 Input and Output descriptors

System calls bringing about read and write operations on files make use of input/output descriptors. A descriptor is allocated to a file by Linux when it is opened, and is released when the file is closed, either explicitly or implicitly when the process is terminated. The process which acts on a file must provide the descriptor at each read or write operation.

Input/output descriptors are single integers, and for the kernel, they represent the entries in a table of descriptors which it manages and which enable it to access control information concerning open files.

Three input/output descriptors have a particular significance: the descriptor 0 represents the standard input generally associated with the keyboard, the descriptor 1 represents the standard output, and the descriptor 2 represents the error output. These two outputs are generally associated with the monitor screen.

6.2
BASIC SYSTEM CALLS
6.2.1 File inputs and outputs

6.2.1.1 Opening and closing files
Files must be open before data can be read or written. The syntax of the call *open* is the following:

```
#include <sys/types.h>
#include <sys/stat.h>
#include <fcntl.h>
#include <unistd.h>


int open (const char *pathname, int flags);
int open (const char *pathname, int flags, mode_t mode);
```

The parameter **pathname** specifies the name of the file to open, according to the opening mode indicated by **flags**, and the parameter **mode** specifies the access permissions to be set in the file when it is created. *open* returns the input/output descriptor corresponding to the open file, or the value –1 if it fails.

The opening mode is expressed as a function of defined constants in the header file **<fcntl.h>**: **O_RDONLY** for read-only access, **O_WRONLY** for write-only access, and **O_RDWR** for access in read or write mode. Other opening options may also be specified by a binary OR operation (operator " | " in the C language):

option	*meaning*
O_CREAT	Creation of a file if it does not exist
O_EXCL	Gives an error if **O_CREAT** is specified and if the file exists already
O_TRUNC	Deletion of the former contents of a file if it existed already
O_APPEND	Opening in write mode, any write is performed at the end of the file
O_NONBLOCK	Opening in non-blocking mode
O_SYNC	Opening of the file in synchronous mode: any update is immediately written to disk

The access permissions to be set (parameter mode) are expressed in terms of binary constants defined in the header file **<sys/stat.h>**:

option	*meaning*
S_ISUID	Bit *setuid*
S_ISGID	Bit *setgid*
S_ISVTX	Bit *sticky*
S_IRUSR	Read permissions for the owner
S_IWUSR	Write permissions for the owner
S_IXUSR	Execution permissions for the owner
S_IRWXU	Read, write and execution permissions for the owner
S_IRGRP	Read permissions for the user group
S_IWGRP	Write permissions for the user group
S_IXGRP	Execution permissions for the user group
S_IRWXG	Read, write and execution permissions for the user group
S_IROTH	Read permissions for the rest of users
S_IWOTH	Write permissions for the rest of users
S_IXOTH	Execution permissions for the rest of users
S_IRWXO	Read, write and execution permissions for the rest of users

In the event of a problem, the variable **errno** can take the following values:

error	*meaning*
EACCES	The specified access is not possible
EEXIST	**pathname** specifies a filename which exists and the options **O_CREAT** and **O_EXCL** have been specified
EFAULT	**pathname** contains an invalid address
EISDIR	**pathname** refers to a directory and the specified access includes writing
ELOOP	A symbolic link loop has been encountered
EMFILE	The maximum number of files opened by the process has been reached
ENAMETOOLONG	**pathname** specifies a filename which is too long
ENOMEM	The kernel has not been able to allocate memory for internal descriptors
ENOENT	**pathname** refers to a non-existent filename and the option **O_CREAT** is not specified
ENOSPC	The filesystem is saturated
ENOTDIR	One of the components of **pathname**, used as a directory name, is not a directory
EROFS	The filesystem is read-mode only and the specified access includes writing
ETXTBSY	**pathname** refers to a binary program which is running, and the specified access includes writing

After using a file, a process must use the system call *close* in order to close it. The *close* syntax is:

```
#include <unistd.h>


int close (int fd);
```

The parameter **fd** corresponds to a input/output descriptor returned by the call *open*. The value 0 is returned in the event of success, If there is a problem, the value –1 is returned. The only error possible is **EBADF,** which indicates that the descriptor specified by **fd** is invalid.

6.2.1.2 *Reading and writing data*
Two calls allow a process to read or to write data to a file which has been previously opened by the call *open*. Linux treats files as a succession of unstructured bytes not having any particular type, and does not impose any restriction on the data that a process may read or write to a file. If the file should be structured, it is the application which must manage this.

The reading of data is accomplished by the call *read*:

```
#include <unistd.h>

ssize_t read (int fd, void *buf, size_t count);
```

The call *read* causes the data to be read from the file whose input/output descriptor is passed in the parameter **fd**. The data that is read is stored in the buffer, whose address is specified in **buf**, and whose size in bytes is indicated in count. The call *read* returns the number of bytes that have been read from the file (0 in the case that the end of the file has been reached), and –1 in the event of error.

In the event of a problem, the variable **errno** can take the following values:

error	*meaning*
EBADF	The specified input/output descriptor is invalid
EFAULT	**buf** contains an invalid address
EINTR	The system call has been interrupted by a reception of a signal
EINVAL	**fd** refers to an object which can not be read
EIO	An input/output error has occurred
EISDIR	**fd** refers to a directory

The writing of data is accomplished by the call *write*. It has the following syntax:

```
#include <unistd.h>

ssize_t write (int fd, const char *buf, size_t count);
```

The data whose address is contained in **buf** and whose size is passed in the parameter **count** are written in the file specified by the input/output descriptor **fd**. *write* returns the number of bytes in the file, or the value –1 in the event of an error.

In the event of an problem, the variable **errno** can take the following values:

error	meaning
EBADF	The specified input/output descriptor is invalid
EFAULT	**buf** contains an invalid address
EINTR	The system call has been interrupted by a reception of a signal
EINVAL	**fd** refers to an object which can not be read
EIO	An input/output error has occurred
EISDIR	**fd** refers to a directory
EPIPE	**fd** refers to a pipe in which is there is no longer a read process
ENOSPC	The filesystem is saturated

The following program uses the file input and output functions to copy the contents of one file into another:

———— CopieFichier.c ————

```
#include <sys/types.h>
#include <sys/stat.h>
#include <fcntl.h>
#include <unistd.h>
#include <errno.h>
#include <stdio.h>

void main (int argc, char *argv[])
{
        int             fd1;
        int             fd2;
        char            buffer[1024];
        ssize_t         n;
        /* Check of arguments */
        if (argc != 3)   {
           printf ("Usage: %s source target\n", argv[0]);
           exit (1);
        }
        /* Opening of source file */
        fd1 = open (argv[1], O_RDONLY);
        if (fd1 == -1) {
           perror ("open 1");
           exit (1);
        }
```

```
        /* Opening of target file */
        fd2 = open (argv[2], O_WRONLY | O_TRUNC | O_CREAT,
                S_IRUSR | S_IWUSR);
        if (fd2 == -1) {
           perror  ("open 2");
           exit  (1);
}

        /* Copy loop (read in source file, write in target file) */
        do {
           n = read (fd1, (void *) buffer, sizeof (buffer));
           if (n > 0)
                   if write (fd2, (void *) buffer, n) !=n
                       perror ("write");
        } while (n > 0);
        /* file closure */
        (void) close (fd1);
        (void) close (fd2);
        /* End of program */
        exit (0);
        }
```

——————————————————————— CopieFichier.c ———————

6.2.1.3 *Positioning within a file*

Read and write calls allow sequential reading and writing of data. There is no primitive which allows direct reading and writing in so far as there is no file structure managed by the kernel.

However, it is possible to alter the reading or writing pointer in a file. In this way, direct reading and writing may be simulated. The system calls *lseek* and *llseek* allow the reading or writing pointer to be positioned:

```
#include <unistd.h>

off_t lseek (int fd, off_t offset, int whence);

loff_t llseek (int fd, loff_t offset, int whence);
```

The parameter **fd** represents the input/output descriptor associated with the file, and **offset** defines the shifting of the reading or writing pointer in bytes with respect to some reference base point specified by **whence**. The latter parameter can take on the following values:

option	meaning
SEEK_SET	Location with respect to the beginning of the file
SEEK_CUR	Location with respect to the current position
SEEK_END	Location with respect to the end of the file

lseek returns the new current position of the pointer relative to the beginning of the file, or the value -1 in the event of a problem.

In the event of an problem, the variable **errno** can take the following values:

error	meaning
EBADF	The specified input/output descriptor is invalid
EINVAL	**whence** specifies an invalid value
EISPIPE	**fd** refers to a pipe

There is no call allowing the current pointer position in a file to be obtained. It is, however, possible to call *lseek* without altering the current position and to make use of the result as follows:

```
#include <unistd.h>

off_t tell (int fd)
{
        return lseek (fd, (off_t) 0, SEEK_CUR);
}
```

The primitive *llseek* is peculiar to Linux. It has the same function to *lseek*, but it allows a pointer offset to be expressed in 64 bits (**loff_t**), even on machines having 32 bit architectures.

6.2.1.4 Saving of modified data

When data is written to a file, it is first of all written to buffers, via the *buffer cache*, then saved regularly on disk by the process *update*. If the file has been opened with the option **O_SYNC**, the changes to be made are written in a synchronous manner on disk.

Saving into buffers gives several performance advantages:

- the processes writing to files are not suspended during the write operations, the kernel sees to it that the data is written to disk asynchronously;
- if several processes access the same files, only the first to do a read operation does this from the disk; other read operations on the same data are achieved by

transferring data from the buffers of the *buffer cache* to the address spaces of the different processes.

Asynchronous writing of data, however, poses a reliability problem: if there is a power loss between the call *write* and the real writing of the data to disk, the modifications are lost.

Linux has available three system calls allowing writing of modified data to disk to be triggered:

```
#include <inistd.h>

int sync (void);

int fsync (int fd);

int fdatasync (int fd);
```

The call *sync* triggers the writing of all modified data, whilst the call *fsync* triggers the writing of modifications corresponding to the file characterised by the input/output descriptor **fd**. *fdatasync* carries out the same processing as *fsync*, but it cannot re-write the control data of the file (such as the date of the last modification for example) and it can thus economise on disk writing.

In the event of an problem, the variable **errno** can take the following values:

error	meaning
EBADF	The specified input/output descriptor is invalid
EINVAL	**fd** refers to an object on which synchronisation is not possible
EIO	An input/output error has occurred

6.2.2 Manipulation of files

6.2.2.1 *Creation of links*
The system call *link* creates a new link to a file. Its syntax is:

```
#include <unistd.h>

int link (const char *oldpath, const char *newpath);
```

link creates a link, whose name is specified by the parameter **newpath,** to a file whose name is passed in the parameter **oldpath.** The existing file and the link must be in the same filesystem and must not be directories.

error	*meaning*
EACCES	The process does not have read access to the directory containing the file specified by **oldpath,** or write access to the directory containing the file specified by **newpath**
EEXIST	**newpath** specifies an existing filename
EFAULT	**oldpath** and **newpath** contain an invalid address
ELOOP	A symbolic link loop has been encountered
EMLINK	The maximum number of links has been reached
ENAMETOOLONG	**oldpath** or **newpath** specify a filename which is too long
ENOENT	**oldpath** refers to a non-existent filename
ENOMEM	The kernel has not been able to allocate memory for its internal descriptors
EPIPE	**fd** refers to a pipe in which is there is no longer a read process
ENOSPC	The filesystem is saturated
ENOTDIR	One of the components of **oldpath** or **newpath,** used as a directory name, is not a directory
EPERM	The filesystem containing the files specified by **oldpath** or **newpath** does not support link creation, or **oldpath** corresponds to a directory name
EROFS	The filesystem is only in read mode
EXDEV	The files specified by **oldpath** or **newpath** are located on different filesystems

6.2.2.2 Deletion of files
The system call *unlink* deletes a link, and therefore a file if it is part of the final link. Its syntax is as follows:

```
#include <unistd.h>

int unlink (const char *pathname);
```

The file specified by the parameter **pathname** is deleted if the process calling it possesses sufficient access permissions, that is it has write access to the directory containing the file.

In the event of a problem, the variable **errno** can take the following values:

error	*meaning*
EACCES	The process does not have write access to the directory containing the file specified by **pathname**
EFAULT	**pathname** contains an invalid address
ENAMETOOLONG	**pathname** specifies a filename which is too long
ENOENT	**pathname** refers to a non-existent filename
ENOMEM	The kernel has not been able to allocate memory for its internal decriptors
ENOTDIR	One of the components of **pathname**, used as a directory name, is not a directory
EPERM	**pathname** specifies the name of a directory
EROFS	The filesystem is only in read mode

6.2.2.3 *Changing the name of a file*

The system call *rename* allows the name of a file to be changed, and therefore to be renamed or to be moved from one directory to another situated in the same filesystem. Its syntax is as follows:

```
#include <unistd.h>

int rename (const char *oldpath, const char *newpath);
```

The source file, whose name is passed in the parameter **oldpath,** is renamed according to the new name passed in the parameter **newpath.** If this latter parameter specifies a name of an existing file, this file is first of all deleted.

In the event of a problem, the variable **errno** can take the following values:

error	meaning
EACCES	The process does not have write access to the directory containing the file specified by **oldpath** or to the directory containing the file specified by **newpath**
EBUSY	**newpath** specifies the name of a directory used as the current directory or the root directory of a process
EFAULT	**oldpath** or **newpath** contain an invalid address
ELOOP	A symbolic link loop has been encountered
ENAMETOOLONG	**oldpath** or **newpath** specify a filename which is too long
ENOENT	**oldpath** refers to a non-existent filename
ENOSPC	The filesystem is saturated
ENOTDIR	One of the components of **oldpath** or **newpath**, used as a directory name, is not a directory
ENOEMPTY	**newpath** specifies the name of a directory which is not empty
EROFS	The filesystem is only in read mode
EXDEV	The files specified by **oldpath** or **newpath** are located on different filesystems

6.2.2.4 Changing the size of a file

A process may modify the size of a file, either by truncating its contents, or by enlarging the file. To do this, two primitives are provided:

```
#include <unistd.h>

int truncate (const char *pathname, size_t length);

int ftruncate (int fd, size_t length);
```

The system call *truncate* modifies the size of the file whose name is specified by the parameter **pathname**. *ftruncate* modifies the size of the open file whose input/output descriptor is passed in the parameter fd. The parameter **length** indicates the new file size in bytes. If the file is larger than the size specified, its contents are truncated, if it is smaller, the contents are padded out.

In the event of an error during execution, the variable **errno** can take the following values:

error	meaning
EACCES	The process does not have write access to file specified by **pathname**
EFAULT	**pathname** contains an invalid address
EIO	An input/output error has occurred
EISDIR	**pathname** refers to a directory
ELOOP	A symbolic link loop has been encountered
ENAMETOOLONG	**pathname** specifies a filename which is too long
ENOENT	**pathname** refers to a non-existent filename
ENOTDIR	One of the components of **pathname**, used as a directory name, is not a directory
EROFS	The filesystem is only in read mode
ETXTBSY	**pathname** refers to a binary program which is running

In the case of *ftruncate*, the following errors are also possible:

error	meaning
EBADF	The specified input/output descriptor is invalid
EINVAL	**fd** refers to a file which is not open in write mode

6.2.2.5 Access permissions to a file

The rights of access to a file are set when the file is created by a call to *open*. They can also by subsequently modified by means of calls *chmod* and *fchmod*. Their syntax is as follows:

```
#include <sys/types.h>
#include <sys/stat.h>

int chmod (const char *pathname, mode_t mode);

int fchmod (int fd, mode_t mode);
```

chmod modifies the access permissions of file whose name is passed in the parameter **pathname**. *fchmod* modifies permissions of access to an open file whose input/output descriptor is specified by the parameter **fd**. The parameter **mode** defines the access permissions to be set and is similar to the third parameter of the call *open*.

The two calls are only authorised for the user/owner of a file and the superuser.

In the event of an error in the system call *chmod*, the variable **errno** can take the following values:

error	meaning
EFAULT	**pathname** contains an invalid address
ELOOP	A symbolic link loop has been encountered
ENAMETOOLONG	**pathname** specifies a filename which is too long
ENOENT	**pathname** refers to a non-existent filename
ENOMEM	The kernel has not been able to allocate memory for its internal descriptors
ENOTDIR	One of the components of **pathname**, used as a directory name, is not a directory
EPERM	The process does not have fileowner permissions, and is not privileged
EROFS	The filesystem is only in read mode

In addition, *fchmod* can return the error **EBADF**, indicating that the descriptor **fd** is invalid.

A process may test whether access is possible to a file. To do this, Linux provides the call *access*, whose syntax is as follows:

```
#include <unistd.h>

int access (const char *pathname, int mode);
```

The parameter **mode** represents the access permissions to be checked, and it is expressed by a combination of the following constants:

error	meaning
F_OK	Test existence of file
R_OK	Test read access
W_OK	Test write access
X_OK	Test execution access

access returns the value 0 if access is possible, and the value –1 if not. In the latter case, the variable **errno** can take the following values:

error	meaning
EACCES	Access is refused
EFAULT	**pathname** contains an invalid address
EINVAL	The value specified by **mode** is invalid
ELOOP	A symbolic link loop has been encountered
ENAMETOOLONG	**pathname** specifies a filename which is too long
ENOENT	**pathname** refers to a non-existent filename
ENOMEM	The kernel has not been able to allocate memory for its internal descriptors
ENOTDIR	One of the components of **pathname**, used as a directory name, is not a directory

6.2.2.6 *Change of the user owner*

When a file is created, the user and group owners are initialised according to the identity of the calling process. Linux provides two system calls allowing file properties to be changed:

```
#include <sys/types.h>
#include <unistd.h>

int chown (const char *pathname, uid_t owner, gid_t group);

int fchown (int fd, uid_t owner, gid_t group);
```

chown allows the user and group owners of a file to be changed, where the file name is passed in the parameter **pathname**. For its part, *fchown* acts on an open file whose input/output descriptor is passed in the parameter **fd**. In both cases, **owner** represents the identifier of the new user/owner, and **group** represents the group identifier. Each of these parameters may be omitted by specifying the value –1.

Only a process having the rights of a superuser may change the user/owner of a file. The owner of a file can only change the group identifier if he is the member of a new group.

In the event of an error in the system call *chown*, the variable **errno** can take the following values:

error	meaning
EFAULT	**pathname** contains an invalid address
ELOOP	A symbolic link loop has been encountered
ENAMETOOLONG	**pathname** specifies a filename which is too long
ENOENT	**pathname** refers to a non-existent filename
ENOMEM	The kernel has not been able to allocate memory for its internal descriptors
ENOTDIR	One of the components of **pathname**, used as a directory name, is not a directory
EPERM	The process does not have fileowner permissions, and is not privileged
EROFS	The filesystem is only in read mode

In addition, *fchown* can return the error **EBADF**, indicating that the descriptor **fd** is invalid.

6.2.3 Management of directories

6.2.3.1 *Creation of directories*
A directory is created by the system call *mkdir* whose syntax is as follows:

```
#include <sys/types.h>
#include <fnctl.h>
#include <unistd.h>


int mkdir (const char *pathname, mode_t mode);
```

The name of the directory to be created is specified in the parameter **pathname**. The parameter **mode** indicates the access permissions to be set for the new directory. It is similar to the third parameter of the call *open*.

In the event of a problem, the variable **errno** can take the following values:

error	meaning
EACCES	The process does not have write access to the parent directory of the directory specified by **pathname**
EEXIST	**pathname** specifies the name of an existing file
EFAULT	**pathname** contains an invalid address
ELOOP	A symbolic link loop has been encountered
ENAMETOOLONG	**pathname** specifies a filename which is too long

Continuation of list of values that **errno** can take	
error	*meaning*
ENOMEM	The kernel has not been able to allocate memory for its internal descriptors
ENOTDIR	One of the components of **pathname**, used as a directory name, is not a directory
EROFS	The filesystem is only in read mode
ENOSPC	The filesystem is saturated

6.2.3.2 Deletion of directories

The system call *rmdir* allows a directory to be deleted. The directory should be empty, with the exception of the entries ".." and "..". The syntax is as follows:

```
#include <unistd.h>

int rmdir (const char *pathname);
```

The parameter **pathname** indicates the directory to be deleted. In the event of a problem, the variable **errno** can take the following values:

error	*meaning*
EACCES	The process does not have write access to the parent directory of the directory specified by **pathname**
EBUSY	**pathname** specifies the name of a directory used as the current directory or the root directory of a process
EFAULT	**pathname** contains an invalid address
ENAMETOOLONG	**pathname** specifies a filename which is too long
ENOENT	**pathname** refers to a non-existent filename
ELOOP	A symbolic link loop has been encountered
ENOMEM	The kernel has not been able to allocate memory for its internal descriptors
ENOTDIR	One of the components of **pathname**, used as a directory name, is not a directory, or **pathname** does not specify the name of a directory
ENOTEMPTY	The directory specified by **pathname** is not empty
EROFS	The filesystem is only in read mode

6.2.3.3 Current directory

All processes are associated with a current directory. The relative file names used by the process are resolved with respect to the directory.

The system calls *chdir* and *fchdir* allow a process to change its current directory. Their syntax is as follows:

```
#include <unistd.h>

int chdir (const char *pathname);

int fchdir (int fd);
```

chdir uses the parameter **pathname** which specifies the name of the new current directory. F*chdir*, for its part, uses the input/output descriptor (parameter **fd**) obtained by a previous call to the primitive *open*.

In the event of a problem with *chdir*, the variable **errno** can take the following values:

error	meaning
EFAULT	**pathname** contains an invalid address
ENOENT	**pathname** refers to a non-existent filename
ENAMETOOLONG	**pathname** specifies a filename which is too long
ELOOP	A symbolic link loop has been encountered
ENOMEM	The kernel has not been able to allocate memory for its internal descriptors
ENOTDIR	One of the components of **pathname**, used as a directory name, is not a directory, or **pathname** does not specify the name of a directory
EPERM	The process has not got execution access to the directory specified by **pathname**

In addition, *fchdir* can return the error EBADF, indicating that the descriptor **fd** is invalid.

There is no system call which enables a process to obtain the name of its current directory, but the library function *getcwd* plays this role. Its syntax is as follows:

```
#include <unistd.h>

char *getcwd (char *buf, size_t size);
```

getcwd returns the absolute name of the current directory in the parameter **buf**, The parameter size specifies the size of the buffer pointed to by **buf**, and the pointer returned by *getcwd* is the parameter **buf** in the event of success. In the event of an error, the value NULL is returned. The only error code that can be returned is **ERANGE** in the event that the buffer size is too small to contain the absolute name of the current directory.

6.2.3.4 Local root directory

All processes have an associated root directory, which may be different from the real root directory. The absolute names of files used by the process are resolved with respect to this directory. Normally, this directory is the same for all processes and corresponds to the root of the file tree structure, but a process which has the rights of superuser may change the root directory in order to confine to sub-levels of the structure the group of files to which it has access, by means of a system call *chroot*.

```
#include <unistd.h>

int chroot (const char *pathname);
```

The parameter pathname specifies the name of the new root directory to use. If successful, *chroot* returns the value 0, and the current process is confined to the files and directories in the sub-levels of the specified directory. In the event of an error, *chroot* returns the value –1.

In the event of a problem with *chroot*, the variable errno can take the following values:

error	*meaning*
EFAULT	**pathname** contains an invalid address
ENOENT	**pathname** refers to a non-existent filename
ENAMETOOLONG	**pathname** specifies a filename which is too long
ELOOP	A symbolic link loop has been encountered
ENOMEM	The kernel has not been able to allocate memory for its internal descriptors
ENOTDIR	One of the components of **pathname**, used as a directory name, is not a directory, or **pathname** does not specify the name of a directory
EPERM	The process is not a privileged one

The main application of *chroot* consists of executing an application in an environment which is constrained due to reasons of security. Anonymous FTP servers use this primitive in order to only allow access to directory sub-levels of their files to unidentified users.

6.2.3.5 *Navigation of directories*

Although directories are managed like disk files by the kernel, it is not possible for a process to directly access the catalogue that they contain. Indeed, the format of the catalogues is dependent on the type of filesystem, and Linux forbids the direct reading of catalogues by the call *read* to avoid incorrect interpretation of their contents by processes.

In order to enable processes to access entries in a directory, Linux provides three system calls, called *opendir, readdir,* and *closedir,* Their syntax is as follows:

```
#include <sys/types.h>
#include <dirent.h>
#include <unistd.h>

DIR *opendir (const char *pathname);

struct dirent *readdir (DIR *dir);

int closedir (DIR *dir);
```

The type **DIR** is defined in the file **<dirent.h>** and represents a descriptor of an open directory. Its contents are not accessible, as is the case with the type **FILE** used by the standard input/output library.

opendir opens a directory in read mode, the name of this directory being specified in th parameter **pathname**, and it returns an open file descriptor.

In the event of a problem, the variable **errno** can take the following values:

error	meaning
EACCES	The process does not have write access to the directory specified by **pathname**
EMFILE	The maximum number of files opened by the current process has been reached
ENFILE	The maximum number of files open in the system has been reached
ENOENT	**pathname** refers to a non-existent filename
ENOMEM	The kernel has not been able to allocate memory for its internal descriptors
ENOTDIR	One of the components of **pathname**, used as a directory name, is not a directory, or **pathname** does not specify the name of a directory

readdir carries out a read operation on a directory entry whose descriptor is passed in the parameter **dir**. It returns a pointer to a structure **dirent**[1] containing the

---

[1] This variable is contained in the address space of the C library, and each call of *readdir* replaces the previous contents.

characteristics of the current directory entry, and if the end of the file is encountered, the value **NULL** is returned.

In the event of an error, the variable **errno** can take the value **EBADF**, indicating that the descriptor specified by **dir** is invalid.

The structure **dirent** is defined in the header file **<dirent.h>** and contains the following fields:

type	field	description
long	d_ino	inode number corresponding to the entry
unsigned short	d_reclen	Size of the structure returned
char []	d_name	Filename contained in the entry

Finally, *closedir* closes the directory whose descriptor is passed in the parameter **dir**.

In the event of an error, the variable **errno** can take the value **EBADF**, indicating that the descriptor specified by **dir** is invalid.

The following program is a simplified emulation of the command *ls*: it opens the current directory, displays the contents of each entry obtained by calling *readdir*, then closes the directory.

──────── ListeRep.c ────────────────────────────

```c
#include <sys/types.h>
#include <dirent.h>
#include <unistd.h>
#include <errno.h>
#include <stdio.h>

void main (void)
{
    DIR            *dir;
    struct dirent *dp;

    /* Opening of the current directory */
    dir = opendir (".");
    if (dir == NULL) {
            perror ("opendir");
            exit (1);
    }
    /* Scanning of the directory */
    dp = readdir (dir);
```

```
        while (dp !=NULL) {
               printf ("%s\n", dp->d_name);
               dp = readdir (dir);
        }
        /* Directory closure */
        closedir (dir);
        /* End of program */
        exit (0);
}
```

———————————————————————————————— ListeRep.c ——————————

The primitive *getdents* has recently been added to the Linux kernel. It carries out the same operation as *readdir*, but allows several consecutive directory entries to be read in a single call. It syntax is as follows:

```
#include <unistd.h>
#include <dirent.h>
#include <unistd.h>


int getdents (int fd, struct dirent *dirp, unsigned int count);
```

The parameter **fd** specifies the input/output descriptor associated with a directory, **dirp** contains the address of the buffer where the results will be stored, and **size** indicates the size in bytes of this buffer. Upon calling *getdents*, one or more variables of the structure type **dirent** are put into the buffer, and the number of bytes initialised is returned. To make use of the results, the list of directory entries created in the buffer has to be scanned.

In the event of a problem, the variable **errno** can take the following values:

error	*meaning*
EBADF	The descriptor specified by **dir** is invalid
EFAULT	**pathname** contains an invalid address

The following program is a variation of the previous one: it opens the current directory, obtains the directory entries by calling *getdents*, displays them, then closes the directory.

————————— ListeRep2.c ——————————————————————————————

```
#include <sys/types.h>
#include <dirent.h>
#include <unistd.h>
#include <errno.h>
```

```c
#include <fcntl.h>
#include <stdio.h>

void main (void)
{
    int             dir;
    struct dirent  *dp;
    char            buf[1024];
    int             i,
                    n;

    /* Opening of the current directory */
    dir = open (".", O_RDONLY);
    if (dir == 1) {
            perror ("open");
            exit (1);
    }
    /* Scanning of the directory */
    n = getdents (dir, buf, sizeof (buf));
    if (n == -1) {
            perror ("getdents");
            exit (1);
    }
    while (n > 0) {
            /* Scanning the list returned by getdents */
            i = 0;
            while (i < n) {
                    dp = (struct dirent *) (buf + i);
                    printf ("%s\n", dp->d_name);
                    i += dp->d_reclen;
            }
            n = getdents (dir, buf, sizeof (buf));
            if (n == -1) {
                    perror ("getdents");
                    exit (1);
}
    /* Directory closure */
    close (dir);
    /* End of the program */
    exit (0);
}
```

6.2.4 Symbolic links

Symbolic links are a special type of file that cannot be manipulated by the same primitives as normal files. Linux provides two system calls enabling symbolic links to be created and to read the name of the files that they point to. Their syntax is as follows:

```
#include (unistd.h>

int symlink (const char *oldpath, const char *newpath);

int readlink (const char *pathname, char *buf, size_t bufsiz);
```

The call *symlink* creates a symbolic link, whose name is specified by the parameter **newpath**, and which points to the file whose name is passed in the parameter **oldpath**. The latter file can be of any type, and may not even exist.

In the event of error, the variable **errno** can take the following values:

error	*meaning*
EEXIST	**newpath** specifies the name of an existing file
EFAULT	**oldpath** and **newpath** contain an invalid address
ELOOP	A symbolic link loop has been encountered
ENAMETOOLONG	**oldpath** or **newpath** specify a filename which is too long
ENOTDIR	One of the components of **oldpath** or **newpath**, used as a directory name, is not a directory
ENOMEM	The kernel has not been able to allocate memory for its internal descriptors
ENOSPC	The filesystem is saturated
EPERM	The filesystem containing the file specified by **newpath** does not support the creation of symbolic links, or the process does not have write access to the directory containing the file specified by **newpath**
EROFS	The filesystem is only in read mode

readlink allows a process to read the name of the file to which a symbolic link points. The name of the link is specified by the parameter **pathname, buf** contains the address of a buffer supplied by the process, and **bufsiz** specifies the number of bytes in the buffer. *readlink* returns the number of bytes which have been placed in the buffer **buf**, or the value –1 in the event of error.

In the event of error, the variable **errno** can take the following values:

error	meaning
EFAULT	**buf** or **pathname** contain an invalid address
EINVAL	The file specified by **pathname** is not a symbolic link
EIO	An input/output error has occurred
ELOOP	A symbolic link loop has been encountered
ENAMETOOLONG	**oldpath** or **newpath** specify a filename which is too long
ENOENT	**pathname** refers to a non-existent filename
ENOTDIR	One of the components of **oldpath** or **newpath**, used as a directory name, is not a directory

6.3
ADVANCED CONCEPTS

6.3.1 inodes

Whilst the user represents files by relative or absolute names, the Linux kernel uses internal identifiers. Each file is identified in a unique way by two numbers:

- the device number: it refers to a device, and therefore the filesystem that it contains;
- the file number: it references, in a unique way, a file present in the filesystem.

Each filesystem, of the Unix type, keeps a table of file descriptors on disk. These descriptors, called inodes, contain the control information used to manage the files, and particularly the file attributes, as well as addresses of blocks of data which make up the contents of a file. The unique file number is used by the kernel as an index in the inode table, in order to convert it into a file descriptor.

When a process calls a system primitive by supplying it with a filename, the kernel has to convert the specified name into a descriptor. To do this, Linux scans each of the directories forming part of the filename, and compares each directory entry with the single name of the following element, each directory entry containing a identifier pair (filename, inode number), as can be seen in figure 6.2. For example, if the name */usr/src/linux/fs/dcache.c* is specified, the kernel carries out the following operations:

1. loading of the inode of the root (/), and looking up the entry "*usr*";
2. loading of the inode of */usr* obtained from the previous step, and looking up the entry "*src*";
3. loading of the inode of */usr/src* obtained from the previous step, and looking up the entry "*linux*";
4. loading of the inode of */usr/src/linux* obtained from the previous step, and looking up the entry "*fs*";

5. loading of the inode of */usr/src/linux/fs* obtained from the previous step, and looking up the entry *"dcache.c"*, which supplies the number of the desired inode.

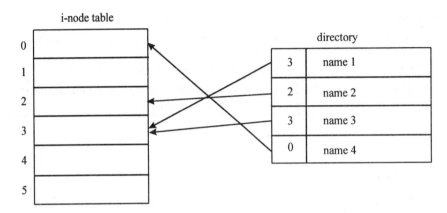

Figure 6.2:   Directory format.

6.3.2 Input/output descriptors

Input/output descriptors returned by the primitive *open* and used by the file input/output system calls have no particular significance for user processes. On the other hand, the kernel keeps descriptor tables of open files.

Linux manages several tables in memory:

- the descriptor of each process (structure **process_struct**) points to a table of files opened by the process;
- each of the elements in this table contains a pointer to an element in the table containing the description of all open files in the system;
- from each of the descriptors of open files, a pointer refers to an element in the table inodes corresponding to files in use.

When a process uses the primitive *open* to open a file, the kernel converts the filename into an identity pair (device number, inode number). It then loads the corresponding inode into memory, if it is not already present in the table of inodes. Linux then allocates a descriptor in the open files table, initialises this descriptor, and points it to the element of the table of inodes allocated at the previous stage. Finally, the kernel allocates a descriptor in the table of files opened by the process and points it to the descriptor of the open file.

When a process supplies the kernel with a input-output descriptor number, Linux uses this number as an index in the table of files opened by the process.

Following this link then allows it access to the corresponding position in open files table, which provides the corresponding entry in the table of inodes. The information contained in the latter descriptor enables the kernel to access the file on disk.

This mechanism is represented in figure 6.3.

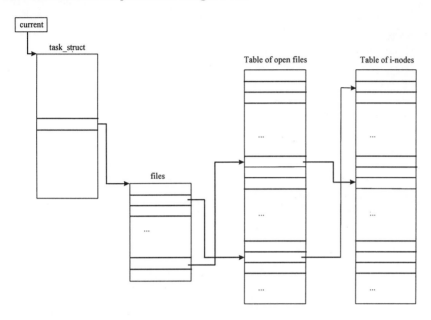

Figure 6.3:   Tables of input/output descriptors.

6.3.3 Sharing descriptors

When a process opens a file, the kernel allocates an entry in the open files table, as well as an entry in the table of process files. It also loads the inode of the file in memory if it is not already in the table of inodes.

When a process creates a child process, its table of files is duplicated for the child. The two processes are then able to carry out inputs and outputs to the files which have been opened by the 'parent' process. The status of the open file (opening mode, current position, etc.) is stored in the open files table, and is therefore shared between the two process. Any change brought about by one process therefore affects the other.

In the sample program *ShareDesc.c*, a process opens a file (the input/output descriptor is stored in the variable **d1**) and it creates a child process which opens another file (the input/output descriptor descriptor is stored in the variable **d2**).

──────── ShareDesc.c ────────

```c
#include <errno.h>
#include <fcntl.h>
#include <stdio.h>
#include <unistd.h>

#define parent_processing ()              /**/
#define child_processing ()               /**/

void main (void)
{
    int         pid;
    int         d1;
    int         d2;

    /* Opening of a file by the parent */
    d1 = open ("/bin/sh", O_RDONLY);
    if (d1 == 1) {
            perror ("open (parent)");
            exit (1);
    }
    printf ("parent: current position = %ld\n",
            (long_ lseek (d1, (off_t) 0, SEEK_CUR));
    /* Child process creation */
    pid = fork ();
    if (pid == -1) {
            perror ("fork");
            exit (1);
    } else if (pid == 0) {
            /* Child process */
            d2 = open ("/bin/ls", O_RDONLY);
            if (d2 == -1) {
                    perror ("open (child)");
                    exit (1)

            }
                    printf ("child: current position = %ld\n",
                            (long) lseek (d1, (off_t) 0, SEEK_CUR));
                    (void) lseek (d1, (off_t) 1000, SEEK_SET);
                    child_processing ();
            } else {
                    /* Parent process */
                    sleep (5);
```

```
        printf ("parent: current position = %ld\n",
                (long) lseek (d1, (off_t) 0, SEEK_CUR));
        parent_processing ();
    }
}
```

———————————————————————— ShareDesc.c ————————

When these operations are performed, the two processes can access the file referenced by **d1**. Only the child process may access the file referenced by **d2**. The relationship between the descriptor tables is shown in figure 6.4. When the child process changes the position of the first file by calling the primitive *lseek*, this change is immediately visible at the level of the parent process.

```
Bbj>ShareDesc
parent: current position = 0
child: current position = 0
parent: current position = 1000
```

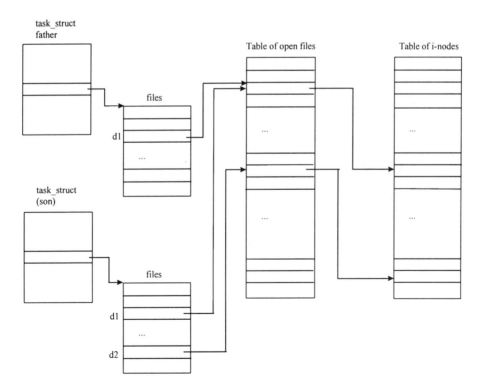

Figure 6.4: Sharing descriptors between related processes.

6.3.4 Locking of files

In the event of several processes accessing the same files in shared mode, it may be necessary to synchronise the processes, that is, to make the read and write operations serial actions, in order to avoid inconsistent results. Linux provides several mechanisms for locking files which enable co-operating processes to synchronise themselves. The locks provided by Linux only apply to co-operating processes. The kernel does not check the locks when normal reads or writes are made using the primitives *read* and *write*, and it is left to the processes to call up the system calls for locking. If a process reads or writes data without obtaining a lock, Linux will not intervene.

Two types of lock exist:

1. Shared locks: several processes may hold a shared lock simultaneously. This type of lock is used by processes which only make read operations in files, and which wish to protect against processes which write.
2. Exclusive locks: only one process may hold an exclusive lock. This type of lock is used by concurrent processes which write, and which wish to prevent simultaneous writing, and to prevent reading during write operations.

6.3.5 Mounting filesystems

Files are formed into hierarchical tree structures made up of branches (directories) and leaves (other types of file). This logical structure model does not correspond to the way that the data is actually physically stored on disk. Indeed, although Linux presents to the user a single tree-based file structure, this single hierarchy may be composed of several filesystems located on different partitions of the disk.

The logical assembly of different filesystems is achieved by a file mounting operation. The latter is generally carried out when the system is booted up, but can also be executed whilst Linux is running, notably to access data stored on removable storage media, such as CD_ROMs for example.

Figure 6.5 represents the mounting operation carried out when the system is initialised. In this figure, two filesystems exist : the root filesystem, and the filesystem containing the hierarchy */usr*. When the mounting is carried out, using the command *mount*, which uses the system call *mount*, the contents of the second filesystem is attached to the root filesystem and becomes accessible in the directory */usr*.

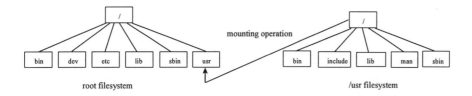

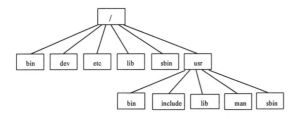

complete hierarchy after mounting /usr

Figure 6.5:   Mounting of filesystems.

6.3.6 Disk quotas

Since disk space is not unlimited, Linux provides a mechanism setting bounds on it: disk quotas. For each filesystem mounted, it is possible for the system administrator to define a limit for the number of files or allocated blocks available to a user, or group of users.

Two types of quota exist:

1. an absolute limit: when this limit is reached, the allocation of further new files or blocks is denied by the kernel;

2. a 'soft' limit: when this limit, which is less than the absolute limit, is reached, a warning message is displayed by the kernel when block allocations are made, and the date of reaching this limit is saved. After a period of grace, (seven days by default), Linux treats the user as if he had reached the absolute limit, that is any further allocation of resources is refused. The user must then delete files to reduce the amount of disk space occupied to below the 'soft' limit.

For each user, the system administrator can define the limits as a function of the number of files held (the number of inodes allocated) and to the number of blocks allocated. These limits must be defined for each filesystem, and are stored in the files *quota.user* and *quota.group*, located in the root directories of the filesystems concerned.

6.4
COMPLEMENTARY SYSTEM CALLS

6.4.1   Reading and writing multiple buffers

The system calls read and write enable a process to read or write data to a file. A process wishing to read data into or write from multiple buffers must use several calls to these primitives, which can give rise to problems:

- the process is obliged to use the same system call several times, which necessitates several changes of execution mode (from user mode to kernel mode and vice versa). The performance is therefore limited.
- Whilst the write process using *write* is discrete, a series of calls can be interrupted and data may be written by another process whilst the current process is suspended in the middle of a sequence of calls to *write*.

For these reasons, Linux offers two system calls enabling read and write operations to be carried out from several non-contiguous buffers in the memory space:

```
#include <sys/types.h>
#include <sys/uio.h>


int readv (int fd, const struct iovec *vector, size_t count);


int writev (int fd, const struct iovec *vector, size_t count);
```

The primitive *readv* enables data in several buffers to be read. The parameter **vector** defines the buffers to use, their number being specified by **count**. The operation carried out is similar to the reading of data using *read*, with the difference that the data read is placed in buffers described by **vector** rather than in a contiguous block of memory. The number of bytes read is returned by *readv*. In the event of a problem, the value –1 is returned.

The primitive *writev* enable data in several buffers to be written. The parameter **vector** defines which ones to use, their number is specified by **count**. The operation carried out is similar to the writing of data using *write*, with the difference that the data is taken from buffers described by **vector**, rather than in only the adjacent memory. The number of bytes written is returned by *writev*. In the event of a problem, the value –1 is returned.

For the two primitives, the parameter **vector** contains the address of a table of buffer descriptors, in which the number of elements is indicated by the parameter **count**. The structure **vector**, defined in the file **<sys/uio.h>**, characterise each of the elements of the table **vector**.

type	field	description
void *	iov_base	Buffer address
int	iov_len	Buffer size in bytes

When data is read, the number of bytes specified by **iovec[0].iov_len** are read and stored starting from the address **iovec[0].iov_base**, then the number of bytes specified by **iovec[1].iov_len** are read and stored starting from the address **iovec[1].iov_base**, and so on.

When data is written, the number of bytes specified by **iovec[0].iov_len** are written and stored starting from the address **iovec[0].iov_base**, then the number of bytes specified by **iovec[1].iov_len** are written and stored starting from the address **iovec[1].iov_base**, and so on.

In the event of error in *readv* or in *writev*, the variable **errno** can take the following values:

error	meaning
EBADF	The input/output descriptor is invalid
EFAULT	**vector** or one of the fields **iov_base** contain an invalid address
EINTR	The system call has been interrupted by the reception of a signal
EINVAL	**count** is greater than **MAX_IOVEC**, or **fd** refers to an object on which reading or writing is not possible
EISDIR	**fd** refers to a directory
EPIPE	**fd** refers to a pipe in which there is no read process
ENOSPC	The filesystem is saturated

6.4.2   Duplication of input/output descriptors

The input/output descriptors returned by the primitive *open* and used by all input/output system calls can be duplicated. This means that a process has the possibility of accessing the same open file by several input/output descriptors.

Two system calls are provided to duplicate the descriptor:

```
#include <unistd.h>

int dup (int oldfd);

int dup2 (int oldfd, int newfd);
```

The call *dup* duplicates the descriptor **oldfd** and returns another descriptor referring to the same open file. The primitive *dup2* makes the descriptor **newfd** equivalent to **oldfd,** and if **newfd** corresponds to an open file, the latter is closed before duplication. *dup* and *dup2* return the new input/output descriptor, or the value –1 if an error occurs.

In the event of error, the variable **errno** can take the following values:

error	meaning
EBADF	The input/output descriptor is invalid
EMFILE	The maximum number of files opened by the current process has been reached

This descriptor duplication mechanism is particularly beneficial for input/output diversions. A process can re-direct its normal input or output to a file, and can then use standard library functions in a transparent manner (*scanf* and *printf* for example), read and/or write operations being carried out in files and not via the keyboard or on the screen.

The following program segment re-directs its normal output to a file called output:

```
int fd;

/* opening of output file */
fd = open ("output", O_WRONLY | O_CREAT | O_TRUNC);
if (fd == -1) {
      perror ("open");
      exit (1);
}
/* redirection of the standard output (descriptor 1) */
if (dup2 (fd, 1) != 1) {
      perror ("dup2");
      exit (1);
}
```

6.4.3 File attributes

Linux provides three system calls enabling the attributes of a file to be displayed. These calls have the following syntax:

```
#include <sys/stat.h>
#include <unistd.h>

int stat (const char *pathname, struct stat *buf);

int fstat (int fd, struct stat *buf);

int lstat (const char *pathname, struct stat *buf);
```

The calls *stat* and *lstat* return the attributes of a file, whose name is passed in the parameter **pathname**, to the buffer whose address is specified by the parameter **buf**. The difference between the two primitives arises from the fact that *stat* follows symbolic links, in other words it returns the attributes of the file pointed to if it is called with the name of a symbolic link, whilst *lstat* returns the attributes of the symbolic link itself.

fstat enables the attributes of the open file to be obtained, the descriptor of which is passed in the parameter **fd**.

In the event of error, the variable **errno** can take the following values:

error	meaning
EBADF	The input/output descriptor is invalid
EFAULT	**buf** or **pathname** contain an invalid address
ENAMETOOLONG	**pathname** specifies a filename which is too long
ENOENT	**pathname** refers to a non-existent filename
ENOMEM	The kernel has not been able to allocate memory for its internal descriptors
ENOTDIR	One of the components of **pathname**, used as a directory name, is not a directory

The structure **stat** is defined in the header file **<sys/stat.h>** and contains the following fields:

type	field	description
dev_t	st_dev	Filesystem identifier
ino_t	st_ino	inode number
umode_t	st_mode	File mode (type of access and access permissions)
nlink_t	st_nlink	Number of links
uid_t	st_uid	User owner identifier
gid_t	st_gid	Group owner identifier

Continuation of the list of fields defining the structure **stat**		
type	*field*	*description*
dev_t	**st_rdev**	Device identifier in the case of a special file
off_t	**st_size**	Size in bytes
unsigned_long	**st_blksize**	Block size in bytes
unsigned_long	**st_blocks**	Number of 1 kilobyte blocks used
time_t	**st_atime**	Date of the last access
time_t	**st_mtime**	Date of the last contents change
time_t	**st_ctime**	Date of the last modification

The fields **st_atime**, **st_mtime**, and **st_ctime** contain the dates expressed as the number of seconds that have elapsed since the 1st of January 1970. The functions provided by the standard library are generally used (*asctime, ctime, gmtime, localtime* and *mktime*) to manage them.

The field **st_mode** contains both the file type and is access permissions. The type may be tested by the macro-instructions defined in **<sys/stat.h>**:

error	*meaning*
S_ISLNK	True if the file is a symbolic link, false if not
S_ISREG	True if the file is a normal file, false if not
S_ISDIR	True if the file is a directory, false if not
S_ISCHR	True if the file is a special character file, false if not
S_ISBLK	True if the file is a special block file, false if not
S_ISFIFO	True if the file is a named pipe, false if not
S_ISSOCK	True if the file is a socket, false if not

Access permissions can be checked by means of constants defined in **<sys/stat.h>**:

option	*meaning*
S_ISUID	*setuid* bit
S_ISGID	*setgid* bit
S_ISVTX	*sticky* bit
S_IRUSR	Read permissions for the owner
S_IWUSR	Write permissions for the owner

Continuation of the list of constants defined in **\<sys/stat.h\>**:	
option	*meaning*
S_IXUSR	Execution permissions for the owner
S_IRWXU	Read, write and execution permissions for the owner
S_IRGRP	Read permissions for the user group
S_IWGRP	Write permissions for the user group
S_IXGRP	Execution permissions for the user group
S_IRWXG	Read, write and execution permissions for the user group
S_IROTH	Read permissions for the rest of users
S_IWOTH	Write permissions for the rest of users
S_IXOTH	Execution permissions for the rest of users
S_IRWXO	Read, write and execution permissions for the rest of users

A binary AND operation ("&" operator in the C language) can be carried out to check access permissions returned in **st_mode**. For example, if it was desired to see if the owner has read and write access to a file, the following test can be applied:

```
if ((st.st_mode & S_IRUSR && (st.st_mode & S_IWUSR))
        /* the owner has read and write permissions */
```

The following program uses the primitive *lstat* to display the size and type of all files whose names have been passed to it in arguments:

——————————————————————————————— TypeFile.c ———————————————

```
#include <sys/stat.h>
#include <unistd.h>
#include <errno.h>
#include <stdio.h>

void main (int argc, char *argv[])
{
     int            i;
     struct stat    st;

     /* Argument Loop */
     for (I = i; I < argc; i++) {
            if (lstat (argv[i], *st) == -1)
                    perror (argv[i]);
```

```
              else {
                     printf ("%s: size = %d, type = ",
                              argv[i], st.st_size);
                     if (S_ISREG (st.st_mode))
                             printf ("file\n");
                     else if (S_ISDIR (st.st_mode))
                             printf ("directory\n");
                     else if (S_ISLNK (st.st_mode))
                             printf ("symbolic link\n");
                     else if (S_ISCHR (st.st_mode))
                             printf ("file mode char\n");
                     else if (S_ISBLK (st.st_mode))
                             printf ("file mode block\n");
                     else if (S_ISFIFO (st.st_mode))
                             printf ("named pipe\n");
                     else if (S_ISSOCK (st.st_mode))
                             printf ("socket\n");

                     else
                             printf ("unknown\n");
              }
       }
       exit (0);
}
```

——————— TypeFichiers.c ————————————————————

6.4.4 Dates associated with files

The dates associated with each file can be changed: any operation on a file can give rise to several dates (atime, ctime, mtime). It is also possible for a process to explicitly modify the dates atime, mtime by using the primitives *utime* and *utimes*:

```
#include <sys/types.h>
#include <utime.h>


int utime (const char *pathname, struct utimbuf *buf);


#include sys/time.h>


int utimes (char *pathname, struct timeval *tvp);
```

These two primitives change the dates of the most recent access and of the most recent modification of the contents of a file, whose name is specified in the parameter pathname. *utime* uses a parameter buf pointing to a variable of the type

utimbuf. This structure is defined in the header file **<utime.h>** and contains the following fields:

type	field	description
time_t	actime	Date of the last access
time_t	modtime	Date of the last change of contents

For its part, the primitive *utimes* uses the parameter **tvp** containing the address of a table of two elements of the type **timeval**. The first element in the table [**typ[0]**] represents the date of the most recent access, and the second element (**typ[1]**) represents the most recent modification of the contents of the file. The structure **timeval** is defined in the header file **<sys/time.h>** and contains the following fields:

type	field	description
long	tv_sec	Number of seconds
long	tv_usec	Number of microseconds

In the event of an error when the primitives *utime* and *utimes* execute, the variable **errno** can take the following values:

error	meaning
EACCES	The process does not have write access to the file specified by **pathname**
EFAULT	**buf, tvp** or **pathname** contain an invalid address
ENAMETOOLONG	**pathname** specifies a filename which is too long
ENOENT	**pathname** refers to a non-existent filename
ENOMEM	The kernel has not been able to allocate memory for its internal descriptors
ENOTDIR	One of the components of **pathname**, used as a directory name, is not a directory

6.4.5 Properties of open files

Linux provides the primitive *fcntl* which enables diverse and varied operations on an open file to be carried out:

```
#include <unistd.h>
#include <fnctl.h>

int fnctl (int fd, int cmd);
int fnctl (int fd, int cmd, long arg);
```

The operation carried out depends on the parameter **cmd**. A range of constants are defined in the file **<fcntl.h>**:

- **F_DUPFD**: this is the equivalent of the primitive *dup2*. The input/output descriptor **fd** is duplicated in the descriptor **arg**.
- **F_GETFD**: returns the flag 'close-on-exec'. If this flag has a value of zero, the file remains open if the current process calls a primitive of the type *exec* to execute a new program, if not, the file is automatically closed upon the call of *exec*.
- **F_SETFD**: sets the flag 'close-on-exec'.
- **F_GETFL**: returns the options used when the file is opened (parameter **flags** of the primitive *open*).
- **F_SETFL**: modifies the options for the opening of a file. Only the options **O_APPEND** and **O_NONBLOCK** may be set.
- **F_GETOWN**: returns the number of the process or the process group of the owning a socket. A process group number is returned in the form of a negative value.
- **F_SETOWN**: sets the process number or the process group of the owning a socket.

fnctl also accepts other options concerning locking of files. These options are detailed in section 6.4.7.

In the event of error, the variable **errno** can take the following values:

error	*meaning*
EBADF	The input/output descriptor is invalid
EINVAL	**cmd** or **arg** specifies an invalid value
EMFILE	The maximum number of files opened by the current process has been reached (in the case of the request F_DUPFD)

6.4.6 Control of the process *bdflush*

The contents of modified buffers is re-written periodically to disk. Two processes are charged with this process: *update*, which executes the primitive *sync* every thirty seconds to re-write the contents of all the buffers that have changed, and *bdflush*. The latter process is an internal kernel process created automatically when the system is booted up: it carries out re-writes of buffers which have changed, taking account of the priorities assigned to them. A buffer containing a filesystem control structure has, for example, a higher priority than a buffer containing ordinary data.

The process *bdflush* is executed automatically by the kernel when the need arise. There is a system call allowing the parameter of *bdflush* to be specified. This system call is not included in the C library and it is necessary to declare it explicitly:

```
#include <syscall.h>

_syscall2(int, bdflush, int, func, long data);
```

This declaration follows the following model:

```
int bdflush (int func, long data);
```

The parameter **func** specifies the function to be executed. If it is equal to 1, a re-writing of buffers that have been altered is performed. If **func** is greater than or equal to 2, its value is interpreted as follows:

- if it is even, the parameter number $\frac{func-2}{2}$ is returned in the integer long whose address is specified in **data**;
- if it is odd, **data**, specifies the value to apply to the parameter number $\frac{func-3}{2}$

The parameters of *bdflush* are numbered 0 to 8:

- 0: maximum number of buffers changed: when this percentage is reached, *bdflush* is activated to re-write the buffers onto disk.
- 1: the number of buffers to re-write to disk at each activation of *bdflush*.
- 2: the number of buffers to put in the list of available buffers, on each occasion that this list is rebuilt.
- 3: number of modifies buffers above which *bdflush* should be activated when the list of available buffers is rebuilt. This parameter is not used by Linux 2.0.
- 4: the percentage of buffers to scan when a look-up of the available *cluster* is being made (see section 6.2.8). This parameter is not used by Linux 2.0.
- 5: length of time during which a buffer is allowed to retain its changes before being re-written to disk. This time is expressed as a number of clock cycles.
- 6: length of time during which a buffer containing a system file descriptor is allowed to retain its changes before being re-written to disk. This time is expressed as a number of clock cycles.
- 7: a constant used to calculate the percentage utilisation of buffers associated with blocks of a certain size.
- 8: this parameter is not used by Linux 2.0.

In the event of error, the variable **errno** can take the following values:

error	*meaning*
EFAULT	Data contains an invalid address
EINVAL	**func** or **data** specify an invalid value
EPERM	The calling process does not have the necessary privileges

6.4.7   Locking

6.4.7.1   *Locking files*

The primitive *flock* allows a complete lock to be placed on a file. Its syntax is as follows:

```
#include <sys/file.h>

int flock (int fd, int operation);
```

flock locks or unlocks access to files whose descriptor is passed in the parameter **fd**. The parameter **operation** specifies the operation to be performed. Several constants are defined in **<sys/file.h>**:

option	*meaning*
LOCK_SN	Request for a shared lock on a file. Several processes may simultaneously have a shared lock
LOCK_EX	Request for an exclusive lock on a file. Only a single process may have an exclusive lock
LOCK_UN	Release of a shared or exclusive lock

In the event of a locking request, the calling process may be suspended. However, if the option **LOCK_NB** is specified the process is not suspended, the primitive *flock* then returns an error if the lock cannot be applied.

In the event of error, the variable **errno** can take the following values:

error	*meaning*
EBADF	The input/output descriptor specified is invalid
EINVAL	**operation** specifies an invalid value
EWOULDBLOCK	The file is locked and the option **LOCK_NB** has been specified

6.4.7.2 Locking a section of a file

The primitive *fcntl* described in section 6.4.5 enables a part of a file to be locked. For this application of the primitive, the argument **arg** should contain the address of the structure **flock**, and this structure is defined in the file **<fnctl.h>** and contains the following fields:

type	field	description
off_t	l_start	Location of the lock in the file
off_t	l_len	Length of the locked zone
short	l_type	Type of lock
short	l_whence	Type of location (**SEEK_SET, SEEK_CUR,** or **SEEK_END**)
pid_t	l_pid	Number of the process acquiring the lock

Several operations are possible:

- **F_SETLK**: sets or releases the lock according to the information passed in the **flock** structure. The structure type can be **F_RDLCK** for achieving a shared lock, **F_WRLCK** for achieving an exclusive lock, and **F_UNLCK** for releasing a lock. If the lock cannot be enabled straightaway, *fnctl* returns the error **EACCES**.
- **F_SETLKW**: is similar to **F_SETLK**. The only difference is that the calling process is suspended while waiting for the lock if it cannot obtain it immediately.
- **F_GETLK**: obtains the description of existing locks. If there is already a lock which conflicts with that specified in the **flock** structure, the contents of the latter are modified and the information characterising the existing lock are placed there.

The function *lockf* offers a simpler interface than the locking options of *fnctl*. Its syntax is the following:

```
#include <fnctl.h>
#include <unistd.h>

int lockf (int fd, int cmd, off_t len);
```

The parameter **fd** specifies the file descriptor, **len** represents the size of the lock with respect to the current setting, and **cmd** can take the following values:

option	meaning
F_ULOCK	Unlocks a section previously locked
F_TLOCK	Locks a section. If the lock cannot be obtained immediately, the error **EACCES** is returned
F_LOCK	Locks a section, and suspends calling process waiting for lock.
F_TEST	Test for the presence of a lock on the specified section: if a lock exists, the error **EACCES** is returned

6.4.8 Mounting of filesystems

Linux provides two system calls enabling filesystems to be mounted and unmounted. Put another way, the filesystems are logically connected or disconnected from the file tree structure. These calls are reserved for processes having superuser permissions.

The syntax of the primitives *mount* and *umount* is as follows:

```
#include <sys/mount.h>
#include <linux/fs.h>

int mount (const char *specialfile, const char *dir,
      const char *filesystemtype, unsigned long rwflag,
      const void *data);

int umount (const char *specialfile);

int umount (const char *dir);
```

The system call *mount* mounts the filesystem onto the device whose name is passed in the parameter **specialfile**. The parameter **dir** indicates the name of the mounting location, that is the directory name from which the filesystem should be made accessible. The filesystem type is passed in the parameter **filesystemtype**, which involves a character string representing a filesystem type recognised by the Linux kernel, such as 'minix', 'ext2', 'proc', or 'iso9660'. The parameters **rwflag** and **data** specify the mounting options and are only taken into account if the most significant 16 bits of **rwflag** are equal to the value **0xCOED**.

The possible mounting options are defined in the header file **<linux/fs.h>** in the form of constants:

option	meaning
MS_RDONLY	Mounting filesystems in read mode only
MS_NOSUID	Bits setuid and setgid are not used
MS_NODEV	No access to special files
MS_NOEXEC	Execution of programs forbidden
MS_SYNCHRONOUS	Synchronous writes

It is possible to combine these different options with the aid of a binary OR operation (operator " | " in the C language). One particular constant, **MS_REMOUNT**, can be used to modify the mounting options of a filesystem which has already been mounted.

The parameter **data** points to a character string containing the additional options. The contents of this string is dependent on the type of filesystem.

In the event of error, the variable **errno** can take the following values:

error	*meaning*
EBUSY	The device specified by **specialfile** is already mounted
EFAULT	**specialfile**, **dir**, **filesystemtype** or **data** contain an invalid address
ENAMETOOLONG	**specialfile** or **dir** specifies a filename which is too long
ENODEV	The type of filesystem specified by **filesystemtype** is not supported by the kernel
ELOOP	A symbolic link loop has been encountered
ENOENT	**specialfile** or **dir** refer to a non-existent filename
ENOMEM	The kernel has not been able to allocate memory for its internal descriptors
ENTBLK	**specialfile** does not specify a special filename
ENOTDIR	One of the components of **specialfile** or **dir**, used as a directory name, is not a directory, or **dir** does not specify the name of a directory
EPERM	The process does not have the necessary privileges

The primitive *umount* unmounts a filesystem which has been previously mounted. It accepts as a parameter both the name of a special file (parameter **specialfile**) and the name of a mount point (parameter **dir**).

In the event of error, the variable **errno** can take the following values:

error	*meaning*
EBUSY	The filesystem specified contains open files
EFAULT	**specialfile**, or **dir** contain an invalid address
ELOOP	A symbolic link loop has been encountered
ENAMETOOLONG	**specialfile** or **dir** specifies a filename which is too long
ENOENT	**specialfile** or **dir** refer to a non-existent filename
ENOMEM	The kernel has not been able to allocate memory for its internal descriptors
ENTBLK	**specialfile** does not specify a special filename
ENOTDIR	One of the components of **specialfile** or **dir**, used as a directory name, is not a directory, or **dir** does not specify the name of a directory
EPERM	The process does not have the necessary privileges

6.4.9 Information on filesystems

The primitives *statfs* and *fsatfs* allows utilisation statistics on filesystems to be obtained. Their syntax is as follows:

```
#include <sys/vfs.h>

int statfs (const char *pathname, struct statfs *buf);

int fstatfs (int fd, struct statfs *buf);
```

statfs calls up utilisation statistics on filesystems containing the file whose name is passed in the parameter **pathname**; *fstatfs* uses an input/output descriptor specified by the parameter **fd**. These two primitives return the information in the variable pointed to by the parameter **buf**. The type of this variable is a structure **statfs**. This structure is defined in the header file **<sys/vfs.h>** and contains the following fields:

type	*field*	*description*
long	f_type	Type of filesystem
long	f_bsize	Block size to use in bytes for optimal input/outputs
long	f_blocks	Total number of data blocks
long	f_bfree	Number of blocks unallocated
long	f_bavail	Number of blocks available to the non-privileged user
long	f_files	Total number of inodes
long	f_free	Number of inodes available
fsid_t	f_fsid	Filesystem identifier
long	f_namelen	Maximum size of filenames
long [6]	f_spare	Unused

In the event of error, the variable **errno** can take the following values:

error	*meaning*
EFAULT	**buf**, or **pathname** contain an invalid address
EIO	An input/outpur error has occurred
ELOOP	A symbolic link loop has been encountered
ENAMETOOLONG	**pathname** specifies a filename which is too long
ENOENT	**pathname** refers to a non-existent filename
ENOMEM	The kernel has not been able to allocate memory for its internal descriptors
ENOTDIR	One of the components of **pathname**, used as a directory name, is not a directory

In addition, the primitive *fstatfs* can return the error **EBADF**, indicating that **fd** specifies an invalid input/output descriptor.

Another primitive, *ustat*, allows similar information to be obtained, but it is implemented solely in order to ensure some compatibility with Unix System V, and in addition it is recommended to use *statfs*. This is why it will not be detailed here.

6.4.10   Information on filesystem types supported

The primitive *sysfs* enables the system to recognise the filesystem types supported by the kernel. Its syntax is as follows:

```
int sysfs (int option, const char *fsname);
int sysfs (int option, unsigned int fs_index, char *buf);
int sysfs (int option);
```

The usage syntax is dependent on the value of the parameter option:

- if **option** has a value of 1, *sysfs* returns the index of the filesystem type specified by **fsname**;
- if **option** has a value of 2, *sysfs* returns the name of the filesystem type corresponding to the index specified by **fs_index** in the buffer pointed to by **buf**;
- if **option** has a value of 3, *sysfs* returns the number of filesystem types supported by the kernel.

6.4.11   Manipulation of disk quotas

The quotas assigned to users can be altered by the primitive *quotactl*:

```
#include <sys/types.h>
#include <sys/quota.h>

int quotactl (int cmd, const char *special, int id, caddr_t addr);
```

The processing performed by *quotactl* depends on the parameter **cmd**. This parameter is initialised by the macro-instruction **QCMD(subcmd, type)** where **type** can be **USRQUOTA** or **GRPQUOTA**; the possible values of **subcmd** are described below. The parameter **special** specifies the name of the device containing the filesystem involved. This filesystem must be mounted beforehand, **id** contains the user or user group identifier to which the operation applies, and the parameter **addr** should contain the address of a data structure dependent on the operation.

The different values of **subcmd** are as follows:

error	meaning
Q_QUOTAON	Activation of the quotas on the filesystem specified by **special**. **addr** should contain the name of the file containing the quotas (normally quota.user or quota.group)
Q_QUOTAOFF	De-activation of the quotas on the filesystem specified by **special**
Q_GETQUOTA	Calling up the limits and the current status of blocks and files allocated for the user or user group indicated by **id** in the filesystem specified by **special**
Q_SETQUOTA	Modification of the limits and the current status of blocks and files allocated for the user or user group indicated by **id** in the filesystem specified by **special**
Q_SETQLIM	Modification of the limits allocated for the user or user group indicated by **id** in the filesystem specified by **special**
Q_SETUSE	Modification of the current status of blocks and files allocated for the user or user group indicated by **id** in the filesystem specified by **special**
Q_SYNC	Re-writing of quota control structures stored in memory by the kernel on disk
Q_GETSTATS	Call up of statistics

In the cases of the options **Q_GETQUOTA**, **Q_SETQUOTA**, **Q_SETQLIM**, and **Q_SETUSE** the parameter **arg** should contain the address of a variable of the structure type **dqblk**. This structure is defined in the file **<sys/quota.h>** and contains the following fields:

type	field	description
unsigned long	**dqp_bhardlimit**	Absolute limit on the number of blocks allocated
unsigned long	**dqp_bsoftlimit**	'Soft' limit on the number of blocks allocated
unsigned long	**dqp_curblocks**	Number of blocks allocated
unsigned long	**dqp_ihardlimit**	Absolute limit on the number of files allocated
unsigned long	**dqp_isoftlimit**	'Soft' limit on the number of files allocated
unsigned long	**dqp_curinodes**	Number of files allocated
time_t	**dqp_btime**	Delay granted following the 'soft' limit on the number of blocks being exceeded
time_t	**dqp_itime**	Delay granted following the 'soft' limit on the number of inodes being exceeded

The operation Q_GETSTATS allows statistics on the internal functioning of quotas to be collected. The parameter **arg** should contain the address of a variable of the structure type **dqstats**. This structure is defined in section 6.5.2.

The calling process must normally possess superuser permissions in order to utilise the primitive *quotactl*. Only **Q_GETSTATS**, **Q_SYNC** and **Q_GETQUOTA**, with **id** holding the identity of the user who is executing the current process, may be executed by a non-privileged process.

In the event of error, the variable **errno** can take the following values:

error	*meaning*
EACCES	The quota definition file is incorrect
EBUSY	**Q_QUOTAON** has been specified on the filesystem or the quotas have already been activated
EFAULT	**addr** contains an invalid address
EINVAL	**type** contains an incorrect value
EIO	An input/output error has occurred
EMFILE	The maximum number of files opened by the current process has been reached
ENODEV	**special** does not contain the name of the device from which the filesystem was mounted
ENOPKG	The kernel was not compiled with the help of quotas
EPERM	The calling process does not have the necessary permissions
ESRCH	A filesystem on which quotas have not been activated has been specified

6.5
GENERAL OVERVIEW OF IMPLEMENTATION

6.5.1 The virtual filesystem

6.5.1.1 *Principle*
Linux supports several filesystem types, whether they are native filesystems such as Ext2, or are filesystems allowing access to data in formats used by other operating systems, such as Minix, or MS/DOS. In order to enable processes to access files in a uniform manner, whatever the filesystem type they are in, the kernel has a software layer whose purpose is to maintain an interface between system calls concerning files and file management code proper. This layer is known as the *Virtual Filesystem* (VFS).

When a process performs a system call on files, it is directed at the VFS. The latter is responsible for performing operations which are independent of the format of the filesystem concerned, and then redirects the request to the module managing the file, as is shown in figure 6.6.

The principle of the VFS is not peculiar to Linux and it may also be used in other filesystems [Kleiman, 1986], but its implementation under Linux is different.

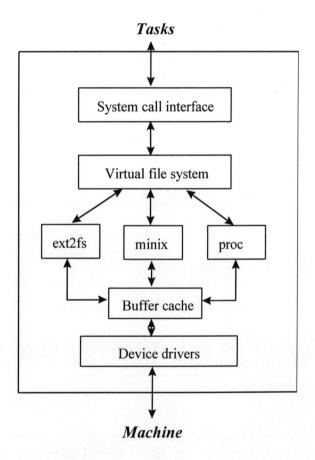

Figure 6.6:   The virtual filesystem.

6.5.1.2 Operations guaranteed by the VFS
The VFS provides functionality which is independent of the physical filesystems. In particular, it implements:

* filename cache:

Each conversion of a filename into a device number and an inode number consumes resources, since it necessitates an iterative exploration of the directories. In the interests of performance, VFS implements a cache of filenames: when a filename is converted into a number of a device and an inode, the result is memorised in a list. When further calls are made to the same filename, the saved result is reused without the need to carry out a new directory look-up. The internal functioning of the cache is explained in section 6.6.1.5.

- the buffer cache:

  Linux maintains a list of buffers in use. When a block is read by a filesystem, the contents of the block are placed in a buffer. This buffer is kept in memory as long as the block is in use, and as long as the memory space that it occupies is not required by another buffer. When the data in a block is modified, the change is made to the buffer, and the buffer is marked as modified but it is not re-written to disk immediately. At regular intervals, the process *update* calls the primitive *sync* to force the buffers that have been modified to be re-written. This principle allows the number of disk reads and writes to be cut down:

  - when a block is read, the VFS first of all checks that it has not already been read. If the block has been loaded into memory, is contents are accessible in a buffer, and no input or output is necessary:

  - in the event of successive modifications to the same data block, the changes are made to the corresponding buffer, and it is not necessary to re-write the block at each change: all the changes are written to disk when the buffer is re-written.

The internal functioning of the *buffer cache* is described in detail in section 6.6.2.
    The internal functions of VFS assure the correct operation of the common parts of system calls operating on files. The algorithm of the majority of these system calls is the following:

```
Checking of the arguments
Conversion of filenames into device and inode numbers
Checking of permissions
Calling of the function of the corresponding filesystem type
```

In order to call functions corresponding to different actions, the VFS uses an object oriented approach: for each filesystem mounted, each open file, and each inode in use, there are associated operations implemented in the system code of the corresponding files. Each entity may be considered to be an object of a certain class, with which are associated methods redefined in each module containing the instances of a filesystem type. Since the Linux kernel is programmed in C, this object approach is implemented by associating a descriptor to each object. This descriptor contains a set of function pointers.

Four sets of operations are defined:

- operations on filesystems: these are operations dependent on the physical format of the filesystem, such as the reading or writing of an inode. These operations are described in detail in section 6.5.3.1;
- operations on inodes that are in use: these are the operations directly linked to inodes, like deleting a file. These operations are described in detail in section 6.5.3.2;
- operations on open files: these are operations to the file input and output primitives, such as reading and writing of data. These operations are described in detail in section 6.5.3.3;
- operations on quotas: these are operations called to validate the allocation of blocks and inodes. These operations are described in detail in section 6.5.3.4.

6.5.2 VFS structures

VFS uses generic structures to describe filesystems and files that are in use.

6.5.2.1 Types of filesystems

Each filesystem type is described by the structure **file_system_type**. This structure is defined in **<linux/fs.h>** and contains the following fields:

type	field	description
struct super_block (*) ()	read_super	Initialisation function
const char *	name	Name of the filesystem type
int	requires_dev	Boolean expression indicating whether the filesystem is linked to a physical device
struct file_system_type *	next	Linking pointer

At the time that the filesystem is initialised, each filesystem type, whose the supporting code has been compiled in the kernel, is registered with the VFS by calling the function **register_filesystem**. This function registers the filesystem type in a string list referenced by the variable **file_systems**. When a filesystem is mounted, VFS searches the string list to find the requested filesystem descriptor, then it calls the function **read_super** which corresponds to it.

6.5.2.2 Mounted filesystems

The kernel keeps two different lists referencing mounted filesystems. The table **super_blocks** contains descriptors in **NR_SUPER** which are used by the VFS for all input and output operations.

The type of these descriptors is the structure **super_block**. This structure is defined in the header file **<linux/fs.h>**, and contains the following fields.

type	field	description
kdev_t	**s_dev**	Device identifier
unsigned long	**s_blocksize**	Blocksize in bytes
unsigned long	**s_blocksize_bits**	Bocksize in bytes expressed as a power of 2
unsigned char	**s_lock**	Locking indicator
unsigned char	**s_rd_only**	Read-only indicator
unsigned char	**s_dirt**	Change indicator
struct file_system_type *	**s_type**	Pointer to the corresponding filesystem descriptor
struct super_operations *	**s_op**	Operations linked to filesystems
struct dquot_operations *	**dq_op**	Operations linked to disk quotas
unsigned long	**s_flags**	Mounting options
unsigned long	**s_magic**	Signature: all filesystems have a 'magic' number which act as a signature: this number enables the presence of a filesystem of a given type on a partition to be recognised
struct inode *	**s_covered**	Pointer to the descriptor of the inode of the mounting point
struct inode *	**s_mounted**	Pointer to the descriptor of the inode of the filesystem root directory
struct wait_queue *	**s_wait**	Variable used to synchronise concurrent accesses to the descriptor
union	**u**	Information depending on the filesystem type

The second list maintained by the kernel keeps in memory the correspondences between the names of devices in which filesystems and the names of the mounting points are located. Elements in this list are of a type having the structure **vfsmount**.

This structure is defined in the file **<linux/mount.h>**, and contains the following fields:

type	field	description
kdev_t	mnt_dev	Device identifier
char *	mnt_devname	Name of the special file representing the device
char *	mnt_dirname	Name of the mounting point
unsigned int	mnt_flags	Mounting options
struct semaphore	mnt_sem	Semaphore used to lock the descriptor
struct super_block *	mnt_sb	Pointer to corresponding superblock descriptor
struct file * [MAXQUOTAS]	mnt_quotas	File descriptors describing quotas
time_t [MAXQUOTAS]	mnt_iexp	Delay granted when the inode quota is exceeded
time_t [MAXQUOTAS]	mnt_bexp	Delay granted when the block quota is exceeded
struct vfsmount *]	mnt_next	Pointer to the following descriptor in the list

6.5.2.3 *Inodes that are in use*

Linux uses an inode descriptor to reference each file in use. This type of descriptor has the **inode** structure, which is, defined in the file **<linux/fs.h>**, and contains the following fields:

type	field	description
kdev_t	i_dev	Device identifier
unsigned long	i_ino	inode number
umode_t	i_mode	File mode (type of access and access permissions)
nlink_t	i_nlink	Number of links
uid_t	i_uid	Identifier of the owner user
gid_t	i_gid	Identifier of the group owner
kdev_t	i_rdev	Identifier of the device if the inode represents a special file
off_t	i_size	File size in bytes
time_t	i_atime	Date of the last access

Continuation of the list of fields associated with the **inode** structure.		
type	*field*	*description*
time_t	i_mtime	Date of the last change of contents
time_t	i_ctime	Date of the last change of inode
unsigned long	i_blksize	Blocksize in bytes
unsigned long	i_blocks	Number of blocks of 512 bytes allocated to the file
unsigned long	i_version	Version number incremented automatically at each new utilisation
unsigned long	i_nrpages	Number of pages loaded into memory since this file
struct semaphore	i_sem	Semaphore used to serialise concurrent accesses to the file
struct inode_operations *	i_op	Operations linked to the inode
struct super_block *	i_sb	Pointer to the corresponding filesystem descriptor
struct wait_queue *	i_wait	Variable used to synchronise concurrent accesses to the inode
struct file_lock *	i_flock	Pointer to the lock descriptors associated with the inode
struct vm_area_struct *	i_mmap	Pointer to descriptors of sections of the inode mapped into memory
struct page *	i_pages	Pointer to descriptors of pages of the inode mapped into memory
struct dquot * [MAXQUOTAS]	i_dquot	Pointer to descriptors of disk quotas associated with the inode
struct inode *	i_next	Pointer to the following inode in the list
struct inode *	i_prev	Pointer to the previous inode in the list
struct inode *	i_hash_next	Pointer to the following inode in the hash list
struct inode *	i_hash_prev	Pointer to the previous inode in the hash list
struct inode *	i_mount	Pointer to the root inode of a filesystem in the case of a mounting point
unsigned short	i_count	Number of inode utilisations
unsigned short	i_flags	Mounting options filesystem containing the inode

Continuation of the list of fields in the file **<linux/fs.h>**		
type	*field*	*description*
unsigned char	**i_lock**	Boolean expression indicating whether the inode is locked in memory
unsigned char	**i_dirt**	Boolean expression indicating whether the inode has been modified
unsigned char	**i_pipe**	Boolean expression indicating whether the inode corresponds to a pipe
unsigned char	**i_sock**	Boolean expression indicating whether the inode corresponds to a socket
unsigned short	**i_writecount**	Number of file openings in write mode for this file
union	**u**	Information dependent on the type of filesystem. This variable also contains the field **generic_ip**, of the type **void ***, which may be used to store the address of private data

The inode descriptors are linked in several lists:

- a global list, the address of the first element of which is stored in the variable **first_node**, containing all the inode descriptors;
- several hash lists : a hash function, acting on the device identifier and the inode number, enables the descriptors to be placed in different lists which are smaller in size than the global list.

6.5.2.4 Open files
Every open file in the system has a corresponding descriptor. The structure **file** is defined in the header file **<linux/fs.h>** and contains the following fields:

type	*field*	*description*
mode_t	**f_mode**	Open mode for a modified file (see below)
loff_t	**f_pos**	Current position in bytes relative to the start of the file
unsigned long	**f_flags**	Open mode for a specified file during the call open
unsigned long	**f_reada**	Number of blocks to be read in anticipated mode

type	field	description
unsigned long	f_ramax	Maximum number of blocks to be read in anticipated mode
unsigned long	f_raend	Position in the file of the first byte following the last page in anticipated mode
unsigned long	f_ralen	Size in bytes of the last data set read in anticipated mode
unsigned long	f_rawin	Window size for anticipated reading
struct file *	f_next	Linking pointer to the next descriptor
struct file *	f_prev	Linking pointer to the previous descriptor
int	f_owner	Number of the process or process group owning a socket
struct inode *	f_inode	Pointer to the descriptor of the corresponding inode
struct file_operations *	f_op	Operations linked to the open file
unsigned long	f_version	Version number incremented at each utilisation
void *	private_data	Pointer to a private data zone which depends on the file management module

The field **f_mode** has particular features: it is based on the mode of opening specified when the call to *open* is made, and is formed by the conjunction of the constants **FMODE_READ** and **FMODE_WRITE**, which indicate respectively whether reading of, or writing to, the file are possible.

The file descriptors are included in a global string list, the address of the first element of which is stored in the variable **first_file**, containing all the file descriptors.

6.5.2.5 Files opened by a process

Each process has an associated table of local descriptors. This table is characterised by the field **files**, and the structure **process_struct**. The definition of this table (structure **files_struct**), which is contained in the header file **<linux/sched.h>**, is the following:

type	field	description
int	count	Number of associated file descriptors
fd_set	close_on_exec	"close-on-exec" flags gathered into a bit string
struct file * [NR_OPEN]	fd	Pointers to open file descriptors

Another structure describes the file management information for each process: this is the **fs_struct** structure, defined in the file **<linux/sched.h>**. It contains the following fields:

type	field	description
int	count	Number of processes refering to this descriptor
unsigned short	umask	Default access permissions used when creating files
struct inode*	root	inode descriptor corresponds to the root of the filesystem for the process
struct inode*	pwd	inode descriptor corresponds to the current directory of the filesystem for the process

6.5.2.6 Lock descriptors

Linux maintains a global list of locks associated with files. The locks assigned to an inode are also listed and referenced by the field **i_flock** of the inode descriptor.

The lock descriptor type (structure **file_lock**) is defined in the header file **<linux/fs.h>** and contains the following fields:

type	field	description
struct file_lock *	fl_next	Pointer to the next lock descriptor in the list associated with the inode
struct file_lock *	fl_nextlink	Pointer to the next lock descriptor in the global list
struct file_lock *	fl_prevlink	Pointer to the previous lock descriptor in the global list
struct file_lock *	fl_block	Pointer to the list of blocked locks waiting for a lock
struct process_struct *	fl_owner	Pointer to the descriptor of the process which created the lock
struct wait_queue *	fl_queue	Wait queue in which processes requesting locks are registered
struct file *	fl_file	Pointer to the descriptor of the file to which the lock is associated
char	fl_flags	Lock mode (see below)
char	fl_type	Lock type (see below)
off_t	fl_start	Marker of the first byte covered by the lock
off_t	fl_end	Marker of the last byte covered by the lock

The field **fl_flags** specifies the locking mode. It may take the following values:

error	meaning
F_FLOCK	The lock was created by the primitive flock. The whole of the file is locked. The lock is associated with a file descriptor and can therefore be shared between a parent and child process. The lock is removed when the last descriptor referring to the file is closed, or when it is cancelled explicitly.
F_POSIX	The lock was created by the primitive **fcntl** or It specifies that a part of the file is locked and is associated with the process.

The field **fl_type** contains the type of lock. It can contain the values **F_RDLCK**, **F_WRLCK**, and **F_UNLCK**.

6.5.2.7 *Disk quota descriptors*

Disk quotas are managed by means of quota descriptors. Each of these descriptors is associated with a particular user of user group. The structure **dquot**, defined in the header file **<linux/quota.h>**, has the following fields:

type	field	description
unsigned int	**dq_id**	User or group identifier to which this quota applies
short	**dq_type**	Quota type, **USRQUOTA** or **CRPQUOTA**
kdev_t	**dq_dev**	Device identifier
short	**dq_flags**	Descriptor status (see below)
short	**dq_count**	Number of utilisations of the descriptor
struct vfsmount *	**dq_mnt**	Pointer to the filesystem descriptor concerned
struct dqbblk	**dq_dqb**	Limits of usage
struct wait_queue *	**dq_wait**	Variable used to synchronise concurrent accesses to the descriptor
struct dquot *	**dq_prev**	Pointer to the previous descriptor in the list
struct dquot *	**dq_next**	Pointer to the next descriptor in the list
struct dquot *	**dq_hash_prev**	Pointer to the previous descriptor in the hash list
struct dquot *	**dq_hash_next**	Pointer to the next descriptor in the hash list

The value of the field **dq_flags** is formed by a combination of the following constants:

error	meaning
DQ_LOCKED	The quota descriptor is locked
DQ_WANT	The process is waiting for this quota descriptor to become available
DQ_MOD	The quota descriptor has been modified
DQ_BLKS	A warning that the limit on the number of blocks has been exceeded has been sent
DQ_INODES	A warning that the limit on the number of inodes has been exceeded has been sent
DQ_FAKE	The quota descriptor contains no limits

In the same way as for inode descriptors, quota descriptors are linked in several lists: a global list containing all the descriptors, and hash lists, is used to speed up searches. The quota management module maintains statistics on the management of quota descriptors. For this, the structure **dqstats**, defined in the header file **<linux/quota.h>**, contains the following fields:

type	field	description
__u32	lookups	Number of times that the quota descriptor has been looked up in the list
__u32	drops	Number of times that the quota descriptor has been freed
__u32	reads	Number of times that the quota descriptor has been read from disk
__u32	writes	Number of times that the quota descriptor has been re-written to disk
__u32	cache_hits	Number of times that the quota descriptor has been found in the list instead of being read from disk
__u32	pages_allocated	Number of pages allocated for the quota descriptors
__u32	allocated_dquots	Number of quota descriptors allocated
__u32	free_dquots	Number of quota descriptors allocated but not used
__u32	syncs	Number of times that quota descriptors have been re-written by an operation **Q_SYNC**

6.5.2.8 *Buffer cache memories*

The *buffer cache* controls the buffers associated with disk blocks. The structure **buffer_head**, declared in the file **<linux/fs.h>** defines the format of buffer descriptors, and contains the following fields:

type	field	description
unsigned long	b_blocknr	Block number on the device
kdev_t	b_dev	Logical device identifier
kdev_t	b_rdev	Physical device identifier
unsigned long	b_rsector	Sector number of the start of the block on the physical device
struct buffer_head *	b_next	Pointer to the following descriptor
struct buffer_head *	b_this_page	Pointer to the following buffer whose contents are in the same memory page
unsigned long	b_state	State of the buffer (see below)
struct buffer_head *	b_next_free	Pointer to the next free descriptor
unsigned int	b_count	Number of utilisations of this block
unsigned long	b_size	Block size in bytes
char *	b_data	Pointer to the contents of the buffer
unsigned int	b_list	List in which the buffer is put (see below)
unsigned long	b_flushtime	Date at which the contents of this buffer should be re-written to disk
unsigned long	b_lru_time	Date at which the contents of this buffer were used for the last time
struct wait_queue *	b_wait	Variable used to synchronise concurrent accesses to this buffer
struct buffer_head *	b_prev	Pointer to the previous descriptor
struct buffer_head *	b_prev_free	Pointer to the previous free descriptor
struct buffer_head *	b_reqnext	Pointer to the next buffer forming part of the same input/output request (see chapter 7, section 7.7.4)

The value of the field **b_state** is formed from a combination of bits referenced by the following constants, defined in the header file **<linux/fs.h>**:

option	*meaning*
BH_Uptodate	The buffer contains valid data
BH_Dirty	The data contained in the buffer has been modified
BH_Locked	The buffer is in use and is locked
BH_Req	If this bit is 0, the buffer has been invalidated
BH_Touched	The buffer has been used recently
BH_Protected	The buffer should not be re-used
BH_FreeonIO	The buffer has been allocated temporarily to an input/output and must be released after this has finished

The functions **clear_bit**, **set_bit** and **test_bit** are used to access this field. Several macro instructions, enabling different flags of this field to be tested, are defined in **<linux/fs.h>**:

macro-instruction	*meaning*
buffer_update	Tests the bit **BH_Uptodate**
buffer_dirty	Tests the bit **BH_Uptodate**
buffer_locked	Tests the bit **BH_Locked**
buffer_req	Tests the bit **BH_Req**
buffer_touched	Tests the bit **BH_Touched**
buffer_has_aged	Tests the bit **BH_Has_aged**
buffer_protected	Tests the bit **BH_Protected**

Buffers are placed in several linked lists according to the contents. The following constants, defined in the file **<linux/fs.h>** represent these lists:

option	*meaning*
BUF_CLEAN	List of un-modified buffers
BUF_UNSHARED	List of buffers which were shared but are no longer
BUF_LOCKED	List of buffers re-written to disk
BUF_LOCKED1	List of buffers containing metadata, that is, filesystem control structures, such as inodes, superblocks, etc
BUF_DIRTY	List of modified buffers
BUF_SHARED	List of shared buffers

In addition, a hash function, based on the device identifier and the block number, is utilised to put buffers into several hash lists, and as a result searches for a buffer are faster.

6.5.2.9 Name caches
Name caches function at two levels:

- a level 1 list, in which are included entries produced when a filename is converted to an inode number, or when directories are read by the call *readdir*. This list is stored in the table **level1_cache**, and the pointer **level1_head** contains the address of the first element.
- a level 2 list, in which are added entries when these are found in the first list. This list is stored in the table **level2_cache**, and the pointer **level2_head** contains the address of the first element.

Each of these lists is managed in *Least Recently Used* mode (LRU): new entries to the list are added to the head of the list, and an entry which is not used is shifted down towards the foot of the list, and is removed from the list when it reaches the end.

To speed up the process of searching in the two lists, a hash technique is used: a hash function combines the device number, the inode number and the name of the entry,and with the help of this function, entries in the two lists are divided into 32 hashed lists, whose pointers are contained in the table **hash_table**.

The structures of the list are defined in the source file *fs/dcache.c*, as well as the functions that it manipulates. An entry in the lists (structure **dir_cache_entry**) contains the following fields:

type	field	description
struct hash_list	**h**	Pointer to the list containing the entry
kdev_t	**dc_dev**	Device identifier
unsigned long	**dir**	Directory inode number
unsigned long	**version**	Directory version number
unsigned long	**ino**	File inode number
unsigned char	**name_len**	Size of entry name in bytes
char [DCACHE_NAME_LEN]	**name**	Filename contained in the directory entry
struct dir_cache_entry **	**lru_head**	Address of the pointer to the head of the list containing the entry, that is **level1_head** or **level2_head**
struct dir_cache_entry **	**next_lru**	Pointer to the next element in the LRU list
struct dir_cache_entry **	**prev_lru**	Pointer to the previous element in the LRU list

The structure **hash_list** contains two pointers used to ensure linking In the hashed lists:

type	field	description
struct dir_cache_entry *	next	Pointer to the next element in the hash list
struct dir_cache_entry *	prev	Pointer to the previous element in the hash list

6.5.3 Generic operations

6.5.3.1 *Operations on superblocks*
The structure **super-operations** contains pointers to functions which are called by the VFS and implemented in filesystem code. The fields of this structure are the following:

- **void (*read_inode) (struct inode *inode)**

  The operation ***read_inode** is called by the VFS when an inode needs to be read from the filesystem. The fields **i_dev** and **i-ino** of the parameter **inode** are initialised by the VFS before the call.

- **int (*notify_change) (struct inode *inode, struct iattr *iattr)**

  The operation ***notify_change** is called by the VFS when the attributes of an inode have been changed. The parameter **iattr** indicates the changes to be made, and its structure is described below.

- **void (*write_inode) (struct inode *inode)**

  The operation ***write_inode** is called by the VFS when an inode needs to be written to the filesystem.

- **void (*put_inode) (struct inode *inode)**

  The operation ***put_inode** is called by the VFS when an inode is no longer used.

- **void (*put_super) (struct super_block *super)**

  The operation ***put_super** is called by the VFS when a superblock is no longer used, that is when the corresponding filesystem is unmounted.

- **void (*write_super) (struct super_block *super)**

  The operation ***write_super** is called by the VFS when the contents of a superblock has been changed and which needs to be re-written to disk, for example when the system call *sync* is made.

- **void (*statfs) (struct super_block *super, struct statfs *buf, int bufsize)**

  The operation **statfs** is called by the VFS to obtain filesystem control information. The parameter **buf** points to a variable of structure type **statfs**, whose definition is given in section 6.4.9.

- **int (*remount_fs) (struct super_block *super, int *flags, char *data)**

  The operation **remount_fs** is called when the filesystem is 'remounted', that is to say when the mounting options are changed by a call to the primitive *mount* with the option **MS_REMOUNT**.

The structure **iattr**, used in the operation **notify_change**, is defined in the file **<linux/fs.h>**. It contains the following fields:

type	*field*	*description*
unsigned int	**ia_valid**	Indication of modifications carried out (see below)
umode_t	**ia_mode**	New mode (type of access and permissions of access)
uid_t	**ia_uid**	New owner identifier
gid_t	**ia_gid**	New group identifier
off_t	**ia_size**	New size in bytes
time_t	**ia_atime**	New date of last access
time_t	**ia_mtime**	New date of last modification of the contents
time_t	**ia_ctime**	New date of last modification of the inode

The field **ia_valid** indicates the changes to take into account. It is made up, by using a binary OR operation, of the following constants, which are defined in **<linux/fs.h>**;

option	meaning
ATTR_MODE	The mode has been modified
ATTR_UID	The owner identifier has been modified
ATTR_GID	The group identifier has been modified
ATTR_SIZE	The size has been modified
ATTR_ATIME	The date of the last access has been modified
ATTR_MTIME	The date of the last modification of the contents has been modified
ATTR_CTIME	The date of the last modification of the inode has been modified
ATTR_ATIME_SET	The date of the last access has been modified by calling *utime* or *utimes*
ATTR_MTIME_SET	The date of the last modification has been modified by calling *utime* or *utimes*
ATTR_FORCE	No check of the validity of modifications should be carried out

6.5.3.2 Operations on inodes

The structure **inode_operations** contains pointers to functions which are called by the VFS and are implemented in filesystem code. The fields of this structure are the following:

- **struct file_operations *default_file_op:**

  This field provides the address of file operations associated with the inode (see section 6.5.3), to be used by default when the file is opened.

- **int (*create) (struct inode *dir, const char *name, int len, int mode, struct inode **result)**

  The operation **create** is called by the VFS to create a new entry in the directory referenced by the parameter **dir**. The name of the entry to be created is specified by the parameters **name** and **len**. **mode** indicates the mode (type and access permissions) of the file to create. The inode corresponding to the created file is returned in the parameter **result**.

- **int (*lookup) (struct inode *dir, const char *name, int len, int mode, struct inode **result)**

  The operation **lookup** is called by the VFS to search for an entry in the directory referenced by the parameter **dir**. The name of the entry to be created is specified by the parameters **name** and **len**. The inode corresponding to the created file is returned in the parameter **result**.

- **int (*link) (struct inode *inode, struct inode *dir, const char *name, int len)**

  The operation link is called to create a link to the inode referenced by the parameter inode. The name of the link to be created is specified by the parameters name and len, and the directory in which the link is to be created is indicated by the parameter dir.

- **int (*unlink) (struct inode *dir, const char *name, int len)**

  The operation unlink is called to delete an entry in the directory referenced by the parameter dir. The name of the link to be deleted is specified by the parameters name and len.

- **int (*symlink) (struct inode *dir, const char *name, int len, const char *symname)**

  The operation symlink is called to create a symbolic link in the directory referenced by the parameter dir. The parameters name and len specify the name of the link to be created. The target name is indicated in symname, in the form of a character string terminated by the character null.

- **int (*mkdir) (struct inode *dir, const char *name, int len, int mode)**

  The operation mkdir is called by VFS to create a sub-directory in the directory referenced by the parameter dir. The name of the sub-directory to be created is specified by the parameters name and len. mode indicates the access permissions of the directory to be created.

- **int (*rmdir) (struct inode *dir, const char *name, int len)**

  The operation rmdir is called to delete a sub-directory in the directory referenced by the parameter dir. The name of the sub-directory to be deleted is specified by the parameters name and len.

- **int (*mknod) (struct inode *dir, const char *name, int len, int mode, int rdev)**

  The operation mknod is called by the VFS to create a special file in the directory referenced by the parameter dir. The name of the sub-directory to be deleted is specified by the parameters name and len. mode indicates the type and access permissions of the directory to be created, rdev contains to the device identifier corresponding to the special file.

- **int (*rename) (struct inode *old_dir, const char *old_name, int old_len, struct inode *new_dir, const char *new_name int mode, int new_len)**

  The operation rename is called in order to rename a directory entry. The parameters old_dir, old_name and old_len specify the name of the entry to be renamed, whilst the new name is indicated in the parameters **new_dir**, **new_name** and **new_len**.

- **int (*readlink) (struct inode *inode, char *buf, int bufsize)**

The operation **readlink** is called to read the contents of the symbolic link referenced by the parameter **inode**. The result is returned in the buffer pointed to by **buf**, and whose length in bytes is indicated by **bufsize**.

- **int (*follow_link) (struct inode *dir, struct inode *inode, int flag, int mode, struct inode **result)**

The operation **follow_link** is called to resolve the symbolic link referenced by the parameter **inode**. The parameter **dir** specifies the inode of the directory from which the interpretation is to be carried out. The inode result is returned in **result**.

- **int (*readpage) (struct inode *inode, struct page *page)**

The operation **readpage** is called to read the contents of a page in memory from the file corresponding to the parameter **inode**.

- **int (*writepage) (struct inode *inode, struct page *page)**

The operation **writepage** is called to write the contents of a page in memory from the file corresponding to the parameter **inode**.

- **int (*bmap) (struct inode *inode, int block)**

The operation **bmap** is called to obtain the number of a physical memory block (that is, the number of a block on disk) corresponding to a logical block, indicated by the parameter **block** and referenced by the parameter **inode**.

- **void (*truncate) (struct inode *inode)**

The operation **truncate** is called to change the size of the file referenced by the parameter **inode**. The VFS changes the field **i_size** if the inode before calling this operation.

- **int (*permission) (struct inode *inode, int perm)**

The operation **permission** is called to check that the calling process possesses sufficient access permissions on the file referenced by the parameter **inode**. The parameter **perm** indicates the required access permissions.

- **int (*smap) (struct inode *inode, int sector)**

The operation **smap** is similar to **bmap,** but it manipulates physical sector numbers on disk rather than block numbers. It is defined in a way so as to enable it to read and write pages in memory from a filesystem of the MS/DOS type.

6.5.3.3 *Operations on open files*
The structure **file_operations** contains pointers to functions which are called by the VFS, and are implemented in filesystem code. The fields of this structure are the following:

- **int (*lseek) (struct inode *inode, struct file *file, off_t offset flag, int whence)**

  The operation **lseek** is called to change the current position of the file referenced by the parameter **file**. The parameter **offset** specifies the displacement expressed in bytes with respect to a baseline represented by **whence.**

- **int (*read) (struct inode *inode, struct file *file, char *buf, int count)**

  The operation **read** is called to read data from the file referenced by the parameter **file**. The parameter **buf** specifies the address of the buffer where the data should be stored, and **count** indicates the number of bytes to be read.

- **int (*write) (struct inode *inode, struct file *file, const char *buf, int bufize)**

  The operation **write** is called to write data to the file referenced by the parameter **file**. The parameter **buf** specifies the address of the buffer holding the, and **count** indicates the number of bytes to be read.

- **int (*readdir) (struct inode *inode, struct file *file, void *dirent, filldir_t filldir)**

  The operation **readdir** is called to read entries from the directory referenced by the parameter **file. dirent** contains the address of the buffer where the data should be put, and the parameter **filldir** is a pointer to a function which saves the result (see section 6.3.5).

- **int (*select) (struct inode *inode, struct file *file, int sel_type, select_table *wait)**

  The operation **select** enables the multiplexing of several input/output descriptors to be carried out at the time that the primitive *select* is executed (see chapter 7, section 7.2.3). It should return the value 1 if the input/output specified by **sel_type** is possible with the file descriptor indicated. If this input/output is not possible, an entry should be added to the multiplexing table **wait** in a waiting queue, and the value 0 returned. The use of this operation is described in detail in chapter 7, section 7.4.4.

- **int (*ioctl) (struct inode *inode, struct file *file, unsigned int cmd, unsigned long arg)**

The operation ioctl is called to perform a control operation on a device (see chapter 7, section 2.4).

- **int (*mmap) (struct inode *inode, struct file *file, struct vm_area_struct *vma)**

The operation mmap is called to map a file's contents onto memory. It is described in detail in chapter 8.

- **int (*open) (struct inode *inode, struct file *file)**

The operation open is called when a file referenced by the parameter file is opened.

- **void (*release) (struct inode *inode, struct file *file)**

The operation release is called at the last closure of the file referenced by the parameter file.

- **int (*fsync) (struct inode *inode, struct file *file)**

The operation fsync is called to re-write memory blocks changed in the file referenced by the parameter file.

- **int (*fasync) (struct inode *inode, struct file *file, int on)**

The operation fasync is called when a process utilises a system call *fcntl* to activate or deactivate asynchronous I/O to the file specified by the parameter file.
When the asynchronous I/O are activated, the signal SIGIO is sent to the process when the reading or writing of data is completed. Only certain device controllers and the *socket* layer of network protocols implement operation.

- **int (*check_media_change) (kdev_t dev)**

The operation check_media_change is used to check whether the unmountable device medium (floppy disk or CD-ROM, for example) which is specified by the parameter dev has been changed by the user. It should return the value 0 if the device has not been changed, and a non-zero value if it has.

- **int (*revalidate) (kdev_t dev)**

The operation revalidate is called after changing a unmountable device medium specified by the parameter dev. It must perform the necessary operations to adapt to the new device (for example, the disk drive controller should carry out a format detect operation on the new floppy disk).

6.5.3.4 *Operations on disk quotas*

The **dquot_operations** operation contains pointers to functions which are called by the VFS. Different filesystems can implement these operations, but a generic version exists in the VFS.

- **void (*initialise) (struct inode *inode, short type)**

  The operation **initialise** is called to initialise descriptors of quotas corresponding to the inode referenced by the parameter **inode**. The parameter **type** specifies the quota type to be initialised: **USRQUOTA**, **GRPQUOTA**, or the value −1 to indicate the two types.

- **void (*drop) (struct inode *inode)**

  The operation **drop** is called to free quota descriptors associated with the inode referenced by the parameter **inode**.

- **int (*alloc_block) (const struct inode *inode, unsigned long count)**

  The operation **alloc_block** is called to check that it is possible to allocate new blocks to the inode referenced by the parameter **inode**. The number of blocks of 1kbyte in size to be allocated is specified by the parameter **count**.

- **int (*alloc_inode) (const struct inode *inode, unsigned long count)**

  The operation **alloc_inode** is called to check that it is possible to allocate new inodes to the owner and to the group of the inode referenced by the parameter **inode**. The number of inodes to be allocated is specified by the parameter **count**.

- **void (*free_block) (const struct inode *inode, unsigned long count)**

  The operation **free_block** is called when blocks associated with the inode referenced by the parameter **inode** are released, in order to update the number of blocks that are available. The parameter **count** specifies the number of blocks to release.

- **void (*free_inode) (const struct inode *inode, unsigned long count)**

  The operation **free_inode** is called when **inodes** associated with the owner and with the group of the inode referenced by the parameter **inode** are released in order update the the number of blocks counted. The parameter **count** specifies the number of blocks to release.

- **int (*transfer) (struct inode *inode, struct iattr *iattr, char direction)**

The operation **transfer** is called when the owner or group associated a file referenced by the parameter **inode** are changed. It transfers the number of blocks and inodes counted from one quota descriptor to another.

6.6
DETAILED DESCRIPTION OF IMPLEMENTATION

6.6.1   Internal functions of VFS

6.6.1.1   *Management of mounted filesystem descriptors*

The management of filesystem descriptors is implemented in the source file *fs/super.c*. This file defines several global variables:

- **ROOT_DEV**, of type **kdev_t**: this variable contains the identifier of the device containing the root filesystem;
- **super_blocks**, table of elements of type **struct super_block**: this table contains the descriptors of mounted filesystems;
- **file_systems**, of type **struct file_system_type ***: this pointer contains the address of the first element in the list of filesystem types supported by Linux;
- **vfsmntlist**, of type **struct vfsmount ***: this pointer contains the address of the first element in the list of filesystem descriptors of mounted files;
- **vfsmnttail**, of type **struct vfsmount ***: this pointer contains the address of the last element in the list of filesystem descriptors of mounted files;
- **mru_vfsmnt**, of type **struct vfsmount ***: this pointer contains the address of the descriptor of the filesystem of mounted files obtained at the last look-up; it is used as a cache for the previous result.

Several functions enable operations on the list of mounted filesystems to be carried out:

- **lookup_vfsmnt**, of type **struct vfsmount ***: this function carries out a look-up of the list of mounted filesystems. It implements a comparison loop in the list pointed to by **vfsmnlist** and returns the address of the descriptor found, or the value **NULL** in the event of a fruitless search.
- **add_vfsmnt**: this function adds an entry to the mounted filesystems. It allocates a descriptor by calling the function **kmalloc**, initialises it, then links it to the list. It returns the address of descriptor allocated, of the value **NULL** in the event of a problem.
- **remove_vfsmnt**: this function deletes an entry to the list of filesystems of mounted files. It first of all carries out a descriptor look-up loop in the list pointed to by **vfsmnlist**. Once it has found the descriptor to be deleted, it removes it from the list by modifying the linkages, then it releases it by calling the function **kfree**.

This module also defines functions controlling the list of filesystem types supported:

- **register_filesystem**: this function is called in order to record a filesystem type. It first of all searches in the list pointed to by **file_systems**. If the filesystem type is found there, it means that it has already been recorded, and the function returns the error message **EBUSY**. If the opposite is the case, it adds the descriptor of the filesystem type at the end of the list.
- **unregister_filesystem**: this function is called in order to delete an entry from the list of filesystem types supported. It first searches for the entry to be deleted. If it finds it, the entry is removed from the list by modifying the linkages and the value 0 is returned. If the opposite is the case, the error **EINVAL** is returned.
- **fs_name**: this function is called in search of an entry, having a specified name, in the list of filesystem types supported. It first of all searches for the entry to be deleted. If the entry is found in the list, its sequence number is returned, if not, the function returns the error **EINVAL**.
- **fs_index**: this function is called in search of an entry, of specified name, in the list of filesystem types supported. It first of all searches for the entry to be deleted. If the entry is found in the list, its name is returned, if not, the function returns the error **EINVAL**.
- **fs_maxindex**: this function returns the number of entries in the list of filesystem types supported.

Finally, management functions for mounted filesystems are defined in this module:

- **get_super**: this function carries out a search for an entry associated with a device in the table **super_blocks**. It returns the address of the corresponding descriptor, or the value **NULL** if it fails.
- **_wait_on_super**: this function ensures synchronism between several kernel mode processes accessing the same filesystem descriptor.
- **sync_supers**: this function triggers the re-writing to disk of all super blocks which have changed. It explores the table **super_blocks,** and it calls the operation **write_super** associated with each changed entry. This ensures synchronism between several kernel mode processes accessing the same filesystem descriptor.
- **put_super**: this function is called when a filesystem is no longer used, typically when it is unmounted. It carries out certain continuity tests, them calls the associated operation **put_super**.

6.6.1.2 *Management of inodes*
The management of inodes is implemented in the source file *fs/inode.c*. This file defines several constants and global variables:

- **NR_IHASH**; the number of hash lists;
- **hash_ltable,** the table of elements of the type **inode_hash_entry**: this table contains the pointers to the hash lists;
- **first_inode**, of the type **struct inode** *: this pointer contains the address of the first descriptor of the list of inodes;

- **nr_inodes,** of the type **int**: this variable contains the number of inodes allocated: it is initially set to 0;
- **inode_wait,** of the type **struct wait_queue ***: this variable is used to await an available inode: if no inode can be allocated, the calling process uses the function **sleep_on** on this variable; a process which frees an inode uses the function **wake_up** on this variable to wake up the processes suspended whilst waiting for inodes;
- **nr_free_inodes,** of the type **int**: this variable contains the number of inodes allocated but not used; it is initially set to 0;
- **max_inodes,** of the type **int**: this variable contains the maximum number of inode descriptors; it is initialised with the constant **NR_INODE** defined in **<linux/fs.h>** but its value can be modified by calling the primitive *sysctl*.

Several internal functions are defined:

- **hashfn**: this function implements the hash function on inodes.
- **hash**: this function calls the function **hashfn**, then returns the pointer to the first element in the corresponding hash list.
- **insert_inode_free**: this function inserts a descriptor at the head of the list.
- **remove_inode_free**: this function deletes a descriptor from the list, by modifying the linkages.
- **insert_inode_hash**: this function inserts an inode in the appropriate hash list.
- **put_last_free**: this function shifts a descriptor to the end of a list. It first calls **remove_inode_free** to delete the inode of the list, then inserts it at the end of the list.
- **grow_inodes**: this function is called when all the descriptors are allocated, and when the kernel needs to allocate other descriptors. It allocates a page of memory by calling the function **_get_free_page** , splits this page up into **inode** structures which it adds to the list of descriptors by calling **insert_inode_free**, then it changes the value of the variables **nr_nodes** and **nr_free_inodes**.
- **lock_inode, unlock_inode, __wait_on_inode,** and **wait_on_inode**: these functions ensure synchronisation between several kernel mode processes accessing the same inode descriptor. They allow inodes to be respectively locked, to be unlocked, or to wait until they are no longer locked.
- **write_inode**: this function is called to write the contents of an inode changed on disk. It locks the inode, calls the operation **write_inode** associated with the filesystem containing the inode, then unlocks it.
- **read_inode**: this function is called to read the contents of an inode from disk. It locks the inode, calls the operation **read_inode** associated with the filesystem containing the inode, then unlocks it.

This module also provides support functions:

- **inode_init**: this function is called when the system is initialised. It sets the hash lists to zero and initialises **first_inode** to the value **NULL**.
- **clear_inode**: this function returns an inode reset to zero. The inode is deleted from the lists by calling **remove_inode_hash** and **remove_inode_free**, it is set to zero, then it is added to the list by a call to **insert_inode_free**.
- **fs_may_mount**: this function checks that a filesystem present on a device may be mounted. It explores the list of inodes by testing each entry, and if at least one inode utilised is located on the specified device, it returns a value of 0, if not, it returns a value of 1.
- **fs_may_umount**: this function checks that a filesystem present on a device may be de-mounted. It explores the list of inodes by testing each entry, and if none of the filesystem inodes, except the root inode, is in use, it returns the value 1, if not it returns the value 0.
- **fs_may_remount_ro**: this function checks that a filesystem may be re-mounted in read mode only. It explores the list of open file descriptors by testing each entry, and if none of the files corresponding to an inode present on the filesystem is open in write mode, it returns the value 1, if not it returns the value 0.
- **inode_change_ok**: this function checks that the calling process has permissions to change the attributes of the inode. The following checks are made:

  - only a superuser can change the owner;
  - only a superuser and the owner can change the file group;
  - in the latter case, the owner must be a member of the group specified;
  - only a superuser and the owner can change the permissions and dates associated with a file.

If the tests are positive, **inode_change_ok** returns the value 1, if not it returns the value 0.

- **inode_setattr**: this function changes the attributes of an inode.
- **notify_change**: this function is called to change the attributes of an inode. If an operation **notify_change** is defined for the filesystem containing the inode, it calls it, if not it calls **inode_change_ok** and **inode_setattr** in order to change the attributes.
- **bmap**: this function is called to find out the number of the physical block corresponding to a logical block number of an inode. If an operation **bmap** is defined for the inode , it is called, if not the value 0 is returned.
- **invalidate_inodes**: this function invalidates inodes corresponding to a filesystem. It searches the list of inodes and releases each entry associated with the specified device, by calling **clear_inode**.
- **sync_inodes**: this function re-writes to disk inodes corresponding to a filesystem. It searches the list of inodes and re-writes each entry associated with the specified device, by calling **write_inode**.

- **iput**: this function is called when a process stops using an inode. If the number of utilisations of the inode (field **i_count**) is greater than 1, it is simply decremented. If the number is less than 1, this means that the inode is no longer used at all and **iput** then wakes up the processes waiting for an inode to become free by calling **wake_up** with the variable **inode_wait**. The operation **put_inode** associated with the corresponding filesystem is called if it is defined, then the contents of the inode are re-written by calling **write_inode** if it has already been changed. Finally, the field **i_count** of the inode is decremented, and **nr_free_inodes** is incremented.
- **get_empty_inode**: this function is called to find an unused inode. If few unallocated inodes remain, the function **grow_inodes** is first called. Then the list of inodes is scanned. All the unused inodes (where the field **i_count** is null) are examined, by checking the value of their fields **i_lock**, **i_dirt**, and **i_nrpages**. If an inode has these three fields null, it is selected.

If at the end of the look-up loop no inode has been located having these three fields null, and if the maximum number of inodes has not been reached, the function **grow_inodes** is called again, and the search starts afresh. If the maximum number of inodes has been reached, but no available inode has been found, the function **sleep_on** is called with the variable **inode_wait** in order to place the calling process on hold waiting for an inode. The process will be woken up when another process frees-up an inode by calling the function **iput**.

When an inode has been found, its contents are initialised, the variable **nr_free_inodes** is decremented, and the address of the inode is returned.

- **get_pipe_inode**: this function is called to find an inode corresponding to a pipe.
- **_iget**: this function is called to find a descriptor corresponding to a mounted filesystem and to an inode number. It performs a look-up in the corresponding hash list, and if no descriptor corresponding to the specified inode is found, a new descriptor is allocated by calling **get_empty_inode**. It is initialised and is inserted into the lists by calling the functions **put_last_free** and **insert_inode_hash**, then its contents are loaded into memory by a call to **read_inode**.

Once an inode has been found or allocated and loaded into memory, its utilisation count (field **i_count**) is incremented, and **nr_free_inodes** is eventually decremented. Finally, the descriptor address is returned.

It should be noted that a parameter specifies whether the mounting points should be traversed.

- **iget**: this function calls **_iget** by specifying that it should traverse the mounting points.

6.6.1.3 *Management of open file descriptors*
Management of the list of open file descriptors is implemented in the source file *fs/file_table.c*. This file defines three global variables:

- **first_file**, of the type **struct file** *: this pointer contains the address of the first descriptor of the list, it is initialised as **NULL**;
- **nr_file**, of the type **int**: this variable contains the number of descriptors utilised: it is initially set to 0;
- **max_files**, of the type **int**: this variable contains the maximum number of file descriptors; it is initialised with the constant **NR_FILE** defined in **<linux/fs.h>** but its value can be modified by calling the primitive *sysctl*.

Several internal functions are defined:

- **insert_file_free**: this function inserts a descriptor at the head after setting the field **f_count** to 0 to indicate that the descriptor is not utilised.
- **remove_file_free**: this function deletes a descriptor from the list by modifying its linkages.
- **put_last_free**: this function inserts a descriptor at the end of a list.
- **grow_files**: this function is called when all the descriptors are allocated, and when the kernel needs to allocate other descriptors. It allocates a page of memory by calling the function **_get_free_page**, splits this page up into **file** structures which it adds to the list of descriptors by calling **insert_file_free**, then it changes the value of the variables **nr_files**.

Service functions are also defined:

- **file_table_init**: this function is called when the system is initialised. It does not perform any processing because the global variables of this module are initialised when they are declared.
- **get_empty_filp**: this function is called when the kernel needs to allocate a file descriptor, when processing the primitive *open* for example. It scans the list looking for an unused descriptor, that is having the field **f_count** set to 0. If the list contains no unused descriptor, and if the number of allocated descriptors is less than the maximum number, it calls **grow_files** to allocate new descriptors, then it restarts its look-up.

When **get_empty_filp** has found an unused descriptor, it puts it at the end of the list by calling **remove_file** and **put_last_free**. It initialises the field **f_count** to indicate that the descriptor is used. Finally, it returns the address of the calling descriptor.

Two functions linked to disk quotas, **add_dquot_ref** and **reset_dquot_ptrs** are also defined in this module. The functions are described in detail in section 6.6.3.

Several service functions are also defined in **<linux/file.h>** and in the source file *fs/open.c*:

- **fget**: this function performs the conversion between a descriptor of a file opened by the current process and a file descriptor by using the open files tableassociated with the current process. It then increments the number of references to the file descriptor, and then returns its address.

- **_fput**: this function is called at the final closure of a file. The operation **release** associated with the file is called if it exists, then **_fput** calls **put_write_access** if the file was open in write mode, and finally the function **iput** is called to release the inode corresponding to the file.

- **fput**: this function is called after a file is used. It decrements the number of descriptor references, and calls if this number becomes zero.

6.6.1.4 *Management of disk quota descriptors*

The management of the list of disk quota descriptors is implemented in the source file *fs/dsquot.c*. This file defines several global variables:

- **nr_quots**, of the type **int**: this variable contains the number of disk quota descriptors allocated, it is initialised to 0;
- **nr_fre_quots**, of the type **int**: this variable contains the number of disk quota descriptors allocated but not used, it is initialised to 0;
- **first_dquot**, of the type **struct dquot ***: this pointer contains the address of first descriptor on the list; it is initialised to **NULL**;
- **hash_table**, table of elements of the type **struct dquots ***: this table contains the pointers to the hash lists;
- **dqstats**, of the type **struct dqstats**: this variable contains the utilisation statistics of disk quotas;
- **dquot_wait**, of the type **struct wait_queue ***: this variable is used to wait for an available descriptor: if no descriptor can be allocated, the calling process utilises the function **sleep_on** on this variable; a process which frees a descriptor uses the function **wake_up** on this variable to wake up the process suspended while waiting for descriptors.

Internal functions for quota management mainly based on the inode management module:

- **hashfn**: this function implements the hash function.
- **hash**: this function calls **hashfn**, then returns the pointer address for the first element in the corresponding hash list.
- **has_quota_enable**: this function calls **lookup_vfsmnt** to find the specified mounted filesystem descriptor, then checks to see if the quotas are activated on this filesystem. If they are, it returns a value 1, if no, a value of 0.
- **insert_dquot_free**: this function inserts a descriptor at the head of the list.
- **remove_dquot_free**: this function deletes a descriptor from the list by modifying its linkage.
- **insert_dquot_hash**: this function inserts a descriptor in the appropriate hash list.
- **remove_dquot_hash**: this function deletes an inode from the appropriate hash list.

- **put_last_free**: this function shifts a descriptor to the end of the list. It first calls **remove_dquot_free** to delete the descriptor from the list, then inserts it at the end of the list.
- **grow_dquots**: this function is called when all the descriptors are allocated and the kernel needs to allocate further descriptors. It adds a memory page by calling **__get_free_page**, divides the page into **dquot** structures which it adds to the list of descriptors by calling insert **_dquot_free**, then it changes the values of variables **nr_dquots** and **nr_free_quots**.
- **lock_dquot, unlock_dquot, __wait_on_dquot** and **wait_on_dquot**: these functions ensure synchronisation between several kernel mode processes accessing the same quota descriptor. They enable descriptors respectively to be locked, to be unlocked, and to wait until they are no longer locked.
- **clear_dquot**: this function returns a descriptor that has been reset to zero. The descriptor is deleted from lists by calling **remove_dquot_ hash** and **remove_dquot_ free**, it is reset to zero, then added to the list by calling **insert_dquot_ free**. locked, respectively.
- **write_dquot**: this function is called to write to disk the contents of a descriptor. It locks the descriptor, calls the operation **lseek** assigned to the quota definition file to position itself, then calls the operation **write** to write the descriptor to disk.
- **read_dquot**: this function is called to read the contents of a descriptor from disk. It locks the descriptor, calls the operation **lseek** associated with the quota definition file to set itself, then calls the operation **read** to read the descriptor from disk.
- **dquot_incr_inodes, dquot_incr_blocks**: these functions increment the number of inodes and the number of blocks in the quota descriptor respectively. The descriptor is then marked as modified.
- **dquot_decr_inodes, dquot_decr_blocks**: these functions decrement respectively the number of inodes and the number of blocks in the quota descriptor. If this operation puts the number of inodes or blocks below the 'soft' limit, the fields **dq_itime**, and **dq_btime**, are respectively reset to zero. The descriptor is then marked as modified.
- **check_idq**: this function when new inodes are to be allocated. It checks that the inodes can be added to the descriptor:
  - if this addition takes the number over the absolute limit, an error message is displayed on the terminal associated with the calling process, and the value **NO_QUOTA** is returned;
  - if the addition takes the number over the 'soft' limit and the allowed delay has expired, an error message is displayed on the terminal associated with the calling process, and the value **NO_QUOTA** is returned;
  - if the addition takes the number over the 'soft' limit, a warning message is displayed on the terminal associated with the calling process, the date of the end of the allowed delay is stored in memory in the field **dq_time**, and the value **QUOTA_OK** is returned.

- – in all other cases, the value **QUOTA_OK** is returned.

- **check_bdq**: this function is called at the time that new blocks are allocated. It checks that the blocks may be added to the descriptor in a similar way to **check_idq**.
- **dqput**: this function is called when a process stops using a quota descriptor. If the number of utilisations of the descriptor (field **dq_count**) is greater than 1, it is simply decremented. If the number is less than 1, this means that the descriptor is no longer used at all and **dqput** then wakes up the processes waiting for an inode to become free by calling **wake_up** on the variable **dquot_wait**. The descriptor is then re-written to disk by calling **write_dquot** if it has already been changed. Finally, the field **dq_count** of the descriptor is decremented, and **nr_free_dquots** is incremented.
- **get_empty_dquot**: this function is called to find an unused descriptor. If few unallocated i-descriptors remain, the function **grow_dquots** is first called to allocate new descriptors. A look-up loop on the list of descriptors is then carried out. All the unused descriptors (where the field **dq_count** is null) are examined by testing the value of the fields **dq_flags** to check if the descriptor has been changed or whether they are locked in memory.
- If at the end of the look-up loop no inode has been located in which these three fields are null, and if the maximum number of inodes has not been reached, the function **grow_dquots** is called again, and the look-up starts afresh. If the maximum number of descriptors has been reached but no available descriptor has been found, the function **sleep_on** is called on the variable **dquot_wait** in order to place the calling process in the waiting mode for a descriptor. The process will be woken up when another process makes an descriptor free by calling the function **dqput**.
- Once a descriptor has been found, it is set to zero by calling **clear_dquot**, the variable **nr_free_dquots** is decremented and the descriptor address is returned.
- **dqget**: this function is called to find a quota descriptor corresponding to a filesystem, a quota type, and a user or group identifier. It first checks that quotas are activated on the filesystem specified and retuns the value **NODQUOT** if this is not the case. A look-up loop is performed in the corresponding hash list. If the entry is found in the list, the number of times it has been used (field **dq_count**) is incremented and its address is returned. If not, a new entry is allocated by calling **get_empty_dquot**. The descriptor is initialised and is inserted into the lists by calling the functions **put_last_free** and **insert_dquot_hash**. Finally, the contents of the descriptor are read from disk by a call to **read_quot**, and the address of the descriptor is returned.
- **dquot_init**: this function is called when the system is initialised. It initialises to zero the hash lists, as well as the variable **dqstats** containing the utilisation statistics.

The quota management module defines two service functions:

- **sync_dquots**: this function is called to re-write to disk all the descriptors of modified quotas. It performs a look-up loop on the descriptor list and re-writes all the modified descriptors by calling **write_dquot.**
- **invalidate_dquots**: this function invalidates all descriptors of quotas associated with filesystems. It performs a look-up loop on the descriptor list, re-writes the corresponding descriptors by calling **write_dquot,** if they have been changed, and frees corresponding descriptors by the function **clear_dquot** .

The source file *fs/dquot.c* defines variables and functions linked to operations on quotas:

- **dquot_initialise**: this function is called to initialise a quota descriptor associated with an inode. It calls **dqget** to find quota descriptor corresponding to the filesystem containing the inode, the type of quota, and the user or group identifier. The descriptor address is stored in memory in the field **i_dquot** of the inode, and the flag **S_WRITE** is raised in the field **i_flags** in order to indicate that a quota descriptor is assigned to this inode.
- **dquot_drop**: this function is called to free quota descriptors assigned to an inode. To do this, it calls the function **dqput**. Then the field **i_dquot** of the inode is reset to **NOQUOT** and the flag **S_WRITE** is raised in the field **i_flags** in order to indicate that the inode does not have an associated quota descriptor.
- **dquot_alloc_block, dquot_alloc_inode**: these functions are called at the allocation of blocks and inodes respectively, to an inode. They call **check_bdq** and **check_idq** to check that the allocation is allowed, then the functions dquot_incr_blocks and dquot_incr_inodes to record the allocation in the corresponding quota descriptor.
  If the allocation fails, these functions return **NO_QUOTA**, if not, they return **QUOTA_OK.**
- **dquot_free_block, dquot_free_inode**: these functions are called at the time that blocks and inodes respectively are released. They call the functions **dquot_decr_blocks,** and **dquot_decr_ blocks** to register the deallocation in the corresponding quota descriptor.
- **dquot_transfer**: this function is called when the owner of a file or file group is changed. In this case, a supplementary inode and its associated blocks must be added to the account of the new owner or new group, and must be subtracted from the number of inodes and blocks belonging to the former owner or group. In the first instance, **dquot_transfer** checks that the transfer may be carried out by calling the functions **check_bdq** and **check_idq**. If this is not the case, the value **NO_QUOTA** is returned. If the transfer is possible, the functions **dquot_decr_blocks** and **dquot_decr_inodes** are called to reduce the number of inodes and blocks accounted for by the former owner or group, then the functions **dquot_incr_blocks** and **dquot_incr_inodes** are called in order to add these numbers to the new owner or group.

The variable **dquot_operations**, of structure type **dquot_operations** ,contains the pointers to these functions.

6.6.1.5 *Name caches*

The management of the name cache is implemented in the source file *fs/dcache.c*. This module defines the constants and global variables used to control the cache:

- **DCACHE_NAME_LEN**: maximum number of characters in names of files placed in the cache;
- **DCACHE_SIZE**: number of entries in the level 1 and 2 lists;
- **DCACHE_HASH_QUEUES**: number of hash lists;
- **level1_dcache**, table of elements of structure type **dir_cache_entry**: this table contains the entries of the level 1 list;
- **level2_dcache**, table of elements of structure type **dir_cache_entry**: this table contains the entries of the level 2 list;
- **level1_head**, table of elements of structure type **dir_cache_entry ***: this pointer contains the address of the first element of the level 1 list;
- **level2_head**, table of elements of structure type **dir_cache_entry ***: this pointer contains the address of the first element of the level 2 list;
- **hash_table**, table of elements of structure type **dir_hash_list**: this table contains the pointers to the hash lists.

Several internal functions are defined:

- **remove_lru**: this function deletes an entry in the LRU list, by changing its linkages.
- **add_lru**: this function inserts an entry in the LRU list, by changing its linkages.
- **update_lru**: this function shifts an entry to the head of the list, by changing its linkages. To do this, it calls successively the functions **remove_lru** and **add_lru**.
- **remove_hash**: this function deletes an element from a hash list by changing its linkages.
- **add_hash**: this function inserts an element from a hash list by changing its linkages.
- **find_entry**: this function carries out a look-up for an entry in a specified hash list. For each element in the hash list, it compares the device number, the number of the directory inode, the directory version number, and the name of the entry together with the parameters that are passed to it.
- **move_to_level2**: this function changes a list entry by deleting it from the level 1 list, and then re-inserting it in the level 2 list. If the entry is already in the second list, it is placed at the head of the list.

Other functions, that can be called by other VFS modules and by filesystems, are also defined:

- **dcache_lookup:** this function is called to resolve an entry. It uses the hash function **hash_fn** in order to determine the hash list to search, then calls the function **find_entry** which performs the look-up. If the entry is found in the list, the function **move_to_level2** is called in order to place it at the head of the level 2 LRU list.
- **dcache_add:** this function is called to insert an entry when a file is created or when a directory is read using *readdir*. It first calls **find_entry** to find out if the entry has already been stored. If so, the entry is put at the head of the list by calling **update_lru**, if not, an entry in the level1 list is deleted and the new entry is added at the top.
- **name_cache_init:** this function is called when the system is initialised. It initialises two linked lists and creates the empty hash lists.

It should be noted that this module does not have a function **dcache_remove,** which could be called when a file is deleted in order to invalidate an entry in the cache. Indeed, Linux uses another technique to automatically invalidate obsolete entries. A version number is assigned to each directory inode loaded in memory. This number is stored in the lists when **dcache_add** is called, and any change in the directory, that is, any addition or deletion of files, causes a change of version number. If a file whose name is present in the cache is deleted in a directory, the version number is changed, and a subsequent call to **find_entry** will fail because the version number of the directory is now different to that which is stored in the cache. In this way, all entries corresponding to a directory are rendered invalid when a file is added or deleted in this directory, and these entries are then progressively eliminated from the LRU lists when other entries are added.

Linux uses an internal variable, called **event,** to manage version numbers. This variable is defined in the file *kernel/sched.c* and is initialised to 0 when the system is booted up. It is incremented at each change to a directory, then assigned to the version number of the corresponding inode.

6.6.1.6 Utility functions for inode management
Several utility functions handle inode descriptors:

- **permission:** this function is called to check that a calling process has the necessary permissions regarding the inode. If an operation **permission** is associated with an inode, it is called, if not the permissions are compared directly with the access permissions specified in the field **i_mode** of the inode.
- **get_write_access:** this function is called to obtain the permission to write to an inode. It searches the process list and checks to see if a process possesses a section of this inode, mapped into its memory space with the option **VM_DENYWRITE.** If this is the case, the error **ETXTBSY** is returned, if not, the field **i_writecount** of the inode is incremented to indicate that a supplementary process is accessing the inode in write mode, and the value 0 is returned

- **put_write_access**: this function is called when a process ceases accessing an inode in write mode. It decrements the field **i_writecount** of the inode.

6.6.1.7 *Management of file names*

System calls handling filenames accept filenames or input/output descriptors as parameters. The functions implementing these calls, as well as the internal VFS and filesystem functions, act on inodes or descriptors of open files. The VFS also provides handling and conversion functions for filenames. These functions are implemented in the source file *fs/namei.c*.

- **getname**: this function is called to copy a filename into the kernel address space. It checks that the name is valid, that is, that it is not just an empty string, and it allocates a page of memory by calling the function **_get_free_page**, then it copies the name into this page.
- **putname**: this function is called to free a filename returned by **getname**. It releases the page allocated by this function by calling **free_page**.
- **lookup**: this function is called to look for an inode corresponding to a directory entry. It first checks that the calling process has the right to search the directory by calling **permission**. Then it deals with the case of a special entry ' .. ': if the directory concerned is the root directory, ' .. ' refers to itself, if the directory is the root of a filesystem, ' .. ' refers to the entry ' .. ' at the mounting point. Finally, **lookup** calls the operation **lookup** associated with the inode of the directory, and returns its result.
- **follow_link**: this function is called to resolve a symbolic link name. It checks that an operation **follow_link** is associated with the inode of the link, calls this operation, then returns its result. If no operation **follow_link** exists for this inode, that means that it is not a symbolic link and the inode itself is returned.
- **dir_namei**: this internal function is called to resolve the name of a directory containing a file whose name is passed as a parameter. It first chooses a directory to start the search from: if the name starts with the character '/' , it is an absolute name and the root directory is chosen as base, if not, it is a relative name and the directory of the calling process is chosen as base. It then performs an iterative resolution loop on each of the components of the filename by calling the function **lookup.**
- **_namei**: this internal function is called to resolve a filename. It calls the function **dir_namei** to find the inode of the parent directory, and calls the function **lookup** to resolve the name of the file in this directory. The parameter **follow_links** specifies what processng is to be carried out on the symbolic links: if it is set, **_namei** then calls **follow_link** to eventually follow a symbolic link.
- **lnamei**: this internal function is called to resolve a symbolic link name. It calls the function **getname** to find the name of the link, then **_namei** to resolve its name by setting the parameter **follow_links.**

- **namei**: this internal function is called to resolve a a filename. It calls **getname** to find the name of the file, then **_namei** to resolve its name without setting the parameter **follow_links**.

6.6.1.8 Management of locks

The source file *fs/locks.c* contains the code for managing locks associated with files. The variable file_lock_table contains the address of the first element in the list of lock descriptors. It is initialised to the value **NULL**.

Several internal functions for managing lists of locks are defined:

- **locks_alloc_lock**: this function allocates a lock descriptor by calling the function **kmalloc**, and initialises it.
- **locks_insert_lock**: this function inserts a lock descriptor in the list of locks associated with an inode, and in the global list of lock descriptors.
- **locks_delete_lock**: this function is called to delete a lock descriptor. First it deletes the descriptor in the global list of locks. It then scans the list of blocked locks which are associated with the descriptor, and wakes up corresponding processes by a call to **wake_up**. Finally, the descriptor is released by calling **kfree**.
- **locks_insert_block**: this function inserts a lock descriptor in the queue of the list of blocked locks which are associated with another lock.
- **locks_delete_block**: this function deletes a lock descriptor from the list of blocked locks which are associated with another lock.
- **posix_remove_locks**: this function deletes all locks enabled by a process on a file. It scans the list of locks and calls **locks_delete_block** for each lock created by the process.
- **flock_remove_locks**: this function deletes all locks enabled on a file decriptor. It scans the list of locks and calls **locks_delete_block** for each lock created on the descriptor of the specified file, if the number of references to the descriptor is equal to 1.
- **posix_make_locks, flock_make_lock**: these two functions initialise a lock descriptor. The descriptor created by **posix_make_locks** contains the addresses of the start and the end of a lock in a file, whilst the descriptor **flock_make_lock** specifies that the whole of a file is locked.
- **locks_overlap**: this function returns a boolean expression indicating if two lock descriptors in the same file have any common parts.
- **locks_conflict**: this function tests if two lock descriptors have any conflict. It first tests to see whether the two locks have a common part (by calling **locks_overlap**). If this is not the case, it returns a value 0, if is, it checks to see if the two locks are compatible. If one of the locks is an exclusive type (that is, if it is of type **F_WRLCK**), the locks are incompatible, and the value 1 is returned. If they are compatible, **locks_conflict** returns a value 0.
- **posix_locks_conflict, flock_locks_conflict**: these functions test if two lock descriptors have any conflict. **posix_locks_conflict** returns a value 0 if the two locks are linked to the same process, and calls **locks_conflict** if this is not the

case. flock_locks_conflict returns the value 0 if the two locks are assigned the same file descriptor, and calls locks_conflict if this is not the case.

- posix_locks_deadlock: this function tests to see if establishing a lock could cause a blockage between two processes, specified by the parameters my_process and blocked_process. It scans the list of lock descriptors: for each descriptor, it searches the list of processes waiting on this lock. If the waiting process is blocked_process and if the lock is held by my_process, a blockage between processes would be provoked by the creation of a lock, and the value 1 is returned. At the end of scanning the list of lock descriptors, if no blockage has been detected, the value 0 is returned

The function locks_remove_locks is also defined in this file. This function is called when a file is closed. It calls the function posix_remove_locks or flock_remove_locks, according to which types of locks are associated with the file.

6.6.2 The *buffer cache*

6.6.2.1 *Description*
The management of the *buffer cache* is implemented in the source file *fs/buffer.c*. This management interacts with memory management, which is presented in chapter 8. Indeed, the contents of buffers are put into memory pages, and the state of memory pages often needs to be consulted or changed. To achieve this, Linux uses the table mem_map, which contains a descriptor for each memory page. This descriptor is decribed in detail in chapter 8, section 8.5.2, but it is necessary to introduce here certain fields utilised by the *buffer cache*:

- count: this field contains the number of references to the page.
- flags: this field contains the state of the page.
- buffers: this field contains the address of the first buffer descriptor whose contents are located on the page.

The management functions of *buffer cache* are divided into several categories:

- management functions for lists of buffers;
- functions called when I/O are performed;
- functions changing the size of *buffer cache*;
- management functions for devices;
- service functions allowing access to buffers;
- functions for re-writing buffer contents to disk;
- management functions for *clusters*;
- the initialisation function for *buffer cache*.

These functions are described in the following sections.

6.6.2.2 Management functions for lists of buffers
Several internal functions support the management of lists in which buffers have
been stored, and several variables are used to maintain these lists:

- **hash_table**: Table containing pointers to the first buffer of each hash list;
- **nr_hash**: Number of hash lists;
- **lru_list**: Table containing pointers to the first buffer of each LRU list;
- **free_list**: Table containing pointers to the first buffer available for each block
  size;
- **unused_list**: Pointer to the first unused buffer;
- **reuse_list**: Pointer to the first unused, but re-usable, buffer;
- **nr_buffers**: Number of allocated buffers;
- **nr_buffers_type**: Table containing the number of buffers recorded in each list;
- **nr_buffers_size**: Table containing the number of buffers allocated for each block;

The functions ensuring the management of these lists are the following:

- **_wait_on_buffer** and **wait_on_buffer**: these functions enable several kernel mode
  processes which access the same buffer to be synchronised.
- **_hashfn** and **hash**: these functions implement the function used for the hash lists.
- **remove_from_hash_queue**: this function deletes a buffer from the corresponding
  hash list.
- **remove_from_lru_list**: this function deletes a buffer from the the corresponding
  LRU list.
- **remove_from_free_list**: this function deletes a buffer from the list of free blocks.
- **remove_from_queues**: this function deletes a buffer from the lists it is located in,
  by calling **remove_from_free_list** or **remove_from_hash_queue**, then
  remove_from_lru_list.
- **put_last_lru**: this function shifts a buffer to the end of its LRU list.
- **put_last_free**: this function inserts a buffer at the end the list of free blocks.
- **insert_into_queues**: this function inserts a buffer in a list, if the buffer is not used,
  put_last_free is called to add it at the end the list of free blocks, if not the buffer is
  inserted in a LRU list.
- **find_buffer**: this function carries out a look-up for a buffer. It scans the
  corresponding hash list and returns the descriptor address, or the value **NULL** if
  it fails.
- **set_writetime**: this function sets the field **b_flushtime** of the buffer descriptor to the
  current date (contained in the variable **jiffies**), if the contents of the buffer have
  been changed. If this is not the case, the field is set to zero.
- **refile_buffer**: this function is called when a buffer is released by a process. It
  examines the state of the buffer, and later changes its LRU list. The date of the
  last use of the buffer (field **b_lru_time**) is set to the current date by this function.
- **put_unused_buffer_head**: this function is called to free a buffer hat is no longer
  used. It adds the buffer to the list of unused blocks pointed to by **unused_list**,

then it uses the function **wake_up** on the variable **buffer_wait** in order to wake up the processes awaiting an available buffer.

- **get_more_buffer_heads**: this function is called to allocate descriptors of supplementary buffers. It loops around as long as it is unable to allocate new buffers. At each round of the loop, it:

    1. tests the variable **unused_list** to determine if unused buffers exist; if this is the case, it returns to the caller;
    2. calls **get_free_page** to find a memory page;
    3. if the allocation fails, it calls **sleep_on** with the variable **buffer_wait** in order to suspend the calling process whilst waiting for an available buffer;
    4. if the allocation succeeds, the allocated page is split into buffer descriptors, and it adds each of the buffers in the list of unused blocks pointed to by **unused_list**.

- **recover_unusable_buffer_heads**: this function inserts buffers to be re-used into the list of unused buffers. It scans the list of buffers to be re-used, pointed to by **reuse_list**, and calls **put_unused_buffer_head** for each buffer.

- **get_unused_buffer_head**: this function is called to find a descriptor of an unused buffer. It calls in turn, **recover_unusable_buffer_heads** and **get_more_buffer_heads**, then it returns the first descriptor in the list of unused buffers, which is pointed to by **unused_list**.

6.6.2.3 *Inputs/Outputs*

Service functions enable other parts of the kernel to trigger inputs and outputs, by using the *buffer cache*. These functions involve as much the creation of buffers in memory pages and inputs and outputs to the memory pages, as the functions of unlocking and release of buffers called at the end of input/output.

The functions are as follows:

- **create_buffers**: this function creates new buffers in a memory page. It allocates buffer descriptors by calling **get_unused_buffer_head**, decomposes the page into buffers, and puts the address of the buffers in the field **b_data** of the descriptors.

- **Free_sync_buffers**: this function is called to free buffers associated with a memory page. It scans the list of these buffers, and each buffer is placed in the list of buffers to re-use, which is pointed to by the variable **reuse_list**.

- **brw_page**: this function is called in order to perform a data read or write operation in, or from, a memory page. It first allocates buffer descriptors corresponding to the contents of the page contents by calling **create_buffers**, then it performs a loop to process the buffers thus created.

Each buffer descriptor is initialised and the flag **FreeOnIO** is set, in order to indicate that a temporary buffer is involved, which should be released at the end of an input/output. Then **get_hash_table** is called in order to see if another buffer in *buffer cache* is referring to the same disk block. If so, the buffer found is used:

- in the case of a data read, its contents are transferred into the page to be read;
- in the case of a data write, the corresponding part of the page contents is transferred into the buffer, and the latter is marked as being changed by calling **mark_buffer_dirty**.

If this is not the case, the buffer assigned to the page contents is recorded in the table.

At the end of this loop, the function **ll_rw_block** (see chapter 7, section 4.2) is called in order to start an input/output. The buffer descriptors created by **brw_page** are passed to it as parameters.

- **mark_buffer_uptodate**: this function is called at the end of a data read, when the input/output has been carried out. It indicates that the corresponding buffer contents are current, by setting the flag **BH_Uptodate** in the field **b_state**, then it scans the buffer whose contents are located in the same memory page. If they are all up to date, the page itself is marked as current.
- **unlock_buffer**: this function is called at the end of an input/output to unlock a buffer. It deletes the flag **BH_lock**, then wakes up the processes waiting for the buffer with a call to **wake_up**.

  In the case of a buffer (whose flag **BH_FreeOnIO** is set), **unlock_buffer** scans the other buffers situated in the same memory page. If they all have a number of references equal to 1, that is they are used only by the page that contains them, they are released by a call to **free_async_buffers**.
- **generic_readpage**: this function is called to read a memory page from a file. A loop is performed to find the addresses of blocks making up the page contents, by calling the operation **bmap** associated with an inode of a file. Once this list of block numbers is calculated, a read operation is executed by calling **brw_page**.

6.6.2.4 Modification of the buffer cache size
With Linux, in contrast to other operating systems, the size of the *buffer cache* is not fixed when the system is initialised. The *buffer cache* is initially empty, and changes size as the system runs. When the kernel requires additional buffers, new memory pages are allocated to the *buffer cache* in order to grow it. When the system is short of memory, it can release certain buffers as well as the memory pages that they are in, which reduces the size of the *buffer cache*.

The functions which change the size of the *buffer cache* are as follows:

- **grow_buffers**: this function is called to enlarge the *buffer cache*. It allocates a memory page by calling **__get_free_page**, then calls **create_buffers** to allocate the buffers, following this it inserts the buffers created in the list of unused buffers.

- **try_to_free_buffer**: this function is called to reduce the memory allocated to *buffer cache*. It scans all the buffers contained in a memory page and tests whether they are used. If they are, it returns the value 0, if not, the buffers are deleted from the lists by calling **remove_from_queues**, then **put_unused_buffer_head**. Finally, the page which contained the buffers is released by a call to **free_page**, and the value 1 is returned.
- **shrink_specific_buffers**: this function reduces the memory allocated to buffers associated with a specific block size. It first of all scans the available buffers and tests the state of each buffer which is placed there. **try_to_free_buffer** is called in order to try to release all the buffers contained in the same memory page. At the end of this look-up of the list of available buffers, **shrink_specific_buffers** scans the LRU lists. It checks whether the buffer has been used recently. If it hasn't, the function **try_to_free_buffer** is called to attempt to free the buffer.
- **refill_freelist**: this function is called to refill the list of buffers of a given size that are available. It first checks whether the number of available buffers is greater than 100. If it is, it decides that there are sufficient available buffers and terminates execution. If not, it calls the function **grow_buffers** in order to allocate new buffers. If the allocations are sufficient, it terminates.

In the case that the *buffer cache* cannot be enlarged, the processing carried out by **refill_freelist** is fairly complex. The function has to select unused buffers and put them in the list of available buffers. For this, it scans the different LRU lists containing buffers, and, for each list, it selects a candidate buffer. This buffer must have a number of references (field **b_count**) equal to 0, its contents must not have been changed (field **b_dirty** is 0), and the page which contains it must not be part of the memory space of a process. At the end of this search through the lists, a candidate buffer is chosen for each list. There is then an 'election' of an appropriate buffer. This election consists of choosing the buffer which has been used the least recently, that is, the one with the oldest date in the field **b_lru_time**.

The selected buffer is deleted from the list by a call to **remove_from_queues**, then inserts the available buffers in the list by calling **put_last_free**. A look-up is then is then carried out in the list in which the buffer was recorded in order to choose another candidate.

After the transfer of the buffer into the available buffers list, **refill_freelist** tests whether it is necessary to repeat the operation. If enough available buffers have been created, the function terminates, if not, it tries to again enlarge the *buffer cache* by calling **grow_buffers**, then it returns to the selection of a buffer at the 'election' stage.

6.6.2.5 *Device management functions*
Two functions act upon buffers assigned to a specified device.

The function **invalidate_buffers** is called to invalidate buffers corresponding to a specified filesystem. It scans the LRU lists, and updates the state of corresponding buffers by modifying the field **b_state**, in order to indicate that the buffers are invalid.

The function **set_blocksize** allows the size of logical blocks present in a device to be specified. It stores this size in memory in an entry in the table **blksize_size** assigned to the device, then it scans the lists of buffers. Any device buffer whose size is not that specified is deleted from the hash list by a call to **remove_from_hash_queue**, then it is inserted into the list of unused buffers.

6.6.2.6 Functions for accessing buffers

The *buffer cache* management module provides service functions which can be used by the VFS and filesystems, for accessing buffers:

- **get_hash_table**: this function is called to find an existing buffer corresponding to a filesystem and a block number. It calls **find_buffer** to look for it. If the correct buffer is found, its utilisation count (field **b_count**) is incremented, then its address is returned, if not get_hash_table returns the value NULL.
- **getblk**: this function is called to find an existing buffer corresponding to a filesystem and a block number. It first calls **get_hash_table** to look for the buffer, then returns the result if it is positive. If this is not the case, that is if there is no buffer corresponding to the request, the function **refill_freelist** is called, and a new look-up is carried out by a call to **find_buffer**. If this new look-up is positive, the process is repeated from the beginning. If it is not, a descriptor is allocated from the list of unused buffers, it is initialised and inserted in the lists by **insert_into_queues**, then its address is returned.
- **brelse**: this function is called to release a buffer. This is later moved to a different LRU list by calling **refile_buffer**, then its utilisation count is decremented .
- **bforget**: this function is called to release a buffer, in the same way as with __brelse, but it inserts it into the list of unused buffers.
- **bforget**: this function simply calls **_bforget**.
- **bread**: this function is called to find an existing buffer corresponding to a device and a block number. It first calls **getblk** to obtain the buffer descriptor, and later calls **ll_rw_block** in order to read the contents of the buffer from disk. It returns the address of the descriptor, or the value **NULL** if it fails.
- **breada**: this function is similar to **bread**, but it enables reading of other blocks to be activated. It calls **getblk** to obtain the specified buffer descriptor, and later calls **ll_rw_block** in order to read the contents of the buffer from disk. For each other block specified, it next calls **getblk** to obtain the buffer descriptor, then triggers the reading of all blocks by calling **ll_rw_block**. It does not wait for the termination of this additional read operation, and returns the address of the buffer descriptor corresponding to the first block.

6.6.2.7 Re-writing modified buffers

The function **sync_buffers** re-writes buffers modified on disk. It can carry out up to three rounds of searches of the lists:

- Throughout the first round, the modified buffers are re-written asynchronously to disk by calling the function **ll_rw_block**. The buffers locked in memory are not included.
- In the following rounds, **sync_buffers** puts itself into waiting mode for the locked buffers using the call **wait_on_buffer**.

The number of look-up rounds carried out depends on the value of the parameter **wait**. The primitive *sync* sets it to 0 in order that **sync_buffers** can trigger I/O without waiting for them to finish, whilst the system call *fsync* sets it to 1 so that **sync_buffers** can carry out several look-up rounds, in order that the modified buffers can be re-written physically to disk at the end of the function.

The parameters of the process *bdflush* are stored in the variable **bdf_prm**. This variable contains the following fields:

type	*field*	*description*
int	nfract	Maximum percentage of buffers modified: when this percentage is exceeded, *bdflush* is activated to re-write buffer to disk
int	ndirty	Maximum number of buffers to re-write at each activation of *bdflush*
int	nrefill	Number of buffers to be put in the list of available buffers each time that this list is rebuilt
int	nref_dirt	Number of buffers modified as a result of which *bdflush* must be re-activated when the list of buffers is rebuilt (this parameter is not used by Linux 2.0)
int	clu_nfract	Percentage of buffers to be scanned when an available cluster is sought (this parameter is not used by Linux 2.0)
int	age_buffer	Time for which a buffer is authorised to keep its modifications before being re-written to disk; expressed in number of clock cycles
int	age_super	Time for which a buffer containing a filesystem descriptor is authorised to keep its modifications before being re-written to disk; expressed in number of clock cycles

Detailed discussion of implementation 217

type	field	description
int	lav_const	Constant used ro calculate the percentage utilisation of buffers assigned to blocks of a given size
int	lav_ratio	This parameter is not used by Linux 2.0

*Continuation of the list of fields in the variable **bdf_prm**.*

By default, the values of these parameters are; 60, 500, 24, 256, 15, 30*HZ, 5*HZ, 1884, and 2.

The variables **bdflush_min** and **bdflush_max** define the minimum and maximum values of the parameters of *bdflush*. They contain the values 0, 10, 5, 25, 0, 100, 100, 1, 1, and 100, 5000, 2000, 2000, 100, 60000, 60000, 2047, 5 respectively.

Several functions enable the functioning of *bdflush* to be managed:

- **wake_up_bdflush**: this function uses the the function **wake_up** to wake up the process *bdflush*, then waits until it has finished its processing by using **sleep_on** on the wait queue **bdflush_done**.
- **sync_old_buffers**: this function re-writes the contents of the buffers to disk. It first of all calls **sync_supers** and **sync_inodes** in order to re-write the filesystem and inode descriptors to disk. It then scans the list of modified buffers. For each buffer, the function **refile_buffer** is called if its contents have not been modified, in order to shift the buffer in the corresponding list. If its contents have been modified, if the buffer has not been locked, and if the writing date has been reached (that is if the value of the field **s_flushtime** is less than or equal to the current date, contained in the variable **jiffies**), the function **ll_rw_block** is called to re-write the contents of the buffer to disk. Finally, at the end of the funcion, the utilisation statistics of each block size are re-calculated.
- **sys_bdflush**: this function implements the system call *bdflush*. It allows a calling process to find or to change one of the parameters controlling the execution of the process *bdflush*.
- **bdflush**: this function implements the process *bdflush*. This process is created when the system is initialised and is executed in kernel mode. After the initialisation of the process descriptor, **bdflush** performs an infinite loop. On each cycle of the loop, it carries out a similar process to that in **sync_old_buffers**, that is, it saves to disk the contents of the modified buffers whose re-writing date has been reached, then it suspends the process *bdflush* by calling **interruptible_sleep_on**, if the number of modified buffers is less than the percentage specified by the parameter **nfract** of *bdflush*. The process will be awoken by the functions **refill_freelist** and **refile_buffer**, which will call **wake_up_bdflush**, when *bdflush* needs to be executed again.

6.6.2.8 *Management of* clusters

Linux uses the notion of *cluster* for the I/O. A *cluster* is a set of buffers whose contents are contiguous in memory, and which correspond to contiguous blocks on disk. The advantage of *clusters* resides in the fact that reading or writing to buffers can be carried out in one I/O, whilst it requires several (one for each block) if the buffers corresponding to contiguous blocks on disk are dispersed in memory. This mechanism of *clustering* is used by the filesystem Ext2 (see section 8.6.5) as well as by direct I/O to devices accessible in block mode (see chapter 7, section 7.4.3). Several functions are available to manage *clusters*:

- **try_to_reassign**: this function tests to see if all the buffers contained on a memory page are available and it associates them with a new *cluster* if this is not the case. It scans the list of buffers contained on a page and checks that each is available. If this is not the case, the value 0 is returned. If all the buffers are available, they are deleted from the hash lists by a call to **remove_from_queue**, their adresses on ·disk (device number and block number) are changed, and they are recorded again in the lists by calling **insert_into_queues**.

- **reassign_cluster**: this function is called to find a new *cluster*. It first calls **refill_freelist** in order to obtain sufficient available buffers, then it scans the list of available buffers. For each buffer in the list, it calls **try_to_reassign** to try to create a new *cluster* in the page containing this buffer.

- **try_to_generate_cluster**: this function tries to generate a *cluster* in a new memory page. It allocates a page by calling **get_free_page**, then calls **create_buffers** in order to create buffers pointing to the contents of the memory page. It then uses **find_buffer** to find out if existing buffers correspond to the device and to the blocks specified. If this is the case, it is impossible to create a *cluster*, the buffers created are released by calling **put_unused_buffer_head**, the memory page is released and the value 0 is returned. In the opposite case, a *cluster* can be created. The buffers created are initialised and are recorded in the lists by calling **insert_into_queues**.

- **generate_cluster**: this function is called to create a *cluster* for a series of specified blocks. It first checks that the specified blocks are contiguous, and that there is no buffer which already refers to these blocks. **maybe_shrink_lav_buffers** is then called in order to reduce the number of buffers used if is too large. If this function has deleted buffers, the function **try_to_generate_cluster** is called to allocate a *cluster*. If the opposite is the case, or if **try_to_generate_cluster** fails, the available memory is tested: if it is limited, the function **reassign_cluster** is called to create the *cluster* from existing buffers, if not, a new *cluster* is created by calling **try_to_generate_cluster**.

6.6.2.9 *Initialisation of buffer cache*

The function **buffer_init** is called when the system is started up in order to initialise the *buffer cache*. It calculates the number of hash lists as a function of the size of available memory, allocates these lists by calling **vmalloc**, and initialises them. Finally, it calls **grow_buffers** in order to allocate some buffers.

6.6.3 Implementation of system calls

6.6.3.1 *Organisation of source files*

System calls handling files are implemented in source files situated in the directory *fs*. The following table summarises the system calls implemented in different files.

source file	system calls
buffer.c	*sync, fsync, fdatasync, bdflush*
dquot.c	*quotactl*
exec.c	*exit, brk, uselib*
fcntl.c	*dup2, dup, fcntl*
ioctl.c	*ioctl*
locks.c	*flock*
namei.c	*mknod, mkdir, rmdir, unlink, symlink, link, rename*
noquot.c	*quotactl*
open.c	*statfs, fstats, truncate, ftruncate, utime, utimes, acces, chdir, fchdir, chroot, fchmod, fchown, open, creat, close, vhangup*
read_write.c	*lseek, llseek, read, write, readv, writev*
readdir.c	*getdents*
select.c	*select (this primitive is described in detail in chapter 7 section 7.4.4)*
stat.c	*stat, newstat, lstat, newlstat, fstat, newfstat, readlink*
super.c	*sysfs, ustat, umount, mount*

Not all the system calls are described in detail in this section. In fact, the processing of certain system calls is very similar, and only a few significant examples are described here.

6.6.3.2 *Handling files*

File handling primitives, implemented in the source file *fs/namei.c*, are relatively simple to understand and all follow the same model. Only the calls *mkdir* and *rename* are described here. The implementation of other system calls is similar.

The function **sys_mkdir** implements the system call *mkdir*. It calls **getname** to establish the name of the directory to create, then the creation is carried out by calling **do_mkdir**. Finally, the name of the directory is released by a call to **putname**.

The function **do_mkdir** is responsible for the creation of the directory. It calls **dir_namei** to obtain the inode of the parent directory, then carries out some tests: it checks that the filesystem has not been mounted in read-mode only, that the calling process has the right to create a sub-directory, and that an operation mkdir is associated with the inode of the parent directory. Once these tests have been performed, the quotas operation initialise is called in order to load the descriptors of associated quotas in the parent directory. Finally, the operation mkdir associated with the inode of the parent directory is called in order to proceed to the creation of the sub-directory.

The function sys_rename implements the system call *rename*. In the same manner as sys_mkdir, it calls *getname* to find the names of files, then do_rename in order to proceed to the changing of filename, and finally putname to free the filenames.

The function do_rename is a little more complex than do_mkdir because it carries out more tests. First of all it calls dir_namei to find out the inode of the parent directory of the file to be renamed. Then, it checks that the calling process has enough permissions with respect to the parent directory, and that the entry to be renamed is neither '.' nor '..'. The same process is carried out on the new filename. Next, do_rename checks that the two directories are located in the same filesystem, and the latter is not mounted in read mode only. The quotas operation initialise associated with the new parent directory is called in order to load the quotas descriptors. Finally, do_rename calls the operation rename associated with the former parent directory to perform the changing of name.

6.6.3.3 *Management of file attributes*

The system calls enabling file attributes to be modified are implemented in the source file *fs/open.c*. Because of their great similarity, only the calls *chmod* and *fchown* are described in detail here.

The function sys_chmod implements the primitive *chmod*. It calls the function namei to find the inode to be modified, then tests to see if it is possible to modify this inode, in other words it checks that the corresponding filesystem has not been mounted in read mode only, and that the inode is not immutable[2] . It then calls the function notify_change by indicating to it that the mode and date of the previous modification to the inode should be changed.

The function sys_fchown, which implements the primitive *fchown* is a bit more complex, since it carries out additional checks. It first of all obtains the inode to be modified by following the pointer reference contained in the open file descriptor. It then checks that the inode may be changed, and initialises the variable newattr, of structure type iattr, containing the new user and group identifiers. If the owner has changed, the mode is updated in newattr in order to overwrite the *setuid* bit; similarly, if the group is changed, the mode is updated in order to overwrite the *setgid* bit. If the quotas operations are associated with an inode, the operation transfer is called in order to take into account the change of owner and group, then the change is implemented by calling the function notify_change.

---

[2] An immutable inode can never be modified.

The source file *fs/stat.c* contains the implementation of the primitives *stat, lstat,* and *fstat.* The functions that implement the latter establish the inode of the file concerned, then return the information that they contain in the buffer whose address is passed as a parameter. The functions **cp_old_stat** and **cp_new_stat** make a copy of the information.

6.6.3.4 File inputs/outputs
The I/O primitives are implemented in several source files:

- *fs/namei.c* contains the function **open_namei,** which contains most of the code of the call *open;*
- *fs/open.c* contains the functions **sys_open** and **sys_close** which implement the primitives *open* and *close;*
- *fs/read_write.c* contains the functions **sys_lseek, sys_llseek, sys_read, sys_write, sys_readv** and **sys_writev** which implement the primitives *lseek, llseek, read, write, readv,* and *writev.*

The function **sys_open** is very simple: it calls **getname** to obtain the name of the file to open, opens the file by calling the function **do_open,** then frees the filename by calling **putname.**

The function **do_open** carries out the file opening proper. It first establishes an open file descriptor, by calling the function **get_empty_filp,** and initialises it. It then calls the function **open_namei** to find the inode corresponding to the file, then it calls the function **get_write_access** to check that the file may be open for writing if the opening mode specifies it. The next stage consists of initialising the field **f_op** from operations on files specified by the inode, and by calling the operation **open** if it is defined. Finally, the address of the file descriptor is inserted into the open files table by the current process.

The function **open_namei** implements a large part of the system call *open.* It calls first of all **dir_namei** to find the inode of the parent directory. If the option **O_CREAT** is specified, the function **lookup** is called, and an error is returned if the file exists, and if the option **O_EXCL** is also specified, then the quotas operation **initialize** and the operation **create** associated with the directory inode, are called to create the file and to find the inode. If the option **O_CREAT** is not specified, the inode of the file is obtained by calling the operation **lookup** associated with the directory. The function **follow_link** is then called in order to follow an ensuing symbolic link, then tests of the conformance of the opening mode with respect to the inode are carried out, Finally, if the option **O_TRUNC** is specified, the file contents are deleted: write access is obtained by calling **get_write_access,** the function **locks_verify_locked** is used to check that no lock is assigned to the inode, the function **do_truncate** is called in order to release the file contents, and the write access is released by calling the function **put_write_access.** Finally, the file inode is returned to the caller.

The function **sys_close** is very simple: it verifies that the I/O descriptor number passed as a parameter is valid, then calls the function **close_fp** to carry out the file closure.

The function **close_fp** starts by finding the inode corresponding to the open file descriptor, it calls the function **locks_remove_locks** to delete the locks assigned to the inode, and it releases the file descriptor by calling **fput**.

The functions **sys_leek** and **sys_llseek** change the current position of a file. They first check that the file descriptor number is valid. If an operation **lseek** is associated with the file descriptor, it is then called, if not, the current position is changed directly by changing the value of the field **f_pos** of the file descriptor.

The function **sys_read** implements data reads from a file. It first of all obtains the file descriptor by calling **fget**, then it checks that the file opening mode allows reading, and that a read operation is associated with the file. If these tests are positive, the function **locks_verify_area** is called to verify that the section to be read is not locked. Then the buffer address provided by the calling process is validated by a call to **verify_area**, and the read operation is carried out by calling the operation **read** associated with the file. Finallly, the file descriptor is released by calling **fput**.

The function **sys_write** is very similar to **sys_read**, except that it carries out a data write operation instead of a read. The main difference is that **sys_write** overwrites the *setuid* and *setgid* bits of the inode, if the data is written by a process that does not have superuser permissions.

The primitives *readv* and *writev* are implemented by the function **do_readv_writev**, and the functions **sys_readv** and **sys_writev** solely carry out tests of the validity of the I/O descriptor number by calling **do_readv_writev** to carry out the I/O. The function **do_readv_writev** first checks its arguments by validating the buffer vector which is passed to it. It then looks for the existence of locks in the section of the file concerned by calling **locks_verify_area**, it then performs a data read or write loop, using buffers specified in the vector passed as a parameter, by calling the operation **read** or **write** associated with the file descriptor.

6.6.3.5 *Reading a directory*
The source file *fs/readdir.c* contains the functions **old_readdir** and **sys_getdents** which implement the primitives *readdir* and *getdents* for reading directory entries.

These two functions are very similar: they verify the validity of the I/O descriptor number, use the function **verify_area** to validate the buffer address passed as a parameter, and call the operation **readdir** associated with the file descriptor. The difference between the two functions rests on the parameter **filldir**, which is passed to the operation **readdir**: old_readdir specifies **fillonedir**, which copies a single directory entry in the buffer, whilst **sys_getdents** specifies **filldir**, which copies directory entries into the buffer until it is full.

6.6.3.6 *Management of locks*
Calls for managing locks associated with files are implemented in the source file *fs/locks.c*. Several functions are provided there:

- **flock_lock_file**: this function creates a lock for an entire file. It scans the list of locks assigned to the corresponding inode, and checks whether a lock already exists. If it does, the value 0 is returned. If a lock of a different type exists, it is deleted by calling **locks_delete_lock**, and a new lock descriptor is then allocated by **locks_alloc_lock**. A look-up loop of lock descriptors associated with the inode is carried out: if a conflict arises between the existing lock and the new one, the calling process is put in waiting mode for the first lock to be deleted. When all the conflicts have been resolved, or if there are no conflicts, the new descriptor is inserted in the list of locks by **locks_insert_lock**.
- **posix_lock_file**: this function creates a lock assigned to part of a file. It scans the list of locks assigned to the corresponding inode, and checks for conflicts and risks of blockage between processes. In the case of such a blockage, the calling process is suspended, whilst waiting for the deletion of the existing lock. After this check, the list of locks assigned to the corresponding inode is again scanned to see if the new lock can be amalgamated with the existing lock, by comparing each lock installed by the current process with the new lock:
    - If the two locks are of the same type, if they have a common part, or if they are adjacent, they are combined into a single lock. The existing lock is deleted by **locks_delete_lock**, and the new descriptor is modified in order to include the zone corresponding to the former lock.
    - If the two locks are of different types, and if the new one includes the former one, the processes waiting on the latter are re-awoken, and the former lock is deleted.
    - If the two locks are of different types, and if the former one includes the new one, the former one is split into two: one part is placed in front of the new lock, and one part after it.
    - Finally, if the two locks are of different types, and if they have a common part, the coordinates of the former lock are modified.

At each change of existing locks, the waiting processes are awoken, since the modification of a lock may authorise them to continue execution.

- **sys_lock**: this function implements the primitive *flock*. It checks the validity of its parameters, and then calls **flock_lock_file** to create a lock.
- **fcntl_getlk**: this function implements the processing of the request **F_GETLK** of the primitive *fcntl*. It first checks the validity of its parameters, then carries out a look-up loop of the lock list associated with the inode. For each existing lock, it calls **posix_locks_conflict** in order to see if the specified lock could be a source of conflict. If it could, the descriptor of the existing lock is returned.
- **fcntl_setlk**: this function processes the requests **F_SETLK** and **F_SETLKW** of the primitive *fcntl*. It first checks the validity of its parameters, creates a lock descriptor by calling **posix_make_lock**, and then calls **posix_lock_file** to associate the lock with the file.

6.6.3.7 *Management of buffer cache*

The system calls linked to *buffer cache* are implemented in the source file *fs/buffer.c*. The processing of re-writes of buffers is split into several functions:

- **sync_dev**: this function re-writes blocks which are associated with a device. To trigger the re-writes, it calls in turn **sync_buffers**, **sync_supers**, **sync_inodes**, and **sync_buffers** to process again the buffers that have been changed by **sync_inodes** and **sync_dquots**.
- **fsync_dev**: this function is similar to **sync_dev**, but it puts itself into wait mode waiting for all the modified buffers to be re-written. It therefore does not finish execution until all the modified buffers have been re-written to disk.
- **sys_sync**: this function implements the system call *sync*. It calls **fsync_dev** by specifying 0 as the device number in order that the blocks belonging to all the devices will be re-written.
- **sys_fsync**: this function implements the system call *fsync*. It checks the validity of the I/O descriptor number which is passed to it as a parameter, then calls the operation **fsync** associated with the file descriptor, if it exists.
- **sys_fdatasync**: this function implements the system call *fdatasync*. It is processing is identical to that of **sys_fsync**.

6.6.3.8 *Management of filesystems*

The system calls for managing filesystem are implemented in the source file *fs/super.c*. The functions defined are as follows:

- **sys_fsys**: this function implements the primitive *sysfs*. According to the value of the parameter **option**, it calls **fs_index**, **fs_name**, or **fs_maxindex**.
- **read_super**: this internal function is called to read and to initialise the superblock of a filesystem to be mounted. It finds the filesystem type descriptor by calling **get_fs_type**, allocates a superblock descriptor in the table **super_blocks**, initialises it, then calls the function **read_super** associated with the filesystem type specified in order to read the superblock from disk.
- **do_umount**: this function is called to unmount a filesystem.

  If the specified filesystem is the root filesystem, it de-activates the quotas by calling **quota_off**, it calls **fsync_dev** to re-write modified blocks, and then changes the mounting options by calling **remount_sb** in order to make the filesystem accessible in read mode only.

  If this is not the case, the quotas are de-activated by calling **quota_off**, then the function **fs_may_umount** is called to check that it is possible to unmount the filesystem. The inodes corresponding to the root directory and to the mounting point are released by calling **iput**. If the superblock has been changed, it is re-written to disk by calling the operation **write_super**. Finally, the function **put_super** is called in order to free the superblock, and the corresponding mounted filesystem descriptor is released by a call to **remove_vfsmnt**.

- **sys_umount**: this function implements the system call *umount*. It first checks that the calling process has superuser permissions, then it converts the specified name into a device number. To do this, it converts the name into an inode by calling **namei**, then it checks the type of inode: if it is a special file, it represents the device containing the filesystem, if not it represents the mounting point.

  Once the number of the device has been obtained, the function **do_umount** is called to unmount the filesystem.

- **do_umount**: this function is called to mount a filesystem. It first of all checks the validity of the mounting options, then converts the name of the mounting point into an inode by calling **namei**. It then carries out validity checks on the inode: it must not be a mounting point that has already been used, and must correspond to a directory. The function **fs_may_mount** is also called to verify that the device may be mounted.

  When these tests have been carried out, the superblock of the filesystem is loaded into memory by calling **read_super**, a mounted filesystem descriptor is allocated by calling **add_vfsmnt**, and the descriptor is updated.

- **do_remount_sb**: this internal function is called to change the mounting options of a filesystem. It checks the validity of the new mounting options, then calls the operation **remount_fs** associated with the the filesystem if it exists. Finally, it updates the mounting options in the superblock descriptor and in the mounted filesystem descriptor.

- **do_remount**: this internal function is called to change the mounting options of a filesystem. It converts the name of the mounting point specified into an inode by calling **namei**, then it calls **do_remount_sb** to change the mounting options.

- **copy_mount_options**: this internal function copies the mounting options (parameter **data** from the system call *mount*) from the address space of the current process to the address space of the kernel.

- **sys_mount**: this function implements the system call *mount*. It first checks that the calling process has user permissions. If the option **MS_REMOUNT** is specified, the function **do_remount** is called to change the mounting options.

  In the case where **MS_REMOUNT** is not specified, the descriptor of the filesystem type is found by calling **get_fs_type**. If this type requires a device, the device name is converted into an inode by calling **namei**, validity checks are carried out on the inode, then the file operation open is called in order to initialise the device. In the opposite case, a 'dummy' device identifier is obtained by calling the function **get_unnamed_dev**.

Finally, **sys_mount** copies the mounting options into the address space of the kernel by calling **copy_mount_options**, then it calls **do_mount** to proceed with the mounting of the filesystem.

The system calls *statfs* and *fstatfs*, which enable information on a filesystem to be obtained, are implemented in the source file *fs/open.c* by the functions **sys_statfs** and **sys_fstatfs**. These two functions convert their first parameter into an inode, either by calling the function **namei**, or by following the reference to the specified I/O descriptor, then they verify that an operation **statfs** is associated with the filesystem containing the inode, and return the result of this operation.

6.6.3.9 Handling input/output descriptors
The I/O descriptor handling primitives *dup*, *dup2* and *fcntl* are implemented in the fource file *fs/fcntl.c*. The functions defined are as follows:

- **dupfd**: this function duplicates an I/O descriptor. It first of all checks the validity of the descriptor number which is passed to it as a parameter, looks for an unused descriptor, then copies the information from the first descriptor. Finally, it increments the utilisation count of the corresponding file descriptor.
- **sys_dup2**: this function implements the system call *dup2*. It first of all checks the validity of the I/O descriptor number, closes it, if it is open, by calling the function **sys_close**, then calls **dupfd** to duplicate the descriptor, by stipulating the descriptor number to be used.
- **sys_dup**: this function implements the system call *dup*. It first of all checks the validity of the specified I/O descriptor number, and carries out different operations according to the value of the parameter **cmd** which is passed to it:

  - **F_DUPFD**: it calls **dupfd** to duplicate the I/O descriptor;
  - **F_GETFD**: it returns the bit of the field **close_on_exec** corresponding to the descriptor;
  - **F_SETFD**: it sets the bit of the field **close_on_exec** corresponding to the descriptor;
  - **F_GETFL**: it returns the field **f_flags** of the file descriptor;
  - **F_SETFL**: it calls the operation **fasync** associated with the file if the flag **FASYNC** is changed, then it changes the value of the field **f_flags** of the file descriptor;
  - **F_GETLK**: it calls **fcntl_getlk**;
  - **F_SETLK**: it calls **fcntl_setlk**;
  - **F_SETLKW**: it calls **fcntl_setlk**.

6.6.3.10 Descriptor inheritance
When a new process is created by the system call *fork*, the context of the parent process is copied. This context includes file descriptors. The functions **copy_fs** and **copy_files**, defined in the source file *kernel/fork.c*, perform this duplication. They are described in chapter 4, section 4.6.2.

If a process clone is created, and the cloning options include **CLONE_FS**, the function **copy_fs** increments the number of descriptor references pointed to by the field **fs** of the current process descriptor. If not, it allocates a descriptor by calling **kmalloc,** recopies to it the contents of the desciptor associated with the parent process, then increments the number of references of the inodes representing root and current directories.

If a process clone is created, and the cloning options include **CLONE_FILES**, the function **copy_files** increments the number of references in the open files table descriptors, pointed to by the field **files** of the current process descriptor. If not, it allocates a table of descriptors of open files by calling **kmalloc**, recopies to it the contents of the desciptors of open files of the parent process. The number of references of each reference recopied is incremented.

When a process is terminated, its context is released. The functions **__exit_fs, close_files,** and **__exit_files,** defined in the source file *kernel/exit.c,* carry out this release.

The function **__exit_fs** decrement the number descriptor references pointed to by the field **fs** of the descriptor of the specified process. If this number becomes zero, the function **iput** is called to free the root and current directories associated with the process (fields **root** and **pwd**), then the descriptor is disallocated by calling the function **kfree.**

The function **close_files** closes the files opened by a process. It performs a loop in the table of file descriptors opened by the process and calls the function **close_fp** for each open file. The function **__exit_files** decrements the number of references of the table of descriptors of open files, pointed to by the field **files** of the process descriptor. If this number becomes zero, the function **close_files** is called to close all open files, then the table of descriptors is released by a call to **kfree.**

6.6.3.11 *Changing directory*
The system calls for changing directories *chdir, fchdir,* and *chroot,* are implemented in the source file *fs/open.c.* These primitives find the inode of the specified directory, either by calling the function **namei,** or by removing the reference to the I/O descriptor passed as a parameter, they then record this inode in the current process descriptor.

The address of the current directory inode descriptor is stored in the field **current->fs->pwd,** whilst the address of the root directory inode descriptor is stored in **current->fs->root.**

6.6.3.12 *Management of disk quotas*
As with the internal management functions and the quotas operations, the system call *quotactl* is implemented in the source file *fs/dquot.c.* The processing of this primitive is composed of several functions:

- **set_dqblk**: this function processes the options **Q_SETQUOTA, Q_SETUSE,** and **Q_SETQLIM**. It first calls the function **dqget** to find the quota descriptor concerned, changes its contents, marks it as changed, then frees it by calling **dqput**.

- **get_quota**: this function implements the option **Q_GETQUOTA**. It obtains the quota descriptor concerned by calling **dqget**, copies the information that it contains into the address space of the calling process using **memcpy_tofs**, then frees the descriptor by calling **dqput**.

- **get_stats**: this function implements the option **Q_GETQUOTA**. It copies the contents of the variable **dqstats** into the address space of the process by using **memcpy_tofs**.

- **add_dquot_ref**: this function, defined in the source file *fs/file_table.c*, is called when filesystem quotas are activated. It scans the list of open file descriptors, and, for each file open in write mode in the specified filesystem, it calls the operation **initialize**.

- **reset_dquot_ref**: this function, defined in the source file *fs/file_table.c*, is called when filesystem quotas are de-activated. It scans the list of open file descriptors, and, for each file open in write mode in the specified filesystem, it assigns the value **NODQUOT** to the field **i_dquot** of the associated inode, and lowers the flag **S_WRITE** of the field **i_flags** in order to indicate that the inode no longer has an associated quota descriptor.

- **quota_off**: this function implements the option **Q_QUOTAOFF**. It scans the mounted file descriptor by calling **lookup_vfsmnt**, and sets to **NULL** the field **dq_op** of the associated superblock descriptor. The functions **reset_dquot_ref** and **invalidate_dquots** are then called to free the descriptors associated with the filesystem. Finally, the quota definition file is closed by a call to **close_fp**.

- **quota_on**: this function implements the option **Q_QUOTAON**. It scans the mounted file descriptor by calling **lookup_vfsmnt**, and checks that the quotas are not already activated on the filesystem. If this is the case, the error **EBUSY** is returned. **quota_on** then simulates the system call *open* on the quota definition file: **open_namei** is called to find the file inode, then an open file descriptor, obtained by calling **get_empty_filp**, is initialised. The file is then opened by calling the file operation **open**, and the file descriptor is stored in the mounted filesystem descriptor. Finally, the function **add_dquot_ref** is called to take into account the quotas for all the file descriptors opened from this filesystem.

- **sys_quotactl**: this function implements the primitive *quotactl*. According to the value of its parameters, it calls the function **quota_on**, **quota_off**, **get_quota**, **sync_quotas**, **get_stats**, or **set_dqblk**.

6.6.4 Filesystems supported

Linux was originally developed under Minix [Tanenbaum 1987], and the first versions of the system only supported this filesystem, which has significant limitations: size limited to 64Mbytes, filenames limited to 14 characters. In order to remove these limitations, several other types of filesystem have been developed:

- *Extended Filesystem*, which expanded the potential of the Minix filesystem, but allowed only mediocre performance;
- *Xia Filesystem*, strongly based on the Minix filesystem, but which extended the possibilities and offered respectable performance;
- *Second Extended Filesystem* [Card *et al.* 1994], which extended the possibilities and allowed very good performance. This filesystem was inspired by the present version in BSD Unix [McKusick et al. 1984}, but has numerous original extensions.

The general characteristics of these filesystems are tabulated below:

	Minix	Ext FS	Ext2 FS	Xia FS
Maximum size	64Mbytes	2Gbytes	4Tbytes	2Gbytes
Maximum file size	64Mbytes	2Gbytes	2Gbytes	64Mbytes
Maximum filename size	14c	255c	255c	248c
Support for three dates	No	No	Yes	Yes
Extension possible	No	No	Yes	No
Variable block size	No	No	Yes	No
Maintained	Yes	No	Yes	No

In addition to these native filesystems, Linux includes support of filesystems offering some capability with other operating systems. This includes MS/DOS, Windows 95, OS/2, Unix System V, BSD Unix, support of the NFS (*Networked Filesystem*)–which enables files to be shared on a network, and support for a type of system of particular files, called */proc*, which allows access to data maintained by the kernel.

In the rest of this chapter, the structure and implementation of the filesystems Ext2 and*/proc* are detailed.

6.6.5 Implementation of the filesystem Ext2

6.6.5.1 *Characteristics of Ext 2*
The filesystem Ext2 provides standard functionality. It supports Unix filesystems (regular files, directories, special files, symbolic links) and offers some advanced functionality:

- attributes can be associated with files to modify the behaviour of the kernel: recognised attributes are the following:

  - protected deletion: when the file is deleted, its contents are overwritten beforehand with random data;
  - *undelete*: when the file is deleted, it is automatically saved in order to be able to restore it later (this is not yet implemented);
  - automatic compression: reading and writing of data to a file brings about a compression on the fly (this is not yet implemented in the standard kernel);

- synchronous writing: any changes to the file is written synchronously to disk;
- clamped: the file can neither by modified, nor deleted;
- addition mode only: the file can only be modified by having been opened in addition mode, and may not be deleted.

- compatibility with the semantics of Unix system V Release 4 or BSD: a mounting option allows the group associated with new files to be chosen: the BSD semantics specifies that the group inherits from the parent, whilst SVR4 uses the number of the primary group of the calling process;
- 'rapid' symbolic links: certain symbolic links do not use data blocks: the target filename is contained directly in the inode on disk, which allows disk space to be economised and the resolution of links to be speeded up, avoiding reading of a block;
- the state of each filesystem is memorised: when the filesystem is mounted, it is marked invalid until it is unmounted. The structure checker, *e2fsck*, uses this state to speed up checks when these are not necessary;
- a mounting counter and a maximum delay between two checks can be used to force the execution of *e2fsck*;
- the behaviour of the management code may be adapted in the event of an error: it can display an error message, 'remount' the filesystem in read mode only in order to avoid corruption of the data, or to avoid confusing the system.

In addition, Ext2 includes numerous optimisations. When reading data, anticipated reads are carried out. This means that the management code requires reading not only the block requested, but also other consecutive blocks. This enables memory blocks that will be used in the following I/O to be loaded into memory. This mechanism is also used when directory entries are read, whether they are explicit (by the primitive *readdir*) or implicit (when resolving filenames in the inode operation **lookup**).

Allocations of blocks and of inodes are also optimised. Groups of blocks are used to regroup related inodes as well as their data blocks. A pre-allocation mechanism also allows consecutive blocks to be allocated files: when a block is allocated, up to 8 consecutive blocks are reserved. In this way, allocations of the following blocks is already achieved and the contents of files can generally be written in contiguous blocks, which speeds up reading them, especially when anticipated reading techniques are employed.

6.6.5.2 *Physical structure of an Ext2 filesystem*

A filesystem of the Ext2 type must exist on a physical medium (floppy disk, hard disk, ..), and the contents of this device is split logically into several parts, as shown in figure 6.7.

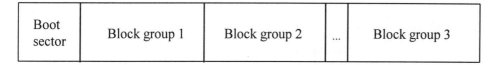

Boot sector	Block group 1	Block group 2	...	Block group 3

Figure 6.7:   Structure of the Ext2 filesystem.

The boot sector contains the machine code needed for loading the kernel when the system is started up, each of the groups of blocks are themselves composed of several elements, as shown in figure 6.8:

- a copy of the superblock: this structure contains the control information of the filesystem and is duplicated in each group of blocks in order to enable the corruption of the filesystem to be easily overcome;
- a table of descriptors: these contain the addresses of blocks containing vital information, such as the *bitmap* blocks and the table of inodes; they are also duplicated in each group of blocks;
- a *bitmap* block for the blocks: this block contains a table of bits: a bit indicating whether the inode is allocated (the bit is 1 in this case) or available (the bit is 0) is assigned to each inode of the group;
- a table of inodes: these blocks contain a part of a table of inodes of the filesystem;
- data blocks: the remainder of blocks in the group is used to store data contained in files and directories.

Super block	Descriptors	Bitmap blocks	Bitmap i-nodes	Table of i-nodes	Data block

Figure 6.8:   Structure of a block group.

A filesystem is organised into files and directories. A directory is a file of a particular type, containing entries. Each of the directory entries contains several fields:

- the number of an inode corresponding to a file;
- the size of an entry in bytes;
- the number of characters making up a filename;
- the name of a file.

Figure 6.9 represents a directory containing the entries '.', '..', 'file1', 'filename_long', and 'f2'.

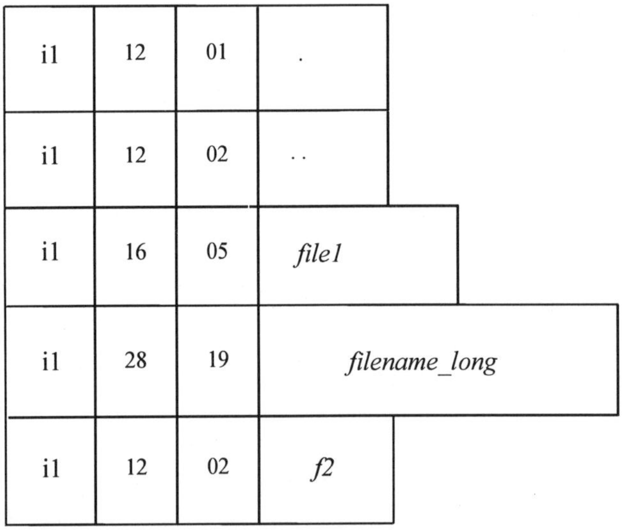

i1	12	01	.
i1	12	02	..
i1	16	05	*file1*
i1	28	19	*filename_long*
i1	12	02	*f2*

Figure 6.9: Directory structure.

6.6.5.3 *The superblock*

The superblock contains control information for the filesystem. It is located at the beginning of the filesystem on disk (offset by 1024) and it is duplicated in each block group in order to allow it to be restored in the event of corruption of the primary copy. The structure **ext2_super_block** defines the format of the superblock. It is defined in the file **<linux/ext2_fs.h>** and contains the following fields:

type	field	description
__u32	s_inodes_count	Total number of inodes
__u32	s_blocks_count	Total number of blocks
__u32	s_r_blocks_count	Number of blocks reserved for the superuser
__u32	s_free_blocks_count	Number of free blocks
__u32	s_free_inodes_count	Number of free inodes
__u32	s_first_data_block	Number of the first data block
__u32	s_log_block_size	Logical block size
__u32	s_blocks_per_group	Number of blocks per group

Continuation of the list of fields defining the structure **ext2_super_block**		
type	*field*	*description*
__u32	s_frags_per_group	Number of fragments per group
__u32	s_inodes_per_group	Number of inodes per group
__u32	s_mtime	Date of the last filesystem mounting
__u32	s_wtime	Date of the last write to a superblock
__u16	s_mnt_count	Number of filesystem mountings
__s16	s_max_mnt_count	Maximum number of filesystem mountings
__u16	s_magic	Filesystem signature
__u16	s_state	State of filesystem
__u16	s_errors	Behaviour of the filesystem in the event of errors
__u16	s_minor_rev_level	Revision number
__u32	s_lastcheck	Date of the last filesystem check
__u32	s_checkinterval	Maximum time between two checks
__u32	s_creator_os	Identifier of the operating system under which the filesystem has been created
__u16	s_def_resuid	Identifier of the user able to utilise blocks reserved for the superuser by default
__u16	s_def_resgid	Identifier of the group able to utilise blocks reserved for the superuser by default

6.6.5.4 *Descriptors of block groups*

Each group of blocks contains a copy of the superblock as well as a copy of the group descriptors. These descriptors contain the coordinates of control structures present in each group.

The structure **ext2_group_desc** defines the group descriptor format. It is defined in the file **<linux/ext2_fs.h>** and contains the following fields:

type	*field*	*description*
__u32	bg_block_bitmap	Block address of bitmap for blocks in this group
__u32	bg_inode_bitmap	Block address of bitmap for inodes in this group
__u32	bg_inode_table	Address of the first block of the inode table in this group
__u16	bg_free_blocks_count	Number of free blocks in this group

Continuation of the list of fields defining the structure **ext2_group_desc**		
type	*field*	*description*
__u16	bg_free_inodes_count	Number of free inodes in this group
__u16	bg_used_dirs_count	Number of directories allocated in this group
__u16	bg_pad	Unused
__u32[3]	bg_reserved	Field reserved for future extension

6.6.5.5 inode structure

The table of inodes is composed of several parts: each part is contained in a group of blocks. This enables particular allocation strategies to be used: when a block needs to be allocated, the kernel tries to allocate it in the same block group as its inode so as to minimise the displacement of the reading head when the file is read.

The structure **ext2_inode** defines the format of an inode. It is declared in the file **<linux/ext2_fs.h>** and contains the following fields:

type	*field*	*description*
__u16	i_mode	inode mode
__u16	i_uid	Owner identifier
__u32	i_size	File size in bytes
__u32	i_atime	Date of the last file access
__u32	i_ctime	Date of the last inode modification
__u32	i_mtime	Date of the last modification of the file contents
__u32	i_dtime	Date of file deletion
__u16	i_gid	Group identifier
__u16	i_links_count	Number of links assigned to the inode
__u32	i_blocks	Number of blocks of 512 bytes allocated to the inode
__u32	i_flags	Attributes associated with the file
__u32	i_reserved1	Field reserved for future extension
__u32 [EXT2_N_BLOCKS]	i_block	Addresses of data blocks allocated to the inode
__u32	i_version	Version number assigned to the inode

Continuation of the list of fields defining the structure **ext2_inode**		
type	*field*	*description*
__u32	i_file_acl	Address of the access control list descriptor associated with the file (this is not implemented in Linux 2.0)
__u32	i_dir_acl	Address of the access control list descriptor associated with a directory (this is not implemented in Linux 2.0)
__u16	i_pad1	unused
__u32[2]	i_reserved2	Field reserved for future extension

The field **i_block** contains the addresses of data blocks assigned to the inode. This table is structured following the classic Unix method [Bach 1993, McKusick *et al.* 1996, Goodheart and Cox 1994, Vahalia 1996]:

- the twelve (value of the constant **EXT2_NDIR_BLOCKS**) first elements of the table contain the addresses of data blocks;
- the sector **EXT2_IND_BLOCK** contains the address of a block which itself contains the address of the following data blocks;
- the sector **EXT2_DIND_BLOCK** contains the address of a block which contains the address of blocks containing the address of the following data blocks;
- the sector **EXT2_TIND_BLOCK** contains the address of a block which contains the address of blocks themselves pointing to indirect blocks.

This addressing mechanism is illustrated in figure 6.10 (which illustrates just two indirect levels for clarity).

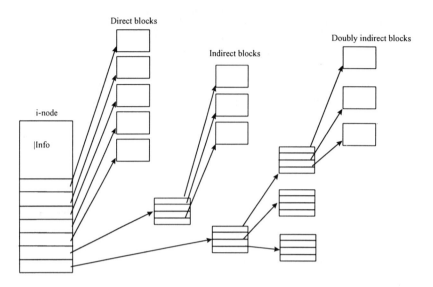

Figure 6.10: Pointers contained in an inode.

6.6.5.6 Directory Entry

Directories are composed of blocks of data, like regular files. However, these blocks are structured logically in a series of entries. The structure **ext2_dir_entry** defines the format of these entries. It is declared in the file **<linux/ext2_fs.h>** and contains the following fields:

type	field	description
__u32	inode	File inode number
__u16	rec_len	Group identifier
__u16	name_len	Length of name
char[ ]	name	Filename

6.6.5.7 Operations linked to filesystems

Operations linked to the superblock of an Ext2 filesystem are implemented in the source file *fs/ext2/super.c*. The variable **ext2_sops** contains the pointers to the functions carrying out these operations.

The functions **ext2_error**, **ext2_panic**, and **ext2_warning** are called by the management code of the filesystem when an error is detected. They display an error message or a warning containing the identification of the device; concerned and the internal function which detected the error by calling the function **printk**.

Several internal functions are used to mount a filesystem:

- **parse_options**: this function analyses the specified mounting options. It analyses the character string passed as a parameter and initialises the mounting options.
- **ext2_setup_super**: this function initialises the superblock descriptor from the filesystem superblock read from disk.
- **ext2_check_descriptors**: this function checks the validity of block group descriptors read from disk. For each descriptor, it checks that the *bitmap* blocks and the table of inodes are contained in the group.
- **ext2_commit_super**: this function is called to save the modifications performed on the superblock. It marks as modified the buffer containing the superblock, by calling **mark_buffer_dirty**. In this way, the contents of the buffer will be written to disk at the next save operation on the *buffer cache*.

The function **ext2_read_super** implements the filesystem operation **read_super**. It is called when the filesystem is mounted. It starts by analysing the mounting options by calling **parse_options**, then reads the superblock from disk, and checks its validity. It next initialises the superblock descriptor. Then, a table of pointers is allocated for the block group descriptors, each descriptor is loaded into a buffer, by calling the function **bread**, and the validity of these descriptors is verified by **ext2_check_descriptors**. Finally, the inode of the root of the file is read from memory by calling **iget**, and **ext2_setup_super** is called to terminate initialisation of the superblock descriptor.

The function **ext2_write_super** implements the operation **write_super**. It updates the fields **s_mtime** (date of the last modification of the superblock) and **s_state** to indicate that the filesystem is mounted, then it calls the function **ext2_commit_super**.

The function **ext2_remount** implements the filesystem operation **remount_fs**. It calls **parse_options** to decode the new mounting options, updates the superblock descriptor, then calls **ext2_commit_super** to indicate that the superblock has changed.

The function **ext2_put_super** implements the filesystem operation **put_super**. It is called when the filesystem is unmounted. It frees the buffers containing the filesystem descriptors, by calling the function **brelse**, then releases the pointers to these buffers by calling **kfree_s**. Next it frees the buffers assigned to the *bitmap* blocks loaded into memory. Finally, it frees the buffer containing the filesystem superblock.

Finally, the function **ext2_statfs** implements the filesystem operation **statfs**: it copies the filesystem utilisation statistics from the superblock descriptor in the variable passed as a parameter.

6.6.5.8 *Allocation and release of blocks and inodes*
The functions allocating or freeing blocks and inodes are implemented in the source files *fs/ext2/balloc.c* and *fs/ext2/ialloc.c*.

These modules define internal functions:

- **get_group_desc**: this function returns the descriptor corresponding to a group of blocks.
- **read_block_bitmap, read_inode_bitmap**: these functions load a *bitmap* block into memory.
- **load_block_bitmap, load_inode_bitmap**: these functions are called to identify a *bitmap* block. They maintain a LRU cache of loaded blocks in the tables **s_block_bitmap** and **s_inode_bitmap**, and call **read_block_bitmap** and **read_inode_bitmap** to load blocks into memory.

The release of blocks is carried out by the function **ext2_free_blocks**. This function verifies that the numbers of blocks to free are valid, then it loads the descriptor and the *bitmap* block of the group concerned by calling **get_group_desc** and **load_block_bitmap**. Then, the bit corresponding to each block to be released is reset to 0 in the *bitmap* block, the quota operation **free_block** associated with the inode is called for each block, and the number of free blocks is incremented. Finally, the superblock and the *bitmap* block are marked as modified by calling **mark_buffer_dirty**.

The function **ext2_new_block** implements the block allocation. This function receives the parameter **goal** which specifies the block number to allocate if it is available. After loading the *bitmap* block, **ext2_new_block** checks to see if the block specified is available. If it is, it is chosen. If not, a search for a free block is conducted in the neighbourhood of this block and, if the look-up fails, an all zeros byte is looked for in the *bitmap* block of the group, that is, 8 consecutive free blocks are sought, or, by default, a single available block. At the end of all these different tests, if no available block has been found, **ext2_new_block** scans all the block groups to find an available block. When a block is found, the quota operation **alloc_block** is called in order to verify that the calling process may allocate the block, then the cooresponding bit in *bitmap* block is set to 1, to indicate that the block is no longer available.

After allocating a block, **ext2_new_block** tries to proceed to a preallocation of consecutive blocks. It carries out an allocation loop on the following blocks by calling the quota operation **alloc_block** and by setting the corresponding bits in the *bitmap* block to 1. Finally, the buffer is allocated for the block by calling **getblk**, its contents are set to 0, and the block group descriptor and superblock information are updated.

The release of an inode is carried out by the function **ext2_free_inode**. This function checks the validity of the inode to be freed, then it loads the descriptor and the *bitmap* block of the group concerned by calling **get_group_desc** and **load_block_bitmap**. Next, the bit corresponding to the inode to be released is reset to 0 in the *bitmap* block, the number of free inodes is incremented, and the quota operation **free_inode** associated with the inode is called. Finally, the superblock and the *bitmap* block are marked as modified by calling **mark_buffer_dirty**.

The function **ext2_new_inode** implements the inode allocation. The allocation algorithm depends on the type of inode:

- If a directory needs to be allocated, a search is carried out to choose the block group having a greater than average number of free inodes, and in which the number of free blocks is a maximum.
- In other cases, **ext2_new_inode** attempts to utilise the group of groups containing the inode of the parent directory. If it is not possible, a quadratic search of a group containing free inodes is carried out. If this search fails, a linear search, group by group, is finally employed.

Once the group of blocks to be used has been chosen, the *bitmap* block is loaded into memory by calling **load_inode_bitmap**, and the first bit having a value 0, corresponding to an unused inode, is searched for: it is set to 1, and the number of available inodes is decremented. The inode descriptor is next initialised and it is inserted into the hash lists by a call to **insert_inode_hash**. Finally, if the quota operations are associated with the filesystem superblock, the operations **initialize** and **alloc_inode** are called to take account of the allocation.

6.6.5.9 Management of inodes on disk

The source file *fs/ext2/inode.c* contains management functions for inodes on disk. The inode operation bmap takes in hand several functions:

- **inode_bmap**: this function returns the address of a block contained in an inode.
- **block_bmap**: this function returns the address of a block obtained from a table contained in a data block. It is used to access indirect block addresses.
- **ext2_bmap**: this function implements the operation **bmap**. It obtains the address of the specified data block by calling **inode_bmap** and **block_bmap**.

Several functions are linked to the allocation of blocks:

- **ext2_diskard_prealloc**: this function is called when a file is closed. It releases blocks pre-allocated by **ext2_new_block** but which have not yet been used by calling **ext2_free_blocks**.
- **ext2_alloc_block**: this function is called to allocate a block. It manages the pre-allocation: if a block has been pre-allocated, and if it corresponds to the block specified by the parameter goal, it is used, if not the pre-allocated blocks are freed by calling **ext2_diskard_prealloc**, and **ext2_new_block** is called in order to allocate a block.
- **inode_getblk**: this function is called to find a buffer containing a block whose address is stored in the inode. It utilises **getblk** to obtain the buffer, if the block is already allocated. If the block is not allocated, and if the calling function specified a block creation, the function **ext2_alloc_block** is called to obtain a new block.

- **block_getblk**: this function is called to find a buffer containing a block whose address is stored in a table contained in a data block. It is very similar to **inode_getblk**.
- **ext2_getblk**: this function is called to find a buffer assigned to an inode. In a manner similar to **ext2_bmap**, it calls **inode_getblk** and **block_getblk** to perform the various remote calls.
- **block_getcluster**: this function tries to create a *cluster* based on several direct inode blocks. It checks that the blocks are contiguous on the disk, and then calls **generate_cluster** to create the *cluster*.
- **ext2_getcluster**: this function tries to create a *cluster* based on several inode blocks. It performs very similar processing to that in **ext2_getblk**, except that it calls **block_getcluster** instead of **block_getblk**.
- **ext2_bread**: this function is called to read a data block assigned to an inode. It calls **ext2_getblk** to find a corresponding memory block, then reads the contents of the block by calling **ll_rw_block** if the buffer contents are not updated.

The function **ext2_read_inode** implements the filesystem operation **read_inode**. It first checks the validity of the inode number to load into memory, then calculates the number of the group containing this inode, and reads the block of the corresponding inode table by calling the function **bread**. The contents of the inode on disk are then copied into the inode descriptor, and the field **i_op** (pointer to the operations linked to the inode) is initialised according to its type.

The function **ext2_update_inode** re-writes an inode to disk. It first checks the validity of the inode to be written, then calculates the number of the block group containing the inode, and it reads the corresponding inode table block by calling the function **bread**. The contents of the inode on disk is then modified in the buffer based on the inode descriptor and the buffer is marked as modified by calling **mark_buffer_dirty**. Finally, if the inode needs to be re-written immediately to disk, the function **ll_rw_block** is called to carry out the physical write operation.

The function **ext2_write_inode** implements the operation **write_inode**. It calls the function **ext2_update_inode** whilst specifying that re-writing the inode should not be carried out immediately. The function **ext2_sync_inode** performs the same process but it requests an immediate re-write when **ext2_update_inode** is called.

The function **ext2_put_inode** implements the filesystem operation **put_inode**. It frees the pre-allocated blocks by calling **ext2_diskard_prealloc**, then tests the number of links in order to find out if the file has been deleted. If so, the delection date of the inode is updated, the inode is re-written to disk by calling **ext2_update_inode**, the contents of the file is released by calling **ext2_truncate**, and finally **ext2_free_inode** is called to release the inode.

6.6.5.10 *Management of directories*
The source file *fs/ext2/dir.c* contains the directory management functions:

- **ext2_check_dir_entry**: this function is called to check the validity of a directory entry. If an error is detected, it displays a message by calling the function **ext2_error**.
- **ext2_readdir**: this function implements the operation **readdir**. It uses the function **ext2_bread** to read each block making up the directory, and implements a strategy of anticipated reading. Each block-read is split up into directory entries which are put into the buffer by using the pointer to the function **filldir** passed as a parameter[3]. **ext2_readdir** uses the version numbers assigned to open file descriptors and with the corresponding inode: if these numbers are different, this means that the directory has been changed (at least a file has been added or deleted), and a re-synchronisation loop is performed in order to place the current pointer position at the beginning of a valid entry.

Other directory mangement functions are also defined in the source file *fs/ext2/namei.c*:

- **ext2_match**: this internal function compares a specified file name with the name contained in a directory entry.
- **ext2_find_entry**: this function is called to search for an entry in a directory. It scans the directory contents, covering each block by calling **ext2_getblk**. A strategy of anticipated reading is followed. Each block is then divided down into directory entries and the function **ext2_match** is called for each entry in order to compare the name it contains with the name searched for. If the name is found, the address of the entry is returned.
- **ext2_lookup**: this function implements the function lookup. It first carries out a filename look-up in the name cache by calling **dcache_lookup**. If the name is found in the cache, the corresponding inode is read by calling **iget**, and is returned. If not, the name is looked for in the directory by calling the function **ext2_find_entry**, the result is added to the name cache by **dcache_add**, the inode is loaded into memory by calling **iget**, and it is returned.
- **ext2_add_entry**: this function is called to create a new entry in a directory. It first performs a directory look-up by reading each block with a call to **ext2_bread**, and by looking for a usable entry, that is, an available entry of sufficient size capable of being divided into two entries. Once a usable entry is found, it is initialised with the name of the specified file.
- **ext2_delete_entry**: this function is called to delete an entry in a directory. It frees the entry by:

    - setting to 0 the inode number of an entry if it is the first entry in a block;
    - merging this entry with the previous one if this is not the case.

---

[3] This parameter contains the addresses of functions **fillonedir** or **filldir**, defined in *fs/readdir.c*, as explained in section 6.3.5.

Numerous other functions, implementing operations on inodes, are defined in *fs/ext2/namei.c*: ext2_create, ext2_link, ext2_mkdir, ext2_mknod, ext2_rename, ext2_rmdir, ext2_symlink, and ext2_unlink. These functions are relatively simple, since they merely link calls from other internal functions, and their operation is not described in detail here.

6.6.5.11   File inputs/outputs

Only the file operation write is implemented explicitly. Reading of data is carried out by calling the function generic_file_read, (which is described in detail in chapter 8, section 8.6.8), because of its interactions with the mechanisms of memory management.

The function ext2_file_write, defined in the source file *fs/ext2/file.c*, implements the operation write. It checks its arguments, then performs a write loop: as long as there is data remaining to be written, it finds a buffer by calling ext2_getblk, recopies a part of the data to be written in this buffer, then marks the buffer as modified by calling mark_buffer_dirty. Once all the data has been written, the file descriptor and the inode are updated.

The function ext2_release_file implements the file operation release. It calls ext2_diskard_prealloc to free blocks pre-allocated by ext2_new_block at the time that the file was last closed.

6.6.6   Implementation of the filesystem */proc*

6.6.6.1   Description

The */proc* filesystem has particular features: it does not grant access to data stored on disk, but makes available, in the form of virtual files, certain information managed by the kernel.

The available files in the */proc* filesystem are the following:

- *cmdline*: arguments passed to the kernel when the system is started up;
- *cpuinfo*: description of processor(s) used;
- *devices*: list of device controllers included in the kernel;
- *dma*: list of *dma* channel used by device controllers;
- *filesystems*: list of filesystems supported by the kernel;
- *interrupts*: list of hard interrupts used by the device controllers;
- *ioports*: list of I/O ports used device controllers;
- *kcore*: memory allocated to the kernel;
- *kmsg*: last messages displayed by the kernel;
- *ksyms*: list of kernel symbols used by modules (see chapter 12, section 12.3.3);
- *loadavg*: system loading;
- *locks*: list of locks assigned to files;
- *meminfo*: process status of central memory;
- *modules*: list of modules loaded in the kernel;

- *mounts*: list of filesystems mounted;
- *pci*: list of devices connected on the PCI bus;
- *profile*: information on kernel *profiling*, used to determine the time spent executing each of the functions;
- *rtc*: information about the real-time clock;
- *stat*: various statistics on operations carried out by the kernel (processor time consumed, number of disk I/O, number of memory page loads, number of hard interrupts processed, number of context changes performed, date and time of system start up, total number of processes created);
- *smp*: information about multi-processor operations;
- *uptime*: time elapsed since system start up;
- *version*: kernel version;

In addition to these files, the directory */proc* contains several directories:

- *net*: files containing information on network protocols;
- *scsi*: files containing information on the control of SCSI devices;
- *sys*: files containing information linked to kernel variables managed by the primitive *sysctl* (see chapter 13, section 2.4);
- One directory per process existing in the system: the name of this directory is the process number, and the directory contains the following files:
    - *cmdline*: list of process arguments,
    - *cwd*: link to the current directory of the process;
    - *environ*: list of variables in the process environment;
    - *exe*: link to the binary file executed by the process;
    - *fd*: directory containing then links to files opened by the process;
    - *maps*: list of memory zones contained in the process address space;
    - *mem*: contents of the process address space;
    - *root*: link to the root directory of the process;
    - *stat, statm, status*: state of the process.
- *self*: link to the directory corresponding to the current process.

6.6.6.2 Entries of /proc
The entries in the directory */proc* (files or directories) are managed dynamically: a list of descriptors is maintained in the memory by the kernel, and has its contents scanned when accessed by */proc*.

The structure **proc_dir_entry**, defined in the file **<linux/proc_fs.h>**, represents the descriptor type. It contains the following fields:

type	*field*	*description*
unsigned short	**low_ino**	inode number assigned to an entry
unsigned short	**namelen**	Size of entry name
const char *	**name**	Entry name
mode_t	**mode**	Type of access permissions
nlink_t	**nlink**	Number of links
uid_t	**uid**	User owner identifier
gid_t	**gid**	Identifier of the group user
unsigned long	**size**	Size in bytes
struct inode_operations *	**ops**	Operations linked to the entry
int (*) (char *, char **, off_t, int, int)	**get_info**	Pointer to the function called for a read
void (*) (struct inode *)	**fill_inode**	Pointer to the function responsible for initialisation of the entry attributes (type, access permissions, user owner and group owner)
struct proc_dir_entry *	**next**	Pointer to the descriptor of the next entry
struct proc_dir_entry *	**parent**	Pointer to the descriptor of the parent directory
struct proc_dir_entry *	**subdir**	Pointer to the descriptor of the first directory entry
void *	**data**	Private data assigned to the entry

The numbers of inodes are allocated statically to the */proc* entries. The header file defined several types for this purpose:

- **root_directory_inos**: numbers of inodes assigned to the */proc* entries, in the range 1 and 127;
- **net_directory_inos**: numbers of inodes assigned to the */proc/net* entries, in the range 128 and 255;
- **scsi_directory_inos**: numbers of inodes assigned to the */proc/scsi* entries, in the range 256 to 511;

In addition, the constants **PROC_DYNAMIC_FIRST** and **PROC_NDYNAMIC** define the numbers of inodes capable of being allocated dynamically.

Inode numbers assigned to directory entries corresponding to processes are calculated from the basis of the process number. This number is offset by 16 bits to the left to generate the base number, and the type **pid_directory_inos** defines a number to be added to this base to obtain the inode number. For example, the inode number of the file *root* contained in the directory assigned to the process having a number p will be p*65536+6, since the constant **PROC_PID_ROOT** has the value 6.

6.6.6.3 Filesystem operations

Operations linked to the filesystem are implemented in the source file *fs/proc/root.c.*

The function **proc_get_inode** is loaded in order to initialise the contents of an inode descriptor: it calls **iget** to load the inode, then initialises certain of these fields from the corresponding entry descriptor. In this function, the address of the entry descriptor is saved in the field **generic_ip** of the inode descriptor in order to be able to access it when inode operations are executed.

The function **proc_read_super** is called when the */proc* filesystem is mounted. It initialises the file descriptor, then calls the function **proc_get_inode** to initialise the inode corresponding to the filesystem root.

The function **proc_put_super** is called when the filesystem is unmounted. It simply resets to zero the field **a_dev** of the descriptor concerned in order to indicate which filesystem is no longer mounted.

The function **proc_read_inode** is called to read the contents of the inode. It calculates a process number by offsetting the inode number by 16 bits to the right, then carries out a look-up of the corresponding process descriptor in the table **process.**

At the end of this look-up, three cases can arise:

1. the process number has not been found;
2. the inode number corresponds to a static entry in */proc*. The field **i_op** of the inode descriptor is then initialised with the address of inode operations specific to the file (for example, **proc_kmsg_inode_operations** for the file */proc/kmsg*);
3. the process number is found: the least significant 8 bits of the inode number are then used to determine which is the directory entry corresponding to the process. The field **i_op** of the inode descriptor is then initialised with the address of inode operations specific to the file (for example, **proc_mem_inode_operations** for the file *mem*).

6.6.6.4 *Directory management*

The source file *fs/proc/root.c* contains functions enabling the contents of directories to be managed.

The global variable **proc_root** contains the root directory of the filesystem.

The function **proc_register** records a new entry in a directory, and the function **proc_unregister** deletes an entry by deleting its descriptor from the list.

The function **proc_register-dynamic** dynamically attributes an inode number to a descriptor then records the corresponding entry in the list.

The initialisation if the list of files and directories located in */proc* is performed by **proc_root_init**. This function calls the function **proc_register** to record the entries contained in */proc*.

The function **proc_lookup** performs a directory scan. It searches the linked list of entries recorded in the directory and compares the specified name with the filename contained in each descriptor. **Proc_root_lookup** carries out a look-up for an entry name in the root directory. It calls **proc_lookup**, then tests its result. If **proc_lookup** has found the specified entry (therefore, if the name refers to a static entry recorded by a call to **proc_register**), the result is returned. In the opposite case, the specified name must represent a directory corresponding to a process. The name is converted to a process number, a look-up for the corresponding process is performed in the table **process**, and the corresponding inode number is built up from the process number.

The function **proc_readdir** is called to obtain a list of entries contained in a directory. It is based on the value of the field **f_pos** of the file descriptor corresponding to the directory: this field contains the entry index to return. **proc_readdir** scans the list of recorded entries in the directory, and calls the function specified by the parameter **filldir**, in order to place the entry names in the buffer provided by the user. The function **proc_root_readdir** implements the call *readdir* for each root directory. If its position in the directory is less than **FIRST_PROCESS_ENTRY**, it calls **proc_readdir** to find the names of recorded entries. Then it scans the table process, converts the process numbers into character strings, and stores them in the buffer provided by a call to the functon specified by the parameter **filldir**.

A single descriptor is used to refer to all directories corresponding to processes: the variable **proc_pid** defines the source file *fs/proc/base.c*. Its contents are initialised by the function **proc_base_init**, called by **proc_root_init**, This function calls **proc_register** to record the entries *cmdline, cwd, environ, exe, fd, maps, mem, root, stat, statm*, and *status*.

6.6.6.5 *Operations on inodes and on files*

The filesystem */proc* utilises pointers to inode and open file operations to distinguish the processing associated with entries. The majority of processes are implemented in the source file *fs/proc/array.c*.

The function **array_read** implements the file operation **read**. It first allocates a memory page, which will act as an intermediate buffer, by calling **__get_free_page**, then it obtains the entry descriptor assigned to an inode. It next calls the operation **get_info** associated with the entry, or the function **fill_array** if no operation is defined. Finally, it recopies the result returned in the buffer provided by the calling process.

The function **fill_array** is called to read the contents of a file, when the corresponding entry does not have a **get_info** operation. It calls **get_process_array** if the inode is contained in a directory corresponding to a process, or **get_root_array** if this not the case. These two functions check the inode number of the file, and call a function which is responsible for converting internal kernel data into a character string.

7

Input/output

System calls described

ioctl, mknod, select

7.1
CONCEPTS

Access to peripheral devices is achieved through special files. A special file appears in the tree structure in the same way as a normal file, but no disk space is allocated to it. Each special file has a corresponding device driver, whose code is integrated in the kernel.

Once a process has opened a special file, read and write requests are not transmitted to the file system but to the corresponding device driver. The latter carries out physical read and write operations on the device, generally in conjunction with its controller, when the process uses the system call **read** and **write**.

Two types of special files exist:

- special files in block mode: they correspond to peripheral devices structured in blocks, like disks, which are accessed by providing a read or write block number. The input/output are carried out via *buffer cache* functions;
- special files in character mode: they correspond to unstructured peripheral devices, like serial and parallel ports, on which data can be read or written byte by byte, generally in a sequential manner.

Each special file is characterised by three attributes:

- its type (block or character);
- its major number: this number identifies the driver controlling the device;

- its minor number: this number allows the driver to be aware of the physical device upon which it should act.

Special files are generally situated in the directory */dev*, an extract of which is reproduced in figure 7.1.

```
. . .
brw-r-----  1 root     disk    3,     0 Oct   3        1993 hda
brw-r-----  1 root     disk    3,     1 Oct   3        1993 hda1
brw-r-----  1 root     disk    3,     2 Oct   3        1993 hda2
brw-r-----  1 root     disk    3,     3 Oct   3        1993 hda3
brw-r-----  1 root     disk    3,     4 Oct   3        1993 hda4
brw-r-----  1 root     disk    3,     5 Oct   3        1993 hda5
brw-r-----  1 root     disk    3,     6 Oct   3        1993 hda6

. . .
crw--w--w-  1 card     users   4,     0 Oct   3        1993  tty0
crw--w----  1 card     tty     4,     1 May  16       12:53 tty1
crw--w--w-  1 card     wheel   4,     2 May  16       12:53 tty2
crw--w--w-  1 card     wheel   4,     3 May  16       12:53 tty3
crw--w--w-  1 card     wheel   4,     4 May  16       12:53 tty4
crw--w--w-  1 card     wheel   4,     5 May  16       12:53 tty5
. . .
```

Figure 7.1 List of special files in the directory /dev.

7.2 SYSTEM CALLS

7.2.1 System calls creation of a special file

The system call *mknod* enables a special file to be created. It syntax is as follows:

```
#include <sys/types.h>
#include <sys/stat.h>
#include <sys/sysmacros.h>
#include <sys/fcntl.h>
#include <sys/unistd.h>


int mknod (const char *pathname, mode_t mode, dev_t dev);
```

The parameter **pathname** specifies the filename to be created, **mode** indicates the authorisation and type of file to be created, and **dev** contains the device identifier corresponding to the special file. The file **<sys/stat.h>** defines the **usable** constants for the type of file:

constant	meaning
S_IFREG	Normal file
S_IFCHR	Special file in character mode
S_IFBLK	Special file in block mode
S_IFIFO	Named pipe (see chapter 10)

The device identifier is composed of its major and minor numbers. Several macro-instructions, defined in **<sys/sysmacros.h>**, enable this identifier to be manipulated:

macro-instruction	meaning
major	Returns the major number corresponding to the device identifier
minor	Returns the minor number corresponding to the device identifier
makedev	Returns the device identifier corresponding to a major number and a minor number

mknod returns the value 0 in the event of success, or −1 if there is an error. The possible errors are the following:

error	meaning
EACCES	The calling process does not have the necessary permissions to create the file specified by **pathname**
EEXIST	**pathname** specifies an existing filename
EINVAL	**mode** contains an invalid type
EFAULT	**pathname** contains an invalid address
ELOOP	A symbolic link loop has been encountered
ENAMETOOLONG	**pathname** specifies a filename which is too long
ENOMEM	The kernel has not been able to allocate memory for internal descriptors
ENOSPC	The filesystem is saturated
ENOTDIR	One of the components of **pathname**, used as a directory name, is not a directory
EPERM	Mode specifies a type different from **S_SIFIFO** and the calling process does not superuser permissions
EROFS	The filesystem is in read-mode only

7.2.2 Input and output in devices

Inputs and outputs to devices are carried out by the same primitives as those used to carry out data reads and writes on ordinary files. A peripheral device is opened by the primitive *open* by specifying the name of the special file. The kernel then returns an input/output descriptor corresponding to the device, and the calling process can access it by system calls *read, write,* and *lseek* if the device supports direct access). After use, the primitive *close* can be used to shut down the device.

7.2.3 Multiplexing inputs and outputs

When one or more devices are accessed, a process may put itself on hold waiting for data. The primitive *select* allows multiplexing of several input/outputs. The syntax is as follows:

```
#include <sys/time.h>
#include <sys/types.h>
#include <unistd.h>

int select (int n, fd_set *readfds, fd_set *writefds, fd_set *exceptfds,
struct timeval *timeout);
```

select puts the process on hold waiting for changed in several groups of descriptors:

- **readfds** contains the list of descriptors from which the calling process wishes to read data;
- **writefds** contains the list of descriptors in which the calling process wishes to write data;
- **exceptfds** contains the list of descriptors for which the current process wishes to be informed of special changes.

The parameter **n** should contain the highest input/output descriptor number present in one of the groups. The parameter **timeout** specifies the waiting delay. If it contains the value **NULL**, the calling process is suspended until a change concerning the descriptors arises.

Several macro-instructions are provided to manage the descriptor groups:

macro-instruction	*meaning*
FD_ZERO	Reset a group to zero
FD_CLR	Deletion of a descriptor in a group
FD_SET	Addition of a descriptor to a group
FD_ISSET	Test for the presence of a descriptor in a group

Upon returning from the call *select*, the descriptor groups are modified to flag the conditions detected, and the number of descriptors concerned is returned.

In the event of error, *select* returns the value −1 and **errno** takes one of the following values.

error	*meaning*
BADF	An incorrect input/output descriptor has been specified in one of the groups
EINTR	A signal has been received during the wait period
EINVAL	**n** contains a negative value
ENOMEME	The kernel has not been able to allocate memory to the internal descriptors

The following program uses the primitive *select* to group up a wait of five seconds for the keyboard entry of at least one character of the standard entry.

——————— LectureCaractere.c ———————

```
#include <sys/time.h>
#include <sys/types.h>
#include <stdio.h>
#include <unistd.h>

void main (void)
{
        fd_set          readfds;
        struct timeval timeout;
        char            c;
        int             r;

        /* Initialisation of the descriptor set */
        FD_ZERO (&readfds);
        FD_SET (0, &readfds);
        /* Wait for 5 seconds */
        timeout.tv_sec = 5;
        timeout.tv_usec = 0;

        /* Wait for a character for 5 seconds */
        r = select (1, &readfds, NULL, NULL, &timeout);

        /* Check for presence of a character */
        if (r == 1) {
```

```
                    /* Read a character */
          read (0, &c, sizeof (c));
          printf ("caractere lu : %c\n", c);
else
          printf ("Aucun caractere tape durant 5 secondes\n");

}
```

——————————————————————————— Lecturecaractere.c ———————

7.2.4 Control over devices

Input and outputs through devices are carried out by standard primitives. There is, however, a system call, called *ioctl*, enabling device parameters corresponding to an input/output descriptor to be modified. The syntax of the system call *ioctl* is the following:

```
#include <sys/ioctl.h>

int ioctl (int fd, int cmd, char *arg);
```

The primitive *ioctl* allows the state of the device associated with the descriptor specified by the parameter **fd** to be changed. The parameter **cmd** indicates the operation to be carried out, and **arg** points to the variable whose type depends on the operation to be carried out.

The codes corresponding to the control operations are defined in the header file **<sys/ioctl.h>**, which itself includes numerous header files. It is not possible to describe in detail all the control operations here because of their diverse nature. The study of kernel header files is advised when writing programs acting on devices.

If successful, *ioctl* returns the value 0. In the event of an error, the value –1 is returned and **errno** takes one of the following values:

error	*meaning*
EBADF	The input/output descriptor specified is invalid
ENOTTY	The operation specified can not be applied to the device corresponding to the descriptor **fd**
EINVAL	The operation specified by **cmd** or the argument **arg** are invalid

According to the operation carried out and the device concerned, other errors, of different types, may also be returned.

7.3.1 Peripherals supported by the kernel

Linux keeps updated the list of device drivers supported which these managers might have included when the kernel was compiled, or which they might have loaded in the form of modules.

To achieve this, it uses two tables: **blkdevs** and **chrdevs**, which contain respectively the device descriptors in block mode and those of devices in character mode. The structure **device_struct**, defined in the source file *fs/devices.c*, characterises the type of each of these table entries. It contains the following fields:

type	*field*	*description*
const char *	**name**	Name of device managed
struct file_operations *	**fops**	Operations on files assigned to the device

7.3.2 Disk input and output

Inputs and outputs carried out on devices in block mode are achieved via the *buffer cache*: blocks are loaded into buffers by calling the functions **bread** and **breada**. The latter call an input/output module in order to read or write blocks to disk.

The role of this module consists of maintaining the list of input/output requests in progress, and those to be carried out. When one or more blocks are to be read or written to disk, the input/output request is added to the list corresponding to the physical device. This list is scanned by the device driver which performs the input/outputs one by one.

In order to optimise the time needed to move the read/write head over the disk, the list of requests in maintained sorted by sector number. In this way, the requests are carried out by neighbouring sectors, thus minimising the displacement of heads, following the elevator seek principle. [Silberschatz and Calvin, 1994].

The structure request, defined in the file **<linux/blkdev.h>**, specifies the type of elements in the request list. It contains the following fields:

type	field	description
volatile int	rq_status	Request status (see below)
kdev_	rq_dev	Device identifier
int	cmd	Command: **READ** or **WRITE**
int	errors	Number of physical errors detected during the input/output
unsigned long	sector	Start sector
unsigned long	nr_sectors	Number of sectors to read or write
unsigned long	current_nr_sectors	Number of sectors remaining to read or write
char *	buffer	Address of data to read or write
struct semaphore *	sem	Semaphore used for the synchronisation of accesses concurrent to this request
struct buffer_head *	bh	Pointer to the buffer containing the data to read or write
struct buffer_head *	bhtail	Pointer to the last buffer of the request
struct request *	next	Pointer to the following request

The field **rq_status** can take the following values:

option	meaning
RQ_INACTIVE	Element in the list available
RQ_ACTIVE	Element in the list busy
RQ_SCSI_BUSY	Request in progress
RQ_SCSI_DONE	Request fulfilled

7.4
DETAILED DESCRIPTION OF IMPLEMENTATION

7.4.1 Management of supported devices

The source file *fs/devices.c* contains the management functions for supported devices. This module maintains the list of drivers present in the kernel.

Two tables are used to maintain the list of supported devices: **blkdevs** contains the descriptors or devices in block mode and **chrdevs** contains the descriptors of devices in character mode.

The functions **register_blkdev** and **register_chrdev** enable device drivers to be recorded. They add a device descriptor to the corresponding table: **blkdevs** for devices accessible in block mode, and **chrdevs** for devices accessible in character mode. The functions **unregister_blkdev** and **unregister_chrdev** allow a device driver to be de-registered, notably in the case when a device management module is deleted in the kernel when being executed, by modifying the corresponding entry in the table **blkdevs** or **chrdevs**.

The functions **get_blkfops** and **get_chrfops** return a pointer to the file operations associated with a device.

The opening of a device is managed by the functions **blkdev_open** and **chrdev-_open**. These functions obtain the file operations associated with the device by calling **get_blkfops** or **get_chrfops**, then carry out the opening by calling the operation **open**. The function **blkdev_release** is called at the last closing of a device in block mode: it obtains the operations on files associated with the device by calling **get_blkfops**, then it calls the operation **release**.

Several variables are exported by this module:

- **def_blk_fops**: operations on files associated with devices in block mode;
- **blk_inode_operations**: operations on inodes associated with devices in block mode;
- **def_chr_fops**: operations on files associated with devices in character mode;
- **chrdev_inode_operations**: operations on inodes associated with devices in character mode.

7.4.2 Input/outputs to disk

The management functions for lists of disk input/output requests are implemented in the source file *drivers/block/ll_rw_blk.c*. Several functions are defined:

- **get_request**: this function looks for a free request descriptor in the global list. The descriptor found in then marked as active and initialised.
- **__get_request_wait, get_request_wait**: the role of these two functions is similar to that of **get_request**, except that they put the calling process on hold if no request descriptor is free.
- **add_request**: this function is called to add an input/output request to the list corresponding to a device, and to maintain this list sorted.
- **make_request**: this function is called to create an input/output request. It first of all tries to merge the request with another already registered in the list, if the sector numbers are adjacent. If this is not possible, it calls **__get_request_wait** to obtain a request descriptor, initialises it, then inserts it the list of the corresponding device by calling **add_request**.
- **ll_rw_block**: this function is called by the *buffer cache*, the file system, and the input/output module, in order to perform an input/output. It checks that the arguments are valid, then creates an input/output request by calling

make_request. The corresponding buffer remains locked as long as the input/output has not been carried out, and it will be unlocked at the completion of the input/output. In this way, the calling process can put itself on hold waiting for the end of the input/output by calling **wait_on_buffer**.

7.4.3 Input/output on peripheral devices in block mode

The functions for the reading and writing of data from devices accessible in block mode are implemented in the source file *fs/block_dev.c*. The functions use primitives from *buffer cache* to access buffers associated with the devices. The functions **block_write**, **block_read**, and **block_sync** implement file operations **write**, **read,** and associated with devices in block mode.

The function **block_write** implements the writing of data to a device. It generates *clusters* for all blocks to be written by calling **generate_cluster** and it uses a mechanism of anticipated reading in order to load the following blocks into memory. It copies data to be written from the address specified by the caller in the buffers created, then it writes buffers by groups by calling **ll_rw_block**.

The function **block_read** implements the reading of data from a device, using an anticipated reading mechanism. It generates *clusters* for all blocks to be read by calling **generate_cluster,** and then creates a single input/output request for all blocks by calling **ll_rw_block**. It next performs a loop through all the buffers from which a read operation has been executed: it waits for the end of reading the block then recopies its contents to the address provided by the caller.

The two functions are rather complex since they use at the same time anticipated reading and *clusters*.

The function **block_fsync** re-writes modified data to a device. It triggers the re-writing of the buffers concerned by calling **fsync_dev**.

7.4.4 Multiplexing input/output

7.4.4.1 Principles

The multiplexing of input/output by the primitive *select* is implemented in the source file *fs/select.c*. Its principle is quite simple: for each input/output descriptor specified, a test is performed to determine whether the input/output is possible. If it is, the current process is placed in the wait queue corresponding to the file.

The list of wait queues in which the current process is suspended is memorised in a multiplexing table. Each entry in the table is defined by the structure **select_table_entry**, defined in the header file **<linux/wait.h>**:

type	field	description
struct wait_queue	wait	Entry in the wait queue corresponding to the current process
struct wait_queue **	wait_address	Address of the wait queue in which the current process is registered

The structure **select_table_struct** defines the format of descriptors of the multiplexing table. It contains the following fields:

type	field	description
int	nr	Number of entries in the table
struct select_table_entry **	entry	Address of the memory page containing the multiplexing table

When the primitive *select* is executed, the current process is recorded in the wait queues corresponding to the descriptors provided, and the multiplexing table contains the list of these wait queues. In this way, when the current process is suspended, it can be woken up by calling functions **wake_up** and **wake_up_interruptible** on any of the wait queues. So the process is woken as soon as an input/output is possible on one of the specified file descriptors.

In order to implement the delay primitive when the primitive *select* is called, the field **timeout** of the current process descriptor may be set. A suspension with a given delay is thus implemented in the manner described in chapter 4, section 4.6.1.

7.4.4.2 Utility functions
The function **select_wait**, defined in the header file **<linux/sched.h>**, adds an entry in the multiplexing table, then records this entry in the specified wait queue.

The function **free_wait** deletes all entries in a multiplexing table of wait queues in which they are recorded. It scans the table, and calls **remove_wait_queue** for each entry.

The function **check** is called to verify whether an input/output on a given file is possible. It calls the operation **select** associated with the file.

7.4.4.3 The file operation select
The file operation **select** has to test whether a specified input/output on a given file is possible. If so, it has to return the value 1, if not it adds an entry to the multiplexing table by calling **select_wait**, and returns a value 0.

As an example, it is useful to study the functioning of the function **random_select**, which implements the operation **select** to generate random numbers. This function is implemented in the source file *drivers/char/random.c,* and its code is as follows:

```
int_random_select(struct inode *inode, struct file*file),
                  int sel_type, select_table * wait)
{
      switch (sel_type) {
      case SEL_IN;
            if (random_state.entropy_count >= 8)
                  return 1;
            select_wait(&random_wait, wait);
            break;
      case SEL_OUT:
             if (random_state.entropy_count <WAIT_OUTPUT_BITS)
                   return 1;
            select_wait(&random_wait, wait);
            break;
      }
      return 0;

}
```

This function distinguishes between two types of access:

- read access (**SEL_IN**): if at least eight random numbers are available, reading is possible and **random_select** returns the value 1.
- write access (**SEL_OUT**): if the random number buffer has not overflowed, writing is possible and **random_select** returns the value 1.

In the case where an input/output is not possible, **select_wait** is called to create an entry in the multiplexing table, and to record this entry in the wait queue **random_wait, random_select** then returns the value 0.

The wait queue **random_wait** is used is used internally by the random number manager. When new random numbers are generated, or when space freed in the buffer, the internal functions call **wake_up_interruptible** to wake up the waiting processes.

7.4.4.4 *Implementation of the primitive* **select**

The function **do_select** implements the multiplexing proper. It first checks the validity of its parameters by controlling the descriptors of specified files, and then it initialises a multiplexing table. It next sets the state of the current process to **PROCESS_INTERRUPTIBLE,** then performs a loop on the group of specified descriptors. For each descriptor, the function check is called in order to ascertain whether input/output is possible. If it is, the number of usable descriptors is incremented. At the end of the loop, the number of usable descriptors is checked: if it is zero, and no signal has been received by the process, schedule is called to trigger a scheduling, then a scan of specified descriptors is resumed. If the number of usable descriptors is not zero, or if the current process has received a signal, the processing stops: the multiplexing table is released, the process state is set to **PROCESS_RUNNING**, and **do_select** returns the number of descriptors calculated.

The primitive *select* is implemented by **sys_select**. This function checks the validity of its parameters, converts the delay specified into a number of clock cycles, then calls **do_select** to proceed to multiplexing proper. After this call, it puts the result of multiplexing in the parameters provided by the calling process.

7.4.5 Interrupt management

The device controller generally transmits an interrupt to the processor when it changes state, for example when an input/output is terminated or when a physical error occurs. The device driver is required to react when it receives such an interrupt.

Linux contains an interrupt management module. This low-level module takes care of the physical programming of the interrupt controller and provides functions enabling interrupts to be handled easily. The source file *arch/i386/kernel/irq.c* contains the functions of this module.

The functions **disable_irq** and **enable_irq** allow the disabling and activation respectively of a hard interrupt. They block all interrupts, screen or un-screen the desired interrupt by programming the interrupt controller, then re-establish the processor status.

The functions diverting an interrupt are similar to functions of signal management (see chapter 5): a device driver can specify a function to be executed when a hard interrupt is received. When this interrupt is received, all associated functions are called one by one to process the event.

The functions **do_IRQ** and **do_fast_IRQ** are called when a hard interrupt is received. They scan the list of interrupt processing functions, and calls each of these functions.

The function **request-irq** enables a device driver to associate a processing function with a hard interrupt: an interrupt descriptor is allocated, initialised, then it is added to the list of interrupt processing functions.

The function **free-irq** enables a device driver to de-activate its hard interrupt processing function. It scans the list corresponding to the interrupt, deletes the corresponding descriptor, then frees it.

7.4.6 Management of DMA channels

When DMA (Direct Memory Access) is invoked, the device controller reads or writes data directly to central memory, using the physical address which is sent to it when the input/output request is made.

A DMA channel is associated with each device controller operation in DMA mode. To dialogue with the controller, the device manager must reserve the channel, in order to be the only one to use it.

Linux provides a mechanism for reserving and releasing the DMA channel. The source file *kernel/dma.c* contain the corresponding functions.

The reserved DMA channels are stored in the table **dma_chan_busy**. Each element in the table is a structure (structure **dma_chan**) and contains the following fields:

type	*field*	*description*
int	lock	Boolean expression indicating whether the channel is reserved
const char *	device_id	Pointer to the string identifying the device manager having reserved the channel

The function **request_dma** enables a device manager to reserve a DMA channel. It checks that the channel number is valid, and then tests to see if the channel is already reserved. If this is the case, the error **EBUSY** is returned, if not the manager name is saved in memory, and the value 0 is returned.

The **free_dma** releases a DMA channel (for example, when a device manager loaded into memory is downloaded from memory). It checks that the channel number is valid, and then marks the channel as available by changing the corresponding sector **dma_chan_busy**

A third function, **get_dma_list** is called by code of the file system */proc*. It returns the ASCII representation of the reserved markers in **dma_chan_busy**, in the following form:

```
2:    floppy
4:    cascade
6:    aha1542
```

7.4.7 Access to input/output ports

The dialogue between a device manager and the corresponding controller is performed by using input/output ports. These ports are addressable through assembler instructions **in** and **out**.

As these device managers are written in the C language, Linux provides several functions, defined in the header file **<asm/io.h>**, enabling input/output ports to be accessed:

- **outb**: writing a byte to a port;
- **inb**: reading a byte from a port;
- **outw**: writing a 16-bit word to a port;
- **inw**: reading a 16-bit word from a port;
- **outl**: writing a 32-bit word to a port;

- **inl**: reading a 32-bit word from a port;
- **outsb**: writing a string of 8-bit bytes to a port;
- **insb**: reading a string of 8-bit bytes from a port;
- **outsw**: writing a string of 16 bit words to a port;
- **insw**: reading a string of 16 bit words from a port;
- **outsl**: writing a string of 32 bit words to a port;
- **insl**: reading a string of 32 bit words from a port;

A variant of each of these functions exists, suffixed by **_p**, and it invokes a pause of some clock cycles after reading and writing from the port.

7.4.8 Example of a device in block mode: the RAM disk

7.4.8.1 Overview
The source file *drivers/block/rd.c* contains the implementation of the RAM disk manager. The constant **NUM_RAMDISKS**, which has the value 16, defines the number of memory disks that can be managed by the module. The variables **rd_length** and **rd_blocksizes** contains the size in bytes of blocks linked to each of the memory disks.

7.4.8.2 Access to the disk memory contents
The function **rd_request** is called to perform an input/output on the contents of a RAM disk: it is responsible for accessing disk contents. The manager uses an original method to store information on disk: rather than declare a memory zone to hold the disk contents and copying the contents into buffers at each reading, the contents of the buffers themselves are used.

These buffers are made available by the functions **block_read** and **block_write** when read and write operations are performed:

- When a read operation is performed, if a buffer corresponding to the block to be read exists, the function **block_read** uses its contents directly, if not a buffer is allocated and **rd_request** initialises it to zero.
- When a write operation is performed, **block_write** transmits a buffer to **rd_request**. This latter function sets the flag **BH_Protected** in order to mark that the buffer is used and must not be released.

As a consequence, the RAM disk contents are effectively stored in the buffers:

- no buffer is assigned to blocks that have never been read, and a buffer initialised to zero is returned in the case of a block read;
- a protected buffer is assigned to each block after being written, and its contents are used when a block is read.

7.4.8.3 File operations

The file operations **read** and **write** are implemented by the functions **block_read** and **block_write**, described in section 7.4.3. The function **rd_request** is called to carry out input/output.

The function **rd_ioctl** implements the file operation **ioctl**. It enables buffers associated with a RAM disk to be invalidated, or to establish the size of disk memory.

The operation open is implemented by the function **rd_open**. This function initialises the RAM disk if its contents should be loaded (see section 7.4.8).

The variable **fs_ops** contains the addresses of these options.

7.4.8.4 Initialisation

The function **rd_init** is called when the system is initialised. It first records the manager by calling **register_blkdev** to which it provides **fd_fops** as a parameter, in order to tell it the file operations associated with RAM disk. It also initialises the field **request_fn** of the table element **blk_dev** corresponding to disk memory, so that the function **rd_request** can be called when processing input/output requests. Finally, it initialises managed disk memory descriptors, by changing the contents of the tables **rd_length** and **rd_blocksizes**.

7.4.8.5 Loading disk memory

The above description relates to the case of a non-initialised RAM disk: when disk contents are accessed, the corresponding buffers are automatically created. Linux also enables the contents of RAM disk to be initialised from a device. This is particularly useful in the case of a start up floppy disk, containing a file system which is loaded into RAM disk created when the system is initialised.

The loading of RAM disk contents is carried out when the kernel is compiled with the option **CONFIG_BLK_DEV_INITRD**. In this case, the function **initrd_load** is called when the system is initialised. It calls **rd_load_image** to load the RAM disk contents. In the opposite case, it is **rd_load** that is called, and this function does not call **rd_load_image** unless the root of the file system is associated with reading the floppy disk.

The function **rd_load_image** loads the RAM disk contents from a device. It calls the function **blk_open** to open the specified device and the RAM disk, it identifies the image type to be loaded by calling **identify_ramdisk_image**, then loads to memory, by calling the operation **read** associated with RAM disk, for each block. When loading is compete, the buffers assigned to the source device are invalidated by a call **to invalidate_buffers**, and the device is closed by calling the associated file operation release.

The function **identify_ramdisk_image** is used to identify the type of device contents to load to disk. It recognises file systems of the type Minix and Ext2, as well as compressed images, created by the command *gzip*. It returns the number of blocks contained in the image.

For disks whose contents have been loaded, a memory zone is allocated when the kernel is initialised (in the source file *arch/i386/kernel/setup.c*) and its co-ordinates are contained in the variables initrd_start (address of the beginning of the zone) and initrd_end (address of the end of the zone).

When RAM disk is loaded, the function rd_open performs a special operation: it increments the number of disk memory references, then returns the variable initrd_fops, indicating that special functions should be used when accessing disk contents.

The operation is then implemented by the function intrd_read. This function copies the contents of the memory zone reserved for RAM disk into the buffer provided by the user, by utilising memcpy_tofs.

The function initrd_release, which implements the operation release, decrements the number of references to RAM disk. If this number becomes zero, the associated memory zone is dis-allocated by calling free_page for each page.

7.4.9 Example of a peripheral in character mode: the printer

7.4.9.1 Functioning
The parallel port manager in the 386 architecture, implemented in the source file *drivers/char/lp.c*, is rather interesting. Indeed, it can use two different methods to carry on a dialogue with the port:

- interrupts: to signal an event, the port sends an interrupt which is processed by the manager:
- polling: rather than use the system of interrupts, the manager carries out wait loops by testing the port state register. This method avoids the production of numerous interrupts(one for each character sent to the printer) and can be shown to be more efficient. Indeed, save and restore operations concerning the current process context, when an interrupt is processed, can be costly in the case of a device generating numerous interrupts.

7.4.9.2 Description of ports
Managed parallel ports are defined by descriptors. The latter are assembled in the table lp_table. The structure lp_struct, defined in the header file <linux/lp.h>, specifies the type of each of the elements. It contains the following fields:

type	*field*	*description*
int	base	Home address of input/output ports utilised
unsigned int	irq	Number of the interrupt used
int	flags	Status of the printer connected
unsigned int	chars	Number of attempts to carry out in printing a character
unsigned int	time	Duration of suspension during a wait phase, expressed in clock cycles
unsigned int	wait	Number of wait loops to perform before a printer acknowledges a character
struct wait_queue *	lp_wait_q	Wait queue used to await the arrival of an interrupt
char *	lp_buffer	Pointer to the buffer containing the characters to be printed
unsigned int	lastcall	Date of the last write to the printer
unsigned int	runchars	Number of characters written to the printer without instigating a suspension
unsigned int	waittime	Field not used
struct lp_state	state	Printer usage statistics

7.4.9.3 *Management functions of the printer with polling*

The function **lp_char_polled** arranges for a character to be sent in *polling* mode. It carries out a wait loop until the printer is ready to receive it, and during this loop, the function **schedule** is called, if the variable **need_resched** is set, in order avoid blocking a higher priority process by imposing an active wait. When the printer is ready, the character is sent to it. This function returns the value 1 if the character has been able to be sent to the printer, and the value 0 if this is not the case.

The function **lp_write_polled** is called to print a series of characters. It performs a loop on each character to be printed. The character is sent by calling **lp_char_polled**, then the result is tested. If the character has been correctly printed, **lp_write_polled** moves on to the next character. In the event of error, a message is displayed by calling **printk**, then the process goes to sleep for a given delay, by changing its state to **PROCESS_INTERRUPTIBLE** by setting the field **timeout** of the process descriptor, and by calling the function **schedule** to instigate a scheduling. At the end of this period of suspension, **lp_write_polled** checks to see if a signal has been received by the process during this sleep. If this is the case, the number of printed characters (or the error **EINTR** if no character has been printed) is returned. If not, it again goes into suspension for a certain delay before resuming the sending character loop. At the end of execution, the function returns the number of characters which have been sent to the printer.

7.4.9.4 Management functions of the printer with interrupts

The function **lp_char_interrupt** sends a character using interrupts. It carries out a loop during which it waits until the printer is ready to receive a character, and then sends it. This function returns the value 1 if the character has been able to be sent to the printer, and 0 if this is not the case.

The function **lp_interrupt** is called when an interrupt is received. It carries out a search in the table **lp_table** in order to determine which printer the interrupt is connected with, then calls the function **wake_up** to wake up the waiting process through the field **lp_wait_q** of the corresponding descriptor.

The function **lp_char_interrupt** is called to print a series of characters. It performs a loop on each character to be printed. The character is sent by calling **lp_char_interrupt**, then the result is tested. If the character has been correctly printed, **lp_write_interrupt** moves on to the next character. In the event of error, a message is displayed by calling **printk**, then the process goes to sleep for a given delay, by changing its state to **PROCESS_INTERRUPTIBLE** by setting the field **timeout** of the process descriptor, and by calling the function **interruptible sleep** through the field **lp_wait_q** of the printer descriptor. In this way, the process will be awoken by the expiry of the specified delay or by the arrival of an interrupt (since **lp_write_interrupt** wakes up the process waiting for **lp_wait _q**. At the end of this period of suspension, **lp_write_interrupt** checks to see if a signal has been received in this sleep period. If this is the case, the number of printed characters (or the error **EINTR** if no character has been printed) is returned. If not, it resumes the sending character loop. At the end of execution, the function returns the number of characters which have been sent to the printer.

7.4.9.5 File input/output operations

The function **lp_write** implements the file operation write. It calls the function **lp_write_interrupt** or **lp_write_polled** according to the printer management mode.

The function **lp_lseek** implements the file operation **lseek**. It returns the error **ESPIPE**.

The function **lp_open** implements the file operation **open**. It first of all checks that the specified printer exists, and that it is not already open under another process, and then initialises the printer. If the printer is to be managed by interrupts, a buffer is allocated by calling **kmalloc**, and its address is saved in the field **lp_buffer** of the printer descriptor, then **lp_open** calls **request_irq** to specify that the function **lp_interrupt** should be called when an interrupt linked to the parallel port concerned is received. Finally, the printer is marked as busy.

The function **lp_release** implements the file operation release. If the printer was managed by interrupts, **free_irq** is called to annul the call to **lp_interrupt** when an interrupt is received, then the buffer pointed to by the field **lp_buffer** of the printer descriptor is released by calling **kfree_s**. Finally, the printer is marked as available.

The function **lp_ioctl** implements the file operation **ioctl**. It enables the parameters linked to the printer to be consulted and modified.

The variable **lp_fops** contains the addresses of these functions.

7.4.9.6   *Initialisation functions*

The function checks the presence of the specified parallel port. If the port exists, it initialises its descriptor.

The function **lp_init** is called when the system is initialised, or when the manager in module form is loaded. It first registers the manager by calling **register_chrdev** to which it transmits the variable **lp_fops,** to tell it which operations are associated to the file. Then, it performs a reconnaissance loop on possible ports by calling **lp_probe.**

8

Memory Management

System calls described

brk, calloc, free, malloc, mlock, mlockall, mmap, mprotect, mremap,
msync, msync , munlock, munlokall, munmap, realloc, sbrk

8.1.1 Process address space

All processes have an associated address space which correspond to the memory
zones allocated to them. This address space includes:

- the code of the process;
- process data, which is divided into two parts; *data* which contains the variables
  which are initialised, and *bss*, containing non-initialised variables;
- the code and the shared library data used by the process;
- the stack used by the process.

In the x86 architecture, Linux allocates three gigabytes to this address space. The
remaining gigabyte is reserved for memory used by the kernel (the code of the
Linux system itself, together with the data that it handles).

The three available gigabytes are split into memory regions used by the
process. The program *AfficheAdresses.c* displays the addresses of various variables
and functions.

───────── AfficheAdressese.c ───────────────────────────

```c
#include <stdio.h>
#include <stdlib.h>

int             i;              /* Variable not initialised (segment BSS)
*/
int             j = 2;          /* Variable initialised (segment DATA) */
extern int      _end;
extern int      _etext;         /* End of code segment */
extern int      _edata;         /* End of data segment */
extern int      _bss_start;     /* Start of BSS segment */

extern char  **environ;         /* Pointer to environment */

void main (int argc, char *argv[])
{
        int k;

        printf ("Address of the function main        =%091x\n",
main);
        printf ("Address of the symbol _etext        =%091x\n",
&_etext);
        printf ("Address of the variable j           =%091x\n",
&j);
        printf ("Address of the symbol _edata        =%091x\n",
&_edata);
        printf ("Address of the symbol __bss_start =%091x\n",
&__bss_start);
        printf ("Address of the variable i           =%091x\n",
&i);
        printf ("Address of the symbol _end       =%091x\n", &_end);
        printf ("Address of the variable k           =%091x\n",
&k);
        printf ("Address of the first argument       =%091x\n",
argv[0]);
        printf ("Address of the first variable       =%091x\n",
environ[0]);
        exit
}
```

────────────────────────────────── AfficheAdresses.c   ─────────

The program listing is as follows:

```
Address of the function main      = 008048474
Address of the symbol _etext      = 008048564
Address of the variable j         = 00804971c
Address of the symbol _edata      = 0080497d8
Address of the symbol __bss_start = 0080497d8
Address of the variable i         = 0080497dc
Address of the symbol _end        = 0080497e0
Address of the variable k         = 0bffff890
Address of the first argument     = 0bffff9a7
Address of the first variable     = 0bffff9b9
```

The positioning of memory regions used by the process can be deduced from this listing, as is shown schematically in figure 8.1.__

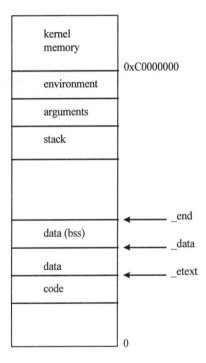

Figure 8.1 Process address space.

8.1.2 Memory allocation

When a process begins execution, its segments have a fixed size. There are, however, memory allocation and memory release functions which enable a process to handle variables whose number and size are not known at the time they were compiled.

The memory allocations and releases are performed by changing the size of the process data segment. When data is allocated, the data segment is enlarged by the necessary number of bytes and the data item can be stored in the memory space thus made available. When a data item positioned at the end of a data segment is no longer used, it is released simply by reducing the size of the segment.

8.2
BASIC SYSTEM CALLS

8.2.1 Changing the size of data segments

A process may change the size of its data segment. Linux provides the system call *brk* for this purpose:

```
#include <unistd.h>

int brk (void *end_data_segment);
```

The parameter **end_data_segment** specifies the address of the end of the data segment. It must be greater than the end of segment code address and less than the address of the end of the stack by 16 kilobytes. If successful, *brk* returns the value 0. In the event of failure, the value –1 is returned and the variable **errno** takes the value **ENOMEM**.

The library function also enables the current process to modify the size of its data segment:

```
#include <unistd.h>
#include <sys/types.h>

void *sbrk (ptrdiff_t increment);
```

The parameter **increment** specifies the number of bytes to add to the data segment, or to subtract if **increment** is negative. The function *sbrk* returns the new end of segment address, or the value –1 in the event of failure. In the latter case, the variable **errno** takes the value **ENOMEM**.

8.2.2 Memory allocation and release functions

Although it is possible to dynamically manage the memory by means of the functions *brk* and *sbrk*, it is relatively painstaking to perform. Indeed, though the allocation of memory is straightforward, since it is sufficient to increase the size of the data segment, the release of memory is more involved, since is necessary to take account of the memory zones used in order to reduce the size of the data segment when necessary. For this reason, the functions of allocation and release provided by the standard library are generally used.

These functions use *brk* and *sbrk* internally to allocate and to release the memory zones, and they manage the structuring of memory blocks.

The functions are based on the following prototypes:

```
#include <stdlib.h>

void *malloc (size_t size);

void *calloc (size_t nmemb size_t size);

void *realloc (void *ptr,  size_t size);
```

The function *malloc* enables a new memory zone to be allocated, and the parameter **size** specifies the size in bytes of the block to allocate. The address of the zone allocated is returned by *malloc*, or the value **NULL** is returned in the event of failure. The contents of the block allocated is indeterminate.

The function *calloc* also enables a new memory zone to be allocated, but it is designed to allocate tables. The parameter **nmemb** specifies the number of cells in the table, and **size** indicates the size of each of the table cells, expressed in bytes. The size of the block to be allocated is thus *nmemb * size*. As with *malloc, calloc* returns the address of the zone allocated, or the value **NULL** in the event of failure. The contents of the block allocated is initialised to zero.

The function *realloc* modifies the size of a memory zone, the parameter **ptr** specifies the address of a memory block, allocated by calling *malloc* or *calloc*, and **size** indicates its new size. The contents of the memory zone is copied into the new allocated block and the address of the new allocated block is returned by *realloc*, and may be different from the address specified in **ptr**. In the event of failure, the value **NULL** is returned, and the zone pointed to by **ptr** is not released.

Finally, the function *free* releases a memory zone. The parameter **ptr** specifies the address of a memory block, allocated by calling *malloc* or *calloc* or *realloc*. After the execution of *free*, the memory zone is released and **ptr** no longer contains a valid address.

8.3
ADVANCED CONCEPTS

8.3.1 Memory regions

As explained in section 8.1.1, the address space of a process is composed of several memory regions. Each region is characterised by several attributes:

- start and end addresses;
- access permissions assigned to it;
- the object associated with it (for example, an executable file containing the code executed by the process).

The memory regions contained in the process address space may be determined by displaying the contents of the file *maps*, situated in the directory of each process in the filesystem */proc*, for example:

```
bbj>cat /proc/self/maps
08048000-0804a000  r-xp  00000000 03:02 7914
0804a000-0804b000  rw-p  00001000 03:02 7914
0804b000-08053000  rwxp  00000000 00:00 0
40000000-40005000  rwxp  00001000 03:02 18336
40005000-40006000  rw-p  00004000 03:02 18336
40006000-40007000  rw-p  00000000 00:00 0
40007000-40009000  r--p  00000000 03:02 18255
40009000-40082000  r-xp  00000000 03:02 18060
40082000-40087000  rw-p  00078000 03:02 18060
40087000-400b9000  rw-p  00000000 00:00 0
bfffe000-c0000000  rwxp  ffff0000 00:00 0
```

The first two fields of each line represent the start and end of the region and the following field states the associated access permissions (the character 'p' indicates that the region may be shared with other processes). The following fields convey the information relating to the object associated with the memory region: the shifting of the beginning of the region in the object, the number of the device containing the object, and the inode number of the object.

In the example given, the first three regions correspond to the program run (code segment, initialised data segment, and non-initialised data segment). The next segment corresponds to the file */usr/share/locale/fr_FR/LC_CTYPE* which is automatically loaded into memory when the system is booted up. The following three segments correspond to the shared C library, */lib/libc.so.5.3.12* (code segment, initialised data segment, and non-initialised data segment). Finally, the last region corresponds to the segment of the stack used by the process.

8.3.2 Memory protection

According to the type of information contained in memory, a different form of protection is associated with each region of memory belonging to the address space of a process.

Memory access permissions are managed directly by the processor: a protection mechanism is associated with each memory page, and the processor checks the validity of each access carried out by the current process.

Linux allows a process to modify the memory protection mechanisms assigned to certain regions within its address space. It provides several types of access permissions:

- **PROT_NONE**: the memory region is marked as inaccessible;
- **PROT_READ**: the current process may read the data contained in the region;
- **PROT_WRITE**: the current process may change the data contained in the region;
- **PROT_EXEC**: the current process may execute code contained in the region.

When a process modifies access permissions assigned to a memory region, the kernel changes the protection information assigned to the corresponding memory pages. The access controls are performed by the processor, which invokes a trap to bar illegal access. This trap is managed by Linux, which then sends the signal **SIGSEGV** to the process at fault.

It should be noted that, within the x86 architecture, not all the access controls are implemented by the processor. In x86 processors, the protection mechanisms **PROT_WRITE** and **PROT_EXEC** imply **PROT_READ**. It is therefore impossible to both authorise a modification of data or the execution of code, and to forbid read access to it.

8.3.3 Locking of memory zones

Linux uses page load on request. This means that pages forming part of the process address space are not all loaded into memory at system boot time. When the process performs a memory access to a page which has not been loaded, the processor invokes a trap. This is managed by Linux, which may respond in the following ways:

- send the signal **SIGSEGV** to the current process, if the memory page referenced does not form part of the process address space, that is if the process has used an invalid memory address;
- allocate an empty page, if, for example, the corresponding memory page is part of the stack segment;
- load the page contents, for example, from secondary memory, from an executable file containing the program that is currently executing.

In a complementary manner, Linux may choose to free a memory page. If the kernel needs central memory, it chooses one or several pages, writes them in due course to secondary memory (if they have been changed), and then releases them.

A process may therefore be suspended by the kernel when the latter needs to load pages or to write them to secondary memory. This mode of operation is not compatible with 'real-time' processes which must not be interrupted or suspended. Therefore, Linux enables a privileged process to lock certain memory pages.

Several system calls allow a process to specify that its pages must not be removed from memory. Once the specified pages are present in memory, the kernel does not consider them when it needs to free-up memory. In this way, the process can not be held up waiting for the loading of a memory page which has been removed from memory.

8.3.4 Mapping of files in memory

The address space of a process contains its code segments, data segments and stack segments by default, as well as code and data segments of the shared libraries that it uses.

A process can create new memory regions in its address space to access file contents. This process is known as file mapping. When a process maps the contents of a file in memory, a new memory region is created in its address space and the contents of the file are made accessible in this region. It is thus possible to directly access file contents by using direct memory reads and writes, without having to go via the primitives *read* and *write*.

This method is particularly advantageous when a process handles a file made up of a series of elements of the same type. By using the input/output primitives on files, the process should be able to use the system call *lseek* to locate the element it wishes to manipulate, then to read or write the data by means of *read* or *write*. If the file is mapped into memory, the process can use the address of the corresponding zone as a starting address, and can make use of an index to access the desired element, in the same way as for a tabulated variable.

Several types of mapping are available:

- shared mappings: several processes map the contents of a file into their address spaces, and any change carried out by a process is immediately visible to the others;
- private mappings: the changes carried out by the process on the file contents are private, and they are not visible by other processes which have mapped the same file onto their address space;
- anonymous mappings: the process has, in effect, created a memory zone which does not correspond to the file contents. When the memory zone is accessed in read mode, Linux allocates pages initialised to zero. The modified pages are saved in the *swap*.

8.3.5 *Swap* devices

When the kernel needs memory, it can overwrite memory pages. If the contents of these pages have been modified, it is necessary to save them to disk: a page corresponding to a file mapped into memory is re-written in the file, and a page corresponding to the data is saved on a *swap* device.

A *swap* device could be a device in block mode, for example a partition on a disk, or a normal file. It must have been previously initialised with the aid of the command *mkswap*.

Linux is capable of using several *swap* devices. When a page needs to be saved, the active *swap* devices are scanned in order to find a place to write the page. The activation of a *swap* device is performed by the system call *swapon*.

In contrast to the majority of other systems, Linux does not confine itself to activating *swap* devices. An active device can be de-activated without having to reboot the system. When this de-activation takes place, all pages saved on the device are re-loaded into memory. The system call *swapoff* performs this de-activation.

8.4.1 Protection of memory pages

A process may modify the access permissions relating to a part of memory which is allocated to it. To this end, Linux provides the primitive *mprotect*, which has the following syntax:

```
#include <sys/mman.h>

int mprotect (caddr_t addr, size_t len, int prot);
```

The system call changes the access protection assigned to the specified memory zone. The parameter **addr** represents the address of the memory zone to be modified, and **len** expresses the size of the zone, measured in bytes. The parameter **prot** specifies the access permissions to set. *mprotect* returns the value 0 in the event of success, or the value –1 in the event of error. In the latter case, the variable **errno** can take the following values:

error	meaning
EACCES	The protection specified by **prot** is not applicable
EFAULT	The address specified by **addr** is not part of the address space of the calling process
EINVAL	**addr**, **len** or **prot** contain an invalid value
ENOMEM	The kernel has not allocated memory for its internal descriptors

Constants, defined in the file **<sys/mman.h>**, represent the different possible protection mechanisms:

constant	*meaning*
PROT_NONE	The zone is marked as inaccessible
PROT_READ	The zone is marked as accessible in read mode
PROT_WRITE	The zone is marked as accessible in write mode
PROT_EXEC	The zone is marked as accessible in execution

At the end of this system call, if the current process tries to access the memory zone in a mode incompatible with the protections set, for example, if it tries to write data to a zone accessible in read mode only, the signal **SIGSEGV** is sent to it.

8.4.2 Locking memory pages

A process with privileges may lock pages in memory. Linux provides several system calls for this:

```
#include <sys/mman.h>

int mlock (conet void *addr, size_t len);

int munlock (conet void *addr, size_t len);

int mlockall (int flags);

int munlockall (void);
```

The primitive *mlock* enables a memory zone to be locked. The parameter **addr** specifies the address of the beginning of the zone, and **len** indicates its size in bytes. At the end of this system call, the specified memory zone is resident in memory and will not be transferred to secondary memory.

The primitive *munlock* enables a memory zone to be unlocked. The parameter **addr** specifies the address of the beginning of the zone, and **len** indicates its size in bytes. The system call *mlockall* locks in memory all pages included in the address space of the current process, that is pages of code segments, data segments and stack segments, as well as the shared libraries, segments of shared memory, and files mapped into memory. The parameter **flag** specifies the locking modes, and is expressed in terms of the following constants, defined in the file **<sys/mman.h>**:

constant	*meaning*
MCL_CURRENT	All pages loaded in memory in the current process address space are locked.
MCL_FUTURE	All pages which will be loaded in memory in future in the current process address space are locked.

The primitive *munlockall* unlocks all the address space of the current process. It nullifies the effect of previous system calls *mlock* and *mlockall*.

All these primitives return the value 0 if successful. In the event of error, the value −1 is returned and the variable **errno** can take the following values:

error	*meaning*
EINVAL	**flags** contains an invalid value
ENOMEM	The available memory does not allow locking
EPERM	The calling process does not have enough privileges to lock memory pages

8.4.3 Mapping to memory

Linux provides several system calls enabling the contents to be mapped to memory:

```
#include <unistd.h>
#include <sys/mman.h>

void *mmap (void *start, size_t len, int prot, int flags, int fd, off_t
offset);

int *munmap (void *start, size_t);

void *mremap (void *old_start, size_t old_len, size_t new_len, unsigned
long flags);
```

The system call *mmap* maps the contents of a file to memory in the address space of the current process. The parameter **start** specifies the address of the memory zone where the contents of the file is to be made accessible. This address is solely an indication to the system, which could decide to use another starting address. The parameter **len** indicates the number of bytes to map into memory. The memory protection measures to apply are defined in the parameter **prot**, with the aid of constants described in section 8.4.1. The parameter **flag** specifies the protection methods. Finally, **fd** indicates the file descriptor, whose contents are to be mapped into memory, and **offset** specifies the byte from which the file should be made accessible. The address from which the file contents are accessible, is returned by *mmap*, and in the event of failure, *mmap* returns the value −1.

Several constants, defined in the file **<sys/mman.h>**, may be used for the parameter **flag**:

constant	meaning
MAP_FIXED	It is essential that the start address corresponds to the parameter **addr**. If this address is unusable, **mmap** returns an error.
MAP_SHARED	The memory mapping is shared with all other processes which map the file into memory. Any change carried out by a process is immediately visible to the others.
MAP_PRIVATE	The memory mapping does not concern the current process. Any change carried out by a process will not be visible to the other processes which have mapped files to memory.
MAP_ANONYMOUS	The memory mapping does nor concern any file. Indeed, the primitive **mmap** is called to create a new memory region whose contents will be initialised to zero.
MAP_DENYWRITE	Any attempt by a process to access the file in write mode will return the error **ETXTBSY**.
MAP_LOCKED	The region created must be locked in memory.

In the event of failure, the variable **errno** can take the following values:

error	meaning
EACCES	The type of mapping or the access protection mode are incompatible with the file opening mode.
EAGAIN	The file is locked or too many of pages are locked in memory.
EBADF	The specified input/output descriptor is invalid.
EINVAL	**start**, **len**, or **offset** contain an invalid value (for example, an address which is not aligned with a page boundary)
ENOMEM	There is not enough memory available.
ETXTBSY	The option **MAP_DENYWRITE** has been specified whilst the file is open in write mode.

The primitive *munmap* deletes the mapping of a file into memory. The parameter **start** specifies the address of the corresponding memory zone, and **len** indicates its size, measured in bytes.

If unsuccessful, *munmap* returns the value –1, and the variable **errno** takes the value **EINVAL**.

The system call *mremap* changes the size of a file. The parameter **old_start** specifies the address of the start of the zone, whose size is given by **old_len**. The new zone size is conveyed in the parameter **new_len**. The parameter **flags** specifies the nature of the changes. Linux 2.0 only provides a single option, **MREMAP_MAYMOVE**, which indicates that the kernel is authorised to change the address of the start of the zone. The *mremap* returns the address of the memory zone, which may be different from the value transmitted in **old_start**, or the value **NULL** is returned in the event of failure. In the latter case, the variable **errno** can take the following values:

error	meaning
EAGAIN	The memory region is locked and may not be moved.
EFAULT	The memory region specified by **old_start** and **old_len** is not part of the address space of the calling process.
EINVAL	**old_start**, **old_len**, or **new_len** contain an invalid value (for example an address not aligned with a page boundary)
ENOMEM	The size of the memory region cannot be enlarged, **MREMAP_MAYMOVE** is not specified.

The program *ExempleMmap.c* uses the primitive *mmap* to access the contents of a file. It opens a file, uses *mmap* to map its contents into memory, then performs a loop to display each byte contained in the file.

——————— ExempleMmap.c ———————

```
#include <fcntl.h>
#include <stdio.h>
#include <unistd.h>
#include <sys/mman.h>
#include <sys/stat.h>

void main (int argc, char *argv[])
{
        int             fd;
        int             i;
        struct stat     st;
        char            *addr;

        /* Argument checking */
```

```
if (argc != 2) {
        fprintf (stderr, "Usage: %s name_of _file\n", argv[0]);
        exit (1);
}
/* Get the file size */
if (stat (argv[1], &st) == -1) {
        perror ("stat");
        exit (2);
        }
/* File opening */
fd = open (argv[1], O_RDONLY);
if (fd == -1) {
        perror ("open");
        exit (3);
}
/* File Mapping in memory */
addr = (char *) mmap (NULL, st.st_size, PROT_READ, MAP_SHARED,
fd,
                        (off_t) 0);
if (addr == NULL) {
        perror ("mmap");
        (void) close (fd);
        exit (4);
}
/* File closure */
close (fd);
/* Display loop of file contents */
for (i = 0; i < st.st_size; i++)
        putchar (addr[i]);
/* Release of file */
if (munmap (addr, st.st_size) == -1) {
        perror ("munmap");
        (void) close (fd);
        exit (5);
}
exit (0);
}
```

———————————————————————— ExempleMmap.c ————————

8.4.4 Synchronisation of memory pages

The system call *msync* causes data contained in a memory region to be re-written to disk. Its standard form is as follows:

```
#include <unistd.h>
#include <sys/mman.h>

int msync (const void *start, size_t len, int flags);
```

The system call *msync* causes changes made to the contents of a file mapped into memory to be re-written to disk. The parameter *start* specifies the address of the start of the zone to be re-written, whose size in bytes is given by the parameter **len**. The update formats are specified by the parameter **flags**. The primitive *msync* returns the value 0 in the event of success, or the value –1 if a problem arises.

Several constants enable the behaviour of *msync* to be changed:

constant	meaning
MS_ASYNC	Re-writing is performed asynchronously: when system calls terminate, the re-writing operation will have been initiated, but it is not certain that the data will have already been written to disk.
MS_SYNC	Re-writing is performed synchronously: when system calls terminate, re-write operations will have been physically written to disk
MS_INVALIDATE	The other mappings to memory are invalidated in such a way as to cause data to be re-read when a process accesses it. As a consequence, modifications that are carried out are visible to other processes.

In the event of failure, the variable **errno** can take the following values;

error	meaning
EFAULT	The memory region specified by **start** and **len** do not form part of the address space of the calling process,.
EINVAL	**start** does not contain an address aligned to a page boundary, or **flags** contains an invalid value

8.4.5 Management of swap device

The system call *swapon* activates a *swap* device. Its standard form is as follows:

```
#include <unistd.h>
#include <linux/swap.h>

int swapon (const char *pathname, int swapflags);
```

The primitive *swapon* activates the device whose name is specified by the parameter **pathname**. This could be a device in block mode, or a normal file. In either case it must have been initialised by the command *mkswap*. The parameter **swapflags** enables the priority of the device to be stated. When a page is to be saved, Linux scans the list of *swap* devices and uses the highest priority one which has non-allocated pages. The value **swapflags** is expressed by adding the priority desired (an integer between 1 and 32767) to the constant **SWAP_FLAG_PREFER**.

If successful, the value 0 is returned. In the event of failure, *swapon* returns the value –1 and the variable **errno** can take the following values:

error	*meaning*
EFAULT	**pathname** contains an invalid address
EINVAL	**pathname** does not refer to a device in block mode, or a normal file
ELOOP	A symbolic link loop has been encountered
ENAMETOOLONG	**pathname** specifies a file name which is too long
ENOENT	**pathname** refers to an non-existent file
ENOMEM	The kernel could not allocate memory to its internal descriptors
ENTDIR	One of the components of **pathname**, used as a directory name, is not a directory
EPERM	The calling process does not have the necessary privileges, or the maximum number of active devices has already been reached

The de-activation of a *swap* device is carried out by calling the primitive *swapoff*. Its standard form is the following:

```
#include <unistd.h>

int swapoff (const char *pathname);
```

The parameter **pathname** specifies the name of a *swap* device to be de-activated.

If successful, the value 0 is returned. If not, *swapoff* returns the value −1 and the variable **errno** can take the following values:

error	*meaning*
EFAULT	**pathname** contains an invalid address
EINVAL	**pathname** does not refer to a *swap* device in block mode, or a normal file
ELOOP	A symbolic link loop has been encountered
ENAMETOOLONG	**pathname** specifies a file name which is too long
ENOENT	**pathname** refers to an non-existent file
ENOMEM	The available memory is too small to reload all the pages contained in the *swap* device
ENTDIR	One of the components of **pathname**, used as a directory name, is not a directory
EPERM	the calling process does not have the necessary privileges

**8.5
GENERAL OVERVIEW OF
IMPLEMENTATION**

8.5.1 Management of page tables

8.5.1.1 Segmentation

With certain architectures, access to memory is carried out using segments. An address is composed of a segment identifier, and an offset within the segment. The processor combines the segment address and the offset to obtain a virtual address.

In the x86 architecture, several segment registers are defined. They contain pointers to segment descriptors which define the protection relating to the segments, as well as the address of the beginning of the segment in memory.

Figure 8.2 shows the conversion of an address composed of a segment identifier and an offset within the segment.

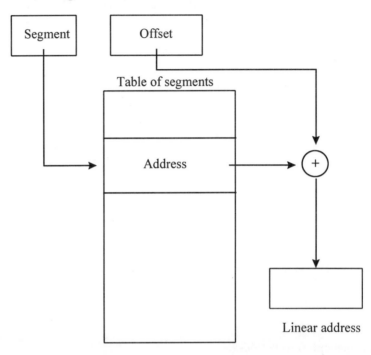

Figure 8.2   Memory segmentation.

Also within the x86 architecture, Linux uses the segmentation mechanism to separate the memory zones allocated to the kernel and to processes. Two segments refer to the first three gigabytes of process address space and their contents may be read and modified in user mode and in kernel mode. Two segments refer to the fourth gigabyte of process address space and its contents may be read and modified solely in kernel mode.

In this way, kernel code and data are protected from erroneous or illicit access on the part of user mode processes.

In user mode, the segment registers **cs** and **ds** point to the two user segments and, in kernel mode, **cs** and **ds** point to the two kernel segments. Changes to the values of segment registers are performed when changing the execution mode when a process moves to kernel mode to execute a system call, for example. Furthermore, this change to kernel mode triggers a change in the segment **fs**. This register points to the data segment of the calling process in order to enable the kernel to read and write in its address space, with the help of specialised functions.

8.5.1.2 Pagination

Linux uses the virtual memory mechanisms provided by the processor on which it is executing. The addresses handled by the kernel and the processes are virtual addresses, and a conversion is carried out by the processor to transform a virtual address into a physical address in central memory.

The conversion mechanism is as follows: a memory address is composed of two parts, a page number, and a offset in the page. The page number is used as an index in a table, called a page table, which provides a page in central memory. To this address is added the offset to obtain the physical address of the memory word in question. Figure 8.3 illustrates this conversion.

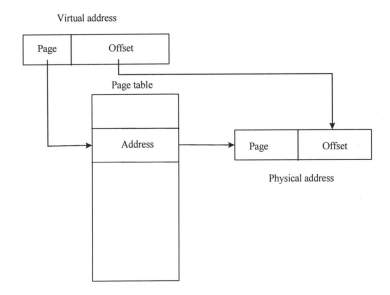

FIGURE 8.3   Conversion of a virtual address to a physical address.

Due to the size of the memory space which is addressable by the processors, the page table is rarely implemented in the form of a single contiguous table in memory. Indeed, since the page table must be resident in memory, this would require far too much memory just for this table. For example, x86 architecture processors can address four gigabytes; the size of memory pages is four kilobytes, and each table entry occupies four bytes: on such processors a complete page table would use 1,048,576 entries, and would occupy four megabytes of memory.

For this reason, the page table is often split into several levels; two at a minimum:

- a page table catalogue contains the addresses of pages which contain part of the page table;
- the parts of the table which are used are loaded into memory.

Figure 8.4 represents the address conversion in the case of x86 architecture, which uses a two-level page table.

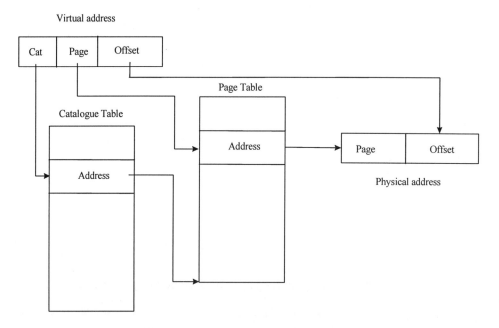

FIGURE 8.4   Two-level table of pages.

The advantage of a multi-level page table arises from the fact that it does not need to be loaded in its entirety into memory. If a process uses 6 megabytes of memory on a x86 processor, only three pages are used for the page table:

- the page containing the catalogue;
- the page containing the part of the page table corresponding to the first 4 mega-bytes of memory;
- the page containing the part of the page table corresponding to the following 4 mega-bytes of memory (of which only half of the entries are used).

8.5.1.3   *Page tables managed by Linux*

Linux manages central memory and the page tables used to convert virtual addresses into physical addresses. It implements a memory management which is largely independent of the processor on which it is executing.

The memory management implemented by Linux operates on page tables at three levels:

- the global table (*page global directory*) whose entries contain the addresses of pages containing intermediate tables;

- intermediate tables (*page middle directory*) whose entries contain addresses of pages containing tables pages;
- tables of pages (*page table*) whose entries contain addresses of memory pages containing code or data used by the kernel or user processes.

Of course, this model does not always match the processor that Linux is running on (x86 processors, for example, use a page table which only has two levels). The kernel performs a mapping of the model implemented by the processor to the Linux model. In x86 processors, for example, the kernel acts as if the intermediate table only contains a single entry.

8.5.1.4 Page sharing

When several processes access the same data, Linux tries its best to share memory pages. For example, if several processes are executing the same program, the program code is only loaded once into memory, and the page table entries of different processes point to the same memory pages.

In addition, Linux implements a technique of copying on write, enabling the minimum number of memory pages to be used. When a process is created, by calling the primitive *fork,* it inherits the address space of its parent. Of course, the code segment is not duplicated, but Linux does not duplicate the data segment either. When processes are duplicated, all pages of the data segment are marked as accessible in read mode only in the page tables of the two processes. When one of the two processes tries to modify data, the processor invokes a memory trap, which is controlled by the kernel. During processing of this trap, Linux duplicates the page concerned and inserts it in the page table of the process giving rise to the trap. In this way, memory pages are only physically duplicated when their contents are changed. Any memory page containing only un-modified data may remain shared between two processes, thus minimising the necessary memory space.

8.5.1.5 Types

The header file **<asm/page.h>** defines the types used to represent the page table entries:

- **pte_t**:   type of page table entry;
- **pmd_t**:   type of intermediate table entry;
- **pgd_t**:   type of global table entry;
- **pgprot_t**:   type used to state memory protection forms.

Although these types can be expressed in the form of integers of four bytes in the x86 architecture, they are defined in the form of structures in order to enable the compiler to check the types of data being handled.

Several macro-instructions enable these types to be accessed:

macro-instruction	*meaning*
pte_val	Returns the contents of a page table entry
pmd_val	Returns the contents of a intermediate table entry
pgd_val	Returns the contents of a global table entry
pgprot_val	Returns the memory protection mode
__pte	Converts an integer into a page table entry
__pmd	Converts an integer into a intermediate table entry
__pgd	Converts an integer into a global table entry
__pgprot	Converts an integer into memory protection

8.5.2 Management of memory pages

8.5.2.1 *Page descriptors*

Linux keeps note of the status of each page making up the central memory. It uses a table of descriptors, pointed to by the variable **mem-map**, which is declared in the source file *mm/memory.c*. Each of the descriptors corresponds to a memory page.

The **page** structure, declared in the header file **<linux/mm.h>**, defines the descriptor format. It contains the following fields:

macro-instruction	*field*	*meaning*
struct page *	**next**	Pointer to the next free page
struct page *	**prev**	Pointer to the last free page
struct inode *	**inode**	inode descriptor corresponding to page contents
unsigned long	**offset**	Page offset in the inode
struct page *	**next_hash**	Address of the descriptor of the following page on the hash list
atomic_t	**count**	Number of references to a page
unsigned	**flags**	Status of a page (see below)
unsigned:16	**dirty**	Boolean expression indicating whether the contents of the page have been changed
unsigned:8	**age**	Counter used to select pages to erase from memory
struct wait_queue *	**wait**	Wait queue used to wait for a page to become available
struct page *	**prev_hash**	Address of the previous page descriptor in a hash list
struct buffer_head *	**buffers**	Address of first descriptor of the buffer whose contents are located in the page

The following constants, declared in the header file **<linux/mm.h>**, define the status of a page:

constant	meaning
PG_locked	The page is locked in memory
PG_error	An error occurred when the page was loaded into memory
PG_referenced	The page has been accessed
PG_uptodate	The page contents are up to date
PG_free_after	The page should be freed at the end of the input/output operation in progress
PG_decr_after	The number of page references should be decremented at the end of the input/output operation in progress
PG_DMA	The page is usable for a DMA transfer (in the x86 architecture, it is contained in the first 16 Mbytes of central memory)
PG_reserved	The page is reserved for a future use, access to it is forbidden

8.5.2.2 Page caches

Linux maintains a page cache in memory. All the memory pages assigned to an inode are recorded in the hash list. They may correspond to the code executed by the processes or to the file contents mapped into memory.

This cache is managed dynamically. When the contents of a page assigned to an inode is to be loaded into memory, a new page is allocated, inserted into the cache, and its contents read from the disk. At later accesses to the page contents, it is no longer necessary to load it since it is already present in memory.

When Linux is short of memory space, it chooses pages to erase from memory. Pages in the cache which have not been accessed for a long time are erased by the functions **page_unuse** (see section 8.6.8) and **try_to_swap** (see section 8.6.9).

From version 2.0 onwards, Linux also uses the page cache mechanism to read files. When the system call *read* is used, reading is carried out by loading into memory pages corresponding to the inode. This enables the page cache and to make use of the pages already in memory.

Only reading data from normal files is performed via the page cache. Writing of data, as well as handling of directories, are performed via the *buffer cache*.

8.5.3 Memory allocation for the kernel

8.5.3.1 Allocation of memory pages

Linux provides the functions **__get_free_pages, get_free_page, free_pages, __free_page**, and **free_page** to allocate and release contiguous pages in central memory.

The kernel maintains a list of available pages in memory by using the principles of the *buddy system* [Knowlton 1965]. Its principle is simple: the kernel maintains a lists of page groups. These groups have a fixed size (they may contain 1, 2, 4, 8, 16 or 32 pages) and refer to contiguous pages in memory.

The fundamental principle of the *buddy system* is as follows: at each request for page allocation, the populated list of page groups having a size immediately greater than the specified size is used, and a page from this list is chosen. This group is composed of two parts: pages of the specified size, and the remainder, of pages that are still available. This remainder may be put into other lists.

When a page group is released, the kernel tries to merge this group with available groups, in order to obtain an available group of maximum size.

In order to simplify the allocation and release of page groups, the kernel only allows allocation of those of predetermined size which match the sizes managed in the lists.

If, for the sake of argument, 8 pages are to be allocated, and that only a group of 32 pages is available, the kernel uses this group, allocates the 8 pages requested, and shares the remaining 24 pages into one group of 16 pages and another of 8 pages. These two groups are inserted into the lists of corresponding groups.

When these 8 pages are released, the kernel tests to see if the 8 adjacent pages are available, that is, whether a page group contains these pages. If it is not the case, an available group is created for the 8 pages released. If an adjacent group exists, its size is modified to include the 8 pages freed, the kernel then tests whether it can merge it with another group of 16 pages, and so on.

The structure **free_area_struct**, declared in the source file *mm/page_alloc.c*, defines the format of descriptors of lists of groups:

type	field	description
struct page *	next	Pointer to the first page contained in the first page group
struct page *	prev	Unused pointer
unsigned int *	map	Pointer to a bit-table: each bit indicates whether the corresponding group has been allocated or is available

The table **free_area** declared in the source file *mm/page_alloc.c*, contains the address of the first available page group descriptor for each group size.

8.5.3.2 *Allocation of memory zones*
Linux provides several types of functions enabling the allocation of memory zones for use principally by the kernel:

- **kmalloc** and **kfree** enable memory zones formed from contiguous pages in central memory to be allocated or released;
- **vmalloc** and **vfree** enable memory zones formed not necessarily from contiguous pages in central memory to be allocated or released. The use of these functions is explained in section 5.5.

For the implementation of **kmalloc** and **kfree**, Linux uses lists of available zones. For each size of zone, a list of pages divided into blocks is maintained. The sizes of zones managed in the x86 architecture are: 32, 64, 128, 252, 508, 1,020, 2,040, 4,080, 8,176, 16,368, 65,520, 131,056. When **kmalloc** is called with a specified size, the corresponding list of the size immediately greater is used.

A descriptor is assigned to each of the lists. The structure **size_descriptor**, declared in the source file *mm/kmalloc.c*, defines the format of this descriptor:

type	*field*	*description*
struct page_descriptor *	**firstfree**	Pointer to the descriptor of the first page group available in the list
struct page_descriptor *	**dmafree**	Pointer to the descriptor of the first page group usable for a DMA access (that is, memory pages situated in the first 16Mbytes of central memory) available in the list
int	**nblocks**	Number of memory blocks contained in a page
int	**nmallocs**	Number of blocks allocated since this list
int	**nfrees**	Number of free blocks in this list
int	**nbytesmalloced**	Number of free bytes in the list
int	**npages**	Number of page groups allocated to the list
unsigned long	**gfporder**	Number of pages to be allocated (expressed in base 2 logarithms)

To each list descriptor is attached a list of memory page groups. Each group contains one or several contiguous pages in central memory. The number of pages in the group is a function of the size of blocks stored in the list: it must be big enough to contain at least one block. This number can be expressed by virtue of the field **gfporder**, by the formula 2^{gfporder}.

The beginning of each page group contains a descriptor. The format of this descriptor is defined by the structure **page_descriptor**:

type	*field*	*description*
struct page_descriptor *	**first free**	Pointer to the descriptor of the next page group in the list
struct block_header *	**dmafree**	Pointer to the descriptor of the first free block in the page group
int	**order**	Number of pages to be allocated (expressed in base 2 logarithms)
int	**nfree**	Number of free blocks in the page group

Each page group is made up of a table of blocks of fixed size. A block defined by the structure **block_header** is found at the beginning of each block:

type	*field*	*description*
unsigned long	**bh_flags**	Status of the block (allocated, usable for a DMA access, or free)
unsigned long	**bh_length**	Block size
struct block_header *	**bh_next**	Pointer to the descriptor of the next block group in the page group

Figure 8.5 represents these data structures, In the figure, two page groups are contained in the first list. The first group contains two free blocks, whilst the second contains a single one.

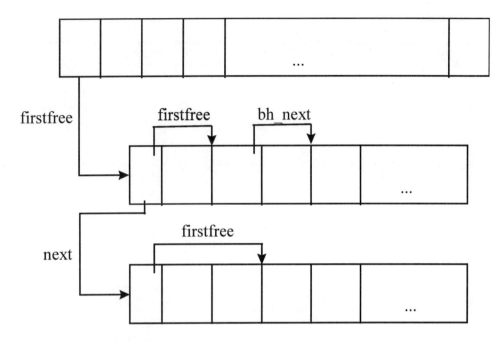

FIGURE 8.5 Lists of available memory blocks.

8.5.4 Process address spaces

8.5.4.1 Memory region descriptors

Process address spaces may be formed from several memory regions, as explained in section 3.1.

The kernel keeps in memory a description of regions utilised by a process. The structure **vm_area_struct**, declared in the header file **<linux/mm.h>**, defines the descriptor format for each region:

type	field	description
struct mm_struct *	**vm_mm**	Pointer to the descriptor of the address space concerned
unsigned long	**vm_start**	Address of the start of the zone
unsigned long	**vm_end**	Address of the end of the zone
pgprot	**vm_page_prot**	Status of the memory region (see below)
unsigned short	**vm_flags**	Address of the end of zone

Continuation of the fields associated with the structure **vm_area_struct**		
type	*field*	*description*
short	**vm_avl_height**	Weight associated with the descriptor in its capacity as AVL node (see section 8.5.4)
struct	**vm_avl_left**	Pointer to the left-hand sub-hierarchy
vm_area_struct struct *	**vm_avl_permission**	Pointer to the right-hand sub-hierarchy
vm_area_struct struct *	**vm_next**	Pointer to the next descriptor in the list of memory zones associated with a process
vm_area_struct struct *	**vm_next_share**	Pointer to the next descriptor in the list of shared memory zones
vm_area_struct struct *	**vm_prev_share**	Pointer to the previous descriptor in the list of shared memory zones
vm_area_struct struct *	**vm_ops**	List of operations on memory zones
unsigned long	**vm_offset**	Address of the start of the memory zone relative to the start of the object mapped into memory
struct inode *	**vm_inode**	inode descriptor mapped to memory in this zone

The value of the field **vm_flags** is expressed as a function of the following constants:

constant	*meaning*
VM_READ	The memory region is accessible in read mode
VM_WRITE	The memory region is accessible in write mode
VM_EXEC	The memory region is accessible in execution
VM_SHARED	The memory region is shared between several processes
VM_MAYREAD	The memory region may be modified so it is accessible in read mode
VM_MAYWRITE	The memory region may be modified to make it accessible in write mode

Continuation of the constants associated with the field **vm_flags**	
constant	*meaning*
VM_MAYEXEC	The memory region may be modified to make it accessible in execution
VM_MAYSHARE	The memory region may be shared between several processes
VM_GROWSDO WN	The memory region grows from below
VM_GROWSUP	The memory region grows from above
VM_SHM	The memory region corresponds to a segment of shared memory
VM_DENYWRITE	The error **ETXTBSY** should be returned in the event of a process trying to write to the file mapped to this region of memory
VM_LOCKED	The memory region is locked

8.5.4.2 Address space descriptors

Linux maintains an address space descriptor. This descriptor is accessible by the field **mm** contained in the process descriptor. Each process normally possesses its own descriptor, but two processes may share the same descriptor if the option **CLONE_VM** is specified when the primitive *clone* is called.

The structure **mm_struct**, declared in the header file **<linux/sched.h>**, defines the format of the descriptor:

type	*field*	*description*
int	**count**	Number of references (that is, the number of processes sharing this descriptor)
pgd_t *	**pgd**	Address of the global table of pages used by the process
unsigned long	**start_code**	Virtual address of the start of code
unsigned long	**end_code**	Virtual address of the end of code
unsigned short	**start_data**	Virtual address of the start of data
unsigned long	**end_data**	Virtual address of the end of data
unsigned long	**start_brk**	Virtual address of the start of memory blocks allocated by calling **brk**
unsigned long	**brk**	Virtual address of the end of memory blocks allocated by calling **brk**
unsigned long	**start_stack**	Virtual address of the start of the stack
unsigned long	**arg_start**	Virtual address of the start of the memory block containing the arguments of the program run

Continuation of the definition of the structure of **mm_struct**		
type	*field*	*description*
unsigned long	**arg_end**	Virtual address of the end of the memory block containing the arguments of the program run
unsigned long	**env_start**	Virtual address of the start of the memory block containing the environment variables
unsigned long	**env_end**	Virtual address of the end of the memory block containing the environment variables
unsigned long	**rss**	Number of pages resident in memory for the process
unsigned long	**total_vm**	Total number of bytes contained in the address space
unsigned long	**locked_vm**	Number of locked bytes in memory
unsigned long	**def_flags**	Default status to use when memory regions are created
struct vm_area_struct *	**mmap**	Address of the first region descriptor forming part of the address space (see below)
struct vm_area_struct *	**mmap_avl**	Address of the AVL root descriptor containing memory region descriptors (see later)

8.5.4.3 Organisation of region descriptors

The region descriptors of a process are referred to by the address space descriptor of a process in two different ways.

A linked list of descriptors is maintained. The field **mmap** contains the address of the first region descriptor assigned to the process, and each descriptor contains the address of the following one in its field **vm_next**. The list is sorted by the address of the end of regions, and is not used to search for a descriptor of a particular region. To speed up the searches, the descriptors are also arranged in an AVL (Adelchild-Velskii and Landis) tree, which allows the complexity of the search to be reduced from a factor in the range $O(n)$ to $O(\log n)$.

An AVL tree is a binary tree which is always balanced. A weight is assigned to each node of the tree, representing the difference between the depths of its left-hand sub-hierarchy and its permission-hand sub-hierarchy, and this weight must always have as a value –1, 0 or 1. If this weight is changed outside of these limits when elements are added or deleted from the tree, rotation operations are carried out to re-balance the AVL tree, as is shown in figure 8.6. A fuller description of

AVL tree characteristics, and manipulation algorithms, may be found in [Froidevaux *et al,* 1993].

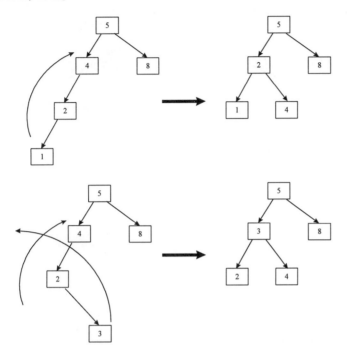

FIGURE 8.6   Examples of rotations in an AVL.

The field **mmap_avl** contains the address of the region descriptor used as root node of the AVL tree.

Figure 8.7 represents the organisation of an AVL tree for a process whose address space contains the following regions:

```
08048000-0804a000  r-xp   00000000 03:02 7914
0804a000-0804b000  rw-p   00001000 03:02 7914
0804b000-08053000  rwxp   00000000 00:00 0
40000000-40005000 rwxp    00000000 03:02 18336
40005000-40006000  rw-p   00004000 03:02 18336
40006000-40007000  rw-p   00000000 00:00 0
40007000-40009000  r--p   00000000 03:02 18255
40009000-40082000  r-xp   00000000 03:02 18060
40082000-40087000  rw-p   00078000 03:02 18060
40087000-400b9000  rw-p   00000000 00:00 0
bfffe000-c0000000  rwxp   fffff000 00:00 0
```

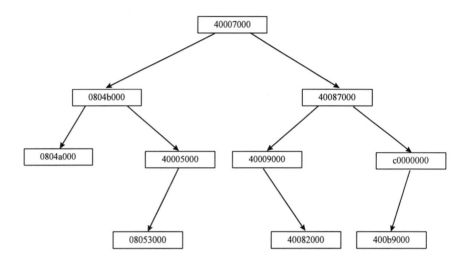

FIGURE 8.7   Organisation of memory regions of a process.

8.5.5 Non-contiguous memory allocation for the kernel

The functions **kmalloc** and **kfree** enable the kernel to allocate and to release memory zones contained in contiguous pages. Although they are very useful for managing small sized zones, they are notoriously inefficient for large zones. Indeed, they use fixed sized blocks and return a block whose size might be much larger than the size requested. For example, if a block of 17 kilobytes is to be allocated (in the x86 architecture), **kmalloc** must use a block of 32 kilobytes, and 15 kilobytes are allocated superfluously.

The functions **vmalloc** and **vfree** do not have this problem. When memory is allocated, several memory pages, which are not necessarily contiguous, are allocated. These pages are then inserted into the segment reserved for the kernel by modifying the page tables. In this way, the amount of memory 'wasted' is less significant.

8.5.6 Management of swap

8.5.6.1 *Format of* swap *devices*
In Linux, any device in block-mode or any normal file can be used as a *swap* device. A *swap* device must always have been initialised by the command *mkswap*. This command creates a catalogue at the beginning of the device. The catalogue has the size of a memory page and is made up of a table of bits. Each of the bits

indicates whether the corresponding page in the device is usable. If, for example the command *mkswap* is executed on a file of four megabytes on an x86 machine which uses a page size of four kikobytes, the catalogue contents are the following:

- the first bit is 1, which indicates that the first page, which contains the catalogue, is not usable;
- the following 1023 bits are 0, indicating that the corresponding pages are usable;
- the following bits are 1, indicating that the following pages do not exist in the file.

The first page also contains a signature: the first 10 bytes contain a character string 'SWAP-SPACE'. This signature enables the kernel to check the validity of a device when it is activated.

The format of a swap device defines the size limit. Given that a bit must exist in the catalogue (which has the size of a page) for each page, the maximum number of pages can be expressed by the formula: (*page_size* − 10) * 8. In the x86 architecture, the maximum size of a *swap* device is therefore in the region of 128 megabytes.

8.5.6.2 *Swap device descriptors*

The kernel keeps a list of active *swap* devices in memory. It uses a table of descriptors, in which each describes a *swap* device.

The structure **swap_info_struct**, declared in the header file **<linux/swap.h>**, defines the format of these descriptors. It contains the following field:

type	*field*	*description*
unsigned int	**flags**	Status of device
kdev_t	**swap_device**	Identifier of device in block mode
struct inode *	**swap_file**	Pointer to the corresponding inode descriptor, in the case of a normal file
unsigned char *	**swap_map**	Pointer to a byte table representing the status of each page
unsigned char *	**swap_lockmap**	Pointer to a bit table indicating for each page whether it is locked or usable
int	**lowest_bit**	Number of the smallest usable page
int	**highest_bit**	Number of the largest usable page
int	**prio**	Priority assigned to the device
int	**pages**	Number of available pages (allocated or not)
unsigned long	**max**	Number of pages on the device
int	**next**	Pointer to the next descriptor in the list

The fields **swap_map** and **swap_lockmap** are used to keep track of the pages used. **swap_map** points to a table of bytes, in which each element contains the number of references to the page. If the number is zero, this means that the page is available, if not, it is allocated.

swap_lockmap points to a table of bits, in which each element indicates whether the corresponding page is locked (if it is 1) or usable (if it is 0). This table is initialised from what is present in the *swap* device catalogue. During input/output of pages on the device, the corresponding bit is set to 1 to prevent any reading or writing during the input/output.

8.5.6.3 *Addresses of* swap *entries*

When a page is written to a *swap* device, an address is attributed to it. This address combines the *swap* device number and the page index used in the device.

Several macro-instructions, declared in the header file **<asm/pgtable.h>**, handle these addresses:

macro-instruction	meaning
SWP_ENTRY	Combination of a device number and a page index to form a **swap** address entry
SWP_TYPE	Return the device number corresponding to a **swap** address entry
SWP_OFFSET	Return the page index corresponding to a **swap** address entry

When a page is to be erased from memory, a page on a *swap* device is allocated to it, and the address of this page must be stored in memory in order that Linux can load the page again later. Rather than use a table to establish the correspondence between memory page addresses and *swap* entries. Linux uses an original method:

- When a memory page is erased, the address of the allocated *swap* entry is saved in the page table, instead of the physical address of the page. This address is designed to indicate to the processor that the page is not present in memory.
- When a memory access is carried out on a page which has been saved on a *swap* device, the processor can tell that the page is not present in memory and it invokes a trap. Linux extracts the address of the *swap* entry from the corresponding entry in the page table, and uses this address to pinpoint a page in the *swap*.

8.5.6.4 *Selection of pages to erase*

In order to erase pages from memory, the process *kswapd* is run. This process is run when the system is started up and executes in kernel mode. It is more or less equivalent to the process *bdflush*, described in chapter 6, section 6.6.2.

The role of the process *kswapd* is not to erase unwanted pages from memory. For most of the time, *kswapd* is dormant and is only awoken when the kernel is short of memory. It scans the list of processes and tries to erase unused pages.

In order to identify the unused memory pages, the kernel uses the field **age** from the memory page descriptor. This counter is incremented when the page is used, and is decremented when it is no longer used. Only the pages having a field **age** of zero can be erased from memory.

8.5.7 Memory operations

Linux not only implements management of page tables independently of the processor, but it also implements general memory management. The memory management module manages memory regions, page tables and the *swap*, but it is not equipped with management mechanisms for the contents of memory regions.

To access the contents of memory regions, the memory management module utilises operations dependent on the memory regions. This method of operating is very similar to that of the virtual filesystem which calls operations on superblocks, inodes, and files, to perform files accesses.

The structure **vm_operations_struct**, declared in the header file **<linux/mm.h>**, defines memory operations associated with memory regions. These operations are the following:

- **void (*open)(struct vm_area_struct * area)**

     The operation **open** is called when a new memory region, referenced by **area**, is created.
- **void (*close)(struct vm_area_struct * area)**

     The operation **close** is called when the memory region, referenced by **area**, is deleted.
- **void (*unmap)(struct vm_area_struct *area, unsigned long start, size_t len)**

     The operation **unmap** is called when the part of the memory region referenced by **area** is deleted from memory. The parameter **start** indicates the address of the beginning of the section to be deleted, and **len** specifies its size.
- **void (*protect)(struct vm_area_struct *area, unsigned long start, size_t len, unsigned int newprot)**

     The operation **protect** is called when the protection measures on a part of the memory region referenced by **area** are changed. The parameter start indicates the address of the beginning of the section to be deleted, and **len** specifies its size. The new protection measures to be applied are specified by the parameter **newprot**.
- **int (*sync)(struct vm_area_struct *area, unsigned long start, size_t len, unsigned int flags)**

     The operation **sync** is called to re-write the contents of a part of the memory region referenced by **area** are changed. The parameter **start** indicates the address of the beginning of the section to be deleted, and len specifies its size. The parameter flags specifies the re-writing method.

- void (*advise)(struct vm_area_struct *area, unsigned long start, size_t len, unsigned int advise)

    The operation advise is not used by Linux 2.0.

- unsigned long (*nopage)(struct vm_area_struct *area, unsigned long address, int write_access)

    The operation nopage is called to load a page into the memory region referenced by area. The parameter address indicates the address to which the page should be loaded, and write_access specifies whether the page will be accessible in write mode or not.

- unsigned long (*wppage)(struct vm_area_struct *area, unsigned long address, unsigned long page)

    The operation wppage is not used by Linux 2.0.

- int (*swapout)(struct vm_area_struct *area, unsigned long page, pte_t pte)

    The operation swapout is called to save to secondary memory the page page of the memory region referenced by area. The parameter pte contains the address of the corresponding entry in the page table.

- int (*swapin)(struct vm_area_struct *area, unsigned long page, unsigned long entry)

    The operation swapin is called to reload into central memory the page of the memory region referenced by area.

8.6
DETAILED DESCRIPTION OF IMPLEMENTATION

8.6.1 Allocation for the kernel

Linux contains several functions enabling memory regions to be dynamically allocated to the kernel, and released.

8.6.1.1 Allocation of memory pages

The source file *mm/page_alloc.c* contains primitives allowing entire memory pages to be allocated and released. Functions in this module manage lists of available pages, following the *Buddy system*, described in section 8.5.3.

The function init_mem_queue initialises a list of page groups, by indicating that the list is empty. The function add_mem_queue adds a page group to the list, and remove_mem_queue deletes a page group from the list it is recorded in.

The function free_pages_ok is called to release a group of pages. It proceeds by updating of the bit tables indicating allocated groups, then adds a group to the list by calling add_mem_queue.

The function __free_page decrements the number of references of the page to release, and calls free_pages_ok if it becomes zero. The function free_pages decrements the number of references of the group of pages to release, and calls free_pages_ok if it becomes zero.

The function **__get_free_pages** is called to allocate a group of pages. It uses the macro-instruction **RMQUEUE** to search a corresponding group of blocks. This the macro-instruction scans all the lists corresponding to group sizes greater than or equal to the size requested. When a group of sufficient size is found, the macro-instruction **EXPAND** splits it into several groups: one is allocated, and the others remain available and are put in corresponding lists. In the event that **__get_free_pages** does not find a group of pages which is large enough, the function **try_to_free_page** is called in order to try to release memory pages, and the process then starts again.

The function **free_area_init** is called when the system is initialised. It allocates the table **mem_map**, containing a descriptor for each page contained in central memory, then allocates the lists of page groups. When created, all the lists are empty.

8.6.1.2 *Allocation of memory regions*
The source file *mm/kmalloc.c* contains the implementation of the functions **kmalloc** and **kfree** which lead to the allocation and release of memory zones for the kernel.

The function **get_malloc_pages** allocates new pages by **calling __get_free_pages**. The function **free_kmalloc_pages** releases pages by calling **free_pages**. It can also place pages in a cache, without releasing them. This cache will be used by **kmalloc** in the event of failure when pages are allocated.

The function **kmalloc_init** is called when the system is installed. It initialises the lists used by **kmalloc**.

The function **kmalloc** allocates a new memory zone. It first scans the list of list descriptors in order to determine the page list to use. If this list is not empty, it allocates the first block, then updates the list, and if is empty, the function **get_malloc_pages** is called in order to allocate new pages to the list. A loop creating free blocks is then performed in the allocated pages, then the first block is allocated. If new pages cannot be allocated, the cache is used: if it contains pages having the specified size, then these are used.

The function **kfree** releases a memory zone allocated by a call to **kmalloc**. The specified block is marked as free, then the number of free blocks in the corresponding pages is incremented. If this number becomes equal to the number of blocks per page, this means that the page contents are entirely free and the latter is released by calling **free_kmalloc_pages**.

8.6.2 **Management of page tables**

The source file *mm/memory.c* contains the management of page tables. It uses a model which is independent of the architecture described in section 8.5.1 c.

The functions which depend on the architecture are defined in **<asm/pgtable.h>**:
pte_none: returns the value 1 if the specified entry in the page table is not initialised;
- **pte_present**: returns the value 1 if the specified page is present in memory;
- **pte_clear**: initialises to 0 the specified entry in the page table;

- **pmd_none**: returns the value 1 if the specified entry in the intermediate table is not initialised;
- **pmd_bad**: returns the value 1 if the specified entry in the intermediate table is wrong;
- **pmd_present**: returns the value 1 if the page containing the intermediate table is present in memory;
- **pmd_clear**: initialises to 0 the specified entry in the intermediate table;
- **pgd_none**: returns the value 1 if the specified entry in the global table is not initialised;
- **pgd_bad**: returns the value 1 if the specified entry in the global table is wrong;
- **pgd_present**: returns the value 1 if the page containing the global table is present in memory;
- **pgd_clear**: initialises to 0 the specified entry in the global table;
- **pte_read**: returns the value 1 if the specified page is accessible in read mode;
- **pte_write**: returns the value 1 if the specified page is accessible in write mode;
- **pte_exec**: returns the value 1 if the specified page is accessible in execution;
- **pte_dirty**: returns the value 1 if the contents of the specified page has been changed;
- **pte_young**: returns the value 1 if the contents of the specified page has been accessed;
- **pte_wrprotect**: renders the specified page inaccessible in write mode;
- **pte_rdprotect**: renders the specified page inaccessible in read mode;
- **pte_exprotect**: renders the specified page inaccessible in execution;
- **pte_mkclean**: resets to 0 the change indicator of the specified page contents;
- **pte_mkold**: resets to 0 the access indicator of the specified page contents;
- **pte_mkwrite**: renders the specified page accessible in write mode;
- **pte_mkread**: renders the specified page accessible in read mode;
- **pte_mkexec**: renders the specified page accessible in execution;
- **pte_mkdirty**: marks the page as modified;
- **pte_mkyoung**: marks the page as accessed;
- **mk_pte**: returns the contents of an entry in the page table by combining the associated memory page address and its protection mode;
- **pte_modify**: modifies the contents of an entry in the page table;
- **pte_page**: returns the address of the memory page contained in an entry in the page table;
- **pmd_page**: returns the address of the memory page containing an intermediate table;
- **pgd_offset**: returns the address of an entry in the global table;
- **pmd_offset**: returns the address of an entry in the intermediate table;
- **pte_offset**: returns the address of an entry in the page table;
- **pte_free_kernel**: releases a page table utilised by the kernel;
- **pte_alloc_kernel**: allocates a page table utilised by the kernel;
- **pte_free**: releases a page table utilised by a process;

- **pte_alloc**: releases an intermediate table utilised by a process;
- **pmd_free**: releases an intermediate table utilised by a process;
- **pmd_alloc**: allocates an intermediate table utilised by a process;
- **pgd_free**: releases a global table utilised by a process;
- **pgd_alloc**: allocates a global table utilised by a process.

The independent functions of the architecture are as follows:

- **copy_page**: copies the contents of a memory page into another;
- **oom**: displays an error message, then sends the signal **SIGKILL** to the process which has exceeded the available memory;
- **free_one_pmd**: releases the page table pointed to by an entry in the intermediate table;
- **free_one_pgd**: releases the intermediate table pointed to by an entry in the global table, by calling **free_one_pmd**;
- **clear_page_tables**: releases the tables assigned to the address space of a user process, by calling **free_one_pmd** for each intermediate table;
- **free_page_tables**: releases the tables assigned to the address space of a user process, by calling **free_one_pmd** for each intermediate table, then by calling **pgd_free**;
- **new_page_tables**: allocates new tables to a process;
- **copy_one_pte**: copies the contents of an entry of the page table to another, by overwriting the write permission if copying by writing is specified;
- **copy_pte_range**: copies the contents of a series of entries of the page table, by calling **copy_one_pte** for each entry;
- **copy_pmd_range**: copies the contents of a series of entries of the intermediate table, by calling **copy_pte_range** for each entry of the intermediate table;
- **copy_page_range**: copies the contents of a memory region, by calling the function **copy_pmd_range** for each intermediate table concerned;
- **free_pte**: releases a page pointed to by an entry in the page table;
- **forget_pte**: releases a page pointed to by an entry in the page table, if this entry is non-null;
- **zap_pte_range**: releases several pages by calling **free_pte** ;
- **zap_pmd_range**: releases a series of entries in the intermediate table by calling the function **zap_pte_range** for each entry of the intermediate table;
- **zap_page_range**: releases the contents of a memory region by calling the function **zap_pmd_range** for each intermediate table concerned;
- **zeromap_pte_range**: initialises several entries in the page table having the same descriptor;
- **zeromap_pmd_range**: allocates page tables and initialises by calling the function **zeromap_pte_range**;
- **zeromap_page_range**: allocates several intermediate tables and calls the function **zeromap_pmd_range** for each table, to initialise the entries in page tables;

- **remap_pte_range**: modifies addresses of pages contained in several entries of the page table;
- **remap_pmd_range**: allocates page tables and changes the addresses contained in them by calling **remap_pte_range**;
- **remap_page_range**: allocates several intermediate tables and changes the table entries by calling **remap_pmd_range**.

8.6.3 Management of memory regions

Memory regions assigned to processes are managed by the functions contained in the source file *mm/mmap.c*.

Two utility functions are defined in the header file **<linux/mm.h>**:

- **find_vma**: this function scans the AVL tree contained in the memory region descriptors assigned to a process to look for a memory region containing the given address, or the first region situated after this address.
- **find_vma_intersection**: this function is called to find the descriptor of a memory region overlapping a given region. It calls **find_vma** to obtain the descriptor of the memory region containing the specified end-point address. If a descriptor is found, it checks to see if the two regions have an overlapping section which is not empty by comparing their start and end-point addresses.

The function **get_unmapped_area** looks for an un-allocated memory region in the address space of the current process, starting from a given address. It calls **find_vma** to obtain the descriptor of the region located immediately after the given address. This process is carried out by varying the address as long as a sufficiently large unused memory zone has not been found.

Several functions of AVL management are defined:

- **avl_neighbours**: this function scans the AVL tree and returns the neighbours of a node, that is, the largest node of the left-hand sub-hierarchy and the smallest of the permission-hand sub-hierarchy.
- **avl_rebalance**: this function performs the necessary rotations to keep the AVL tree balanced.
- **avl_insert**: this function inserts a new node into the tree.
- **avl_insert_neighbours**: this function inserts a new node into the tree and returns its neighbours.
- **avl_remove**: this function deletes a node in the tree.

The function **build_mmap_avl** constructs the AVL tree which contains the descriptors of memory regions of a process by calling **avl_insert** for each region.

The function **insert_vm_struct** adds a memory region into the address space of a process. It calls **avl_insert_neighbours** to insert the descriptor of the region in the

AVL tree, then inserts this descriptor into the list of regions by linking it to the descriptors of neighbouring regions.

The function **remove_shared_vm_struct** deletes a memory region descriptor of an inode.

The function **merge_segments** is called in order to merge process memory regions having two given addresses. It finds the first memory region by calling **find_vma**, then scans all regions situated before the end-point address. For each region, it checks whether the following region is adjacent and whether the characteristics of the two regions are identical. If they are, it merges the two regions into a single one.

8.6.4 Processing of traps

The processor invokes a trap in the event of certain memory accesses:

- access which is incompatible with the form of protection assigned to a memory page;
- access to a page which is not present in memory.

The functions called when a memory trap is processed are defined in the source file *mm/memory.c*:

- **do_wp_page**: this function is called to control copy writing, when a process accesses in write-mode a page which is shared and is protected for read-mode only. It allocates a new memory page by calling **__get_free_page**, then it checks to see if the page which the trap concerns is shared between several processes. If it is, its contents are copied to the new page, and the latter is inserted into the page table of current processes by **set_pte**, and the number of references to the former page is **decremented** by calling **free_page**. In the event that the page concerned is not shared, its protection mode is simply altered to make it possible to write to it.
- **do_swap_page**: this function is called to reload into memory the contents of a region situated in the swap memory space. If an operation **swapin** is associated with the memory region containing the page, it is called. In the opposite case, it is the function **swap_in** which is called. In both cases, the page allocated is inserted into the address space of the current process.
- **do_no_page**: this function is called when a page which is not present in memory is accessed. It first checks to see if the page has been deleted from memory and is contained in the swap address space. If it is, **do_swap_page** is called to reload into memory the contents of the page, if not, **do_no_page** tests to see if a memory operation **nopage** is associated with the region containing the page. If it is, this operation is called to load the contents of the page into memory, and the page is inserted in the page table of the current process. If no operation **nopage** is associated with the memory region containing the page, a new page containing zeros must be allocated: the page is allocated by calling **__get_free_page**, its

contents are initialised to 0, and it is inserted into the page table of the current process.

- **handle_pte_fault**: this function is called to process a memory trap. It ascertains whether the trap concerns a page which is not present, and if so, it calls **do_no_page**, or whether the page is shared and should be copied, in which case it calls **do_wp_fault**.
- **handle_mm_fault**: this function is called when a memory trap is processed in machine architectures having a memory manager which is separate from the processor. It calls **handle_pte_fault**, then updates the cache of the memory manager.

The function **do_page_fault**, declared in the source file *arch/i386/mm/fault.c* for the x86 architecture, is called to process memory traps. It first obtains the descriptor of the memory region concerned by calling **find_vma**, then tests the type of error:

- If the error is caused by an access to a page which is not present in the segment of the stack, the function **expand_stack** is called to increase the size of the stack.
- If the error is due to an access in write-mode to a memory region confined to read-mode, the error is made known to the current process by sending it the signal **SIGSEGV**.
- If the error is due to an access in write-mode to a memory region confined to read-mode, in order to implement a copy write, the function **do_wp_page** is called, to carry out the copy.
- If the error is caused by an access to a page which is not present in memory, the function **do_no_page** is called in order to load the page in memory.

8.6.5   Access to the process address space

As presented in section 5.1.1, Linux uses memory segmentation mechanisms to protect the address spaces of the process and the kernel, in certain architectures. The kernel may therefore not directly access data referenced by an address provided by a process.

Several processes enable the kernel to access the address space of processes. These functions, defined in the header file **<asm/segment.h>**, are as follows:

- **memcpy_fromfs**: reading of the data from the address space of the calling process;
- **memcpy_tofs**: writing of the data to the address space of the calling process;
- **get_user**: reading of an integer composed of 1, 2 or 4 bytes from the address space of the calling process;
- **put_user**: writing of an integer composed of 1, 2 or 4 bytes to the address space of the calling process;
- **get_fs**: returns the register value of the segment **fs**, pointing to the data segment of the calling process ;

- **get_ds**: returns the register value of the segment **ds**, pointing to the data segment of the calling process;
- **set_fs**: changes the register value of the segment **fs**, pointing to the data segment of the calling process.

In addition to these access functions, the function **verify_area**, defined in the source file *mm/memory.c*, is used by the kernel to test the validity of the pointer provided by the calling process. It uses **find_vma** to find the descriptor of the region containing the address specified, and it checks that the protection mode assigned to the region is compatible with the access mode requested (read or write). **verify_area** performs this check on several regions if the zone to be verified extends over several regions. In the event that the memory protection forms are not compatible with the access requested, the error **EFAULT** is returned.

It should be noted that **verify_area** takes account of the operating charcteristics of the processor upon which Linux is executing. In certain processors, such as the i386, memory protection is ignored in kernel mode. On such a processor, if access in write mode is specified, **verify_area** calls **do_wp_page** to duplicate the shared pages.

8.6.6 Modifying memory regions

8.6.6.1 *Creating and deleting memory regions*
The source file *mm/mmap.c* contains the implementation of system calls enabling memory regions to be created and deleted (primitives *mmap* and *munmap*). It also contains the implementation of the system call *brk*.

The function **do_map** carries creates a memory region. It first checks the validity of its parameters. In the case where the contents of a file are to be mapped onto memory in a new region, it also checks that the file opening mode is compatible with the mapping format. A region descriptor is then allocated and initialised. If the memory region has to correspond to a file mapped into memory, the operation **mmap** assigned to the file inode is called. Finally, the region descriptor is inserted into the process address space by calling **insert_vm_struct**, and **merge_segments** is called to merge the memory regions if this is possible.

The function **unmap_fixup** releases a part of the memory region, whose descriptor has already been deleted from the address space of the current process. Four cases can arise:

- the whole region is to be released: the associated memory operation **close** is then called;
- a section located at the beginning of the region is to be released: the address of the beginning of the region is updated in the region descriptor;
- a section located at the end of the region is to be released: the address of the end of the region is updated in the region descriptor;

- a section situated in the middle of the region is to be released: in this case, the region is divided into two. A new region descriptor is allocated and is initialised. The descriptor of the original region is updated. Finally, the new descriptor is inserted in the address space by calling insert_vm_struct.

In the last three cases, unmap_fixup creates a new descriptor for the modified region, and inserts it into the address space of the current process.

The function do_unmap releases the memory regions situated within a specified range. It first scans the list of regions contained in the range, saves their descriptors in the list to memory, and deletes them from the address space of the current process by calling avl_remove. After this loop, it scans the list of descriptors saved earlier. For each region, the memory operation unmap is called, the corresponding pages are deleted from the page table by calling zap_page_range, the function unmap_fixup is called, and the region descriptor is released.

The function sys_munmap implements the system call *munmap* by simply calling do_munmap. The implementation of the system call *mmap* is contained in the source file *arch/i386/kernel/sys_386.c*, for the x86 architecture. The function old_map checks the validity of its parameters, then calls the function do_map.

The function sys_brk implements the primitive *brk*. It verifies that the address supplied is located within the data segment, and that it does not exceed the limits imposed by the process. In the case that the end-of-data segment address is reduced, the function do_munmap is called to release the specified memory zone. In the case of the size of the data segment needing to be enlarged, the function find_vma_intersection is called to check that the zone to be allocated does not come into conflict with an existing region. Then the memory region of the data segment is extended by calling the function do_map.

8.6.6.2 *Locking of memory regions*

The source file *mm/mlock.c* contains the functions implementing locking of memory regions.

The function mlock_fixup_all locks or unlocks an entire region of memory. It modifies uniquely the field vm_flags of the region descriptor.

The function mlock_fixup_start locks or unlocks a zone situated at the beginning of a region. The region should be composed of two parts: the first representing the part whose state changes, and the second representing the part that doesn't change. A descriptor is allocated for a new region, then initialised. The contents of the original region descriptor is also modified in order that the region starts after the region created. Finally, the descriptor of the new region is inserted in the process address space by calling insert_vm_struct.

The function mlock_fixup_end locks or unlocks a zone situated at the end of a region. The region should be composed of two parts: the first representing the part whose state does not change, and the second representing the part that is modified. A descriptor is allocated for a new region, then initialised. The contents of the original region descriptor is also modified in order that the region ends before the region created. Finally, the descriptor of the new region is inserted in the process address space by calling **insert_vm_struct**.

The function **mlock_fixup_middle** locks or unlocks a zone situated at the beginning of a region. The region should be composed of three parts: the first representing the part whose state does not change, and the second representing the part that does change, and the third represents the end of the original region, whose state does not change. Two region descriptors are allocated and initialised. The descriptor of the original region is also modified, the new the descriptors are inserted in the process address space by calling **insert_vm_struct**.

The function **mlock_fixup** changes the locking mode of part, or of all of a memory region. If the state of the region doesn't change, it immediately terminates execution. If it does, it calls one of the earlier functions according to the siting of the zone to be locked or unlocked in the region.

The function **do_mlock** is called to change the locking mode of a part of the process address space. It first checks that the calling process possesses sufficient privileges, then test the validity of its parameters. It then carries out a scan loop of the memory regions included in the specified range. For each region, the function **mlock_fixup** is called in order to change the locking of part, or of all of the region. On completion of this loop, the function **merge_segments** is called in order to merge adjacent regions if the change of state of the different regions has made them compatible.

The primitives **sys_mlock** and **sys_munlock** implement the primitives *mlock* and *munlock* by calling **do_mlock**.

The function **do_mlockall** modifies the locking of the complete address space of a process. It first checks the calling process possesses the necessary privileges, the it carries out a scanning loop on all the memory regions situated in the address space of the process. For each region, the function **mlock_fixup** is called in order to change the locking of the region. At the end of this loop, the function **merge_segments** is called in order to merge adjacent regions if the change of state of the different regions has made them compatible.

The functions **sys_mlockall** and **sys_munlockall** implement the primitives *mlockall* and *munlockall* by calling **do_mlockall**.

8.6.6.3 *Memory protection changes*
The system calls modifying the protection assigned to memory regions are implemented in the source file *mm/mprotect.c*.

Several functions modify the protection modes assigned tomemory pages:

- **change_pte_range**: this function changes memory protection contained in a series of entries in the page table.
- **change_pmd_range**: this function changes memory protection contained in a series of entries in the page table corresponding to a range. It calls the function **change_pte_range** to carry out these modifications.

- **change_protection**: this function changes memory protection of pages corresponding to a memory region, by calling change_pmd_range.

The protections assigned to memory regions are changed by four functions, whose operation is similar to the functions of modification and locking:

- **mprotect_fixup_all**: modification of the protection associated with the entirety of a memory region;
- **mprotect_fixup_start**: modification of the protection associated with a zone situated at the beginning of a memory region;
- **mprotect_fixup_end**: modification of the protection assigned to a zone situated at the end of a memory region;
- **mprotect_fixup_middle**: modification of the protection assigned to a zone situated in the middle of a memory region.

The function **mlock_fixup** calls one of the four above functions according to the zone to be modified internal to the memory region. It then calls **change_protection** to modify the protections assigned to corresponding memory pages.

The function **sys_protect** implements the primitive *mprotect*. It checks the validity of its parameters, then performs a loop on the memory regions within the specified range. For each memory region, **mlock_fixup** is called in order to modify the protections. At the end of this loop, the function **merge_segments** is called in order to merge adjacent regions if the change of state of the different regions has made them compatible.

8.6.6.4   *Re-siting of memory regions*
The source file *mm/mremap.c* contains the functions which implement the re-positioning of memory zones. These re-locations are invoked by the primitive *mremap*.

Several page table management functions are defined:

- **get_one_pte**: returns the address of a page table entry corresponding to a given address;
- **alloc_one_pte**: allocates an entry corresponding to a given address, in the page table;
- **copy_one_pte**: copies the contents of a page table entry into another entry;
- **move_one_page**: calls **get_one_pte** then **copy_one_pte** to copy the page table entry;
- **move_page_tables**: calls **move_one_page** for each page included in the given range.

The function **move_vma** resites a memory region. It allocates a new memory descriptor, obtains an unused address by calling **get_unmapped_area**, and moves the contents of the page table by calling **move_page_tables**. The new descriptor is then initialised, inserted into the process address space by calling **insert_vm_struct**, then the function **merge_segments** is called to merge the adjacent memory regions. Finally, the old memory region is freed by a call to **do_unmap**.

The function **sys_mremap** implements the system call *mremap*. If the new size specified is less than the old, **sys_mremap** merely calls **do_unmap** to liberate the superfluous memory. If this is not the case, it calls **find_vma** to obtain the descriptor of the memory region concerned. It modifies the address of the end of the region, if that is possible, i.e. if there is no region situated in the required space. If the change of size is not possible, and if the option **MREMAP_MAYMOVE** is specified, the function **move_vma** is called to move the memory region.

8.6.7 Creation and deletion of address space

When a process is created by system call *fork*, the process address space is duplicated. When a process is terminated, its address space is released.

The functions **dup_mmap** and **copy_mm**, contained in the source file *kernel/fork.c* (see chapter 4, section 8.6.2), duplicate the address space of the parent process. The function **dup_map** scans the list of memory region descriptors assigned to the process. A new descriptor is allocated for each region, its contents are initialised and the page tables are copied by calling **copy_page_range**. At the end of this loop, the AVL tree containing the region descriptors is constructed by calling **build_mmap_avl**. The function **copy_mm** duplicates the address space descriptor of the parent process, if the child process is not a clone. It then creates the page table of the child process by calling **new_page_tables**, then calls **dup_mmap** to copy the memory regions.

The function **exit_mmap**, defined in the source file *mm/mmap.c*, is called to free the memory regions contained in the process address space, when the latter terminates. It scans the list of region descriptors, calls the memory operations **unmap** and **close** assigned to each region, deletes the corresponding page tables by calling **zap_page_range**, and then releases the descriptor of the region.

The function **_exit_mm** contained in the source file *kernel/exit.c* (see chapter 4, section 8.6.2), is called to release the process address space. It first decrements the number of references to the address space descriptor. If the number becomes zero, it calls **exit_mmap** to delete the memory regions associated with the process, releases the page tables by calling **free_page_tables**, and releases the address space descriptor.

8.6.8 Mapping of files into memory

The source file *mm/filemap.c* contains the routines managing the page cache and the files mapped to memory.

The page descriptors assigned to files mapped into memory are recorder in several hash lists. The table **page_hash_table** contains the address of the first element in each list.

Several functions, defined in the header file **<linux/pagemap.h>**, enable the lists to be managed:

- **_page_hashfn**: this function implements the hash table, based on an inode descriptor and a offset within the file.
- **find_page**: this function performs a scan of a page in the hash lists and returns its descriptor. It sets the flag **PG_referenced** in the descriptor.
- **remove_page_from_hash_queue**: this function deletes a page descriptor from its hash list.
- **add_page_to_hash_queue**: this function adds a page descriptor to the hash lists. It sets the flag **PG_referenced** in the descriptor.
- **remove_page_from_inode_queue**: this function deletes a page descriptor from the list of pages attached to an inode.
- **add_page_to_inode_queue**: this function adds a page descriptor to the list of pages attached to an inode.
- **wait_on_page**: this function suspends the current process whilst waiting for a page if the descriptor of the latter is locked.

The function **release_page** decrements the number of references to a page. This number must be greater than 1 when the call is made. It is a rapid version of **__free_pages**.

The function **invalidate_inode_pages** invalidates all pages assigned to an inode. It performs a loop on the list of pages assigned to an inode, deletes each page of the lists by calling **remove_page_from_hash_queue**, then calls **__free_page** to release each page.

The function **truncate_inode_pages** deletes all pages assigned to an inode, beyond a specified offset. It performs a loop on the list of pages assigned to an inode, and calls **remove_page_from_hash_queue** then **__free_page** for each page involved. It is called when the system call *truncate* is executed.

The function **shrink_mmap** is called in order to free memory pages. It cycles through memory pages and examines pages assigned to an inode or those containing buffers. It checks the number of references of each of the corresponding pages. If this number is equal to 1, it checks to see if the page has been referenced recently. If it has, **shrink_mmap** tries to release the page.

- if the page is assigned to an inode, it is deleted from the cache by calling the function **remove_page_from_hash_queue** then **remove_page_from_inode_queue**, and the page is released;
- if the page contains buffers, the function **try_to_free_buffer** is called in order to release the caches contained in the page, and the page itself.

The function **page_unuse** is called to attempt to free a memory page. If there are 2 references to the page and if the page is assigned to an inode, it is deleted from the lists by calling in turn the functions **remove_page_from_hash_queue** and **remove_page_from_inode_queue**.

The function **update_vm_cache** updates the contents of the memory pages assigned to an inode when the file contents are changed by calling the primitive *write*. It scans the list of pages assigned to an inode and tests to see if the contents of each page are part of the section that has been modified by a write operation. If it has, the contents of the page are updated.

The function **add_to_page_cache** adds a descriptor to the page cache by calling **add_page_to_hash_queue** then **add_page_to_hash_queue**.

The function **try_to_read_ahead** performs an anticipated read operation on the page. It allocates a page by calling **__get_free_page** if necessary. It then calls **find_page** to look for the page in the cache, and if it does not find it, a page read is performed by calling the inode operation **readpage**.

The function **generic_file_read** implements the data read operation from a file, using the page cache to read the data in memory. It performs a loop by calling **find_page** to look for the page corresponding to the data to be read. If the page is not found in the cache, a page is allocated by calling **__get_free_page**, this page is added to the cache by calling **add_to_page_cache**, and its contents are read from disk by calling the operation **readpage** assigned to the inode. Once the page has been read from disk, or if the page has been found in the cache, its contents are copied to the buffer.

The function **filemap_nopage** implements the memory operation **nopage** for the files that are mapped to memory. It first carries out a scan of the specified page in the cache by calling **find_page**. If the page is not found in the cache, a page is allocated by calling **__get_free_page**, this page is added to the cache by **calling add_to_page_cache**, and its contents are read from the disk by calling the operation **readpage** assigned to the inode. Once the page has been read from the disk, or if the page has been found in the cache, **filemap_nopage** checks to see if he page can be shared between several processes. If it can (for example for a private mapping), the page is duplicated: a new page is allocated and its contents are initialised based on the contents of the first page.

The function **do_write_page** re-writes to disk the contents of a page associated with a file mapped into memory. For this, it calls the operation **write** associated with the specified file.

The function **filemap_write_page** writes the contents of a page to a file. It creates a temporary open file descriptor, then calls **do_write_page** to perform the write operation.

The function **filemap_swapout** implements the operation **swapout** associated with files mapped into memory. It calls **filemap_write_page** to write the contents of the page, then resets to 0 the corresponding entry in the page table by calling **pte_clear**.

The function **filemap_swapin** can only by called during a page write operation. Indeed, if the page has been erased from memory, its entry in the page table is null and it is the operation **readpage** that will be called. If, on the other hand, the page is being saved by **filemap_swapout**, its entry its not null, and this indicates nevertheless that the page is not present. In this case, filemap_swapin re-initialises the contents of the entry corresponding to the page.

The re-writing of modified pages is carried out by several functions:

- filemap_sync_pte: this function re-writes a page to disk by calling the function filemap_write_page.
- filemap_sync_pte_range: this function re-writes a series of pages to disk by calling the function filemap_sync_pte for each page.
- filemap_sync_pmd_range: this function re-writes a series of pages to disk by calling the function filemap_sync_pte_range.
- filemap_sync: this function implements the memory operation sync associated with files mapped to memory. It uses filemap_sync_pmd_range to re-write to disk all pages contained in the given range.

The function filemap_unmap implements the memory operation unmap associated with files mapped to memory. It simply calls filemap_sync to re-write the modified pages to disk.

The function generic_file_map implements the file operation mmap associated with files. It checks that the memory mapping can be carried out, then initialises the field vm_inode of the memory region descriptor. The number of references to the inode is incremented, and the pointer vm_ops is initialised with the address of the variable file_private_mmap, in the case of a private mapping, or of file_private_mmap, in the case of a shared mapping.

Finally, the source file *mm/filemap.c* contains the implementation of the system call *msync*. The function msync_interval calls the memory operation sync associated with a region, and the function file_sync to force re-writing to disk if the option MS-SYNC is enabled. The function sys_msync checks the validity of its parameters, then calls msync_interval for each memory region located in the specified range.

8.6.9 Management of swap

8.6.9.1 *Management of* swap *devices*
The source file *mm/swapfile.c* contains the functions controlling files or devices used to save pages erased from memory.

The table swap_info contains the characteristics of active *swap* devices. The variable swap_list contains the device index marked with the highest priority.

The function scan_swap_map looks for an available page in the given device. It scans the table indicating the status of pages and returns the number of an available page.

The function **get_swap_page** is called to allocate a page on a *swap* device. It scans the list of available devices and calls **scan_swap_map** for each device. When a page is found, its *swap* address is returned.

The function **swap_free** is called to free a page on a *swap* device. It decrements the byte containing the number of references to the page.

The functions **unuse_pte**, **unuse_pmd** and **unuse_pgd** are called when a *swap* device is de-activated. It scans the page tables and reloads in memory all the pages present on the given device. The function **unuse_vma** utilises **unuse_pgd** to reload all pages corresponding to a memory region.

The function **unuse_process** scans the list of memory regions contained in the process address space. It calls **unuse_vma** for each region.

The function **try_to_unuse** is called to reload into memory all pages present on the given device. It scans the table of processes and calls the function **unuse_process** to reload the address space of each process.

The function **sys_swapoff** implements the primitive *swapoff* which de-activates a *swap* device. It first checks that the calling process has the required privileges, then looks for the device descriptor in the table **swap_info**, and deletes it from the list. It next calls **try_to_unuse** to reload into memory all the pages saved on the device. If that doesn't work, the device descriptor is again put into the list, and an error is returned. If successful, the file operation **release** associated with the device is called, and the descriptor is released.

The function **sys_swapon** implements the primitive *swapon* which activates a *swap* device. It first checks that the calling process possesses the required privileges, then looks for a free descriptor in the table **swap_info**, and initialises the descriptor. A memory page is next allocated, the *swap* device catalogue is read from this page, and the signature of the *swap* device is verified. After this check, a loop is performed in order to count the pages available on the device, the page status byte table is allocated and initialised. Finally, the descriptor of the device is inserted into the list.

8.6.9.2 *Input/output on* swap *pages*
The source file *mm/page_io.c* contains the page input/output functions acting on *swap* devices.

The function **rw_swap_page** reads or writes a page in the *swap* device. It checks that given device is active, and that the page number is valid, then locks the page concerned in the *swap* device descriptor. Next, it checks the type of *swap* device:

- If it is a device in block mode, the function **ll_rw_page** is called to read or write the contents of the page.
- If it is a *swap* file, the operation **bmap** associated with the file is called to ascertain the addresses of blocks making up the page, and **ll_rw_swap_file** is called to read or write the blocks. This function, defined in the source file *drivers/block/ll_rw_blk.c*, generates input/output requests for specified blocks.

The function **swap_after_unlock_page** is called when a page read or write in a *swap* device is terminated. It unlocks the page concerned in the *swap* device descriptor.

The function **ll_rw_page** is used to read or write a page in a device in block mode. It locks the page in memory by setting the flag **PG_locked**, then calls the function **brw_page** to carry out an input/output.

The functions **read_swap_page** and **write_swap_page**, declared in the header file **<linux/swap.h>**, call **rw_swap_page** to carry out a page read or write.

The function **swap_in**, defined in the source file *mm/page_alloc.c* is called to load a memory page for a process. It allocates a memory page, and calls **read_swap_page** to load its contents. The address of the page is then recorded in the entry of the page table concerned.

8.6.9.3 *Erasing memory pages*

The source file *mm/vmscan.c* contains the functions which select page for erasure from memory, and write them to a *swap* device.

The function **try_to_swap_out** is called in order to try to erase a given page. If the page is reserved or locked, or has recently been accessed, it is not erased from memory. If this is not the case, its status is tested, and if the page has been modified, it has to be saved to disk: if a memory operation **swapout** is associated with the region containing the page, it is called; if not, a *swap* entry is allocated by calling **get_swap_page**, and the function **write_swap_page** is called to write the page. In the case where the page has not been modified, the function **page_unuse** is called to delete it from the page cache, then the page is freed by **free_page**.

The functions **swap_out_pmd** and **swap_out_pgd** scan the page table of a process and attempt to erase each page. They halt execution as soon as a page has been erased. The function **swap_out_vma** calls **swap_out_pgd** to attempt to erase a page from a memory region and stop execution as soon as a page has been erased.

The functions **swap_out_process** is called to erase a page from the address space of a process. It scans the list of memory regions contained in the address space of a process, calls **swap_out_vma** for each region to halt execution as soon as a page has been erased.

The function **swap_out** is called to erase a page forming part of the address space of one of the existing processes. It scans the process table and calls the function **swap_out_process** for each process having pages resident in memory. When a page has been able to be erased, or when it has not been able to be erased, execution is stopped.

The function **try_to_free_page** is called to try to free any memory page, It calls in turn, **shrink_mmap, shm_swap,** and **swap_out** to achieve this.

The function **kswapd** implements the process *kswapd* which erases pages from the memory in the background. This process performs an infinite loop during which it is suspended by a call to **interruptible_sleep_on**, then tries to free memory pages by calling **try_to_free_page** when it is awoken.

The function **swap_tick** is called at each clock cycle. It wakes the process *kswapd* to free up memory if the number of pages available is less than the allowed threshold.

9

POSIX terminals

9.1.1 General overview

The term *terminals* is used to designate for entities which range from simple consoles to machines that any user works at, from the window **xterm**, to the serial link connecting a person to a machine via a modem. Terminals may be thought of as conduits between users and applications, and the complexity of their use arises from the diversity of devices that they can communicate with. However, they also act as an indicator of machine power.

On any Unix machine, terminals are represented by special files known as *character mode* files(see chapter 7, section 7.1, for more details on this type of device), in which it is possible to read, when a user presses keyboard key for example, or write, when data is sent via modem over a serial port.

In general, five types of terminal can be identified under Linux, as follows:

- virtual consoles, which are normally used when a user is physically connected to a machine: **tty1** → **tt63**;
- master pseudo-terminals: **ptyp0** → **ptysf**;
- slave pseudo-terminals which are used over a distant connection or in a window X-Window: **ttyp0** → **ttysf**;
- serial ports used by modems, mice: **ttyS0** → **ttyS63** and **cua0** → **cua63**. The fact that two terminals for each port will be explained later;
- particular terminals: consoles, specific serial cards[1], certain particular mouse types, such as models PS/2 …

---

[1] Some cards exist which allow more than the two ports normally implemented on PCs. In the event that the machine possesses one of these cards, particular terminals are assigned to it. For example, peripherals **ttyC0** to **ttyC31** are dedicated to *Cyclades* cards.

Linux has some special terminal management features. Indeed, if the management of virtual terminals and pseudo-terminals is rather similar to that on other Unix systems, the management of serial ports is different (two devices per port). The first category **ttySx** is used for opening calls. For example, it is possible to be connected to certain machines by a modem, and in this case, it is a **ttySx** file on the distant machine which will be used to 'reply' to the connection. Files of type **cuax** are used on the machine at which the user is based to operate the modem.

When a process opens a special **ttySx** file, it is put on hold until the corresponding device is ready. A connection establishment program (*getty*) on a serial port, is therefore suspended until a connection takes effect and the connected modem raises a DTR (*Data Terminal Ready*) signal. In contrast, no suspension is invoked if a process opens a special **cuax** file. It is therefore the ports which will be called on to perform 'outgoing' calls.

A big problem, which has frustrated many developers, arises from the configuration of these different terminals because, given their variety, the code is not very portable between the different existing Unix versions. The POSIX.1 standard has normalised the manipulation operations by being based mainly on the existing functionality of System V (see [AT&T, 1989], and especially [Lewine, 1991]), whilst adding high-level primitives which avoid excessive use of the call *ioctl*.

If the term *Posix Terminals* is taken to cover the 'physical' mechanisms of serial port management, the standard has set out clearly the notions of sessions and groups of processes. These notions have enabled people to distinguish at the level of the operating system processes executing in the background and those executing in the foreground. This distinction also allows it to be determined whether a process belongs to a user session, or whether it is itself the leader of the session.

9.1.2   Configuration of a terminal

9.1.2.1   *Canonic mode and non-canonic mode*

Before describing the details of terminal configuration, it is necessary to present two modes of utilising a terminal: *canonic* mode and *non-canonic* mode.

Canonic mode is simplest: data input at a terminal is organised in the form of lines. A line is delimited by a line-feed (LF) character, and end-of-file (EOF) character, or an end-of-line (EOL) character. These different types of characters are described in section 9.1.3.

This means that a program wishing to read a line on a terminal must wait until a complete line has been captured before being able to process it. The number of characters is unimportant, what matters is that it should be a complete line that is sent. It is, however, possible to read only a limited number of characters (without any loss of information). Reading may also stop if a signal is received. In this mode, the mechanism for deleting characters or lines is normally invoked (the characters **ERASE, WERASE, KILL** will be described later).

In the non-canonic mode, input characters are not processed in the form of lines. The values MIN and TIME are employed to determine how the characters are received, but MIN and TIME are only usable when the line is not configured in canonic mode. They determine how a process should process received characters, and their behaviour is rather complex. MIN represents the minimum number of characters which must be received before a read cycle is complete, and TIME represents a *timer* count in tenths of a second which is used to make data available after a certain period. The two values are linked, and four different scenarios exist:

1. MIN > 0 and TIME > 0: TIME is then used as a *timer* between each character. It is activated after the first character is received, and is reset after each new arrival. If MIN characters are received after the expiry of the period TIME, then a read cycle is complete, and if not, the characters received are returned to the user. If the number of characters read is less than the number of characters presented, then the *timer* is not reset and the read cycle is immediately completed.

2. MIN>0, TIME = 0: in this case, only MIN is used. A read cycle is only complete when MIN characters have been received.

3. MIN = 0, TIME > 0: since MIN = 0, TIME is used as a read *timer* which is activated as soon as a read is carried out. A read cycle is complete as soon as a single character is received, as long as the proper time count has elapsed. In this case, no characters are sent back. Therefore, if no characters are received in the period TIME * 0.10 seconds, the read fails.

4. MIN = 0, TIME = 0: return of characters is immediate. The minimum number of characters requested (or available) is returned.

9.1.2.2 *The* termios *structure*

The configuration of a POSIX terminal is not particularly straightforward, as a result of the large number of variants that may exist. This is for a variety of reasons, from the high data rate, to the type of coding used etc.

The header files enabling the functionality of POSIX terminals to be exploited are numerous. However, the majority of primitives, structures and constants used reside in the header file <termios.h>. The latter includes the files <linux/termios.h>, <asm/termios.h> and <asm/termbits.h>, which put the real definitions into effect.

The configuration of a terminal is carried out by means of the structure termios. It also enables the configuration to be inspected and its parameters changed. The details are tabulated below:

type	*field*	*description*
tcflag_t	**c_iflag**	Input modes
tcflag_t	**c_oflag**	Output modes
tcflag_t	**c_cflag**	Control modes
tcflag_t	**c_lflag**	Local modes
cc_t	**c_line**	Line protocol[2]
cc_t [NCCS]	**c_cc**	Control characters

The field types for this structure are actually **unsigned int** for **tcflag_t**, and **unsigned char** for **cc_t**. The 'real' types of these fields are only given as indicators and must under no circumstances be used in source code, because they may depend upon the way they are implemented.

9.1.2.3 How communication operates

Before continuing with the details of the different values that the fields of this structure may take, it is necessary to understand how a communication with a terminal is set up and how it functions.

Exchange of data between a process and a POSIX terminal is carried out, as figure 9.1 shows, via two buffers. These buffers enable the data transfer between a process and a terminal to be speeded up (as long as the terminal has not been configured differently). When a character is transferred from a buffer to the terminal, it undergoes a transformation depending on the characteristics of the terminal, and the inverse transformation takes place when a character originates in the terminal. Indeed, in order to carry out a correct dialogue with the 'hardware' which exists, it is necessary to adapt (speed, 7 or 8-bit coding, control bit, parity bit etc.) to the communication protocol of the terminal. As a consequence, reading and writing are transparent, since the conversion operation is encapsulated and is not visible to the developer, except when the terminal is initialised. This greatly eases communications.

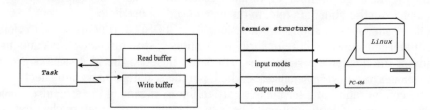

FIGURE 9.1:   Communication between process and terminal.

---

[2] Caution: this field is only present for reasons of compatibility with the former structure **termio**. It is not present on other Unix systems.

9.1.2.4 *Configuration of input modes*

The input modes, which are represented by the field **c_iflag** in the **termios** structure, enable the definition of the processing necessary (conversions, format etc.) in order to transmit a character from a terminal to a buffer.

To configure this field, the developer has a number of options available, which are declared in the header file **<linux/tty.h>**. In the following table, all the options which it is possible to use to configure a serial line are presented. However, some are specific to the POSIX.1 standard, whilst others are extensions (SVR4, BSD...). Where the POSIX.1 standard is not followed, the table entry is left empty.

macro-instruction	meaning	standard
BRKINT	If **IGNBRK** is not fixed, reception of a **BREAK** character causes the signal **SIGNT** to be sent and the input and output buffers are emptied. If this is not the case, reading a **BREAK** character is equivalent to a \0 character.	POSIX.1
ICRNL	If **IGNR** is not set, a **CR** character received is converted to a **NL** character.	POSIX.1
IGNBRK	The characters **BREAK** are not taken into account, but simply ignored.	POSIX.1
IGNR	Ignore the **CR** character.	POSIX.1
IGNPAR	Ignore parity and windowing errors.	POSIX.1
IMAXBEL	Sound a beep when the input buffer is full.	POSIX.1
INLCR	Convert character NL to CR.	POSIX.1
INPCK	Activate parity checking. If this option is not set, error checking is not performed.	POSIX.1
ISTRIP	Delete 8th bit.	POSIX.1
IUCLC	Change upper case to lower case letters.	POSIX.1
IXANY	Activate all characters.	POSIX.1
IXOFF	Activate flow control XON/XOFF on the input: the characters **START** and **STOP** are automatically sent by the system to avoid data loss.	POSIX.1

Continuation of the list of options for configuring a serial line.		
macro-instruction	*meaning*	*standard*
IXON	Activate flow control XON/XOFF on the output: it the character **STOP** is received, the data stream is suspended until the character **START** is sent.	POSIX.1
PARMRK	Mark parity errors. If **IGNPAR** is not set, a byte having a parity or a windowing error is sent to the application in the form of three successive characters; \377, \0 and the errored character. In the case where **IGNPAR** and **PARMRK** are not fixed, reading a character having a parity or a windowing error is equivalent to reading the character \0.	POSIX.1

9.1.2.5 Configuration of output modes

The output modes, which are represented by the field **c_oflag** in the **termios** structure, enable the definition of the necessary processing (conversions, format etc.) to achieve transmission of a character from a buffer to a terminal.

To configure this field, the developer has a number of options available, which are declared in the header file **<linux/tty.h>**.

macro-instruction	*meaning*	*standard*
BSDLY	Delay after a character **backspace.**	POSIX.1
BS0, BS1	Masks for **BSDLY.**	
CRDLY	Delay mask after a carriage return .	
CR0, CR1, CR2, CR3	Masks for **CRDLY.**	
FFDLY	Delay after the character **FF.**	
FF0, FF1	Masks for **FFDLY.**	
NLDLY	Delay mask after a character **NL** .	
NL0, NL1	Masks for **NLDLY.**	
OCRNL	Transforms characters **CR** to **NL.**	
OFDEL	The fill character if the ASCII character DEL, if not it is the character NULL.	
OFILL	Sends fill characters to cause a delay.	

Continuation of the list options for output mode field configuration		
macro-instruction	*meaning*	*standard*
OLCUC	Transforms lower case into upper case.	
ONLCR	Transforms characters **NL** to **CR NL**.	
ONLRET	The character **NL** is interpreted as being a character **CR**.	
ONOCR	Does not display the character **CR** in column 0.	
OPOST	Activates processing of characters.	POSIX.1
TABDLY	Delay after tabulation.	
TAB0, TAB1, TAB2, TAB3, XTABS	Masks for **TABDLY**. The mask **XTABS** transforms a tabulation into 8 spaces.	
VTDLY	Delay after a vertical tabulation.	
VT0, VT1	Masks for **VTDLY**.	

9.1.2.6 *Configuration of control modes*

The control modes are defined by the field c_cflag of the structure termios, and enable the response of the hardware the program has to communicate with to be defined.

To configure this field, the developer has available several options declared in the header file <linux/tty.h>:

macro-instruction	*meaning*	*standard*
CBAUD	Communication line rate	
B0, B50, B75, B110, B134, B150, B200, B300, B600, B1200, B1800, B2400, B4800, B9600, B19200, B38400	Masks for **BSDLY**.	
CBAUDEX	Extension declaring the modem communications speed	
B57600, B11520, B230400, B460800	Speed mask.	
CIBAUD	Mask for data input speed (not used)	
CLOCAL	Ignores line control of the modem.	POSIX.1

Continuation of the list of options for configuring the control field		
macro-instruction	*meaning*	*standard*
CREAD	Activates the receiver.	POSIX.1
CRTSCTS	Flow control	POSIX.1
CSIZE	Size of character coding	POSIX.1
CS5, CS6, CS7, CS8	Masks for **CSIZE**	POSIX.1
CSTOPB	Two stop bits instead one	POSIX.1
HUPCL	Automatic disconnection when the last process under control terminates.	POSIX.1
PARENB	Parity activated.	POSIX.1
PARODD	Odd parity. If this mask is not indicated, parity is even.	POSIX.1

9.1.2.7 Configuration of local modes

These modes are paramount because they specify how characters are interpreted.

macro-instruction	*meaning*	*standard*
ECHO	If mask set, typed characters visible.	POSIX.1
ECHOCTL	If **IEXTEN** is set, all control characters different from **TAB, NL, START,** and **STOP, CR** and **BS** take their ASCII value plus 100 in octal.	POSIX.1
ECHOE	If **ICANON** set, the character **ERASE** deletes previous character, and char. **WERASE** deletes previous word.	POSIX.1
ECHOK	If **ICANON** is set, the character **KILL** deletes the current line.	POSIX.1
ECHOKE	If **ICANON** is set, the character **KILL** is sent out to delete each of the characters of the line, as specified by **ECHOE** and **ECHOPRT**.	
ECHONL	If **ICANON** is set, the character **NL** is sent even if **ECHO** is not set.	POSIX.1
ECHOPRT	If **ICANON** and **IECHO** are both set, characters are displayed as they are deleted (this serves to view the characters that are deleted).	POSIX.1

Continuation of the list of options for configuring the local mode		
macro-instruction	*meaning*	*standard*
FLUSHO	Output buffer emptied. Option toggled when character **DISCARD** received.	
ICANON	Activates the canonic mode, that is, use of terminal in interactive mode. This activates certain special characters such as **EOF, EOL, EOL2, ERASE, KILL, REPRINT, STATUS** and **WERASE**. Finally, toggling in this particular mode means that characters coming from the terminal are inserted in buffer in the form of a line terminated by the characters **NL** and **LF**.	POSIX.1
IEXTEN	Activates the processing system defined by the implementation of the device.	POSIX.1
ISIG	When the **characters INTR, QUIT, SUSP** (or **DSUSP**) are received, the signals **SIGINT, SIGQUIT**, and **SIGTSP** are sent respectively.	POSIX.1
NOFLSH	De-activates the system for emptying input and output buffers when the signals **SIGINT** or **SIGQUIT** are received. It also de-activates the system for emptying the input buffer when the signal **SIGSUSP** is received.	POSIX.1
PENDIN	All characters in the input buffer are returned when the next character is sent.	
TOSTOP	Sends the signal **SIGTTOU** to the process group of a background process attempting to write to the control terminal.	POSIX.1
ICASE	If **ICANON** is set, the terminal is operating only in upper case. All characters received at the terminal input are converted to upper case, except characters preceded by a '\'. At the output, characters in upper case are preceded by a '\' and lower case letters are converted to upper case.	

9.1.3 Special characters and the *c_cc* table

Certain particular characters have been used in explaining the values that different fields can take. The POSIX.1 standard defines 11 characters which are treated in a special way. Other standards add certain characters to this list, which are also accomodated by Linux. However, their use is not advised since they do not conform to POSIX.

POSIX.1 also enables the value of these characters to be changed. (except **NL** and **CR**). To bring this about, all that is necessary is to modify the entries in the table **c_cc**, of the **termios** structure. In the following example, the control character **QUIT** has been disabled, and the character **INTR** has been redefined[3].

———— Modifieccc.c ————————————————————

```c
#include <termios.h>
#include <unistd.h>
#include <stdio.h>

void main()
        struct termios term;

        /* Get the terminal configuration */
        if (tcgetattr (STDIN_FILENO, &term) == -1 {
                perror ("tcgetattr");
                exit (-1)
        }
        /* modification of the composition of c_cc */
        term.c_cc[VINTR] = 65; /* change */
        term.c_cc[VQUIT] = _POSIX_VDISABLE; /* de-activate */

        /* update the structure */
        if (tcsetattr (STDIN_FILENO, TCSAFLUSH, &term) == -1 {
                perror ("tcgetattr");
                exit (-1)
        }
}
```

———————————————————————————— Modifieccc.c ————————

The example above illustrates the modification of a character, but above all the disabling of the effect of another. This is achieved by giving it the value **_POSIX_VDISABLE**, a constant which is defined by the standard POSIX.1 and which enables the action of a character to be easily suppressed.

—————————————————

[3] Use of this example on a terminal is strongly discouraged. Indeed the behaviour of the communication channel will be altered as a result of these changes. It would be better to carry out a test on a window *xterm* dedicated for this purpose.

To end this section, and before treating functions dealing with access to and manipulation of terminals, the table below lists each of the characters, along with their effect.

Character	meaning	c_cc	activated by	Value	standard
CR	Carriage return		**ICANON**	\r	POSIX.1
DISCARD	No longer use the output	VDISCARD	**IEXTEN**	^O	
DSUSP		VDSUSP	**ISIG**	^Y	
EOF	End of file: all characters typed before can now be read	VEOF	**ICANON**	^D	POSIX.1
EOL	End of line	VEOL	**ICANON**		POSIX.1
EOL2	Another end of line character	VEOL2	**ICANON**		POSIX.1
ERASE	backspace character	VERASE	**ICANON**	^H	POSIX.1
INTR	Interruption signal **SIGINT**	VINTR	**ISIG**	^? ^C	POSIX.1
KILL	Line deletion	VKILL	**ICANON**	^U	POSIX.1
LNEXT	All subsequent characters are ignored	VLNEXT	**ICANON**	^V	POSIX.1
MIN	see section 1.2.1	VMIN		4	POSIX.1
NL	Carriage return		**ICANON**	\n	POSIX.1
QUIT	Signal QUIT	VQUIT	**ISIG**	^\	POSIX.1
REPRINT	re-displays all characters	VREPRINT	**ICANON**	^R	
START	Re-authorises the emission of characters to the terminal	VSTART	**IXON/ IXOFF**	^Q	POSIX.1
STATUS	Request for status	VSTATUS	**ICANON**	^T	
STOP	Suspends emission of character to terminal	VSTOP	**IXON/ IXOFF**	^S	POSIX.1

Continuation of the list of characters					
Character	*meaning*	*c_cc*	*activated by*	*Value*	*standard*
SUSP	Signal **SIGTSTP**	VSUSP	**ISIG**	^Z	POSIX.1
TIME	see section 1.2.1	VTIME		N.D.	
WERASE	Erasure of the last word typed on the line.	VWERASE	**ICANON**	^W	

These characters are treated as special because their presence in a communication session affects the conversion of code received. Some of these are not defined under the POSIX.1 standard, as indicated in the table. However, in the interests of portability, Linux interworks with them without problems.

9.1.4 The command stty

The command *stty* enables all the parameters of the terminal a user is connected to be established. Indeed, this command enables parameters to be read from a terminal, and also to be modified.

```
gandalf# stty -a
speed 9600 baud; rows 24; columns 80; line = 0;
intr = ^C; quit = ^\; erase = ^?; kill = ^U; eof = ^D; eol = <undef>;
eol2 = <undef>; start =^Q; stop = ^S; susp = ^Z; rprnt = ^R; werase = ^W;
lnext = ^V; flush = ^O; min = 1; time = 0;
-parenb -parodd cs8 -hupcl -cstopb cread -clocal -crtscts
-ignbrk -brkint -ignpar -parmrk -inpck -istrip -inlcr -igncr icrnl ixon
-ixoff
-iulc -ixany -imaxbel
opost -olcuc -ocrnl onlcr -onocr -onlret -ofill -ofdel nl0 cr0 tab0 bs0
vt0 ff0
isig icanon iexten echo echoe echok -echonl -noflsh -xcase -tostop -
echoprt
echoctl echoke
```

9.1.5 The command setserial

The command *setserial* enables information about a serial port (which is a particular type of terminal) to be obtained.

For example, the information regarding the serial port used by a mouse is shown below:

```
gandalf# setserial -a /dev/mouse
/dev/mouse, Line 0, UART: 16550A, Port: 0x03f8, IRQ:4
        Baud_base: 115200, close_delay 50, divisor: 0
        Flags: spd_normal skip_test
```

9.1.6 Terminal groups–the session

The notion of groups of processes and groups of sessions were introduced in chapter 4, section 4.1.7.

A control terminal distinguishes one of the process groups in the session to which it is associated to form the foreground process group. All other process groups in a session are therefore designated as background processes. The foreground process group plays a particular role in the management of characters which need to be captured. By default, when a control terminal is associated to it, the process can read and write data on the terminal. Of course, there can be only one process of this type at a time on a given terminal.

The background process groups must conform to the line discipline when they wish to access their control terminal. This causes the process which is performing a read operation to stop, since it is in the background. In this event, it receives the signal **SIGTTIN**. When the **TOSTOP** bit of the control terminal is set, background process groups wishing to write to the control terminal receive the signal **SIGTTOU**, and are therefore also suspended. In addition, the signals **SIGINTR**, **SIGQUIT** and **SIGUSP** are not sent to it by the terminal.

9.1.7 Pseudo-terminals

A pseudo-terminal is a software layer which enables two terminals to communicate. It has two components: a master terminal, and a slave terminal. From a device point of view, the slave pseudo-terminal is associated with a *tty*, whilst the master pseudo-terminal is associated with a *pty*. The main difference between a pseudo-terminal and a real terminal is that all that is written on a pseudo-terminal is available to be read by the slave terminal, as figure 9.2 illustrates. Equally, all that is written on the slave terminal can be read on the master terminal.

FIGURE 9.2: Reading/writing on a pseudo-terminal.

Master pseudo-terminals can be accessed via the files */dev/ptyp0* to */dev/ptysf* and slave pseudo-terminals can be accessed via the files */dev/ttyp0* to */dev/ttysf* .

Pseudo-terminals have the advantage of being usable exactly like normal files, that is, with standard system calls like *read* and *write*. However, the master pseudo-terminal may only be opened once because two processes are not able to open the same master pseudo-terminal. If this is attempted, the error **EBUSY** is returned. Pseudo-terminals are mainly used by network servers and windowing systems such as X-Windows. For example, the main command *rlogin* consists of opening a network connection to a daemon *rlogind* which is executing on another machine. This daemon launches a process to execute the command *login*, and communicates with it by means of pseudo-terminals:

- *rlogind* owns the master pseudo-terminal and writes to it to all the packets received from the network; it also reads data written by the child process and transmits it on the network;
- *rlogin* owns the slave pseudo-terminal and sends its display to it; it also reads from it on its standard input, data transmitted by *rlogind*.

Figure 9.3 illustrates this mechanism.

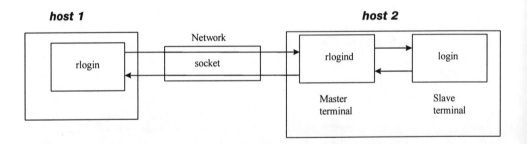

FIGURE 9.3:   Using a pseudo-terminal with *rlogin*.

9.2
POSIX FUNCTIONS

Before the POSIX.1 standard was made applicable to terminals, configuration was carried out by the system call *ioctl*. However, readability was poor, and the code was particularly difficult to implement. With the definition of these POSIX.1 functions, configuration and access to terminals is much simpler. In the description of terminal handling functions, the use of the system call *ioctl* will also be included, although this is the old method, and though it is preferable not to use it.

9.2.1 Access to and modification of terminal attributes

Two methods enabling the configuration of a terminal to be captured, and its configuration to be changed have already been illustrated in a previous example (see section 9.1.3).

```
#include <termios.h>
#include <unistd.h>

int tcgetattr (int fd, struct termios *termios_p);

int tcgetattr (int fd, int optional_actions, struct termios *termios_p);
```

The first function enables the terminal configuration to be reset. All that is needed for this is to identify the file descriptor and a pointer to an allocated **termios** structure. This function is equivalent to using the request **TCGETS**.

```
int tcgetattr (int fd, struct termios *termios_p)
{
        return ioctl (fd, TCGETS, termios_p);
}
```

The function *tcsetattr* enables the configuration of the required terminal to be carried out. The first and third parameter represent the same things as in the previous function. The second parameter allows the method of implementing the configuration to be specified:

- **TCSANOW** (request **TCSETS**): the change is carried out immediately;
- **TCSADRAIN** (request **TCSETSW**): the change is carried out after all write operations to the file descriptor have been completed. It is preferable for the developer to use this option when changing terminal output attributes;
- **TCSAFLUSH** (request **TCSETSF**): the change is carried out after all write operations to the file descriptor have been completed. The read buffer is emptied if characters still remain in it.

This function call is equivalent to the following code:

```
int tcsetattr (int fd, int optional_actions, struct termios *termios_p);
{
        switch (optional_actions) {
                case TCSANOW;
                        return ioctl (fd, TCSETS, termios_p);
                case TCSADRAIN;
                        return ioctl (fd, TCSETSW, termios_p);
```

```
                          case TCSAFLUSH;
                                  return ioctl (fd, TCSETSF, termios_p);
                          default:
                                  errno = EINVAL;
                                  return -1;
        }
        }
```

It is important to note that, after the behaviour of a terminal has been altered, all processes accessing the terminal will adopt this new behaviour.

The values returned from these two methods are 0 in the event of success, and if a problem arises, the values are –1 , and the variable is set.

The following errors may be generated when POSIX functions are used for manipulating terminals:

error	*meaning*
EINVAL	Bad parameter
ENOTTY	The device is not a terminal
EIO	Input/output error
ESPIPE	Direct setting is not possible
ENOMEM	Out of memory
ENODEV	The device corresponding to the terminal does not exist
EPERM	Insufficient user permissions to carry out the operation
EBUSY	Terminal busy

9.2.2 An example of line configuration

Before continuing further, the following is a short program example illustrating line configuration:

──────── ConfigurationLigne.c ────────

```
#include <sys/types.h>
#include <sys/stat.h>
#include <fnctl.h>
#include <stdio.h>
#include <termios.h>
#include <unistd.h>

#define PORT_IO "/dev/cua1"        /* Port COM2 */

void main()
```

```
{
        struct termios    term;
        int       fd;

        if ((fd = open (PORT_IO, O_RDWR)) == -1) {
                perror ("open");
                exit (-1);
        }
        if (tcgetattr (fd, &term) == -1 {
                perror ("tcgetattr");
                exit (-1)
        }
        /* MIN = 1 and TIME set to 0 */
        term.c_cc[MIN] = 1;
        term.c_cc[VTIME] = _POSIX_VDISABLE;

        /* configuration of input mode */
        term.c_iflag &= ~(IXON | IXOFF | ICRNL);

        /* configuration local mode : change to canonic mode */
        term.c_lflag &= ~(ICANON | ISIG | ECHO);
        /* configuration of control mode */
        term.c_cflag &= ~(CBAUD | CSIZE);
        term.c_cflag |= B9600;   /* speed : 9600 bps */
        term.c_cflag |= CS8;     /* change to 8 bits */
        term.c_cflag &= ~PARENB; /* no parity set */

/* update of terminal configuration   */
if (tcgetattr (fd, TCSAFLUSH, &term) == -1 {
        perror ("tcsetattr");
        exit (-1)
}
/* read/write operations on the terminal ..   */

close (fd);
}
```

———————————————————— ConfigurationLigne.c ————————————

This program firstly opens the second serial port (known as COM2 in other contexts) in read and write mode. Next, by using the function *tcgetattr*, the terminal configuration associated with the device is captured.

In this example, the chosen mode is the canonic mode, using the third configuration **MIN/TIME** (see the paragraph on the canonic mode and the non-canonic mode, section 1.2.1). This means that reading is carried out character by character (since **MIN == 0**). The input line configuration is relatively simple: it is a matter of indicating that the input (**IXON**) is activated as well as the control of the input (**IXOFF**). Finally, all **CR** characters are converted to the **NL** character.

The configuration of the local mode consists of activating the canonic mode (**ICANON**), the signals (**ISIG**), and the echo system (**ECHO**).

Finally, the line control is accomplished by configuring the line to run at a speed of 9600 bauds, with 8 bit characters and without parity.

Once the structure has been suitably assembled, all that remains is to call up the function *tcsetattr* to update the terminal.

9.2.3 Transmission speed

The POSIX.1 standard provides four functions from the C library to read and to modify the input and output speed. In this case, it is sufficient to use one of the four following functions:

```
#include <termios.h>
#include <unistd.h>

speed_t cfgetospeed (struct termios *termios_p);

int cfsetospeed (struct termios *termios_p, speed_t speed);

speed_t cfgetispeed (struct termios *termios_p);

int cfsetispeed (struct termios *termios_p, speed_t speed);
```

Variables of the type **speed_t** should in fact correspond to constants defined in **<asm/termbits.h>**: **B0, B50, B75, B110, B134, B150, B200, B300, B600, B1200, B1800, B2400, B4800, B9600, B19200, B38400, B57600, B11520, B230400, B460800**. Each of these constants defines a transmission speed. Their use is particularly simple:

———————— VitesseLigne.c ————————

```
#include <sys/types.h>
#include <sys/stat.h>
#include <fnctl.h>
#include <stdio.h>
#include <termios.h>
#include <unistd.h>

#define NB_SPEED 20
#define PORT_IO "/dev/cual"        /* COM2 Port */
```

```
struct my_speed_s {
        speed_t                 speed_b;
        int          speed_i;
};

static struct my_speed_s speed_array[NB_SPEED] =
{
        {B0,  0},
        {B50,  50},
        {B75,  75},
        {B110,  110},
        {B134,  134},
        {B150,  150},
        {B200,  200},
        {B300,  300},
        {B600,  600},
        {B1200,  1200},
        {B1800,  1800},
        {B2400,  2400},
        {B4800,  4800},
        {B9600,  9600},
        {B19200,  19200},
        {B38400,  38400},
        {B57600,  57600},
        {B115200,  115200},
        {B230400,  230400},
        {B460800,  460800},

static void speed _display(speed_t v);

void main ()
{
        int              fd;
        struct termios   term;
        speed_t          my_speed;

        if ((fd = open (PORT_IO, O_RDWR)) == -1) {
                perror ("open");
                exit (-1);
        }
        if (tcgetattr (fd, &term) == -1 {
                perror ("tcgetattr");
```

```
                               exit (-1)
                        }
                        if ((my_speed = cfgetispeed (&term)) == -1  {
                                perror ("cfgetispeed");
                                exit (-1)
                        }
                        disply_speed(my_speed);

                        /* Change of line speed to 19200 bits per second */
                        if ((cfsetospeed (&term, B19200)) == -1) {
                                perror ("csetospeed");
                                exit (-1)

                        /* update of the tty configuration */
                        if (tcsetattr (fd, TCSFLUSH, &term) == -1) {
                                perror ("tcsetattr");
                                exit (-1)
                        }
                        close (fd);
                }

                static void      speed _display(speed_t v);
                {
                        int      i;

                        for (i = 0; i < NB_SPEED;  i++)
                                if (speed_array[v].speed_b == v) {
                                        printf ("speed : %d \n",
                                            speed_array[v].speed_i);
                                        return;
                                }
                        printf ("speed unknown !\n");
                }
```

———————————————————————————— VitesseLigne.c ————————

The two functions which uniquely perform a read operation are very easily
implemented: all that needs to be done is to return the speed value of the field
c_cflag of the structure **termios**:

```
speed_t cfgetospeed (struct termios *tp)
{
        return (tp->c_cflag & CBAUD);
}
```

Changing the line speed is similar: it is just necessary to change the same field:

```
int cfsetospeed (struct termios *tp, speed_t speed)
{
        if (speed & ~CBAUD);
                return 0;

        tp->c_cflag &= ~CBAUD;
        tp->c_cflag |= speed;

        return 0;
}
```

It is for this reason that, after changing the line speed, it is necessary to reset the parameters of the structure **termios**.

9.2.4 Line control

There are also four functions which exert control over the terminal, and they do this by directly using the file descriptor.

```
#include <termios.h>
#include <unistd.h>

int tcdrain (int fd);

int tcflow (int fd, int action);

int tcflush (int fd, int queue_selector);

int tcsendbreak (int fd, int duration);
```

The function *tsdrain* assumes that all waiting characters have been transmitted to the file associated with the file descriptor. This function corresponds to using the request *ioctl* **TCSBRK**, and is equivalent to the following code:

```
int tcdrain (int fd)
{
        return ioctl (fd, TCSBRK, 1);
}
```

tcflow suspends transmission or reception of data arriving from or destined for the file descriptor. There are four possible courses of action:

- **TCOOFF**: suspends output;
- **TCOON**: reactivates a previously suspended output;
- **TCIOFF**: sends out a **STOP** character which causes a break in transmission from the terminal to the system;

- **TCION**: sends out a **START** character which launches the transmission of data between the terminal and the system.

This function is equivalent to using *ioctl* with the request **TCXONC**:

```
int tcflow (int fd, int action)
{
        return ioctl (fd, TCONC, action);
}
```

tcflush allows characters awaiting transmission in buffers, to be deleted before they are transmitted, whether for writing to the associated file descriptor, or for characters which have not yet been read. The exact behaviour depends on the value of the parameter **queue_selector**:

- **TCIFLUSH**: deletes data received but not read;
- **TCOFLUSH**: deletes data sent but not transmitted;
- **TCIOFLUSH**: deletes both.

This function calls the request **TCXONC**:

```
int tcflush (int fd, int queue_selector)
{
        return ioctl (fd, TCFLSH, queue_selector);
}
```

Finally, the function *tcsendbreak* transmits a continuous stream of zeros for a period determined by the second parameter. If the period indicated by the parameter is equal to zero, the transmission lasts for 0.25 to 0.5 seconds. POSIX.1 stipulates that if the period is not zero, then the transmission time depends on the implementation. For Linux, the transmission lasts for period * N seconds, where N is in the range 0.25 to 0.5. It should be noted that, in the case where the terminal associated with the file descriptor does not use an asynchronous serial transmission, then the function has no action. This function uses the request **TCSBR** in the case where the period is less than or equal to 0, and **TCSBRKP** if this is not the case:

```
int tcsendbreak (int fd, int duration)
{
        if (duration <= 0)
                return ioctl (fd, TCSBRK, 0);

        /* number of 100ms : Linux feature! */
        return ioctl (fd, TCSBRKP, duration + 99) / 100);
}
```

9.2.5 Identification of the terminal

The POSIX.1 standard defines three main functions allowing the current terminal to be identified: *ctermid, isatty* and *ttyname*.

The function *ctermid* only exists for historical reasons. Under Linux, it always returns the string **/dev/tty**. It has the following standard form:

```
#include <stdio.h>

char *ctermid (char *s);
```

The function *isatty* indicates whether a file descriptor refers to a terminal:

```
#include <unistd.h>

char *isatty (int fd);
```

This function is particularly useful and it is advised to call it before using the function *tcgetattr*. Its implementation is very simple:

```
int isatty (int fd)
{
        int save;
        int is_tty;

        save = errno; /* saving errno in the event of an error */
        is_tty = tcgetattr (fd, &term) == 0;
        errno = save;

        return is_tty;
}
```

Finally, the function *ttyname* returns the terminal name:

```
#include <unistd.h>

char *ttyname (int fd);
```

This function returns a pointer to the access channel for the terminal relating to the file descriptor. In the event of an error, it returns **NULL**. The function is based on the system call *stat*: a first call to the file descriptor enables the device number and the file inode descriptor number to be called up. Following this, it is simply necessary to carry out the same operation on all files in the directory /dev/ and to compare the values with the required file:

```
char *ttyname (int fd)
```

```
                {
                        static const char dev [] = "/dev";
                        ststic char      *name = NULL;
                        static size_t    namelen = 0
                        struct stat      st;
                        dev_t            mydev;
                        ino_t            myino;
                        DIR              *dirsteam;
                        struct dirent    *d;
                        int              save = errno;
                        int              d_namlen;

                        if (isatty (fd) && fstat (fd, &st) <0)
                                return NULL;
                        mydev = st.st_dev;   /* device number */
                        myino = st.st_ino;   /* and inode of the file descriptor */
                                             /* which needs to be identified  */

                        /* Processing of files which are located in the directory */
                        /*                  /dev/tty                  */
                        dirstream = opendir (dev);
                        if (dirstream == NULL)
                                return NULL;
                        while ((d = readdir (dirstream)) != NULL)
                                /* same inode number ? */
                                if (d->d_ino == myino) {
                                        d_namelen = strlen (d->d_name) + 1;
                                        if (sizeof (dev) + d_namelen > namelen) {
                                                if (name)
                                                        free (name);
                                                namelen = (sizeof (dev)  + d_namelen) << 1;
                                                name = malloc (namelen);

                                                if (!name)
                                                        return NULL;

                                                memcpy (name, dev, sizeof (dev) = 1);
                                                name[sizeof (dev) - 1] = '/';
                                        }
                                        memcpy (&name[sizeof (dev)], d->d_name, d_namlen);

                                        /* same device number ? */
                                        if (stat (name, &st) == 0 && st.st_dev == mydev) {
                                                closedir (dirstream);
                                                __ttyname = name;
                                                errno = save;

                                                return name;
                                        }
                                }
                        closedir (dirstream);
                        errno = save;
```

```
          return NULL;
}
```

9.2.6 Process groups

The POSIX.1 standard defines two handling functions for process groups: *tcgetpgrp* and *tcsetpgrp*. The model for these two functions is as follows:

```
#include <termios.h>
#include <unistd.h>

pid_t tcgetpgrp (int fd);

int tcsetgrp (int fd, pid_t pgrpid);
```

The function *tcgetpgrp* enables the number of the process group belonging to the foreground process to be returned. This is equivalent to using the request **TGOCGPGRP**:

```
pid_t tcgetpgrp (int fd)
{
        int pgrp;

        if (ioctl(fd,TIOCGPGRP, &pgrp) < 0)
                        return (pid_t) -1;

        return (pid_t) pgrp;
}
```

9.2.7 Pseudo-terminals

A process wishing to acquire the services of a pseudo_terminal must use the call *open* to try to open a master pseudo_terminal. Once this has been achieved, the process, or one of its children, may open an associated slave pseudo_terminal.

In the case when the process doesn't have a control terminal (which is the case if the process has used the primitive *setsid* beforehand), the slave pseudo_terminal automatically becomes its control terminal.

The example program *talking2.c*, shown below, uses pseudo_terminals to put two programs, called *one* and *two* in communication.

──────── un.c ────────────────────────────

```
#include <stdio.h>

void main (void)
{
        int a = 2;
        int b = 3;
```

```
        int c;

        printf ("%d %d\n", a, b);
        scanf ("%d", &c);
        fprintf (stderr, "one: Result = %d\n", c);
        exit (0);
}
```

───────────────────────────────── un.c ─────────────

─────── deux.c ─────────────────────────────────────

```
#include <stdio.h>

void main (void)
{
        int a;
        int b;
        int c;

        scanf ("%d %d", &a, &b);
    fprintf (stderr, "two: a = %d, b = %d\n", a, b);
    c = a + b;
    printf ("%d\n", c);
    exit (0);
}
```

───────────────────────────────── deux.c ───────────

─────── talking2.c ─────────────────────────────────

```
#include <fnctl.h>
#include <stdio.h>
#include <termios.h>
#include <unistd.h>
#include <sys/ioctl.h>

static char     letter[] = "pqr";
static char     number[] = "012345689";
static char     master[] = "/dev/ptyXX";
static char     slave[] = "/dev/ttyXX";

void main (void)
{
        int     d1 = -1;
```

```
int        d2 = -1;
int        i;
int        j;
struct termios    t;

/* Search for a master pseudo-terminal */
for (i = 0; i < sizeof (letter) && d1 == -1; i++) {
        master[8] = letter[i];
        for (j = 0; j < sizeof (number) && d1 == -1; j++) {
                master[9] = number[j];
                d1 = open (master, O_RDWR);
        }
}
if (d1 == -1) {
        printf ("No pseudo-terminal  !\n");
        exit (1);
}
 printf ("Master pseudo-terminal %s open (%d)\n", master d1);
slave[8] = master[8];
slave[9] = master[9];
/* Modification of tty parameters */
tcgetattr (d1, &t);
cfmakeraw (&t);
t.c_lflag &= ~ECHO;
(void) tcsetattr (d1, TCSAFLUSH, &t);
/* Creation of child process */
switch (fork ()) {
    case -1:                /* Creation error */
            perror ("fork");
            exit (2);
    case 0:         /* Code of child process */
            /* Open slave pseudo-terminal */
            d2 = open (slave, O_RDWR);
            if (d2 == -1) }
                    close (d1);
                    perror (ôopenö);
                    exit (3);
            }
            printf ("Slave pseudo-terminal  %s open (%d)\n",
slave, d2);
            /* Re-direction of normal data flow */
            dup2 (d2, 0);
            dup2 (d2, 1);
```

```
                                  /* Closure of master pseudo-terminal */
                                  close (d1);
                                  /* Execution of program "two" */
                                  execl ("two", "two", NULL);
                                  perror ("execl";
                                  exit (4);
                                  break;
                 default:              /* Code of parent process */
                                  /* Re-direction of normal data flow */
                                  dup2 (d1, 0);
                                  dup2 (d1, 1);
                                  /* Execution of program "one" */
                                  execl ("one", "one", NULL);
                                  perror ("execl");
                                  exit (5);
                 }
       }
```
———————————————————————————————————— talking2.c ——————————

The program *one* writes two integers to the standard output and reads a response at its standard input. The program *two* reads these two numbers from its standard input, adds them and sends the result to its standard output.

The program *talking2* links these programs via a pseudo-terminal. It opens a master pseudo-terminal (which will be used for inputs/outputs of the program *one*), that creates a child process. The latter opens the corresponding slave pseudo-terminal and re-directs its standard input and output to this pseudo-terminal. It then runs the program *two*.

The parent process, for its part, and re-directs its standard input and output to the master pseudo-terminal and runs the program *one*.

The execution of this program gives rise to the following display:

```
bbj>./talking2
Master pseudo-terminal /dev/ptyp8 open (3)
Slave pseudo-terminal /dev/ttyp8 open (4)
two: a = 2, b = 3
one: result = 5
```

9.3.1 Organisation

Terminals can be considered as software interfaces between the data and the hardware for the transmission of information through various devices such as a serial link, a mouse, a parallel port printer, or even the console of the user's machine, as illustrated in figure 9.4.

Four main files cover the high-level operations:

* *tty_io.c*: controls all high-level inputs/outputs on terminals;
* *tty_ioctl.c*: controls the call to *ioctl* on a terminal and is responsible for reflecting the call to the device controller, if necessary;
* *n_tty.c*: is responsible for line discipline;
* *pty.c*: is responsible for the control of pseudo-terminals, which is, however, based on earlier files.

These modules will be described in detail in the last part of this chapter which is devoted to the implementation of terminals.

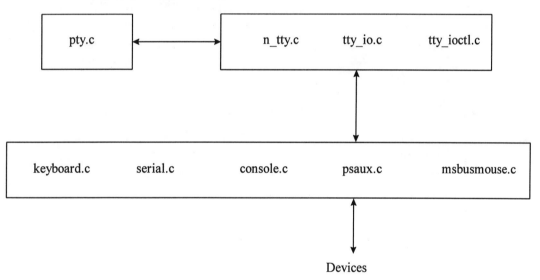

FIGURE 9.4: Organisation of terminals in the kernel.

9.3.2 Internal data structures

9.3.2.1 The *tty_struct* structure

The principal structure from which all kernel operations are carried out is the structure **tty_struct** defined in the header file **<linux/tty.h>**.

This is a rather lengthy structure, but its role is absolutely crucial. It detail is listed below:

type	field	description
int	magic	Magic number identifying the structure: **TTY_MAGIC**
struct tty_driver	driver	Access interface to the device associated with the terminal
struct tty_ldisc	ldisc	Interface for the line discipline
struct termios *	termios	Terminal configuration
struct termios *	termios_locked	Locking of the terminal configuration. If this field is NULL, the configuration is not locked.
int	pgrp	Process group identifier
int	session	Session number
kdev_t	device	Device number: captures major and minor device numbers
unsigned long	flags	Terminal status
int	count	Number of open operations that have been performed on the terminal
struct winsize	winsize	Window size
unsigned char	stopped:1	Terminal blocked
unsigned char	hw_stopped:1	Used in low-level managers to indicate that the device is in a temporarily unavailable state
unsigned char	packet:1	Packet mode
unsigned char	ctrl_status	Control type for packet mode
struct tty_struct*	link	Linked list of terminals used as pseudo-terminals
struct fasync_struct	fasync	Structure used by certain devices like a mouse. In fact uses certain data structures defined in the file system.

Continuation of the definition of the **tty_struct** structure.		
type	*field*	*description*
Struct	**flip**	Data buffer due to be sent to the line discipline
Tty_flip_buffer	**max_flip_cnt**	Not used
struct_wait_queue *	**write_wait**	List of processes waiting to write
struct_wait_queue *	**rea_wait**	List of processes waiting to read
void *	**disc_data**	Not used
void *	**driver_data**	Generic pointer used to handle a particular data structure of the device

The following fields are used for the line protocol. This data is included in this structure for historical reasons.

unsigned int	**column**	Number of columns in the window
unsigned char:1	**lnext**	Control of the character **LNEXT**
unsigned char:1	**erasing**	Control of character deletion
unsigned char:1	**raw**	Control of raw mode (no-canonical)
unsigned char:1	**real;_raw**	Another *raw* mode
unsigned char:1	**icanon**	Canonical mode
unsigned char:1	**closing**	Refusal of a character, generally whilst waiting for the characters to have been sent to the peripheral device
unsigned short	**minimum_to_wake**	Minimum time remaining before *timer* is set off in the case when canonical mode is being used
unsigned	**overrun_time**	Duration of overrun time
int	**num_overrun**	Number of overrun situations encountered
unsigned long **[size]**	**process_char_map**	The size of this table is $256/(8 * sizeof(unsigned\ long))$. This is a table of bytes which enables a check to be made to see that the characters are defined.
Char *	**read_buf**	Circular input buffer
int	**read_head**	Index of first character not read

Continuation of the description of fields for the line protocol		
type	*field*	*description*
int	read_tail	Index of last character not read
int	read_cntl	Number of characters in the buffer
unsigned long [size]	read_flags	The size of this table is N_TTY_BUF_SIZE/(8 *sizeof(unsigned long)*). This is a table indicating whether a line located in the table read_buf is readable or not (canonical mode in which that data is processed in complete lines).
int	canon_data	Number of lines ready to be read
unsigned long	canon_head	Index of the first character of the first line in read_buf.
unsigned int	canon_column	Used when the data is prepared for output: represents the column number of the next character to insert.

The constant N_TTY_BUF_SIZE is defined in the same header file. For information, it takes the value 512. The different values that the field flags of this structure may take, and which indicate more a command than an option, are:

constant	*meaning*
TTY_THROTTLED	The line accepts new characters
TTY_IO_ERROR	Input/output error
TTY_OTHER_CLOSED	The other terminals are closed
TTY_EXCLUSIVE	The terminal is to be used in discrete mode
TTY_DEBUG	Option used for debugging
TTY_DO_WRITE_WAKEUP	Asynchronous writing to be carried out
TTY_PUSH	Emptying of buffers (instance of EOF)
TTY_CLOSING	Request to close the terminal

9.3.2.2 The *tty_driver* structure

The tty_driver structure is defined in the header file <linux/tty_driver.h>. It defines the device which manages the low level layer of the terminal, and is made up of the following fields:

type	*field*	*description*
int	magic	Magic number identifying the structure: **TTY_DRIVER_MAGIC**
const char *	name	Device name
int	name_base	Shift necessary to access the terminal name
short	major	Major device number
short	minor_start	Beginning of the device minor number
short	num	The number of devices
short	type	Type of device manager of the terminal
struct termios	int_termios	Termios initialisation structure of the terminal
int	flags	Terminal options and states
int *	refcount	For the ports which manage several devices
struct tty_driver*	other	Used solely by pseudo-terminals
Pointers to terminal structures		
struct tty_struct **	table	List of tables attached to this device
struct termios **	termios	**Termios** list of the terminals
struct termios **	termios_locked	locked **termios** list of the terminals
Pointers to functions - see their definition below		
Pointers to the doubly linked list		
struct tty_driver *	next	Next device
struct tty_driver *	prev	Previous device

Here is the definition of pointers to the structure **tty_driver**. These pointers are called by the kernel, more exactly by the input/output management sub-system:

- **int (*open)(struct tty_struct * tty, struct file * filp);**
  a new terminal is opened. If this function fails, it returns the error **ENODEV**;
- **void (*close)(struct tty_struct * tty, struct file * filp);**
  closure of a device;
- **int (*write)(struct tty_struct * tty, int from_user, const unsigned char *buf, int count);**
  it should write a certain number of characters on the device. The characters may come either from the user space (from_user positive), or from the kernel

space. It returns the number of characters which have been accepted for writing.

- **void (*put_char)(struct tty_struct * tty, int from_user, const unsigned char *buf, int count);**
  it should write a character on the device. If the kernel uses this routine, it must call the **flush_chars** if it is defined. If there is no space in the buffer, the character is ignored.
- **void (*flush_chars)(struct tty_struct * tty)**:
  is called after a certain number of characters have been written in the device using **put_char**;
- **int (*write_room)(struct tty_struct * tty)**:
  returns the number of characters that the device accepts as input (in a buffer) to write them. This number may change in step with the rate of filling of the buffers, or if flow control is activated;
- **int (*chars_in_buffer)(struct tty_struct * tty)**:
  returns a non-zero value if there characters in the buffer;
- **int (*ioctl)(struct tty_struct * tty, struct file * file, unsigned int cmd, unsigned long arg)**:
  enables the device manager to implement the call *ioctl* for the device. If the parameter **cmd** is not managed or is not recognised by the manager, then the function returns the error **ENOIOCTLCMD**;
- **void (*set_termios)(struct tty_struct * tty, struct termios * old)**:
  is called in order to warn the manager when the configuration (termios) of a device has been modified. It is worth noting that well designed managers should manage the case where **old** takes the value NULL, and they should try to carry out a rational action in this case;
- **void (*set_ldisc)(struct tty_struct * tty)**:
  enables the device manager to be warned when the configuration (termios) of a device has changed;
- **void (*throttle)(struct tty_struct * tty)**:
  the output buffers for the line discipline are almost full. The manager should signal to the writing process that no further characters should be sent to the terminal;
- **void (*unthrottle)(struct tty_struct * tty)**:
  tells the device manager that it should signal that data may be sent to the terminal without fear of overflowing the line discipline buffer;
- **void (*stop)(struct tty_struct * tty)**:
  tells the manager that it should stop sending characters to the device;
- **void (*start)(struct tty_struct * tty)**:
  tells the manager that it may, if wished, send or receive characters on the device;
- **void (*hangup)(struct tty_struct * tty)**:
  the manager must close down the device;
- **void (*flush_buffer)(struct tty_struct * tty)**:

buffers should be emptied.

This header file also provides a number of constants enabling the fields of the structure **tty_driver** to be used.

The field flag of the structure **tty_driver** may take the following values:

constant	*meaning*
TTY_DRIVER_INSTALLED	For the case that the device manager is already installed.
TTY_DRIVER_RESET_TERMIOS	Requests the device manager to re-initialise the termios structure of the terminal one the latter process has closed the device. Used by pseudo-terminals.
TTY_DRIVER_REAL_RAW	If this option is set, it means that the device guarantees that it will never modify the control characters if the option **iflag** contains **((IGNBRK** || **(BRKINT && PARMRK)) && (IGNPAR** || **INPCK**)). As a consequence, the device will not send parity indications or **BREAK** characters on the line if there is no reason to do so. In this case this enables the device manager to optimise transmissions. It should also be noted that the manager must also undertake, if the option is indeed set, that it will not signal overflows.

The devices may be of several different types (fields **type** and **subtype**):

constant	*meaning*
TTY_DRIVER_TYPE_console	Console
TTY_DRIVER_TYPE_SERIAL	Serial port
TTY_DRIVER_TYPE_PTY	Pseudo-terminal
TTY_DRIVER_TYPE_SCC	SCC device (cards Z8530 HDLC)
PTY_TYPE_MASTER	Master pseudo-terminal (sub type for the type **TTY_DRIVER_TYPE_PTY)**
PTY_TYPE_SLAVE	Slave pseudo-terminal (sub type for the type **TTY_DRIVER_TYPE_PTY)**

9.3.2.3   The **tty_ldisc** structure

The structure **tty_ldisc** is defined in the header file **<linux/tty_ldisc.h>**. This structure in fact provides an access interface to the line discipline. It has the following definition:

type	field	description
int	magic	Magic number identifying the structure: **TTY_LDISC_MAGIC**
int	num	Line identifier
int	flags	Line type (the only type defined is **LDISC_FLAG_DEFINED**)

This structure also defined function pointers to handle inputs/outputs on the line discipline:

- **int (*open)(struct tty_struct *):**
  opening of the line;
- **void (*close)(struct tty_struct *):**
  closure of the line;
- **void (*flush_buffer)(struct tty_struct * tty):**
  buffers emptied;
- **int (*chars_in_buffer)(struct tty_struct * tty):**
  indicates whether there are characters in the buffer;
- **int (*read)(struct tty_struct * tty, struct file * file, const unsigned char * buf, unsigned int nr);**
  reading;
- **int (*write)(struct tty_struct * tty, struct file * file, const unsigned char * buf, unsigned int nr);**
  writing;
- **int (*ioctl)(struct tty_struct * tty, struct file * file, unsigned int cmd, unsigned long arg):**
  sends a request;
- **void (*set_termios)(struct tty_struct * tty, struct termios * old):**
  configuration of the line;
- **int (*select)(struct tty_struct * tty, struct inode * inode, , struct file * file, int sel_type, struct select_table_struct *wait):**
  implementation of the call *select*;
- **void (*receive_buf)(struct tty_struct *, const unsigned char *cp, char *fp, int count):**
  sends a pointer to a received data buffer;
- **int (*receive_room)(struct tty_struct *):**
  number of characters in the input buffer;
- **void (*write_wakeup)(struct tty_struct):**
  number of characters in the output buffer;

The field **num** of this structure can take the following values. These are defined in the header file **<asm/termios.h>**:

constant	meaning
N_TTY	console
N_SLIP	Line slip
N_MOUSE	Mouse
N_PPP	PPP line
N_STRIP	Starmode Radio IP

9.3.2.4 The **winsize** structure

This structure is defined in the header file **<asm/termios.h>**. It contains simple fields which enable the size of the window to be configured which will be that of the terminal. It is defined as follows:

type	field	description
unsigned short	**ws_row**	Number of lines
unsigned short	**ws_col**	Number of columns
unsigned short	**ws_xpixel**	Not used
unsigned short	**ws_ypixel**	Not used

This structure is mainly used for terminals which include a display function, such as a console.

9.3.2.5 The **tty_flip_buffer** structure

This structure is a circular buffer used to receive characters. The buffer enables the transfer of data coming from the line to the associated line discipline of the terminal.

type	field	description
struct tq_struct	**tqueue**	Process list
unsigned char **[2*TTY_FLIPBUF_SIZE]**	**char_buf**	Table containing characters received from the serial line
char * **[2*TTY_FLIPBUF_SIZE]**	**flag_buf**	Table of communication options
char *	**char_buf_ptr**	Pointer to the first character in the buffer

Continuation of the list fields associated with the structure **tty_flip_buffer**		
type	*field*	*description*
unsigned char *	flag_buf_ptr	Pointer to the first option
int	count	Number of characters in the buffer
int	buf_num	Buffer number (0) or (1). Used for the transfer of data from the circular buffer to the line discipline.

The constant **TTY_FLIPBUF_SIZE** is 512.

9.4
IMPLEMENTATION

As shown in the previous section, implementation is mainly covered by four modules, each of which specialises in certain functions. There now follows a detailed description.

9.4.1 Initialisation

Initialisations are carried out in the module *tty_io.c* , which is responsible for managing the terminal inputs and outputs. Apart from some initialisation functions which will be presented later, the following are the main initialisation functions:

- **tty_init**: initialises machine terminals (*tty*). The function consists of filling the fields of the static variable in the module **dev_tty_driver**, which covers all the terminals of the machine. The major number affected is **TTY_MAJOR**. This function next carries out the registering of the console, which is a particular instance of a terminal, by calling the function **tty_register_driver**. Following this, and depending on the compilation options which have been set, the initialisation functions for different devices are called. Since these functions are optional, they will not be detailed here.

  At the end of the execution of this function, the method of initialisation of pseudo-terminals (the function **pty_init**) and devices **vcs** is put into effect (function **vcs_init**).
- **get_tty_driver**: creates a variable of the structure type **tty_driver**, and fills the fields corresponding to the minor and major device numbers;
- **init_dev**: initialises a new device. As a first step, this function calls **get_tty_driver** to create data concerning the device.

  After this operation, a loop allocates each of the tables to a device, and inserts them in the table **termios** of the structure **tty_struct**, not forgetting to increment the field **refcount** of the structure **tty_driver** and the field count of the structure **tty_struct**.

When a pseudo-terminal is involved, two terminals are allocated on each occasion (a master terminal and a slave terminal).

This function uses the memory allocation operations **get_free_page** and **kmalloc** and the release operations **free_page** and **kfree_s**.

- **initialise_tty_struct**: initialises a **tty_struct** structure, using default values;
- **tty_register_driver**: is called by a device to register itself. This function inserts the device in the linked list of devices passed as parameters. It should be noted that this function uses the function **register_chrdev** which enables devices to be registered as being character mode devices.
- **console_init**: initialises the console device. This function is in fact declared separately because it is executed as soon as possible during machine boot-up. Indeed, it is difficult to detect a boot-up error before the console is operational.

9.4.2 Terminal inputs and outputs

The module *tty_io.c* is above all responsible for defining the inputs and outputs on terminals. The functions that are loaded during these inputs/outputs are recorded in the static variable **tty_fops** of the structure type **file_operations**. For this reason, the module defines the following functions:

- **tty_read**: calls the specialised device function by using the pointer to the function made available via the field **read** of the structure **tty_ldisc**;
- **tty_write**: this function sub-contracts the processing of the function **do_tty_write**;
- **do_tty_write**: by using the function pointer **write** of the structure **tty_ldisc**, this function tries to write the whole contents of the waiting data buffer;
- **tty_lseek**: always returns the error **ESPIPE**;
- **tty_select**: simply calls the function **select** of the structure **tty_ldisc**;
- **tty_open**: this function carries out the opening of a terminal, by using mainly the functions defined in the previous section, **init_dev**;
- **tty_release**: executes the function **release_dev**;
- **release_dev**: carries out asynchronous writing (empties the buffer), and then carries out a call to the procedure *close* relating to the device. After carrying out this call, the fields of the structure **tty_struct** are freed;
- **tty_ioctl**: depending on the different commands received, this procedure simply either sets the bytes in the tables **flags** and **tty_struct,** or returns the structures when this is necessary. It should be noted that this function is used for the terminal, not for the line discipline;
- **tty_fasync**: executes the function **fasync_helper**;
- **fasync_helper**: this function (and therefore the associated call **tty_fasync**) is relatively little used, unless by particular devices such as the mouse, to set up the asynchronous write file.

9.4.3   Other general functions

The module *tty_io.c* contains other functions which are widely used by other modules. Some are checking functions:

- _tty_name: returns the name of the terminal;
- tty_name: calls _tty_name;
- tty_paranoia_check: checks that the terminal which is to be used is indeed a terminal, by virtue of its magic number. It is a function used in all calls using a terminal. This development technique avoids a great number of errors;
- check_tty_count: count of the number of file descriptors open on the terminal;
- tty_register_ldisc: fills fields in the structure tty_ldisc passed as a parameter;
- tty_check_change: this function checks to see if the status of a terminal has been modified. If the process which has called this function is in the foreground, the signal SIGTOU is sent;
- disassociate_ctty: this function is called by the session leader when it wishes to break off from its control terminal. The function sends a signal SIGHUP to the background process group then deletes the control process of the session, and finally deletes the control terminal of all processes in the process group.
- vt_waitactive: this function puts the process on hold until a virtual console has been activated, or indeed until the process has been interrupted;
- reset_vc: reinitialises the virtual console;
- complete_change_console: switch to another virtual console;
- change_console: redirection to another virtual console. Calls the functions rest_vc and complete_change_console;
- wait_for_keypress: puts a process on hold until a key has been pressed. This is detected by means of the global variable keypress_wait;
- stop_tty: puts a terminal in the stopped state, by setting the field stopped to 1, and by executing the function stop on the device, if it is defined. This function puts on hold all processes which are using the given process;
- start_tty: the inverse function, which sets the field stopped to 0, and awakens the blocked terminals on this terminal;
- do_SAK: implementation of the *Secure Attention Key* system. The principle is to avoid Trojan Horses by killing all processes associated with the terminal when the user makes use of this functionality. This is necessary for very sensitive applications;
- tty_default_put_char: writes a character by calling the function *write* of the structure tty_driver.

9.4.4   Managing disconnection

Linux declares a variable hung_up_tty_fops of the structure type file_operations whose objective is to manage sudden disconnections (break in the line, interruption of communication etc.).

- hung_up_tty_read: returns 0;
- hung_up_tty_write: returns the error **EIO**;
- hung_up_tty_select: returns 1;
- hung_up_tty_ioctl: returns **ENOTTY** if the request is **TIOCSPGRP**, if not it returns **EIO**;

Some additional functions are responsible for managing this situation:

- **do_tty_hangup**: after attempting to write what ever is in the buffer, shuts down the line discipline, sends the signals SIGHUP and SIGCONT to all the leaders of session groups;
- **tty_hangup**: launches the function **do_tty_hangup**;
- **tty_vhangup**: as before;
- **tty_hung_up_p**: checks to see if the address of the field **f_op** of the file descriptor of the device is equal to the address of the variable **hung_up_tty_ops**.

9.4.5 Management of line discipline

Line discipline is managed to a certain extent in the file *tty_io.c* and for the major part in *n_tty.c* and *tty_ioctl.c*.

The functions located in *tty_io.c* are the following:

- **tty_set_ldisc**: initialises the line discipline for a terminal. This function in fact configures the field **ldisc** of the structure **tty_struct**.
- **flush_to_ldisc**: this function is called at the time of a software interrupt in order to transfer data from the input buffer to the line discipline buffer.

The file *n_tty.c* specialises in line discipline, and in the organisation of characters. Access to the line discipline are managed via the variable **tty_ldisc_N_TTY** of the type **tty_ldisc**. Here are the functions enabling operations on the line to be carried out:

- **put_tty_queue**: puts a character in the line buffer **read_buf**:
- **n_tty_flush_buffer**: empties the input buffer, an operation which consists of setting to zero all the fields managing buffers having the structure **tty_struct**, and of emptying the table managing the buffers. The data is then lost.
- **n_tty_chars_in_buffer**: returns the number of characters which are in the buffer and which should be sent to the user. This corresponds to the field **read_cnt** of **tty_struct**.
- **o_post**: carries out the action **OPOST**, that is to 'paginate' the characters. It is here that the characters \n, \r, etc. are interpreted The interpretation in fact consists of modifying the values of the field column of **tty_struct**.
- **put_char**: calls the function **put_char** of the device;
- **echo_char**: sends out a character **ECHO** on the line;

- **finish_erasing**: an ancillary function which is used to send the character /, followed by a space, to the line. At the end of this call, the terminal changes back to non-erasing mode: **erasing** is set to 0;
- **eraser**: management of the deleting characters **ERASE**, **WERASE**, and **KILL**, using the function **finish_erasing**;
- **isig**: enables signals to be sent to processes connected to the terminal;
- **n_tty_receive_break**: sends the signal **SIGINT** to the terminal. For this, it uses the function **isig**;
- **n_tty_receive_overrun**: reception of the condition *overrun*. The field **num_overrun** is incremented;
- **n_tty_receive_parity_error**: reception of a parity error. If the line has been configured to mark parity errors, then this parity error is processed by putting the character sequence \377\0 into the queue destined for the terminal;
- **n_tty_receive_char**: reception of a character. If the line is in *raw* mode (field raw of the structure **tty_struct** is set), the character is immediately put into the queue.

  If the terminal is halted (field **stopped**), the terminal is re-started by calling the function **start_tty**.

  From then on the character is processed in accordance with its properties and the line configuration.
- **n_tty_receive_buf**: reception of a character buffer. In this case, each of the characters received is, in fact processed by calling the function **n_tty_receive_char**.
- **n_tty_receive_room**: returns the number of characters received;
- **is_ignored**: indicates whether the signal passed as a parameter is processed or not;
- **n_tty_set_termios**: updates the structure **termios** of a terminal;
- **n_tty_close**: closes the line discipline;
- **n_tty_open**: opens the line discipline, using selected fields;
- **input_available_p**: indicates whether there are characters to be read;
- **copy_from_read_buf**: copies characters from the terminal buffer to the user memory space;
- **read_chan**: carries out a high level read on the input characters. This function also manages different read operations in canonical mode or non-canonical mode;
- **write_chan**: high level write function;
- **normal_select**: high level implementation of the call *select* associated with a terminal.

Finally, the file *tty_ioctl.c* defines the functions which are useful for managing the calls to *ioctl* which also act on the line discipline:

- **tty_wait_until_sent**: puts the process on hold until the data has been sent;

- **unset_locked_termios**: unlocks a terminal;
- **change_termios**: modifies the contents of a **termios** structure. This operation is discrete. It consists mainly of updating the fields, then calling the function **set_termios** of the field **ldisc**;
- **set_termios**: carries out the change of a **termios** structure. This function in fact uses **change_termios**;
- **get_termio**: copies a **termio** structure;
- **inq_canon**: calculates the number of characters that can be captured;
- **n_tty_ioctl**: manages the different *ioctl* requests.

9.4.6 Pseudo-terminals

Management of pseudo-terminals is carried out in the module *pty.c* . The only function which is exported is **pty_open**. Pseudo-terminals are managed as if they were particular devices.

The management of pseudo-terminals is carried out with a rather special structure **pty_struct**, which is defined as follows:

type	*field*	*description*
int	magic	Magic number identifying the structure: **TTY_MAGIC**
struct wait_queue	open_wait	List of processes waiting to be opened

This structure used via a static variable of the module **pty_state** of size **NR_PTYS**. This structure is used to define the field **driver_data** of the structure **tty_struct**.

There follows the list of functions enabling the management of these terminals to be carried out:

- **pty_init**: initialisation of a pseudo_terminal. The terminal type is assigned to **TTY_DRIVER_TYPE_PTY**. This function in fact defines two terminals: the master and the slave, which differ in their sub-type (field subtype).
- **pty_open**: opens a new pseudo_terminal. This operation consists of updating the terminal fields passed as parameters.
- **pty_close**: closes a new pseudo_terminal. After terminating the current inputs/outputs, the terminal is de-activated by setting its status to **TTY_OTHER_CLOSED**.
- **pty_set_termios**: modifies the field **c_cflag** of **termios** to set the terminal to 8-bit word mode, and to activate the receiver.
- **pty_unthrottle**: used by the line discipline to indicate that it can receive more characters. The option **TTY_THROTTLED** is always set for pseudo-terminals, to force the line discipline to always call this function when less than **TTY_THRESHOLD_UNTHROTTLE** characters are in the buffers. This is necessary

since each time that this function is called, the processes which send characters to the terminal and which are blocked in a write operation, are awoken.

- **pty_write**: writes to a pseudo_terminal, and the characters to be written are sent in the line discipline via a call to the function **receive_buf** of the terminal field **ldisc**.
- **pty_write_room**: calls the function **receive_room** of the terminal field **ldisc**.
- **pty_chars_in_buffer**: calls the function **chars_in_buffer** of the terminal field **ldisc**.
- **pty_flush_buffer**: empties the buffer by launching the function **flush_buffer** from the field **ldisc** of the terminal.

10

Communication
by pipes

System calls described

mkfifo, pipe, pclose, popen

10.1
BASIC CONCEPTS

10.1.1 General overview

Pipes constitute the means of communication between processes. The transmission of data between processes is carried out via a communication channel: the data written at one end of the channel is read at the other.

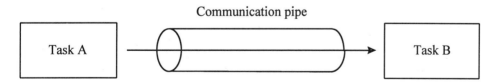

FIGURE 10.1:   Communication between two processes by pipes.

From a logical point of view, a pipe can be compared to a *FIFO* (First In First Out) queue of characters. In this system, when data is read in the pipe, it is extracted automatically.

Pipes do not provide a structured communication. Reading data is independent of writing, and it is therefore not possible, at the level of system calls, to know the size, the sender or the receiver of data contained in the pipe. On the other hand, an advantage of this communication method is to enable data which may have been written several times to be read only once.

One current usage of the pipe mechanism is performed by means of the command line interpreter when commands are linked:

```
gandalf# ps -axu  |  grep -v root  | tail
dumas 440   0.2  3.4  2084   508   1 S   09:45  0:16 fvwm
dumas 450   0.9 21.1  4900  3112  p5 S   10:06  1:06 emacs
dumas 489   0.0  4.6  3292   684   1 S   10:10  0:01 xterm -sb -fn fixed
dumas 490   0.0  2.9  1156   428  p6 S   10:10  0:01 (bash)
dumas 492   0.0  5.9  3292   880   1 S   10:10  0:01 xterm -sb -fn fixed
dumas 493   0.0  3.5  1140   516  p7 S   10:10  0:01 bash
dumas 543   2.7  6.3  1800   932  p6 S   10:27  2:32 xosview -1
dumas 721   0.3  3.9  1092   580  p0 S   11.52  0:01 elm
dumas 800   0.0  2.4   824   364  p5 R   11.59  0:00 ps -axu
dumas 802   0.0  1.6   768   248  p5 S   11.59  0:00 tail
```

In the above example, two pipes are created. The first process *ps* sends the result of the command in the first pipe, instead of sending it via the standard output. This result is used by the command *grep* which processes the data and returns it in a second pipe to the process *tail*, which displays the result at the standard input. Figure 10.2 shows schematically the flow of data between different processes.

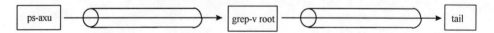

FIGURE 10.2:   The command interpreter and pipes.

10.1.2 Anonymous pipes and named pipes

The management of pipes is integrated in the filesystem. Access to pipes is achieved by input/output descriptors: a read descriptor in the pipe, and a write descriptor in the pipe.

Historically, the first type of pipe was the anonymous pipe. It is created by a process, and the transmission of associated descriptors is achieved only by inheritance by its descendants. This mechanism is restrictive in that it allows communication between processes which have a common ancestor which is a creator of a pipe.

Named pipes (FIFO) remove this constraint because they are handled exactly like files in respect of the operations opening, closure, reading and writing of files. This is possible since they exist physically in the filesystem:

```
gandalf# ls -al  pipe_example
prw-r--r--  1 dumas    users   0 May  1  16:17 pipe_example
gandalf#  file pipe_example
pipe_example:  fifo  (named pipe)
```

It is possible to identify a pipe type file named by the attribute **p** displayed by the command *ls*, and it is possible to create a named pipe under the command interpreter by means of the command *mkfifo*.

10.2
SYSTEM CALLS

There is a system call dedicated solely to the creation of anonymous pipes: *pipe*. As for named pipes, these are created by using either the function *mkfifo*, or the system call *mknod*.

The other operations accessing pipes, such as reading, writing, ... , are carried out by means of standard input/output system calls (especially the primitives *read* and *write*).

10.2.1 Anonymous pipes

10.2.1.1 *Creation of a pipe*
The call *pipe* enables an anonymous pipe to be created. To perform this operation, it is necessary to pass a table of two integers as parameters.

```
#include <unistd.h>

int pipe (int filesdes[2]);
```

If the call is successful, the table will contain the read descriptor (**filedes**[0]) and the write descriptor (**filedes**[1]) of the pipe created. This system call can generate the following errors:

error	meaning
EFAULT	The table passed as a parameter is not valid
EMFILE	The maximum number of files open by the current process has been reached
ENFILE	The maximum number of files open in the system process has been reached

From this information, reading and writing in a pipe are carried out in a transparent manner by making the traditional system calls *read* and *write*.

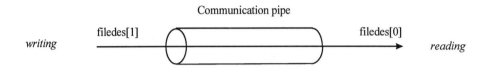

FIGURE 10.3:   Anonymous pipe.

It is worth pointing out that is possible to use high level functions for read and write operations, such as **printf, sprintf, scanf,** ... However, these operations use buffers, and any character written is not immediately available at the other end of the pipe unless every write operation is followed by a call to **fflush.**

Using a pipe for a single process is only of limited interest, but the creation of an anonymous pipe is followed by the creation of a process which inherits the descriptors regarding the pipe and can therefore communicate with the creator of the pipe. It is important to carry out these operations in this order because otherwise the pipe can only be accessed by one of the two processes.

Each process therefore has a read descriptor and a write descriptor in the same pipe. In order to communicate correctly, the processes must choose a transmission direction. Each therefore uses only one of the descriptors. One process writes in the pipe, and the other reads. Unused descriptors can be closed by the system call *close*. Once closed, the descriptor is no longer allowed to access the pipe.

By default, reading in the pipe, is blocking. The reading process remains blocked until it has read the amount of data specified in the call *read*. Two communicating processes must therefore adopt a protocol in order to avoid blocking each other.

10.2.1.2 An example of usage
To illustrate the process, the following program implements the example of the beginning of the chapter, which consists of carrying out at a software level the operations represented by calls to the commands *ps, grep*, and *tail*.

The program carrying out this operation uses the call *fork* twice to create a child and a grandson, as shown in figure 10.4. In this way, each process is charged with the execution of a program.

P1

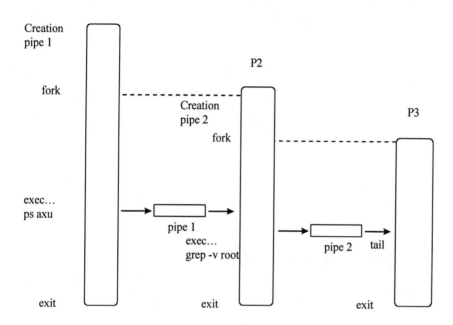

FIGURE 10.4: Example of anonymous pipes.

In addition, the system call *dup2* (see chapter 6, section 6.4.2), which enables an entry in the table of file descriptors to be duplicated, is used to redirect standard inputs/outputs to pipes.

——————— exempletube.c ———————

```c
#include <sys/stat.h>
#include <stdio.h>
#include <unistd.h>


#define CLOSE_ALL(_fd_) close(_fd_[0]); close(_fd_[1])

static void  child  (int fd1[2]);

void main()
{
        int fd[2];
```

```
                    /* Creation of the first pipe : pipe 1 */
                    if (pipe (fd) == -1) {
                            perror ("pipe");
                            exit (-1);
                    }
                    /* Creation of a child process P1 which is going to
            execute *
                    * the child function (fd)                     */
                    switch (fork ()){
                            case -1:
                                    perror ("fork");
                                    exit (-1);
                                    break;

                            case 0:
                                    child  (fd);
                                    break;
                            default:
                                    /* Redirection of the standard output
            descriptor *
                                    to pipe 1                     */
                                    dup2 (fd[1], STDOUT_FILENO); /* stdout */

                                    /* Closure of all pipe 1 descriptors */
                                    CLOSE_ALL (fd);

                                    /* execution of : ps axu */
                                    execlp ("ps", "ps", "axu", NULL);
                                    perror ("execlp");

                                    exit (-1);
                                    break;
                    }
            }
            static void  child (int fd1[2]);
            {
                    int fd[2];

                    /* Creation of the second pipe */
                    if (pipe (fd2) == -1) {
                            perror ("pipe");
                            exit (-1);
                    }
```

```
            /* Creation of a process P2,  grandchild of *
             * the main process                       */
            switch (fork ()){
                    case -1:
                            perror ("fork");
                            exit (-1);
                            break;
                    case 0:
                            /*  Closure   of   the   standard   input
description of pipe 1 */
                            CLOSE_ALL (fd1);

                            /*  Redirection  of  the  standard  input
descriptor *
                             * to pipe 2                    */
                            dup2 (fd2[0], STDIN_FILENO); /* stdin */

                            /* Closure of all descriptors of pipe 2 */
                            CLOSE_ALL (fd2);

                            /* execution of : tail */
                            execlp ("tail", "tail", NULL);

                            perror ("execlp");
                            exit (-1);
                            break;

                    default:
                            /*  Redirection  of  the  standard  input
descriptor *
                             * to pipe 1                    */
                            dup2 (fd1[0], STDIN_FILENO); /* stdin */

                            /*  Redirection  of  the  standard  output
descriptor *
                             * to pipe 2                    */
                            dup2 (fd2[1], STDOUT_FILENO); /* stdout */


                            /* Closure of all descriptors of pipes 1
and 2 */
                            CLOSE_ALL (fd1);
                            CLOSE_ALL (fd2);
```

```
                                    /* execution of : grep -v root */
                                    execlp  ("grep",  "grep",  "-v",  "root",
           NULL);

                                    perror ("execlp");
                                    exit (-1)
                                    break;

               }
       }
```

————————————————————————————— *exempletube.c* ————————

The process executing this program generates two other processes by means of the system call *fork*. In the first process, called the parent, the standard entry is redirected to the standard entry of the child process. The child redirects the standard output to the standard input of its own child. Finally, each of them run the required program, by calling *execlp*.

This example underlines the simplicity of using and handling anonymous pipes. The linking operation which is a command interpreter facility is implemented in this way, using the character |.

10.2.1.3 Pipe creation and program execution
It is common for pipes to communicate with an external program, as has been done in the previous example. Two library processes are provided to simplify this process:

```
#include <stdio.h>

FILE *popen (const char *command, const char *type);

int pclose (FILE *stream);
```

The function *popen* creates a pipe, and then a child process. This process executes the command specified by the parameter **command**. An input/output corresponding to the pipe created is returned, depending on the value of the parameter **type**:

- if **type** is the string "r", the descriptor is accessible in read mode, and allows access to the standard output of the command;
- if **type** is the string "w", the descriptor is accessible in write mode, and allows access to the standard output of the command.

The function *pclose* can be called to close the pipe. It uses the function *fclose* for closure, then triggers the termination of the associated child process, which had been created by the call to *popen*.

10.2.2 Named pipes

The creation of a named pipe is carried out by means of the C library function *mkfifo*. When *stat* is called, the field **st_mode** of the structure **stat** corresponding to the file type has the value **S_IFIFO**:

─────────── Montrefifo.c ────────────────────────────────

```
#include <sys/stat.h>
#include <stdlib.h>
#include <stdio.h>
#include <unistd.h>

static void  usage (char *prg);

void main(int argc, char **argv)
{
    struct stat st;

    if (argc != 2)
            usage (argv[0]);

    if (stat (argv[1], &st) == -1)  {
            perror ("stat");
            exit (-1);
    }
    if (S_ISFIFO (st.st_mode))
            printf (" %s is of type named pipe ! \n", argv[1]);
    else
            printf (" %s is not of named pipe type : %o \n",
                    argv[1]), st.st_mode & S_IFMT);

}
static void  usage (char *prg);
{
    fprintf (stderr, "%s Filename : is the file of FIFO type ?\n",
            prg);
    exit (-1)
}
```

──────────────────────────────── Montrefifo.c   ─────────

The standard form of the function *mkfifo* is as follows:

```
#include <sys/stat.h>

int mkfifo (const char *path, mode_t mode);
```

However, this is not a system call. Indeed, the function is implemented in a very simple manner, using the call *mknod* described in chapter 6, section 6.2.1.

The implementation of the function is carried out using the following call:

```
mknod(path, mode | S_FIFO, 0);
```

It should be noted that the user may create a named pipe by using either *mkfifo*, or the command *mknod*.

Like any file, named pipes allow blocking inputs and outputs (by default) or non-blocking inputs and outputs (by specifying the option **O_NODELAY** or **O_NONBLOCK** when opened using *open*). All file handling operations are valid for a named pipe, except calls to *lseek*.

10.3
GENERAL OVERVIEW OF IMPLEMENTATION

The implementation of pipes is realised in a rather special manner because of the great similarity between the behaviour of anonymous pipes and named pipes. However, to really understand the implementation of pipes, it is necessary to go through the chapter on filesystems. Indeed, a pipe is a particular file in filesystems.

From the point of view of the inode of the pipe, the field **i_pipe** is set to 1, which identifies the inode. The field **u** of the inode, in the case of a pipe (anonymous or not) is constituted from the structure **pipe_inode_info** described in the file **<linux/pipe_fs_i.h>**.

type	*field*	*description*
struct wait_open *	**wait**	Variable used for synchronising simultaneous accesses to the pipe
char *	**base**	Pointer to memory page intended for pipe data
unsigned int	**start**	Position in the memory page
unsigned int	**len**	Number of bytes waiting in the pipe

type	field	description
unsigned int	lock	Pipe lock
unsigned int	rd_openers	Number of processes which have opened the named pipe in read mode
unsigned int	wr_openers	Number of processes which have opened the named pipe in write mode
unsigned int	readers	Number of processes which have read access to the pipe
unsigned int	writers	Number of processes which have write access to the pipe

To a user, the size of a pipe appears to be infinite. However, for performance reasons, it is limited to 4 kbytes (the value of the constant **PIPE_BUF** defined in the file **<linux/limits.h>**). This limit represents the maximum value necessary for carrying out a discrete write operation to the pipe. The user may write more data to the pipe, but he will not be guaranteed a complete operation.

10.3.1 Named pipes

The creation of a named pipe is equivalent to the creation of any sort of file, and it is detailed in the file *fs/fifo.c*.

The read and write operations are found in the file intended for anonymous pipes *fs/pipe.c* since the operations to be carried out are exactly the same.

10.3.2 Anonymous pipes

The creation of an anonymous pipe is achieved in the first instance by creating a new inode in the filesystem. This inode is initialised with the different relevant fields such as the creator identifiers.

The important point is that the inode has a number of null links. As a consequence, this file is not visible in the filesystem, and the only way of accessing it, from the point of view of the programmer, is to possess a file descriptor.

10.4
DETAILED DESCRIPTION
OF IMPLEMENTATION

10.4.1   Creation of a pipe inode

The creation of a pipe inode is performed by the function **get_pipe_inode** of the file *fs/inode.c*. As a first step, an inode is allocated by . calling the function **get_empty_inode**. The operation consists of allocating a memory page to contain the data, and the allocation is carried out by the function **__get_free_page**.

The field **i_op** which contains the list of operations associated with the inode, is set to **pipe_inode_operations**. This variable contains, by default, a pointer to the variable **rdwr_pipe_fops** for creating an anonymous pipe. But, according to the type of pipe created and the creation options, it can contain pointer to other operations.

The process of creating of an inode finishes by initialising the characteristics of a pipe, that is, the setting of access permissions, dates etc.

10.4.2   Creation of a named pipe

The creation of a named pipe is performed by the function **fifo_open**, defined in the source file *fs/fifo.c*. This function is called by means of the initialisation function of a named pipe: **init_fifo**.

The creation of a named pipe depends on creation options. The options authorised on the inode are established in accordance with these options:

- read only: **connecting_fifo_fops** in the case of a non-blocking read, and **read_fifo_fops** if this is not the case;
- write only: **write_fifo_fop** ;
- read and write: **rdwr_fifo_fops**.

10.4.3   Creation of an anonymous pipe

An anonymous pipe is created more simply by the function **do_pipe** of the file *fs/pipe.c*. This call has to construct a table of two file descriptors which correspond to the input and the output of the anonymous pipe.

The creation of an anonymous pipe consists, in the first instance, of creating an inode for the pipe by means of the function **get_pipe_inode** described previously. Next, two file descriptors are allocated by means of the function **get_empty_filp**.

Finally, the file descriptor having an index 0 receives **read_pipe_fops**, because it is dedicated to reading, and the descriptor having index 1 receives **write_pipe_fops** .

10.4.4   Input/output operations

The read and write operations are carried out via a buffer of size **PIPE_BUF**. In accordance with the reading and writing of data in the pipe, the window containing the pipe data moves in a circular manner inside the buffer.

All input/output operations, whether they concern named pipes or anonymous pipes, are located in the file *fs/pipe.c*. Details of this and their functioning are given below:

- **pipe_read**: runs through the memory page copying data contained in the buffer intended for the user. During this operation, the pipe is locked.

  In the case where the read is non-blocking, the error **EAGAIN** is returned if the pipe is locked or if it is empty. If this is not the case, the calling process is put on hold whilst the pipe is empty.

  Once the data is available, the pipe is locked, the data is copied into the buffer provided by the calling process, then the pipe is unlocked.
- **pipe_write**: writes to the pipe data passed as parameters from the buffer within the limit of the remaining available size. During this operation, the pipe is locked.

  This function performs a loop as long as not all the data have been written to the pipe.

  At each cycle of the loop, it checks to see id there are still reading processes in the pipe. If not, the signal *SIGPIPE* is sent to the calling process. If it is, the pipe is locked, the data is copied into the buffer provided by the calling process, then the pipe is unlocked.
- **pipe_ioctl**: the only operation of the type *ioctl* which is allowed is the operation designated by **FIOREAD** which enables the number of data bytes currently stored in the pipe to be established. The contents of the field len of the structure **pipe_inode_info** is then returned.
- **pipe_select**: for the operation of multiplexing associated with the call *select*, this function checks certain validity conditions before indicating whether it is necessary to take make/take more input/output to the pipe:

  - multiplexing in read mode: it is necessary that the pipe is not empty, and that at least one process has access to the pipe in read mode;
  - multiplexing in write mode: it is necessary that the pipe is not full, and that at least one process has access to the pipe in read mode;
  - exceptions: the pipe must be accessible at least one process in read and in write mode.

- **connect_read**: this function is used exclusively by named pipes when, at the creation of the pipe, no process has opened the pipe in write mode. It only modifies the realisable operations on the inode by assigning the field **f_op** to **read_fifo_fops**. After this modification, a call to the read function in a table is launched (**pipe_read**);
- **connect_select**: in the same context as the function above, this function only modifies the field **f_op** when multiplexed reading.

Functions used when descriptors are closed include the following:

- **pipe_read_release**: decrements the number of processes having read access to the pipe;
- **pipe_write_release**: decrements the number of processes having write access to the pipe;
- **pipe_rdwr_release**: decrements the number of processes having read and write access to the pipe.

Functions used when a new process is created, inheriting the pipe:

- **pipe_read_open**: increments the number of processes having read access to the pipe;
- **pipe_write_open**: increments the number of processes having write access to the pipe;
- **pipe_rdwr_open**: increments the number of processes having read and write access to the pipe.

11

IPC System V

System calls described

msgctl, msgget, msgsnd, msgrcv, semctl, semget, semop

This chapter is devoted to one of the key mechanisms of the Unix system: IPCs (Inter Process Communication). IPCs enable data to be exchanged and shared, but also to synchronise processes in a way that is relatively easy to use.

Historically, IPCs appeared in the System V versions of Unix. They are nowadays present in all Unix variants.

11.1
BASIC CONCEPTS

11.1.1 Introduction

In earlier chapters, the topics of pipes and signals have been tackled. These concepts are limited to the domain of communication. For example, it is not possible for any arbitrary process to read or write in a pipe unless it is the child of the process which created it. Furthermore, in the management of signals, the only information that is transported is a simple number, which renders signals unsuitable for transferring data.

IPCs enable data of all types to be handled, to be sent from one process to another, or indeed to be shared. In reality, IPCs are composed of three mechanisms:

1.Message queues

A message queue may be considered to be like a letter box. In other words, as long as it has the necessary permissions, an application can lodge a message there (a number, a character string or even the contents of some data structure, etc.) and other applications may read this message.

2. Shared memory

Management of shared memory enables a memory zone to be made common to several applications. Normally, when a memory zone is allocated (using *malloc* for example), it is local to the process, this means that no other application working on the system can be accessed. The management of shared memory enables memory zones to be created which are accessible to several processes in read mode as well as write mode.

3. Semaphores

Semaphores help overcome one of the biggest problems facing a multi-process system: process synchronisation. Indeed, several processes are operating at the same time and can access the same data. This can cause certain problems, such as simultaneous access to data, mutual blocking etc.

It is worth pointing out a big difference between other communication systems and IPCs: the latter do not use the file management system. When an IPC is created or handled, it is not used like a file, and therefore not by way of *open, read,* etc. The only way to handle an IPC, is by knowing its identification key.

11.1.2 Management of keys

IPCs are based on a particular mechanism: *key management*. To create IPCs, or simply to access them, it is necessary to possess an identifier, known as a *key*. This key is a number which identifies the IPC uniquely at the system level, and it is therefore necessary to possess it in order to access the resource.

To generate a key, the library function *ftok* is called.

```
include <sys/types.h>
include <sys/types.h>

key_t ftok (char *pathname, char proj);
```

This function takes a filename as an argument. The second parameter allows one file to generate several different keys. Starting from the filename, it returns the unique identifier of the IPC. It is this identifier which should be used to manage the IPC.

The number is calculated with the following formula:

$$clef = (st\_ino \ \& \ oxFFFF) \ | \ ((st\_dev \ \& \ oxFF) << 16 \ ) \ | \ (proj << 24)$$

The calculation is carried out using a combination of the file inode number, the number of the device on which the file is located, and the last parameter, in such a way that a unique number is generated.

There now follows an example of the use of this function:

——————— CreerClef.c ———————————————————————————

```c
#include <stdio.h>
#include <sys/types.h>
#include <sys/ipc.h>
#include <sys/stat.h>

void usage(char *prg)
{

    printf (" %s existing_file_name \n", prg);
    exit (1);
}

void main (int argc, char **argv)
{
    struct stat data;

    if (argc !=2)
            usage (argv[0]);

    if (stat (argv[1], &data) == -1) {
            printf (" Can't access %s \n", argv[1]);
            exit (2);
}
    printf ("Inode number of file  :  %s \n",
            (int) data.st_ino;
    printf ("Key with 0 ; %x \n", (int) ftok (argv[1], '\0'));
    printf ("Key with a ; %x \n", (int) ftok (argv[1], 'a'));


}
```

————————————————————————————— CreerClef.c ———————

Here is an example execution:

```
gandalf> % CreateKey zorglub.c
File in-node number : 38e6
Key with 0 : 238e6
Key with a : 610238e6
```

11.1.3 Access permissions

Along with any memory zone, file, or other entity in Unix, an IPC possesses access permissions to ensure the confidentiality of information transmitted. This system of access permissions authorises, for example, access to a queue of messages to a particular group of users.

Each IPC has an **ipc_perm** structure which contains data relating to access permissions. It is possible to modify these permissions at the time that the IPC is created. The detail of the structure is given below:

type	*field*	*description*
key_t	**key**	Only key
ushort	**uid**	Owners effective user identification
ushort	**gid**	Owners effective group identification
ushort	**cuid**	Creator's effective user identification
ushort	**cgid**	Creator's effective group identification
ushort	**mode**	Access permissions
ushort	**seq**	Number of input operations

The standard fields identifying the owner, the resource creator, and the access permissions, are found in this structure. The access permissions are important since they allow other processes to be able to read and write data.

11.2
SYSTEM CALLS

The handling of IPCs is carried out via system calls. Although the three types of IPC are very different, they use similar system calls, and these can be grouped into three categories:

- Creation: *msget, semget, shmget*
- Control: *msgctl, semctl, shmctl*

- Communication: *msgsnd, msgrcv, semop, shmop*

Seven constants are frequently used:

Call types	Meaning	Constant
Creation	New queue	**IPC_PRIVATE**
	Creation of an IPC if the key is not already used.	**IPC_CREAT**
	Creation of an object if it doesn't already exist.	**IPC_EXCL**
	Used for loadable modules.	**IPC_KERNELD**
msgsnd, msgrcv, semop	No waiting.	**IPC_NOWAIT**
Control	Deletion of object resources	**IPC_RMID**
	Fixes options in **ipc_perm**	**IPC_SET**
	Reading of **ipc_perm**	**IPC_GET**
	Returns a structure **msginfo**, or **shminfo, seminfo**	**IPC_INFO**

11.2.1 Message queues

Message queues are generally compared to a system of letter boxes. The principle is relatively simple: a process places one, or several, messages on a 'letter box'. Another process (or even several) may then read each of these messages, in their order of arrival, according to the message type that he wants. This directly analogous to reading ordinary mail: one can start from the top or the bottom of the pile, start with the bills or the post cards[1] ...

To manipulate a message queue, other than system calls, three structures are required.

11.2.1.1 Basic structures

The structure **msqid_ds** corresponds to a message queue object. It is thanks to this structure that it is possible to handle the object created. It is defined in the header file **<linux/mag.h>**, but for reasons of portability, it is sufficient to include the header file **<sys/msg.h>**. There now follows an example of this structure:

---

[1] Starting by the bills can spoil your day, so it is better start elsewhere ...?

type	field	description
struct ipc_perm	msg_perm	Access permissions to the object
struct msg *	msg_first	Pointer to the first message in the queue
struct msg *	msg_last	Pointer to the last message in the queue
time_t	msg_stime	Date of the last call to *msgsnd*
time_t	msg_rtime	Date of the last call to *msgcrv*
time_t	msg_ctime	Date of the last modification of the object
struct wait_queue *	wwait	Queue of processes waiting to write
struct wait_queue *	rwait	Queue of processes waiting to read
ushort	msg_cbytes	Number of bytes currently in the queue
ushort	msg_qnum	Number of messages in the queue
ushort	msg_qbytes	Maximum number of bytes in the queue
ushort	msg_lspid	Number of the last process having carried out a *msgsnd*
ushort	msg_lrpid	Number of the last process having carried out a *msgrcv*

This header file also contains the definition of the structure msginfo. It is used when calling *msgctl*, using IPC_INFO as argument. This structure is in particular used by the program *ipcs*, and it is usually reserved by system programs for statistics gathering or machine monitoring.

It is made up of the following fields:

type	field	description
int	msgpool	Size of the data in a queue in kbytes
int	msgmap	Number of entries in the message table
int	msgmax	Maximum size of the messages in bytes
int	msgpmnb	Maximum size of the message queue
int	msgmni	Maximum number of message queue identifiers
int	msgssz	Size of a message segment
int	msgtql	Number of system message headers
ushort	msgseg	Maximum number of segments

The structure msgbuf stores a message of its type. It represents the model to be used for sending or receiving messages from a queue:

type	field	description
long	mtype	Message type
char[1]	mtext	Message contents

This structure is never used in applications. In fact, any data structure placed in a message queue must absolutely have the message type as its first field. This is always a positive number, of the type **long**, and it enables a message to by selected from the queue according to its type.

Message queues are also used by the kernel within the framework of loadable modules, and of *kerneld* (see chapter 12, section 12.4.1).

11.2.1.2 Creation and look-up of message queues
The system call *msgget* has two roles:

    1. Creation of new message queues;

    2. Search for existing message queues (created by another application, for example) by means of its key.

In both cases, the operation requires possession of the key. The model for this system call is the following:

```
#include <sys/types.h>
#include <sys/ipc.h>
#include <sys/msg.h>

int msgget (key_t key, int option);
```

The first argument represents the key to the already existing message queue, or the one which is to be created. If the key passed has the value **IPC_CREAT**, then a queue is created. If it is a different key, there are two possibilities:

    1. The key is not already used by another message queue: in this case, **IPC_CREAT**should be taken up as the option. This will create the queue, with the key passed as a parameter. Certain access permissions may be fixed by the options.

    2. The key is being used by a message queue. Either **IPC_CREAT** or **IPC_EXCL** should be passed as the parameter. In this case the message queue may be read or written to, if the associated access permissions permit it, of course.

If everything proceeds as it should, *msgget* returns the message queue identifier. If this is not the case, **errno** can take the following values:

error	meaning
EACCESS	A message queue exists for this key, but the calling·process does not have access permissions to the message queue
EEXIST	A message queue already exists for this key, and the options **IPC_CREAT** and **IPC_EXCL** have both been fixed
EIDRM	The message queue has been marked for erasure
ENOENT	No message queue exists for the key, and the option IPC_CREAT has not been given
ENOMEM	A new message queue could have been created, but the system does not have enough memory for the new structure
ENOSPC	The maximum number of message queues has been reached

This call returns the message queue identifier.

11.2.1.3 Control of message queues

After creating a message queue, it is possible to handle it by modifying access permissions to the queue, for example. Above all, it should be remembered that IPCs are managed in the table by message queues. The system call *msgctl* enables certain fields in this table to be accessed and modified, for the queues for which access permissions are set.

The model for this call is as follows:

```
#include <sys/types.h>
#include <sys/ipc.h>
#include <sys/msg.h>


int msgctl (int msqid, int cmd, struct msqid_ds *buf);
```

The first argument *msqid* represents the message queue identifier given by calling *msgget*. The second argument *cmd*, indicates the type of operation to be carried out on the message queue. The list of operations which may be carried out on the message queue is given below:

- **MSG_STAT** (or **IPC_STAT**): copies the table associated with the message queue at the address pointed to **buf**, of structure type *msqid_ds*.
- **IPC_SET**: allows certain members of the **msqid_ds** structure to be fixed. This operation automatically updates the field **msg_ctime** which saves the date of the last modification to entries in the process table. It is possible to access three

fields in the structure: **msg_perm.uid, msg_perm.gid** and **msg_perm.mode**. An additional field - **msg_qbytes** - may be modified, but only by the super-user.

- **IPC_RMID**: enables the message queue and the data it contains to be erased. Only processes whose user identifier corresponds to a super-user, a creator or the owner of the message queue, may erase a message queue.
- **MSG_INFO** (or **IPC_INFO**): conforms to the **struct msginfo** structure passed a as parameter. This is used, for example, by the program *ipcs*.

11.2.1.4 Broadcast of messages

The system call *msgsnd* enables a message to be posted to the message queue. It follows the model below:

```
#include <sys/types.h>
#include <sys/ipc.h>
#include <sys/msg.h>

int msgsnd (int msqid, struct msgbuf *msgp, int msgsize, int msgopt);
```

For this operation to work normally, the message queue identifier must have been obtained, along with the access permissions to write to the queue. The second parameter corresponds to the data that is required to be posted to the queue. The parameter **msgsize** corresponds to the size of the object sent to the queue.

If the option **IPC_NOWAIT** is passed, this only has an effect when the queue is full. In this case, the call is not blocking (unlike a call without this parameter) and the error **EAGAIN** is returned.

The list errors which may be returned following this call are listed below:

error	meaning
EAGAIN	The message may not be sent because the wait queue is full and the option `IPC_NOWAIT` has been set
EACCES	No write permission
EFAULT	The address pointed to by **msgp** is not accessible
EIDRM	The queue no longer exists: it has been erased
EINTR	The process has received a signal and the system call has therefore failed
EINVAL	Bad queue identifier, or the data type to be sent to the message queue is not positive
ENOMEM	Insufficient memory to make a copy of the object

This call returns the value 0 if successful.

11.2.1.5 *Message reception*

The call *msgrcv* enables the message queue to be read. It has the following standard form.

```
#include <sys/types.h>
#include <sys/ipc.h>
#include <sys/msg.h>

int msgrcv (int msqid, struct msgbuf *msgp, int msgsz, long msgtyp, int
msgflg);
```

If there are sufficient process permissions, this system call enables messages to be retrieved which will be copied in **msgp**. The memory zone pointed to by **msgp** has a maximum size **msgsz**.

Two types of option can be given in the field **msgflg**:

- **MSG_NOERROR**: if the size of the message is greater than size specified in the field **msgsz**, and if the option **MSG_NOERROR** is set, then the message will be truncated. The part cut off will be lost. In the event of this option being absent, the message is not extracted from the queue and the calls fails, returning the error **E2BIG**.
- **IPC_NOWAIT**: this option enables an active wait to be avoided. If the queue ever becomes empty, the error **ENOMSG** is returned. If this option is not activated, the call is suspended until data of the type requested arrives in the message queue.

The type of message to be read should be specified in the field (**msgtyp**):

- If **msgtyp** is equal to 0, it is the first message in the queue, that is, the oldest message, which will be read, whatever its type.
- If **msgtyp** is **negative**, then the first message in the queue having the smallest type less than or equal to the absolute value **msgtyp** which is returned.
- If **msgtyp** is **positive**, then the first message in the queue having a type strictly equal to **msgtyp** which is returned. In the case where the option **MSG_EXCEPT** is given, then it is the first message having a different type which will be returned.

The errors which may result from using this system call are listed below:

error	meaning
EINVAL	The message queue identifier is invalid, **mtype** is less than zero, or **msgsz** is less than zero or greater than the maximum size of a **MSGMAX** message.
EFAULT	The memory zone pointed to by **msgp** is not accessible
EIDRM	Whilst the process was waiting for a message, the message queue was destroyed
EACCES	The process does not have the necessary permissions to access the message queue.
E2BIG	The message size is greater than **msgsz** and the option **MSG_NOERROR** has not been set.
ENOMSG	The option **IPC_NOWAIT** has been set and no message has been found in the queue.
EINTR	Whilst the process was waiting for a message, the process received a message

11.2.1.6 An example of system calls in use

Having described the different system calls, there now follows a simple example of their use. The principle is to create a server which will copy into the same message queue two files passed to the command line. Two clients are created; they each retrieve a file, and save it. Figure 11.1 summarises the example which follows:

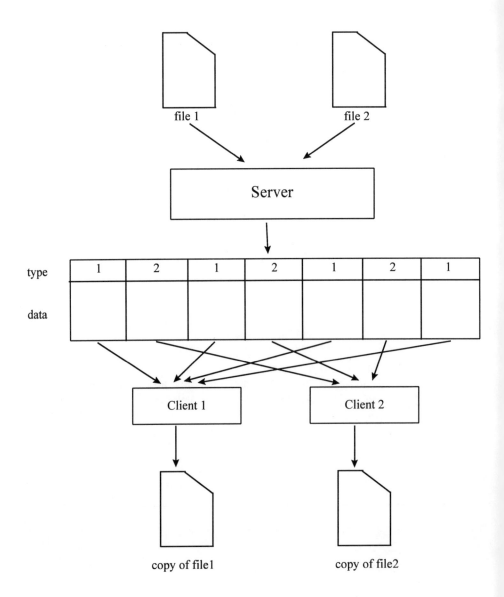

FIGURE 11.1:   Example of message queue manipulation.

The file *Copy.h* contains common declarations, the server is implemented in the file *Copyserver.c* and the file *CopyClient.c* contains the client source code.

──────── Copie.h ──

```
#ifndef COPY_H
#define COPY_H

#define FILE_KEY "CopyServer"      /* Filename which will be used to
                                    generate the message queue key */
#define PROJ_FTOK 'a'      /* parameter ftok       */

#define TYPE_FILE1  1      /* File type 1 in the message queue  */
#define TYPE_FILE2  2      /* File type 2 in the message queue  */
#define TYPE_END1   3      /* Client 1 has finished reading the file
     */
#define TYPE_END2   4      /* Client 2 has finished reading the file
     */


#define SIZE_BUF 256       /* Block size */

typedef struct data _s data_t
struct data_s {
    long type;              /* message type */
    int size;                 /* amount of data transferred
                            -1 == EOF       */
    char buf[SIZE_BUF];  /* message              */
};

#endif
```

── Copie.h ──────────

──────── CopieServeur.c ────────────────────────────────────

```
#include <stdio.h>
#include <stdlib.h>
#include <fcntl.h>
#include <errno.h>
#include <unistd.h>
#include <sys/stat.h>
#include <sys/types.h>
#include <sys/ipc.h>
#include <sys/msg.h>

#include "Copy.h"
```

```
static void usage (char *prg)
{
        printf (" Example of an application using message queues \n");
        printf (" → Server \n");
        printf (" %s <file1> <file2> \n\n", prg);
        exit (-1);
}

static void  my_error (char *msg, char *call)
{
        fprintf (stderr, "Error Server %s :%d \n", msg, errno);
        perror (call);
        exit (-1);
}

static void  close_all (int id_file, int fd1, int fd2)
{
        msgctl (id_file, IPC_RMID, NULL);
        close (fd1);
        close (fd2);
}

void main (int argc, char **argv)
{
        int        fd1;
                   fd2;
        int        id_file;
        key_t      key;
        data_t     data1;
                   data2;
        int        end1 = 1,
                   end2 = 1;

        if (argc != 3)
                   usage (argv[0]);

        /* File opening */
        if ((fd1 = open (argv[1], O_RDONLY)) == -1
                   my_error ("Error open1 ", "open");

        if ((fd2 = open (argv[2], O_RDONLY)) == -1   {
                   close (fd1);
                   my_error ("Error open2 ", "open");
```

```
        }
        /* Key generation */
        if ((key = ftok (FILE_KEY, PROJ_FTOK)) == -1) {
                      close (fd1);
                      close (fd2);
                      error ("Error ftok", "ftok");
        }
        /* Creation of message queue */
        if ((id_file = msgget (key, IPC_CREAT | IPC_EXCL | 0666)) == -1) {
                      close (fd1);
                      close (fd2);
                      error ("Error at msgget",  "msgget");
        }
        printf ("Server : Message queue(%d) created : copy of %s and %s
\n",
                id_file, argv[1], argv [2]);

        data1.type = TYPE_FILE1;
        data2.type = TYPE_FILE2;

        data1.data_sz = data2.data_sz = -1;

        /* Copy loop */
        while ((data1.data_sz) || (data2.data_sz)) {
        if (data1.data_sz) {
              data1.data_sz = read (fd1, data1.buf,
                                    SIZE_BUF * sizeof (char));

              if (data1.data_sz == -1) {
                    close_all (id_file, fd1, fd2);
                    my_error ("Error read1", "read");
              }
              if (msgsnd (id_file, (struct msgbuf *) &data1,
                          sizeof (data_t), 0) == -1
                    my_error ("Error msgsnd file 1", "msgsnd";
              }
        if (data2.data_sz) {
              data2.data_sz = read (fd1, data2.buf,
                                    SIZE_BUF * sizeof (char));

              if (data2.data_sz == -1) {
                    close_all (id_file, fd1, fd2);
                    my_error ("Error read2", "read");
```

```
                }
                if (msgsnd (id_file, (struct msgbuf *) &data2,
                                sizeof (data_t), 0) == -1
                        my_error ("Error msgsnd file 2", "msgsnd");
        }
}


printf ("Server : data transmission to message queue completed\n");
printf ("Server : waiting for clients to finish reading \n");

/* Waiting for the child processes to flag they have terminated */
while ((end1) || (end2)) {
            struct msgbuf  rec;

        if (msgrcv (id_file, &rec, sizeof (struct msgbuf),
                TYPE_END1, IPC_NOWAIT) != -1)
                            end1 = 0;

        if (msgrcv (id_file, &rec, sizeof (struct msgbuf),
                TYPE_END2, IPC_NOWAIT) != -1)
                            end2 = 0;
    }
    printf ("Server : disconnection of the two child processes  \n");

    close_all (id_file, fd1, fd2);
}
```

———————————————————————————————— CopieServeur.c ————

———————— CopieClient.c ——————————————————————————————

```
#include <stdio.h>
#include <stdlib.h>
#include <fcntl.h>
#include <errno.h>
#include <unistd.h>
#include <sys/stat.h>
#include <sys/types.h>
#include <sys/ipc.h>
#include <sys/msg.h>

#include "Copy.h"
```

```
static void usage (char *prg)
{
        printf (" Example  of  an  application  using  message  queues
\n");
        printf (" → Client \n");
        printf (" %s 1 |2 <file_copy> \n\n", prg);
        exit (-1);
}

static void my_error (char *msg, char *call, int no_client)
{
        fprintf (stderr, "Client error%d%s :%d \n", no_client, msg,
errno);
        perror (call);
        exit (-1);
}

static void  disconnection (int id_file, int no_client)
{
        struct msgbuf disconnection_msg;

        if(no_client == 1)
            disconnection_msg.mtype = TYPE_END1;
        else
            disconnection_msg.mtype = TYPE_END2;

        msgsnd (id_file, &disconnection, sizeof (struct msgbuf), 0);
}

static void  close_all (int id_file, int fd, int no_client)
{
        disconnection (id_file, no_client);
        msgctl (id_file, IPC_RMID, NULL);
        close (fd);
}

void main (int argc, char **argv)
{
    int         fd;
    int         id_file;
    int         ret;
    key_t       key;
    data_t      data;
```

```
        int              no_client; / Client 1 or 2 */
        int              type_client /* Identification of the client
for the server */

        if (argc != 3)
                usage (argv[0]);

        /* Retrieve client number */
        no_client = atoi (argv[1];
        if ((no_client != 1) && (no_client != 2))
                usage (argv[0]);

        if no_client == 1)
                type_client = TYPE_FILE1;
        else
                type_client = TYPE_FILE2;

/* Key generation */
if ((key = ftok (FILE_KEY, PROJ_FTOK)) == -1)
        my_error ("Error ftok", "ftok", no_client);

/* Connection to the message queue */
if ((id_file = msgget (key, IPC_EXCL)) == -1) {
        my_error ("Error at msgget",  "msgget", no_client);

fprintf (stderr, "Client%d connected to the message queue
                \n",no_client);

/* File opening */
if ((fd = open (argv[2], O_WRONLY | O_CREAT | 0666)) == -1)
        my_error ("Error on open", "open", no_client);

/* Read loop */
while (1) {
        if (msgrcv (id_file, (struct msgbuf *) &data,
                sizeof(data_t),type_client, 0) == -1)
              my_error ("Error during reception", "msgrcv",
                        no_client);

        if (data.data_sz == 0) /* EOF */
                break;
        ret = write (fd, data.buf, data.data_sz * sizeof (char));

        if (ret == -1) {
                close_all (id_file, fd, no_client);
```

```
                my_error ("Error during writing", "write",
                          no_client);



            }
        }
        close (fd);

        printf ("Client%d : Disconnection \n", no_client);

        disconnection (id_file, no_client);


    }
```

——————————————————————— CopieClient.c ———

An example of usage is presented below.

```
gandalf> CopyServer CreateKey.c Copy.h &
Server : Message queue created : copy of CreateKey.c and Copy.h

gandalf> CopyClient 1 file1 &
Client1 connected to the message queue

gandalf> CopyClient 2 file2 &
Client1 connected to the message queue

Server: send to the message queue terminated
Server: Waiting for clients to have finished reading à
Client2: Disconnection
Client1: Disconnection

Server: Disconnection of two child processes achieved
```

11.2.2 Semaphores

Linux uses semaphores internally for synchronising kernel mode processes (see chapter 4, section 4.5.3). It also provides processes with handling functions for semaphores.

In some circumstances, processes need to be provided with several resources to continue their action, for example they may need to access a data buffer and a shared memory segment if they wish to move data from one place to another. It is then necessary for processes to use two semaphores and to execute two P operations (one for the buffer and the other for the memory) in order to be able to call on the two resources. This situation could cause a mutual blocking in the following case: a process has exclusive access to the buffer and access to the memory is desired, whilst another has exclusive access to the memory and access to the buffer is required.

To solve this problem, the operations P and V are not carried out on a single semaphore, but on a table of semaphores. As a result, a process can continue only if operations have progressed correctly on all elements of the table. From the user's point of view, this must obviously occur in a atomic manner, that is in a single system call.

The System V semaphores implement all this functionality with extensions which enable processes to wait until a semaphore is set to zero.

11.2.2.1 Basic structures

These structures are defined in the header file **<linux/sem.h>** but as for message queues, it is sufficient to include the file **<sys/sem.h>**. When a System V semaphore is created, a set of semaphores is created. The structure **semid_ds** is the control for such a set of semaphores. It contains system information, pointers to operations to be carried out on the set, as well as a pointer to the **sem** structures which are stored in the kernel and contain information on each semaphore.

type	*field*	*description*
struct ipc_perm	**sem_perm**	Permissions
time_t	**sem_otime**	Date of the last operation
time_t	**sem_ctime**	Date of the last change using *semctl*
struct sem *	**sem_base**	Pointer to first semaphore of the set
struct sem_queue *	**sem_pending**	Operations waiting to be carried out
struct sem_queue **	**sem_pending_last**	Last operation waiting to be carried out
struct sem_undo *	**undo**	Operations aborted in the event of termination
ushort	**sem_nsems**	Number of semaphores in a set

The structure **sembuf** represents an operation on a semaphore (increment, decrement, or wait for the value null), it is therefore used when calling *semop*. It contains the following fields:

type	field	description
ushort	sem_num	Semaphore number in the group
short	sem_op	Operation on a semaphore
short	sem_flg	Options

The **semun** structure is a combination, it is used when calling *semctl* to store or to recover information about the semaphores.

type	field	description
int	val	Value for `SETVAL`
struct semid_ds *	buf	Data buffer for `IPC_STS` and `IPC_SET`
ushort	array	Table for `GETALL` and `SETALL`
struct seminfo *	_ _buf	Data buffer for `IPC_INFO`
void *	_ _pad	Alignment pointer of the structure

As can be seen, the semaphore value may be modified; the sign of the field **val** defines the action specified:

- if **val** is negative, it is a **P** operation;
- if **val** is positive, it is a **V** operation;
- if **val** is null, the process is blocked until the value of the semaphore is null (this feature is used for example to rendez-vous between processes).

The definition of the structure **seminfo** is also available. This structure enables the current or the limit values of the system to be called up by means of a call to *semctl*. These calls are not generally carried out directly, but are left for system utilities such as the command *ipcs* (see section 3.2.1) to perform. In Linux, only four fields have significant values for the call *semctl* with **IPC_INFO** as an argument, and only two fields are significant with **SEMINFO**. The following table describes the significant fields in the structure:

type	field	description
int	semmap	Unused
int	semmni	Maximum number of semaphore groups (`SEMMNI=128`) (**IPC_INFO**)
int	semmns	Maximum number of semaphores (`SEMMNS=SEMMNI * SEMMSL`) (`IPC_INFO`)
int	semmnu	Unused

type	field	description
int	**semmsl**	Maximum number of semaphores per group (**SEMMNS=32**) (**IPC_INFO**)
int	**semopm**	Unused
int	**semume**	Unused
int	**semusz**	Number of semaphores currently defined (**SEMINFO**)
int	**semvmx**	Maximum value of the semaphore counter (**SEMVMI-32767**) (**IPC_INFO**)
int	**semaem**	Number of semaphores currently defined (**SEMINFO**)

11.2.2.2 Creation and look-up of semaphore groups

The system call *semget* enables either the creation of semaphore groups, or the recovery of the identifier of a group already in existence. This function behaves like the function *msgget* but for a table of semaphores. It has an additional argument which indicates the number of semaphores to be created in a table. It should be noted that semaphores are numbered from zero within the group. The general form of the function is as follows:

```
#include <sys/types.h>
#include <sys/ipc.h>
#include <sys/sem.h>


int semget (key_t key, int nsems, int semflg);
```

This call returns the identifier of the semaphore group or the value -1 if an error occurs. In the latter case, the variable **errno** takes one of the following values:

error	meaning
EACCES	A semaphore group exits for this key, but the process does not have sufficient permissions to access the group.
EEXIST	A semaphore group exits for this key, but the options **IPC_CREAT** or **IPC_EXCL** are group.
EIDRM	A semaphore group has been erased.
ENOENT	The semaphore group does not exist and the option **IPC_CREAT** is not group.
ENOMEM	The semaphore could be created but the system has insufficient space to store the structure.
ENOSPC	The semaphore could be created but the maximum number of semaphore groups (**SEMMNI**) or the maximum number of semaphores (**SEMMNS**) would be exceeded.

11.2.2.3 Semaphore operations

Three operations were introduced in section 2.2.1: Incrementing, decrementing and waiting for the value zero to be reached. The system call *semop* allows these three operations to be performed on some of the semaphores in a group. The form of the call is as follows:

```
#include <sys/types.h>
#include <sys/ipc.h>
#include <sys/sem.h>

int semop (int semid, struct sembuf *sops, unsigned nsops);
```

The first argument represents the group on which the operations are to take place. The second argument is a table of the **sembuf** structures containing the list of operations. Finally, the last argument is the number of operations to be carried out when the call is made (in fact, this gives the size of the table pointed to by the second argument).

All these operations should be carried out in a step-by-step fashion. Where this is not possible, either the process is suspended until it becomes possible, or, if the flag **IPC_NOWAIT** is set (field **sem_flag** of the structure **sembuf**) for one of these operations, the system call is interrupted without any operation being completed.

For each operation performed, the system checks whether the flag is set, If so, it creates a structure to keep a trace of this operation and to be able to cancel it at the end of process execution.

If the system call proceeds correctly, the value returned is 0, if not, it is –1, and **errno** takes one of the following values:

error	*meaning*
E2BIG	The argument **nsops** is larger than **SEMOPM**, and the maximum number of operations allowed for this call is thus exceeded.
EACCES	The calling process does not have access permissions to one of the semaphores specified in one of the operations.
EAGAIN	The flag IPC_NOWAIT is set and the operations have been carried out immediately.
EFAULT	The address specified by the field **sops** is invalid.
EFBIG	The semaphore number (field **sem_num**) is incorrect for one of the operations (either negative, or larger than the number of semaphores in the group).
EIDRM	A semaphore no longer exists.

Continuation of the list of values for **errno**	
error	*meaning*
EINTR	The process has received a signal whilst waiting for access to the semaphore.
EINVAL	Either the semaphore requested does not exist (argument **semid**), or the number of operations to be carried out is negative or zero (argument **nsops**).
ENOMEM	The flag SEM_UNDO is set and the system is unable to allocate memory to store the structure cancelling the operation.
ERANGE	The value added to the semaphore counter cause the maximum value allowed for the counter **SEMVMI** to be exceeded.

11.2.2.4 *Control of semaphores*

The system call *semctl* enables semaphore groups to be interrogated, modified or deleted. It also enables semaphores to be initialised, obtains information on the number of semaphores awaiting incrementing or decrementing to zero. The call model is the following:

```
#include <sys/types.h>
#include <sys/ipc.h>
#include <sys/sem.h>

int semctl (int semid, int semnum, int cmd, union semun arg);
```

According to the value of **cmd**, the parameter **semnum** represents either the number of semaphores or the semaphore number: **arg** may also be interpreted in different ways. The parameter **cmd** indicates which operation is to be carried out, and its value may be:-

- **IPC_STAT**: enables information regarding a semaphore group to be obtained. **semnum** is ignored, and **arg** is a pointer to the zone containing the information. The process must have read access to carry this operation out.
- **IPC_SET**: enables certain values of the semaphore group structure to be modified. The fields which may be changed are **sem_perm.uid**, **sem_perm.gid**, and **sem_perm.mode**. The field **sem_ctime** is automatically updated. The process must be either the creator or the owner of the group, or be a super-user.
- **IPC_RMID**: enables a semaphore group to be erased. The process must be either the creator or the owner of the group, or be a super-user. All processes waiting

for one of the semaphores in the group are woken up and they receive the error message **EIDRM**.

- **GETPID**: allows the value **sempid** of the semaphore **semnum** to be returned. It is the identifier of the last process to have carried out the system call *semop* on this semaphore. The process must have read access to carry this operation out.
- **GETNCNT**: allows the value **semncnt** of the semaphore **semnum** to be returned. This represents the number of processes waiting for the semaphore counter to increase. The process must have read access to carry this operation out.
- **GETZCNT**: allows the value **semzcnt** of the semaphore **semnum** to be returned. This represents the number of processes waiting for the semaphore counter to become zero. The process must have read access to carry this operation out.
- **GETVAL/SETVAL**: enables the value of the semaphore **semnum** of the set **semid** to be read or set. **arg** contains the value of the semaphore read or changed. Where there have been changes, the operation cancellation structures are erased, the processes waiting for the semaphore are woken up if the value becomes zero or positive, and the field **sem_ctime** is updated. The process must have read and write access.
- **GETALL/SETALL**: enables the value of the semaphores of the set **semid** to be read or set. **arg** contains the result or value of the operation; the parameter **semnum** is ignored. The process must have read and write access to the group.

The system call returns –1 in the event of an error, and the variable **errno** contains one of the following values:

error	meaning
EACCES	The calling process does not have sufficient permissions to carry out this operation
EFAULT	The address specified by `arg.buf` or `arg.array` is invalid
EIDRM	The semaphore group has been erased
EINVAL	The value of `semid` or of `cmd` is incorrect
EPERM	The process does not have sufficient permissions for the operation (command `IPC_SET` or `IPC_RMID`)
ERANGE	`cmd` has the value `SETALL` or `SETVAL` and the value of the counter of one of the semaphores to be modified is less than zero or greater than `SEMVI`

If successful, the system call returns a positive value or zero depending on the parameter **cmd**:

GETPID	Value of **sempid**
GETVAL	Value of **semval**
GETNCNT	Value of **semncnt**
GETZCNT	Value of **semznt**

11.2.3 Shared memory

An important innovation brought by IPCs is management of shared memory. In a normal program, an allocated memory zone is owned by the process which executes it. No other process may access it. The principle of shared memory is to enable processes to share a part of their address space.

Although shared memory provides a very powerful system for sharing memory zones, it necessitates an access synchronisation mechanism to be put in place. Indeed, it is conceivable that two processes might try to write to the same point in memory at the same time: it is highly likely that the correct ordering of data would be violated. A solution to these problems is to use semaphores.

Shared memory can only be handled by means of two particular structures.

11.2.3.1 Basic structures
The structures **shmid_ds** and **shm_inf** are defined in the header file **<linux/shm.h>**. However, it is sufficient to include the file **<sys/shm.h>** to be able to access it. The **shmid_ds** structure is represented by an entry in the shared memory table. The details are given in the table below:

type	*field*	*description*
struct ipc_perm	**shm_perm**	Access permissions
int	**shm_segsz**	Segment size (bytes)
time_t	**shm_atime**	Date of the last attachment
time_t	**shm_dtime**	Date of the last detachment
time_t	**shm_ctime**	Date of the last modification
unsigned_short	**shm_cpid**	Number of the creating process
unsigned_short	**shm_lpid**	Number of the process which carried out the last operation
short	**shm_nattch**	Number of attachments
unsigned_short	**shm_npages**	Segments size (number of memory pages)
unsigned_long *	**shm_pages**	Tables of pointers to memory windows
struct vm_area struct *	**attaches**	Attachment descriptors

The last three fields are private: they are used by the kernal to organise shared memory.

The same header file defines the **shminfo** (not to be confused with the structure **shm_info** used solely by the kernel). It is used when calling *shmctl* using **IPC_INFO** as an argument. This structure is used for example by the program *ipcs*. Otherwise it is rarely used (except for the system data gathering or monitoring programs). The details are listed below:

type	*field*	*description*
int	shmax	Maximum segment size (bytes)
int	shmin	Minimum segment size (bytes)
int	shmni	Maximum number of segments
int	shmseg	Maximum number of segments per process
int	shmall	Maximum number of segments in numbers of memory pages

11.2.3.2 Creation and look-up in shared memory zones

The system call *shmget* creates a new memory zone or indeed obtains access to an existing one. The general form of this call is as follows:

```
#include <sys/ipc.h>
#include <sys/shm.h>

int shmget (key_t key, int size, int option);
```

The parameter **size** represents the size of the shared memory segment required. The third parameter corresponds to the standard parameter for creating an **IPC**.

It should be pointed out that is this system call is used to obtain a reference to an already existing shared memory, the size specified should be equal or less than that of the existing memory.

If this is not the case, the allocated size should be a multiple of PAGE_SIZE, which corresponds to the size of a memory page (4kbytes in the x86 architecture).

If successful, this system call returns the identifier of the shared memory. If there is an error, the variable **errno** may be set to the following values:

error	*meaning*
ENOMEM	Insufficient memory
EINVAL	Parameters not valid (**SHMMIN** > size or size > **SHMMAX**)
ENOENT	No shared memory segment exists for the given key
EEXIST	The value **IPC_CREAT** - **IPC_EXCL** has been given whereas the shared memory segment already exists
EIDRM	The memory segment has been marked as erased
EACCES, EPERM	Not enough access permissions
EFAULT	Incorrect parameters
ENOSPC	All shared memory identifiers have been used, or the allocation of a shared memory of the given size has exceeded **SHMALL**

11.2.3.3 Attachment of a memory zone

The system call *shmat* enables a shared memory to be attached to a process. This operation in fact consists of attaching a virtual memory zone to the address space of the calling process.

The general form of this system call is as follows:

```
#include <sys/types.h>
#include <sys/ipc.h>
#include <sys/shm.h>

void *shmat (int shmid, const void *shmaddr, int option);
```

The second parameter, **shmaddr**, enables the address of the shared memory to be specified:

- if **shmaddr** is zero, the operating system tries to find a memory zone which is free (this being the most reliable method);
- if not, the operating system tries to attach the shared memory to the specified address. In the case when the option **SHM_RND** is specified, the system tries to attach the memory zone to a **SHMLBA** multiple address which is the nearest to that specified.

It should be pointed out that this system call allows the use of a special option: **SHM_RDONLY**. This option specifies that the process may only access the shared memory segment in read mode. Without the option, the segment is attached in read and write mode. There is no way of carrying out an attachment in write mode only.

When this system call is made, the following parameters of the structure **shmid_ds** are updated:

- **shm_atime** takes the current date;
- **shm_lpid** takes the pid of the current process;
- **shm_nattach** is incremented by one.

shmat returns the address of the memory segment that may be reconfigured. In the case where *shmat* returns a value null, **errno** is set to the following values:

error	*meaning*
EACCES	Not enough access permissions
EINVAL	Invalid key or address
ENOMEM	Insufficient memory
EIDRM	Segment marked as erased

11.2.3.4 Detachment of a memory zone
The system call *shmdt* enables a process to detach a shared memory zone from its address space.

The general form of this call is as follows:

```
#include <sys/types.h>
#include <sys/ipc.h>
#include <sys/shm.h>

int shmdt (const void *shmaddr);
```

When the call is made, the following fields of the **shmid_ds** structure are updated:

- **shm_dtime** takes the current date;
- **shm_lpid** takes the pid (process identifier) of the current process;
- **shm_nattach** is decremented by one.

11.2.3.5 Control of shared memory zones
The system call *shmctl* governs the management of a shared memory. The general form of this call is as follows:

```
#include <sys/ipc.h>
#include <sys/shm.h>

int shmctl (int shmid, int cmd, struct shmid_ds *buf);
```

The following list gives the different commands possible. They correspond to different usage:

- **IPC_STAT**: enables information about the shared memory segments to be obtained. This information is copied to the memory zone pointed to by **buf**. It should be noted that, to be successful, the process must have read access to the memory segment.
- **IPC_SET**: enables changes to be applied that the user has carried out at the level of fields **uid, gid,** or the field mode **shm_perms**. Only the lowest order 9 bits are used. The field **shm_ctime** is also changed. Only the owner, the creator, and the super-user are allowed to carry out this operation.
- **IPC_RMID**: enables a shared memory segment to be marked as erased. This segment will not be effectively erased until the last attachment has been deleted.

Two specific Linux options should be added to these commands, and these options may only be taken up by the super-user. They either allow or forbid the *swap* of a shared memory segment:

- **SHM_LOCK**: forbids the *swap* of a shared memory segment:
- **SHM_UNLOCK**: allows the *swap* of a shared memory segment:

11.2.3.6 Interaction with other system calls
A process's shared memory zones are taken into consideration when other system calls are made:

- *fork*: the child process inherits the shared memory zones attached to its parent;
- *exec, exit*: all the segments are detached (but not erased).

11.2.3.7 An example of use
This section gives an example illustrating the use of shared memory segments, as well as semaphores. A segment of memory shared between several processes is a critical resource, and it is therefore necessary to protect access to it. Semaphores are a way of managing this access.

Consider a shared memory zone, which may accessed in read or write mode. The constraints placed to ensure that the information read or written is coherent are as follows:

- several processes may read from the segment simultaneously;
- when a process writes, it must be the only one accessing the segment.

One solution to this problem consists in using two semaphores, one for read access, and the other for write access. The write access semaphore is a binary semaphore because writing is exclusive. The read access semaphore is an *N*-ary semaphore, where *N* represents the number of simultaneous authorized accesses.

The use of the two semaphores is not separate because read access is linked to write access. This is overcome by using a semaphore group containing the two semaphores referred to.

The file *Commun.h* contains the definition of the group, as well as the necessary constants for the creation of access keys to the different IPCs.

─────── Commun.h ───────────────────────────────

```
 #ifndef COMMON_H
#define COMMON_H


#define NAME Common_H

#define PROJ_FTOK_SEM 'a'  /* parameter ftok           */
#define PROJ_FTOK_MEM 'O'  /* parameter ftok           */


define AREA_SIZE 20 /* Area shared size */

define N 5 /* Number of simultaneous readers */

/* Set initialisation values ;
* 1 writer
* N simultaneous readers
*/

ushort init_sem[]={1,N};

/* request for access to the zone in write mode */

struct sembuf request_write = {0, -1, SEM_UNDO}, {1,-N, SEM_UNDO}};
struct sembuf stop_write = {1, +1, SEM_UNDO},{1,+N, SEM_UNDO}};;


/* request for access to the zone in read mode */

struct sembuf request_read = {1, -1, SEM_UNDO};
```

```
struct sembuf stop_read = {1, +1, SEM_UNDO};

#endif
```

———————————————————————————————— Commun.h ————

Two other files make up the example:

- *Writer.c* which creates a shared zone and executes the writer:
- *Reader.c*: which attaches the shared zone and creates the number of readers passed as a parameter.

————————— Ecrivain.c ——————————————————————————

```
#include <stdio.h>
#include <stdlib.h>
#include <unistd.h>
#include <errno.h>
#include <sys/ipc.h>
#include <sys/sem.h>
#include <sys/shm.h>


#include "Common.h"

int             shmid,
                semid;

static void usage ()
{
    printf ("Example of an application using semaphores and shared
memories \n");
    printf (" → Readers/Writer \n");
    printf ("Writer \n\n");
    exit (-1);
}

static void error (char *msg)
{
    fprintf (stderr, "Error Writer %s :%d \n", msg, errno);
    exit (-1);
}

void writing (char *source, char *destination, int nb_bytes)
```

```
{
    int i;

    semop (semid, write_request, 2);

    printf (
                "Start of writing in the shared zone of %d bytes"
                "by the process %d\n"
                ,nb_bytes, getpid ());

    for (i = 0; i < nb_bytes; i++)
            destination[i] - source[i];

    sleep (1);
    printf (       "End of writing in the shared zone by the %d\n",
            getpid ());
    semop (semid, stop_writing, 2);
}

void init_writer ()
{

int  key_mem,
     key_sem;
/* Key generation for accessing shared memory */
if ((key_mem = ftok (NAME, PROJ_FTOK_MEM)) == -1)
            error ("Error during ftok shared memory ");

/* Key generation for semaphore */
if ((key_sem = ftok (NAME, PROJ_FTOK_SEM)) == -1)
            error ("Error at semaphore ftok");

if ((shmid = shmget (key_mem, SIZE, IPC_CREAT | IPC_EXCL | 0644)) ==
    -1)
            error ("Error at shmget");

if ((semid = semget (key_sem, 2, AREA_SIZE, IPC_CREAT | IPC_EXCL |
0666))
    == -1)
            error ("Error semget");

if (semctl (semid, 2, SETALL, init_sem) == -1)
            error ("Error semctl");
```

```
        }

void  writer ()
{

     char    buf[20];
     char    *addr;
     int     i,
             j;

     if ((addr = shmat (shmid, NULL, 0)) == (char *) -1)
             error ("Error at shmat");

     for (j = 0; j < 4; j++) {
             for (i = 0; i < 20; i++)
                     buf[1]++;
             writing (buf, addr, 20);
     }
}

void  main (int argc, char *argv[])
{

     int     i,
             nb_process;

     if ((argc !=1)) {
             usage ();
             exit (1);
     }
     init_writer ();
     writer ();
     sleep (5);
     if (semctl (semid, 0, IPC_RMID, 0) == -1
             error ("Error at semctl");
     if (shmctl (shmid, 0 IPC_RMID, NULL) == -1
             error ("Error shmctl");

     exit (0);

}
```

———— Lecteur.c ————————————————————

```
#include <stdio.h>
#include <stdlib.h>
#include <unistd.h>
#include <errno.h>
#include <sys/ipc.h>
#include <sys/sem.h>
#include <sys/shm.h>

#include "Common.h"

int  shmid,
     semid;

static void usage (void)
{
    printf ("Example of an application using semaphores and shared
memories \n");
    printf (" → Readers/Writer \n");
    printf ("Reader <nb_readers> \n\n");
    exit (-1);
}

static void  error (char *msg)
{
    fprintf (stderr, "Error Reader %s :%d \n", msg, errno);
    exit (-1);
}

void reading (char *source, char *destination, int nb_bytes)
{
    int i;

    semop (semid, &read_request, 1);

    printf (
                "Start of reading in the shared zone of %d bytes"
                "by the process %d\n"
                ,nb_bytes, getpid ());

    for (i = 0; i < nb_bytes; i++)
            destination[i] - source[i];
```

```
        sleep (2);
        printf ("End of reading in the shared zone by the %d\n", getpid
());
        semop (semid, stop_read, 1);
        sleep (1);
}


void init_readers (void)
{
        key_t key_mem,
              key_sem;

        /* Key generation for shared memory */
        if ((key_mem = ftok (NAME, PROJ_FTOK_MEM)) == -1)
                error ("Error at shared memory ftok");

        /* Semaphore key generation */
        if ((key_sem = ftok (NAME, PROJ_FTOK_SEM)) == -1)
                error ("Error at semaphore ftok");

        if ((shmid = shmget (key_mem, AREA_SIZE, 0)) == -1)
                error ("Error at shmget");

        if ((semid = semget (key_sem, 2, 0)) == -1)
                error ("Error at semget");
}


void reader (void)
{

        char    buf[20];
        char    *addr;
        int     i,

        if ((addr = shmat (shmid, NULL, SHM_RDONLY)) == (char *) -1)
                error ("Error at shmat");

        sleep (1);
        for (i = 0; i < 4; i++)
                for (i = 0; i < 20; i++)
                        reading (addr, buf, 20);
        exit (0);
}
```

```
void main (int argc, char *argv[])
{

    int i,
        nb_process;

    if ((argc < 2)) || (argc > 2)) {
            usage ();
            exit (1);
    }
    init_readers ();
    nb_process = atoi (argv[1]);

    for (i = 1;  i <= nb_process; i++) {
            switch (fork ()) {
                    case 0;
                            reader ();
                            break;
                    case -1;
                            error ("Error at fork");
                    default;
                            break;
            }
    }
    exit (0);

}
```

———————————————————————————— Lecteur.c ————————

In these two programs, the use of the system call *sleep* serves solely to desynchronise the processes. There is no constraint on the order of executing reads and writes.

The execution of the example for one writer and three readers gives a check that the program is functioning correctly. The read operations of the shared zone may be interlaced, whilst the write operations are always exclusive.

```
scylla (2)>./Writer & ; ./Reader 3
[1] 1172
Start of writing in the 20 byte shared memory by the process 1172
scylla (2)> end of writing in the shared memory by the process 1172
Start of writing in the 20 byte shared memory by the process 1172
End of writing in the shared memory by the process 1172
Start of writing in the 20 byte shared memory by the process 1176
Start of writing in the 20 byte shared memory by the process 1175
Start of writing in the 20 byte shared memory by the process 1174
End of writing in the shared memory by the process 1174
End of writing in the shared memory by the process 1175
End of writing in the shared memory by the process 1176
Start of writing in the 20 byte shared memory by the process 1172
End of writing in the shared memory by the process 1172
Start of writing in the 20 byte shared memory by the process 1174
Start of writing in the 20 byte shared memory by the process 1176
Start of writing in the 20 byte shared memory by the process 1175
End of writing in the shared memory by the process 1174
End of writing in the shared memory by the process 1176
End of writing in the shared memory by the process 1175
Start of writing in the 20 byte shared memory by the process 1172
End of writing in the shared memory by the process 1172
Start of writing in the 20 byte shared memory by the process 1175
Start of writing in the 20 byte shared memory by the process 1174
Start of writing in the 20 byte shared memory by the process 1176
End of writing in the shared memory by the process 1176
End of writing in the shared memory by the process 1174
End of writing in the shared memory by the process 1175
Start of writing in the 20 byte shared memory by the process 1175
Start of writing in the 20 byte shared memory by the process 1174
Start of writing in the 20 byte shared memory by the process 1176
End of writing in the shared memory by the process 1176
End of writing in the shared memory by the process 1174
End of writing in the shared memory by the process 1175
```

11.3.1 Kernel compilation option

Although IPCs have been in use for some time, they have to be specified for inclusion when the kernel is compiled, though IPCs are normally included in standard issue kernels. It would be perverse not to add them to the kernel because certain applications need these communication tools in order to function (*perl* for example).

When configuring the kernel (**make config**), the reply *y* should be made to the following question:

```
System V IPC (CONFIG_SYSVIPC) [y/n]
```

After recompiling the kernel and rebooting the system, the IPCs are included in the kernel.

11.3.2 The programs *ipcs* and *ipcrm*

11.3.2.1 ipcs
This command enables three IPC tables managed by the kernel to be displayed.

```
Gandalf(gandalf)→ ipcs

------ Shared Memory Segments ---------
shmid  owner   perms  bytes   nattch status
------ Semaphore Arrays ---------
semid owner   perms   nsems   status
------ Message Queues ----------
msqid  owner   perms   used-bytes      messages
256    dumas   666     13078           54
257    dumas   600     1378            25
```

In the above example, two message queues have been created on the system.

The command *ipcs* provides standard IPC handling functions:

- -s: semaphore display
- -m: shared memory display
- -q: message queue display
- -a: the above three facilities (default option)

As well as these four options, this command manages five others which enable a different display to be realised:

- **-t** ⇒ *time*: allows certain information to be obtained, such as the date of the last change, etc :

```
gandalf> ipcs -q -t
------ Message queues Send/Recv/Change/ Times -------
msqid          owner   send                recv               change
0      dumas   Jan 3 10:49:30 Not set           Jan 3 10:54:35
```

- **-p** ⇒ *pid*: indicates which IPCs are attached to the process:

- **-c** ⇒ *creator*: gives information on the creator of the IPC:

```
gandalf> ipcs -q -c
------ Message queues: Creators/Owners -------
msqid          perms   cuid    cgid     uid      gid
128   666      dumas   etu      dumas   etu
```

- **-l** ⇒ *limits*: displays resource limits regarding the management of the IPC:

```
gandalf> ipcs -1

------ Shared Memory Limits -------
max number of segments = 128
max seg size (kbytes) = 16384
max total shared memory (kbytes) = 16777216
min seg size (bytes) = 1

------ Semaphore Limits -------
max number of arrays = 128
max number semaphores per array = 32
max number semaphores system wide = 4096
max ops per semop call = 32
semaphore max value = 32767

------ Message: Limits -------
max number queues system wide = 128
max size of message (bytes) = 4096
default max size of queue (bytes) = 16384
```

- **-u** ⇒ *creator*: gives information on the creator of the IPC:

```
Gandalf (beetlejuice) → ipcs -u

------ Shared memory Status -------
segments allocated 4
pages allocated 2
pages resident 1
pages swapped 1
Swap performance: 5 attempts  5 successes


------ Semaphore status -------
used arrays = 3
allocated semaphores = 5


------ Message: Status -------
allocated queues = 1
used headers = 62
used space = 16386 bytes
```

11.3.2.2 ipcrm

The command *ipcrm* allows an IPC to be erased, though it is necessary to be the creator of the IPC or a super-user to be able to carry out this operation.

Its syntax is simple:

```
        ipcrm [ shm   msg   sem ] id
```

For example, in order to delete the message queue having the identifier 657 (see section 11.3.2), it just needs the following keyboard input:

```
gandalf> ipcrm msg 657
resource deleted
```

The message queue is automatically deleted if the caller has sufficient permissions.

11.4

The System V IPC source files can be found in the directory *ipc* in the kernel tree structure. They are made of four modules

- *msg.c*: message queue management,
- *sem.c*: semaphore management,
- *shm.c*: shared memory management,
- *util.c*: initialisation and access permission management functions.

11.4.1 Common functions

One part of the source codes is shared between different IPC modules. The common section of this is collected together in the file *util.c*. This module fulfils several roles:

1. initialises three IPC types (for a function called only once when the kernel is launched);
2. checks access permissions;
3. in the event that the IPCs have not been built in when the kernel was compiled *(which is not advised since several programs have need of them)*, this module allows only function declarations to be carried out.

Initialisation (function **ipc_init**) consists of launching a specific initialisation function for each of the IPCs. It is called when initialising the kernel using the function main located in the file *init/main.c*.

The access permissions management function **ipc_perms** is responsible (amongst other things) to check that sufficient permissions exist to access the desired IPC.

11.4.2 Algorithms

The IPCs are implemented in the form of three tables (one per IPC type) of sizes MSGMNI, SEMNI and SHMMNI. These three tables, each of constant size, are tables of pointers to IPC manipulation **functions (msqid_ds, semid_ds, and shmid_ds)**.

The initialisation of the IPC structures, when the machine is booted up, consists of calling the function **ipc_init**. The code of this function is of little interest since it only contains a call to each of the three initialisation functions **shm_init, msg_init** and **sem_init**, located in their respective files.

This initialisation assigns the value **IPC_UNUSED** to each cell of the table. This therefore marks all the IPC resources as free. Each element of the table can have three types of value:

- **IPC_UNUSED**: resource free;
- **IPC_NOID**: the resource is either in the process of being allocated, or it should be deleted;
- the address of the structure containing data relating to the managed resource.

Figure 11.2 represents the shared memory table, and this is exactly the same for the other two IPC types, to the nearest type.

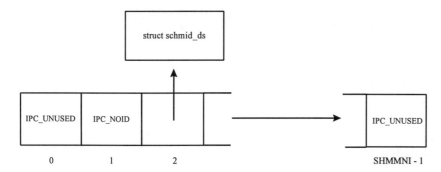

FIGURE 11.2:   Shared memory table.

11.4.3 Key management

The different system calls linked to IPCs use a key to identify resources. The problem is to associate this key with its index in the corresponding table. This operation is carried out by means of the **findkey** functions, which are located in each of the three modules.

  This function scans each of entries in the relevant table, and three separate cases may then be identified:

- **IPC_UNUSED**: move on to the next value,
- **IPCCNOID**: this value is set when a structure is in the process of being modified. In this case, the process is put on hold until the operation is finished,
- It relates to a data structure: in this case, the key to this structure is located in the field **sem_perm.key** (whatever the type of IPC used). It is then sufficient simply to make a comparison.

In the event that the value of the key does not correspond to any of the existing keys, this function returns –1.

11.5.1   Message queue

The file *msg.c* contains the collection of functions implementing message queues. As well as performing message queue management, the implementation of system calls is also included: **sys_msgsnd, sys_msgrcv, sys_msgget** and **sys_msgctl**.

Message queues are also necessary for the process *kerneld* which enables on-demand loading of modules in the kernel. A number of processes are intended for this process: **kerneld_exit, kd_timeout** and **kerneld_send**. Their use is not described in detail here.

The file also contains the initialisation function (called at system boot-up) and the close down function (called at the end of execution of each process), which are linked to message queues.

11.5.1.1   Internal representation of message queues

Message queues are stored in the table **msgque**. This table contains pointers to the structure **msqid_ds**. However, this table has a limited size, and is fixed at the value of the constant **MSGMNI**.

The message queue of index n is, in fact, made up of elements such as access permissions. But the two primary elements are two particular pointers to the queue:

- a pointer to the first element in the queue;
- a pointer to the last element in the queue.

All message queue management may be reduced to a simple management of linked lists.

A schematic internal representation of message queues is shown in figure 11.3.

11.5.1.2   Initialisation

The initialisation function **msg_init** is called by the function **ipc_init** at system boot-up when the IPCs are initialised. It puts the value **IPC_UNUSED** into each element of the table **semary** and sets a number of internal variables to 0, such as for example the amount of memory occupied by data stored in message queues.

11.5.1.3   Creation of a message queue

The function **sys_msgget** enables a new message queue to be created. For this, it performs a call to the function **newque** which either creates a new message queue if none already exists, or modifies the status of the wait queue existing already. The creation operation ends with the attribution of different access permissions.

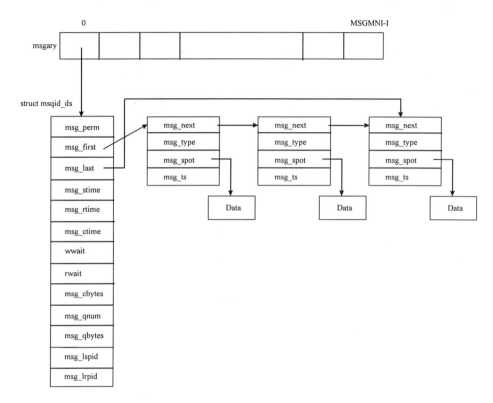

FIGURE 11.3:   Internal representation of message queues.

11.5.1.4 *Sending a message*

The call *msgsnd* in fact corresponds to the function call **real_msgsnd,** which carries out a simple insertion of elements into the data list. This operation can of course only take place if the memory space and authorisation conditions are met.

At the end of the call, the fields **msg_cbytes,** which represent the memory space occupied by the queue data, and **msg_qnum,** representing the number of messages in the queue, are updated.

11.5.1.5 *Reception of a message*

Received messages, resulting from the call *msgrv,* are processed by the function **sys_msgrcv.** In practice, this function calls another function, **real_msgrcv,** which effectively manages the reception of a message in the queue. After usage checks (access permissions, verification that the required queue exists), the queue is scanned in search of the type requested. Once located, the element concerned is extracted from the queue and returned.

11.5.1.6 *Control of a message queue*

Control of message queues is carried out by means of the system call *msgctl*. Implementation of this call is quite simple: the large majority of commands that may be passed to this call are mainly at the information level.

The more specialised command **IPC_SET** enables certain parameters situated in the structure **msqid_ds** to be set. This operation is performed using a simple memory copy by means of the function **memcpy_fromfs**. The command also updates access permissions and time of access to the message queue. The only really interesting command is that carrying out message queue deletion, which is realised by using **IPC_RMID**. Here, the function **freeque** releases resources, and this occurs in three stages: firstly a search is made for the message queue and its existence verified, then each of the memory zones managed by the queue is erased, and finally the queue itself is deleted. This operation is similar to a deletion operation on a linked list.

11.5.2 Semaphores

The source file *sem.c* contains the group of functions which implement semaphores, including **sys_semget, sys_semctl** and **sys_semop**. The file also contains the initialisation function (called at system boot-up), and the close-down function (called at the end of execution of each ask).

11.5.2.1 *Internal representation of semaphores*

The semaphores are stored by the system in the table **semary**. This table contains pointers to the structure **semid_ds**. Its size therefore indicates the maximum number of semaphore groups that may be created: **SEMNI**. Each **semid_ds** structure contains three lists:

- the list of semaphores in the group (**base**), stored in memory in the form of a table just after the semaphores descriptor;
- the list of operations which are waiting (**sem_pending**) managed in the form of a doubly-linked list;
- the list of requests that can be undone (**undo**).

11.5.2.2 *Initialisation*

The initialisation function **sem_init** is called by the function **ipc_init** at system boot-up when the IPCs are initialised. It puts the value **IPC_UNUSED** in each element of the table **semary** and initialises the semaphore counters to 0.

11.5.2.3 *Creation of semaphores*

The function **sys_semgget** manages the creation of new semaphores, by performing a call to the function **newary** which looks for a free cell in the table **semary** and dynamically allocates memory to the new semaphore. This function also initialises information relating to the time and to the ownership of the semaphore.

A schematic internal representation of semaphores is shown in figure 11.3.

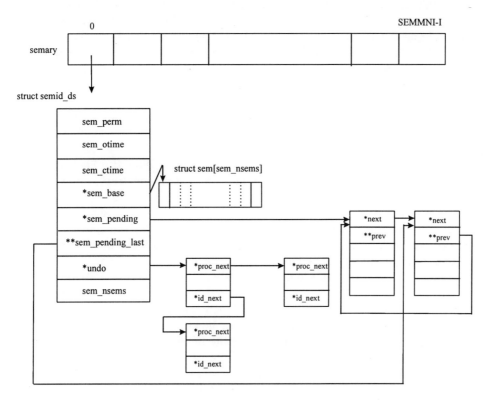

FIGURE 11.4: Internal representation of semaphores.

11.5.2.4 *Control of semaphores*

The function **sys_semctl** carries out semaphore control. For the most cases (operations **GET***, **IPC_STAT** or **IPC_SET**), this is very simple because it is merely a matter of modifying relating information. These operations consist of transferring data to/from the user space to/from the kernel space. The operation **IPC_RMID** deletes the semaphore and all associated resources. However, two of the operations, **SETVAL** and **SETALL** are somewhat complex, since they change the value of the semaphore counter, and it may therefore be necessary to wake up processes waiting for access to the semaphore, in the event that the counter is incremented or if it becomes zero. This is the role of the function **update_queue,**. a function which is described in detail in the next section.

11.5.2.5 *Changing semaphore values*

Modifications to semaphore values are carried out by the system call *semop*. This is the most complex call to perform and there are several difficulties to overcome.

An operation may block a process, and a wait queue is therefore needed to store processes waiting for access to the semaphore. This queue is implemented in the form of a doubly linked list. It is accessed by the fields **sem-pending** and **sem_pending_last** of the structure **semid_ds**. The list is also accessible for each process via the process table (field **semsleeping** of the structure **process_struct**). The functions **insert_into_queue** and **remove_from_queue** enable this list to be reconfigured, by inserting and removing elements respectively.

The operations to be carried out should form a coherent set. A check that they have been performed is made by the function **try_semop**, a function which returns 0 if the operations are possible, 1 if the process should be put into standby mode, or the error message **EAGAIN** if the request has been made using the flag **IPC_NOWAIT**.

The system must manage the cancellation of requests if the flag **EM_UNDO** is set, and for this, after the system call **try_semop**, the system constructs a linked list of operations which may be cancelled by the process. This list is accessible by the fields **semundo** of the structure of the semaphore, and for each process it is accessible via the process table (field **semundo** from the semaphore structure **process_struct**). The cancellation of operations takes effect when processes finish so as to free resources that are no longer used.

Next, the system carries out the operations requested (calling the function **do_semop** if the function **try_semop** succeeded), or indeed it puts the process on hold in the linked list and puts it to sleep (function **sleep_interruptible**).

After calling the function **do_semop**, it may be necessary to wake up the process which was put to sleep. This is realised by the function **update_queue**, which scans the wait queue associated with the semaphore passed as a parameter and tries to carry out the operations requested by a process in the sleeping state; if this is possible the sleeping process is reloaded into the queue of processes waiting to be executed (function **wake_up_interruptible**). The function repeats the process as long as it can wake up at least one process in the list.

11.5.2.6 *Termination of semaphores*

When a process terminates, the system calls the function **sem_exit** so as to cancel the operations that the process would have carried out on the semaphores (with the flag **SEM_UNDO**). The function checks to see that the process is not sleeping and is not waiting for access to a semaphore, by means of the field **semsleeping** of the structure **process_struct,** and it removes it from the queue if this is the case. Because the cancellation of operations liberates resources, the function calls **update_queue** in order to wake up processes waiting for these resources.

11.5.3 Shared memory

The source file *shm.c* contains the group of functions which implement shared memories. The management of shared memories is performed by means of a number of system calls: **sys_smget, sys_shmctl, sys_shmat** and **sys_shmdt**.

As well as functions initialising the structure of shared memory pages, functions allocating and releasing a shared memory segment: **newseg** and **killseg** are also defined.

Other more specific shared memory functions are also found in this module: for example functions enabling a zone of shared memory to be swapped: **shm_swap_in** and **shm_swap**.

The management of shared memory utilises a circular list of the different attachments available. The management of this list is performed by means of two operations: **insert_attach**, enabling an element to be inserted, and **remove_attach**, enabling one to be removed.

11.5.3.1 Internal representation of shared memory

Shared memories are implemented in the form of a table of pointers (**shm_segs**) to structures of the type **shmid_ds**. This table contains a maximum of **SHMMNI** elements.

The fundamental elements of the structure are:

- the segment size in bytes, and number of pages;
- a table of pointers to different *windows*;
- a circular list of shared memory attachments.

An internal representation is shown in schematic in figure 11.5.

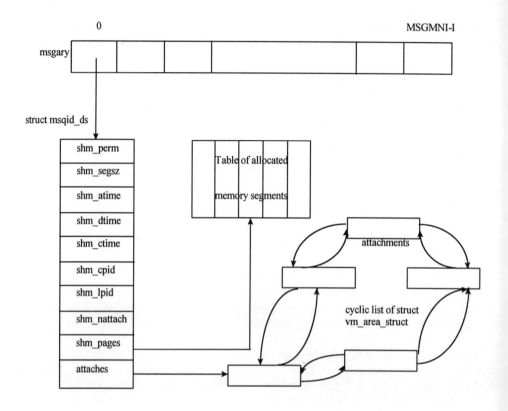

FIGURE 11.5:   Internal representation of shared memories.

11.5.3.2 Intialisation
The initialisation function **shm_init** is called at system boot time when the **IPCs** are initialised. It puts the value **IPC_UNUSED** in each element of the table **shmary** and sets a number of internal variables to 0, such as for example the number of segments used.

11.5.3.3 Creation of a shared memory zone
The creation of a new shared memory zone is implemented in the code of the call *shmget*. If the shared memory associated with the key does not exist, a call to the function **newseg** creates a new shared memory. This function allocates a new structure **shmid_ds,** as well as pointers to the memory segments. The call returns the reference to this shared memory.

If the event of a successful call to the function findkey, consisting of a search to see if a shared memory has already been allocated with the key passed as a parameter, the identity of the shared memory is then returned.

11.5.3.4 Attachment of a memory zone
The call *shmat* attaches a segment of shared memory to a process, using, the virtual memory system for this. The variable shmd of type vm_area_struct is created. This structure enables the type of memory employed to be identified (see the chapter on memory management, chapter 8). By means of a call to the function shm_map, the memory zone is mapped into the process space.

The variable is inserted into the list of attachments to the shared memory, using a call to the function insert_attach. This list makes known the set of processes allowed to access the given shared memory zone.

11.5.3.5 Removal of a memory zone
The removal of a shared memory zone is realised using the call *shmdt*. The corresponding kernel function sys_shmdt calls the function do_munmap defined in the source file *mm/mmap.c* (see chapter 8, section 8.6.6).

This operation, though invoking memory management, is actually carried out in the shared memory module by means of the virtual memory system, in fact, the variable shm_vm_ops of type vm_operations_struct declares the function freeing the shared memory that is allocated: shm_close.

This function removes from the attachment list the memory segment allocated by calling remove_attach, then deletes the segment by calling killseg if it is no longer used and if the option SHM_DEST is activated (this corresponds to a call of this function following a request to delete the segment).

The function remove_attach removes the memory zone from the circular list.

The function killseg deletes each of the pages by calling the freeing function free_page.

11.5.3.6 Control of shared memory zones
For the majority of options, the control of a shared memory zone (*shmctl*) consists of copying information. The option IPC_RMID, however, results in the deletion of shared memory by calling the function killseg.

However, two functions are peculiar to Linux in that they address the possibility of changing the shared memory management mode at the *swap* level. If the option SHM_UNLOCK is enabled, then the shared memory is unlocked, that is, it is again *swapable*. If, on the other hand, the option SHM_LOCK is enabled, then this is not the case. These two operations are performed by changing the option in the field mode of the shared memory permissions, by means of the constant SHM_LOCKED.

11.5.3.7 Inheritance in shared memory zones
When calling *fork*, shared memory zones must be inherited by the child processes. This operation is carried out when the memory zones of the parent process are

scanned at the time that the child is created. The function **do_fork** calls the function **copy_mm** which in turn calls the function **dup_mmap**. By means of the field **mm->mmap->vm_ops,** the function **do_fork** finds the function to call in order to recognise the new process and its shared memory zones. The function **shm_open** is called, and it adds an attachment to this already allocated zone.

12

Loadable modules

System calls described

get_kernel_syms, create_module, delete_module, init_module

12.1.1 Overview

At a macro level, the Linux kernel is made up of components which are not all needed by users all the time. This is why, when it builds the kernel, Linux asks users to say which elements they wish to include. Obviously, the aim of this is to insert only those managers which are necessary according to the machine configuration and its usage. In this way, the kernel size can be kept as small as possible for a given machine, and indeed the smaller the kernel, the more memory is available to users. In addition, booting up a specially adapted machine, having only the managers loaded for the peripherals the machine possesses, is much more rapid than it would otherwise have been.

However, any modification of the kernel, such as adding or deleting peripheral managers or file systems necessitates a recompilation of the kernel. At least, this was true of the early versions of Linux, until the implementation of loadable modules.

The principle of loadable modules is to generate in the first instance a minimal kernel, and then to load managers in a dynamic manner according to need. This enables the system to have an 'extended' kernel, as indicated schematically in figure 12.1. This system of loadable modules also exists in other Unix operating systems, such as Solaris, though in a different form.

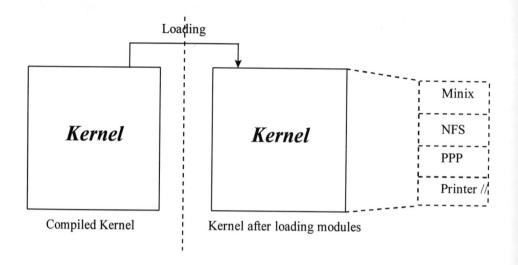

Figure 12.1:   Loading modules.

Figure 12.1 shows the capability given to the kernel in being able to load modules. During a session, the user or users of the machine may not need the *NFS, Minix, PPP* or the *parallel printer* resources at a particular time. However, at a later point, the user may need to use one or more of them. All that is then required is to load the modules, which will then become 'dynamically integrated' into the kernel. When they are no longer used, the modules may then be unloaded.

12.1.2 Compilation

The generation of modules is realised in a particular way. Linux enables most of the components of which it is constituted to either be integrated into the kernel, or to specifically non-integrated, or indeed to be generated in the form of a module.

It should be noted that the kernel must be configured in such a way that it can manage modules, and for this, it is necessary to activate the following option.

```
*
* Loadable module support
*
Enable loadable module support (CONFIG_MODULES) [Y/n/?]
```

If the option is not activated, it will not be possible to use loadable modules on a configured machine.

In the compilation of modules themselves, if, for example, it is desired to put the MS-DOS file system into a module form when the machine is configured, it is just necessary to specify this with the letter M for Module when making the selection:

```
DOS FAT fs support (CONFIG_FAT_FS) [M/n/y/?] M
MSDOS fs support (CONFIG_MSDOS_FS) {M/n/?] M
VFAT (Windows-95) fs support (CONFIG_VAT_FS) {M/n/?] M
```

Once the compilation of the kernel has been launched, it is necessary to compile the modules. The entire generation of the kernel must therefore be carried out following these steps:

```
gandalf# make config
gandalf# make dep
gandalf# make clean
gandalf# make zImage
gandalf# make modules
gandalf# make modules_install
```

Once these operations have been carried out, the modules are identified as file objects, located in the library **/lib/modules**.

12.1.3 Command line operation: manual loading

Linux provides a primary method of using modules: this concerns the first version of these modules. The aim is to allow the super-user to load and unload modules manually as he wishes. This technique is rather cumbersome since the operation must be carried out manually. Furthermore, the normal user does not have sufficient permissions to perform this operation.

Linux provides three main commands enabling modules to be handled: *nsmod, lsmod* and *rmmod*.

The command *insmod* allows the module to be loaded, *lsmod* displays the contents of the file */proc/modules*, and *rmmod* unloads the required module.

The command *lsmod* not only indicates the names of each of the modules loaded in memory, but also the number of memory pages occupied by the module, as well as the number of processes using it. Given that a memory page takes up 4kbytes, it is easy to calculate the memory saved when these modules are not loaded.

These commands are simple to work with, as illustrated by the following example:

```
gandalf# insmod fat
gandalf# nsmod
Module:        #pages: Used by:
fat             6        0
gandalf# rmod fat
gandalf# lsmod
Module: #pages: Used by:
```

However, (apart from **lsmod**) these operations have the disadvantage of being reserved for super-users and of being tedious to carry out.

12.1.4 On-demand loading

The on-request loading system is a recent development in the Linux system. It enables loading of different modules to be automatically carried out according to demand. Its installation requires the activation of the option **CONFIG_KERNELD** and of System V IPCs when compilation is performed. Indeed, the daemon *kerneld* uses message queues to communicate with the kernel: loading and unloading of a module is carried out by *kerneld*, but orders are sent by the kernel via a special message queue (see the section on implementation for more details).

The installation of this technique on the machine implies running the programme *kerneld* when the system is booted up. It is also necessary to perform certain operations to build the list of loadable modules installed. More details may be found in [Dumas 1996], and in the documentation supplied with the module kit: examples of ready-to-use modules are provided.

Dynamically loadable modules need two programmes when they are installed on a machine:

- *depmod*, which enables a dependancy file to be generated based on the symbols located in the module group. These dependances will be used later by the second command;
- *modprobe*, which enables a module, or group of modules to be loaded, but also to load basic modules needed for a smooth boot-up of the machine (for example, NFS, etc.).

In the following example, the kernel is only supported by the MS-DOS file system in the form of a module. However, an MS-DOS format partition will be set up in the example in a completely transparent manner.

```
gandalf# lsmod
Module: #pages: Used by:

gandalf# mount -t msdos /dev/fd0 /mnt

gandalf# lsmod

Module: #pages: Used by:
msdos           2                 1 (autoclean)
fat             6         [msdos] 1 (autoclean)

gandalf# ls -al /mnt
drwxr-xr-x      2 root root          7168  Jan  1  1970  .
drwxr-xr-x     21 root root          1024  Jun  1  03:34  . .
-rwxr-xr-x      1 root root         19693  Jun  4  17:45 bouquin.sty
-rwxr-xr-x      1 root root          3012  Jun  4  17:45 livre.sty

gandalf# umount /mnt

gandalf# lsmod
Module: #pages: Used by:
msdos           2                 0 (autoclean)
fat             6         [msdos] 0 (autoclean)

gandalf# sleep 60

gandalf# ls mod
Module: #pages: Used by:
```

When the file system is set up, the two modules needed for using the *MS-DOS* file system are automatically loaded by the daemon *kerneld*. Straight after removing the partition, the number of references is zero because in this case no processes are using the modules. They will be unloaded automatically a few seconds later.

The timeout between the last usage and unloading is defaulted to 60 seconds, but it is possible to set a chosen elapsed time using the option **delay**. Once the daemon is launched using this option, modules are unloaded according to this parameter.

Many of the details of use of this daemon may be found in [Storner, 1996].

12.2
ADVANCED CONCEPTS

12.2.1 Design of loadable modules

12.2.1.1 *Overview*
Loadable modules are notable in that they allow a minimal kernel to be built and to load and unload a part of the kernel in accordance with the needs of users working on the machine.

However, this is only one feature of the system, since it is also frequently used to develop some peripheral managers.

Indeed, in traditional developments, it is necessary to modify the kernel, to recompile it, and then to re-boot the system and test the changes, all of which wastes a lot of time. Kernels allow only the recompilation of the required module before re-loading it. After testing its functionality, it is a simple matter of unloading it, modifying it, and so on. It is thus unnecessary to re-boot the system. Of course it is important that the module does not produce errors in the kernel, or it will then be necessary to re-boot.

The short example which follows presents the design of a loadable module which is capable of providing the time on a given peripheral (*/dev/time* for example). The time will be expressed in terms of the number of seconds which have elapsed since January 1st 1970.

12.2.1.2 *Example*
The source code reserves the use of the peripheral having a major number 60 and minor number 0. The call to *read* on this file produces a return of the present time.

──────── Module-heure.c ────────

```
/* This loadable module gives the current time using a simple
gandalf# cat /dev/time */

#include <linux/module.h>
#include <linux/kernel.h>
#include <linux/errno.h>
#include <linux/sched.h>


/* Major and minor numbers */
#define HOUR_MAJOR 60
#define HOUR_MINOR 0
/* Input/output operations on the device */
static int time_fs_read (struct inode *inode, struct file *file,
                         char *buf, int nbytes);
```

```
static struct file_operations time_fops =
{
    NULL,
    time_fs_read,
    NULL,
    NULL,
    NULL,
    NULL,
    NULL,
    NULL,
    NULL,
    NULL
} ;


/*Initialisation */
int time_init (void)
{
    if (register_chrdev (HOUR_MAJOR, "time", &time_fops)) {
            printk ("time : unable to get major %d\n", HOUR_MAJOR);
            return -E10;
    }
    printk ("time module loaded (major=%d)\n", HOUR_MAJOR);
    return 0;
}


#ifdef MODULE
/* Module initialisation */
int       init_module (void)
{
    return time_init ();
}


/* Module unload */
void      cleanup_module (void)
{
    unregister_chrdev (HOUR_MAJOR, "time");
    printk (" time module unloaded \n");
}


#endif

/* Device read : simply return current time */
static int time_fs_read (struct inode *inode, struct file *file,
```

```
                                    char *buf, int nbytes)
{
      unsigned int   minor = MINOR (inode->i_rdev);
      char                  tmp[32];

      if (nbytes == 0)
             return 0;

      if (minor != HOUR_MINOR)
             return -ENODEV;

      MOD_INC_USE_COUNT;     /* one extra process is using this module
   */

      sprintf (tmp, "%d\n", (int) (CURRENT_TIME));
      memcpy_tofs (buf, tmp, strlen (tmp));

      MOD_INC_USE_COUNT;     /* Use terminated */

      return strlen (tmp) + 2; /* number of bytes used in the buffer */
}
```

———————————————————————————— Module-heure.c ————————

12.2.1.3 Compilation and execution

Compilation is performed fairly simply. It involves firstly compiling the object files, and then generating the archive:

```
gandalf# make
gcc -c -D_ _KERNEL -I/usr/src/linux-pre2.0.8/include -Wall
-Wstrict-prototypes -02 -fomit-frame-pointer -fno-strength-reduce
-pipe -m486 -malign-loops=2 -malign-jumps=2 -malign-function=2 -DPCU=686
-DMODULE module-time.c

ld -m elf_i386 -r -o monmodule.o module-time.o
```

The important options are **-DMODULE** and **-D_ _KERNEL_ _** which specify the code which will be generated in the form of a loadable module. The options shown in this example are those used when the kernel is compiled[1].

File creation, module loading and execution are all carried out very simply:

————————————————————————————

[1] Specifically, the machine this example refers to is a PC with a 686 processor.

```
gandalf# mknod /dev/time c 60 0
gandalf# insmod time-module
gandalf# lsmod
Module:        #pages: Used by:
module-time    1             0
gandalf# cat/dev/time | head ûlines=1
833371919
gandalf# rmmod time-module
```

Firstly, the peripheral, having 60 as the major number and 0 for the minor number, has to be created. Then it is a question of using the special commands dedicated to handling loadable modules.

Certain traces have been left in this example. In an earlier use, the following messages may have been left in the trace file[2]:

```
May 29 13:33:25 gandalf kernel: time module loaded (major=60)
May 29 13:33:30 gandalf kernel: time module unloaded
```

12.2.2 System calls specific to modules

Four system calls exist for manipulation of loadable modules, however, they do not appear in any library. These system calls are used by loadable module handling programmes, such as *insmod*, ... It should be noted that only the super-user may use them. The call declarations, the structures and the macro-commands are located in the header file **<linux/module.h>**.

12.2.2.1 *get_kernel_syms*
This system call has several roles: it can either return the number of symbols available in the kernel, or one of these symbols themselves.

The general form of this call is as follows:

```
#include <linux/module.h>

int get_kernel_syms (struct kernel_sym *table);
```

---

[2] This depends on the configuration of the daemon *syslogd* but it often refers to the files */var/adm/messages* or */var/adm/syslog*.

If the table passed as a parameter is NULL, the system call with return the number of symbols which are actually available in the kernel. This technique can be used to allocate memory space needed to create the table receiving the data.

The **kernel_sym** structure has the following definition:

type	*field*	*description*
unsigned long	**value**	Symbol value
char [SYM_MAX_NAME]	**name**	Symbol name

If this parameter is passed to the system call, all symbols and module names known to the kernel are copied into the table. The entries are arranged in Last In First Out (LIFO) order of modules loaded in the kernel. The field *value* contains the address in the kernel of the structure which describes the module.

12.2.2.2 create_module

This module serves by allocating a certain number of bytes in the kernel address space to receive the module. The call also creates kernel structures for managing this module. The module then exists in the kernel, but has a status of **MOD_UNITIALIZED,** that is, it is not usable for the moment.

The general form of this call is as follows:

```
#include <linux/module.h>


int create_module (char *module_name,  unsigned long size);
```

12.2.2.3 init_module

This call fulfils the role of module loader and enables the module to be loaded into the kernel. It has the following general form:

```
#include <linux/module.h>


int init_module (char *module_name, unsigned long size)
            unsigned codesize, struct mod_routines *routines,
            struct symbol_table *symtab);
```

The call loads the module called **name** into the kernel. The module code is contained in the parameter **code**, of size **codesize**. It is therefore only after this call that the module is usable. The two parameters which follow relate pointers to initialisation and module unloading routines. The **mod_routines** structure is composed of the following fields:

type	field	description
int (*) (void)	init	Initialisation routine
void (*) (void)	cleanup	Deletion with unloading routine

The size of module symbols passed as parameters is expressed by the structure **symbol_table** according to the following definition:

type	field	description
int	size	Total size, including the table of links
int	n_symbols	Number of symbols
int	n_refs	Number of references
struct internal_symbol [0] [0]	symbol	Table of symbols

Each symbol in this table is represented by the **internal_symbol** structure:

type	field	description
void *	addr	Symbol address
const char *	name	Symbol name

Each module is referenced in the following form:

type	field	description
struct module *	module	Pointer to the module structure
struct module_ref *	next	Pointer to the following module

This concerns the internal kernel structure.

Finally, each module is represented in the form of the following structure:

type	field	description
struct module *	next	Pointer to the following module
struct module_ref *	ref	List of modules which use this module
struct symbol_table *	symtab	Table of module symbols
const char *	name	Module name
int	size	Module size in memory pages
void *	addr	Module address
int	state	State of module
void (*) (void)	cleanup	Routine launched at module unloading

A loadable module may be in three states. Only the **MOD_RUNNING** state allows a module to be actually used.

constant	meaning
MOD_UNINITIALIZED	Module created but not initialized
MOD_RUNNING	Module being used
MOD_DELETED	Module deleted

12.2.2.4 delete_module

This call unloads the module named by the kernel. It should be noted that this operation may fail if certain processes still have access to the module.

The general form is as follows:

```
#include <linux/module.h>

int delete_module (char *module_name);
```

12.3
IMPLEMENTATION OF
LOADABLE MODULES

12.3.1 Overview

The implementation of loadable modules divides into several parts:

- the implementation of the system calls *kernel/module.c*;
- the management of virtual files */procmodules* and */proc/ksyms* in *kernel/module.c*;
- the communication system with *kerneld* in *ipc/msg.c*;
- the daemon *kerneld*.

The heart of the module is located in the file *kernel/module.c*. It manages notably the list of modules loaded into the kernel, and concerns the **variable module_list** and the **module** structure type.

When the system is booted up, the function **init_modules** is launched, This function consists of initialising the global (or static) variables such as:

- **module_list**: list of loaded modules;
- **symbol_table**: table of kernel symbols.

12.3.2   Implementation of system calls

12.3.2.1   *create_module*
This system call consists of allocating the necessary memory (this is an allocation in the memory zone of the kernel) in which to store the code of the loadable module.

After the memory allocation, a new element in the list of modules is created, having a state fixed at **MOD_UNITIALIZED**. This element is then inserted in the list **module_list**.

12.3.2.2   *init_module*
This call carries out the physical loading of the module, starting by putting the code, passed as a parameter, into the list of modules (field **addr** which corresponds to the memory space allocated by means of *create_module*). As a consequence, the code becomes an integral part of the kernel.

The complex part of loading of a module lies not in the loading itself (which is quite simple as has just been described), but in the update of the table of kernel symbols.

Indeed, the Linux kernel contains a table of function symbols to make known at which address a particular function is located. Therefore, once the kernel code has been loaded, it is necessary to update the table of symbols to indicate the address at which each of the functions of the module is located.

The operation consists of creating a new table of symbols of the type **symbol_table**, which is described in detail in section 12.2.2. In fact, this amounts to a duplication of the table of symbols contained in the module since it is passed as a parameter. This table is then associated with the module resident in the kernel. In this way, any symbol included in the module is then accessible by any kernel function.

12.3.2.3   *delete_module*
The deletion of a module is a particularly delicate operation. This call uses two functions which will be described later: **get_mod_name** and **find_module** which retrieve the name of the kernel and a pointer to the structure of the module respectively.

The call can have two outcomes. It may only unload a single module, if its name is specified. If the name is not specified, it scans the whole list of modules and tries to unload each unused module in turn.

After retrieving the name and the pointer to the module, and in the case where the module is not used, the state of the module field is set to **MOD_DELETED**. A call to the unloading function **free_modules** is then carried out.

This function scans the list of all modules and deletes those which are marked **MOD_DELETED**. The deletion of a module is performed in two stages. Firstly, if the references to the module are used by other modules, a call to **drop_refs** is performed. This function re-orders references between modules. Secondly, the function **free_modules** deletes the table of module symbols, then erases the module code. The module is then deemed 'unloaded' since its code no longer exists in the kernel.

12.3.2.4 *get_kernel_syms*

This system call first scans the list of modules loaded and counts the number of symbols present. This operation is simple since each module knows the number of symbols it possesses (field **n_symbols** in the table of module symbols).

Next, if the table passed as a parameter is not null, all names and all addresses of the different symbols contained in the loaded modules are copied in it. This operation is carried out by scanning the list. Only modules in the state **MOD_RUNNING** are considered.

12.3.3 Management of virtual files

The virtual files */proc/modules* and */proc/ksyms* are implemented in the source file *kernel/module.c*. These files can only be accessed in read mode.

When reading the file */proc/modules*, the function **get_module_list** is called. It scans the list of modules and fills the buffer passed as a parameter. This buffer is in fact the text that will be displayed when this file is consulted.

When the file *ksyms* is accessed, the function **get_ksyms_list** is called. As before, a scan of the list of modules and of each of their tables of symbols enables the list of symbols to be built up.

12.3.4 Anciliary functions

Certain functions are used in this module (or externally), but they are of minor interest:

- **get_mod_name**: copies a module name from a user space to a kernel space;
- **find_module**: returns a module pointer whose name has been passed as a parameter;
- **register_symtab_from**: inserts a table of symbols into the list.

12.4
AUTOMATIC LOADING OF
MODULES (kerneld)

12.4.1 Overview

The automatic module loading system is rather complicated since it uses several mechanisms. However, the principle is relatively straightforward. At some point, the kernel requires certain functionality which is available from a loadable module, and it is therefore necessary to load it. The operation is actually carried out by a user-mode process, *kernel*. The loading order is sent by the kernel to the daemon via a message queue (see chapter 11, section 11.2.1).

As figure 12.2 shows schematically, the loading operation is performed in three stages:

- For the kernel to carry out the load operation, it uses the function **request_module.**
- A message is sent to the message queue. The content of the message is made up of the constant **KERNELD_REQUEST_MODULE**, together with the name of the required module.
- The daemon reads the message and performs the load by calling the programme *modprobe*.
- In due course the daemon sends a reply to the kernel.

This method of loading modules has certain advantages. Indeed, it may happen that the daemon has several orders to load in the message queue, and in this case all the modules are loaded at once. In addition, the kerneld code is relatively simple because the loading operations are external to the kernel. Finally, error management is greatly simplified. However, the fact that it is a daemon executed in user mode (and which is therefore interruptible) which performs the loading process, means that the process which triggered the loading may be put on hold. This wait ends when the daemon has finally succeeded in loading the required modules.

12.4.2 Implementation details

Implementation is shared between the modules *ipc/msg.c* and **<linux/kerneld.h>**. Although the latter is a header file, certain functions are defined in it. The major part of the implementation in fact resides in the daemon, whose source codes are distributed separately[3].

---

[3] The primary distribution site is http://www.pi.se/blox/modules.

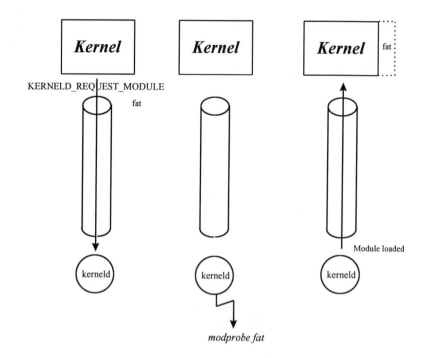

Figure 12.2:   Communication between the kernel and kerneld.

Below are listed the functions contained in the header file.

- **request_module:** loads a module whose name is passed as a parameter. The command **KERNELD_REQUEST_MODULE** is used. In addition, a particular option (**KERNELD_WAIT**) allows the function to be exited only when the module has been loaded, or if an error has occurred. The command is usually converted into a call to *modprobe* by the daemon.
- **release_ module:** requests a module to be unloaded. This operation consists of using the command **KERNELD_RELEASE_MODULE**. The daemon then launches the programme *rmmod* to carry out the operation.
- **delayed_release_ module:** if the module is not used for a period of time (default 60 seconds), the module is unloaded. The command used to carry out this operation **KERNELD_DELAYED_RELEASE_MODULE**, which leads to the execution *rmmod*.
- **cancel_release_ module:** tries to cancel a request to unload a module. This call may be made if the kernel wishes to avoid the automatic unloading of the module, by means of the command **KERNELD_CANCEL_RELEASE_MODULE**.
- **ksystem:** carries out a so-called 'inverted' system call. This enables certain information to be transmitted to the daemon, by means of the command **KERNELD_SYSTEM**.

- **kerneld_route**: specially designed for networks, this function allows an entry in the routing table to be created, which is used for example in network connections using the PPP protocol. The command used is **KERNELD_REQUEST_ROUTE**.
- **kerneld_blanker**: allows an external screen-saver to be used. It uses the command **KERNELD_BLANKER**.

This header file also defines the **kerneld_msg** structure which contains the message which transits between the kernel and the **daemon**. This structure has the following fields:

type	field	description
long	mtype	Command type
long	id	If this field is not null, then the kernel awaits a response
short	version	Protocol version. If the field is 0, the old protocol is being used. The protocol used from now on will be number 2.
short	pid	Pid of the process which triggers module loading
char *	text	Passage of information

All the functions described above rely mainly on the function **kerneld_send** which is located in the module *ipc/msg.c*. It consists of 'posting' the message queue of type **IPC_KERNELD**. This is a message queue reserved for communications between the kernel and the daemon. Sending and receiving messages is performed by means of the functions **real_msgend** and **real_msgrcv**. These functions were described in detail in chapter 11, section 5.1.4. The data which moves through this message queue is expressed using the structure **kerneld_msg**.

The implementation of the daemon *kerneld* is beyond the scope of this book since it is external to the kernel. However, it functions very simply, and may be summarised as follows: by means of an active wait in read mode in the message queue, it receives orders to load or to unload modules. Data passed to the message queue use the **kerneld_msg** structure described in section 12.4.2. However, the daemon does not actually load the modules, but uses programmes provided for this purpose.

13

System administration

System calls described

adjtimex, gettimeofday, gethostname, getdomainname, reboot, setdomainname, sethostname, settimeofday, stime, syslog, sysctl, time, uname

13.1
BASIC CONCEPTS

Linux keeps certain information permanently. This is to safeguard correct operation of the kernel, and also correct functioning of processes.

13.1.1 Information intended for processes

Certain data is made available for processes. By putting it in the kernel address space, it is at the same time protected and readily available. Among the data stored here are the machine name, the domain name, the operating system name as well as the version number, the compilation date, etc.

It should be pointed out that the domain name is rather ambiguous since it may be used in the context of the DNS (Domain Name System) or the NIS (Networked Information Services), see [Moreno, 1995] for more details. One problem arises concerning configuring programs making use of this information, since a program may refer to the domain name in one case or the other but the effect is not the same.

This data is directly accessible by means of the commands *hostname*, *domainname*, and *uname*.

The first two have a particular role.

- display a value:

```
gandalf#% hostname
gandalf
```

- change the value, if the user is a super-user:

```
gandalf# domainname freenix.fr
gandalf# domainname
freenix.fr
```

The command *uname* allow this information to be made available, and it has numerous options. For example, to access all this data, one would type:

```
gandalf# uname -a
Linux gandalf 2.0.14 #1 Wen Aug 21 00:37:52 MET DST 1996 i486
```

The system call giving access to this data is *uname*.

13.1.2   Information controlling execution

Several types of information are retained in the kernel:

- *the time*: this is represented as the number of seconds elapsed since the 1st of January 1970 00:00 UTC. Two main calls are used to access this data: *gettimeofday* and *settimeofday*. However, Linux provides two other calls to maintain compatibility: *time* and *stime*.
- *display mode for kernel messages*: the kernel sends messages to the administrator about operations carried out on the machine. The system call *syslog* allows the level of detail about messages to be displayed to be defined.
- *machine status information*: certain information is useful in order to understand the performance and functioning status of the machine. This relates to the memory available, the load, the *swap* used etc. The system call *sysinfo* provides this information, a part of which may be visualised by means of the commands *uptime* and *free*.
- *clock synchronisation*: there is a system for synchronising the system clock: *xntpd*. Indeed, computer clocks have long term gain or loss of time, and in a group of several machines, it is difficult to arrange to have the same time on all of them, however, *xntpd* enables them to be synchronised. This daemon utilises a particular system call: *adjtimex*. The kernel retains certain useful data, such as the clock precision, its frequency etc. This system is based on the NTP (Network Time Protocol) protocol which is described in detail in [Mills, 1992].

13.1.3 Change of status in the kernel

A particular system call modifies the status of the machine: *reboot*. In fact, it may be advantageous to reboot the machine from time to time[1]. Several Unix commands enable this operation to be carried out (*reboot, shutdown,* etc.). A specific feature of Linux worth noting is the ability of rebooting the machine with the well known **CTRL ALT DEL** (the so-called *'three finger salute'*).

13.1.4 Dynamic configuration of the system

13.1.4.1 Overview

Linux provides a very powerful system call, *sysctl*, which allows certain system parameters to be dynamically configured, such as the machine name, the maximum number of open files, *swap* management, etc.

13.1.4.2 An alternative method

The dynamic configuration of the system may also be achieved by means of the virtual file system */proc*, whose operation has been described in detail earlier in chapter 6, section 6.6.6. All information accessible via the system call *sysctl* is available in the form of files in the directory */proc/sys*.

For example, certain information regarding the machine is directly accessible:

- */proc/sys/kernel/hostname*: machine name

```
gandalf# cat hostname
gandalf
```

- */proc/sys/kernel/domainname*: machine name

```
gandalf# cat domainname
freenix
```

- */proc/sys/kernel/version*: machine name

```
gandalf# cat version
#1 Wed Aug 21 00:37:52 MET DST 1996
```

---

[1] To change the kernel version, for example.

13.2
ADMINISTRATION SYSTEM
CALLS

Linux allows user processes to handle information maintained by the kernel, and all these processes may access this data in read mode, but only privileged processes may modify it.

13.2.1 Information relating to the workstation

Various information regarding the workstation itself, that is its name, its domain, the system version etc.
, may be obtained by means of the system call *uname*. This call uses the **utsname** structure defined in the header file **<sys/utsname.h>**. The fields making up this structure are as follows:

type	*field*	*description*
char *	sysname	Name of the operating system
char *	nodename	Workstation name
char *	release	Operating system number
char *	version	Version number of the kernel and its compilation date
char *	machine	Hardware platform identifier
char *	domainname	Name of the domain to which the workstation belongs

The system call syntax for *uname* is as follows:

```
#include <sys/utsname.h>


int name (struct utsname *buf);
```

The data is returned to the structure, whose address is passed as a parameter. The system call *uname* returns the value 0 if successful, or the value −1 in the event of failure (the only error code able to be returned is EFAULT in the case where the parameter **buf** contains a valid address).

The following program displays data returned by *uname*. It is a simplified equivalent of the command *uname:*

——————— ShowUname.c ———————————————————

```
#include <stdio.h>
#include <sys/utsname.h>
#include <linux/errno.h>

void main (void)
{
    struct utsname buf;
    int             err;

    err = uname (&buf);
    if (err != 0)
            printf ("Error uname\n");
    else {
            printf ("sysname      = %s\n", buf.sysname);
            printf ("nadename     = %s\n", buf.nodename);
            printf ("release            = %s\n", buf.release);
            printf ("version            = %s\n", buf.version);
            printf ("machine            = %s\n", buf.machine);
            printf ("domainname   = %s\n", buf.domainname);
    }
}
```

——————————————————————————— ShowUname.c ———————

Running this program produces the following display:

```
bbj>ShowUname
sysname = Linux
nodename      = bbj
release       = 1.2.13
version       = #1 Fris Aug 11 18:50:10 1995
machine = i486
domainname    = freenix.fr
```

A privileged process may modify certain information obtained by calling *uname*. The system calls *sethostname* and *setdomainname* enable the workstation name and the domain name to be changed, respectively. The syntax of these calls is as follows:

```
#include <inistd.h>

int sethostname (const char *name, size_t len);

int setdomainname (const char *name, size_t len);
```

These two system calls take as arguments the new workstation name and the new domain name (parameter **name**), as well as the number of characters composing the name (parameters **len**). In the event of failure, the error **EPERM** indicates that the calling process does not possess the required privileges to modify this information, and the error **EINVAL** indicates that the size of the name exceeds the system limit. The following program changes the name of the workstation and the domain name according to the parameters which are passed to it: it first displays this information, modifies it, then re-displays it.

——————— ShowUtsname.c ———————————————

```
#include <stdio.h>
#include <unistd.h>
#include <sys/utsname.h>
void main (int argc, char *argv [])
{
    struct utsname buf;
    int            err;

    if (argc != 3) {
            printf (ôUsage: %s hostname domain_name\nö, argv[0]);
            exit (1);
    }
    err = uname (&buf)
    if (err !=0)
            printf ("Error uname\n");
    else {
            printf ("nodename     = %s\n", buf.nodename);
            printf ("domainname = %s\n", buf.domainname);
    }
err = sethostname (argv[1], strlen (argv[1]));
if (err != 0)
            printf ("Error sethostname\n");
err = uname (&buf);
if (err != 0)
            printf ("Error setdomainname\n");
err = uname (&buf);
if (err != 0)
            printf ("Error uname\n");
else {
```

```
        printf ("nodename    = %s\n", buf.nodename);
        printf ("domainname = %s\n", buf.domainname);
    }
}
```

────────────────────────── ShowUtsname.c ──────────

Running the program results in the following display:

```
bbj# ./ShowUtsname workstation domain
nodename      = bbj
domainname    = freenix.fr
nodename      = workstation
domainname    = domain
```

Two functions, *gethostname* and *getdomainname*, enable the names of the workstation and the domain to be obtained. These functions are implemented in the C library, and are not the system calls processed by the kernel: **gethostname** and **getdomainname** confine themselves to returning information sent back by the system call *uname*. Their syntax is as follows:

```
#include <unistd.h>

int gethostname (char *name, size_t len);

int getdomainname (char *name, size_t len);
```

13.2.2 Control of execution

13.2.2.1 Time

The system calls *gettimeofday* and *settimeofday* enable the time elapsed since January 1st 1970 to be retrieved, or for this duration to be fixed. Two other system calls may also be used for this: *time* and *stime*. These two calls are only retained for reasons of compatibility, since *gettimeofday* and *settimeofday* can carry out the same operation.

The syntax of these two calls is as follows:

```
#include <sys/time.h>
#include <unistd.h>

int gettimeofday (struct timeval *tv, struct timezone *tz);

int settimeofday (const struct timeval *tv, const struct timezone *tz);
```

Two structures are used, and their presence influences the progress of the system call. To be able to handle these two structures, it is appropriate to include the file **<sys/time.h>** (these two structures are in fact declared in the file **<linux/time.h>**).

The structure **timeval** allows the time to be expressed in terms of the number of seconds and microseconds elapsed since January 1st 1970. Its format is defined in chapter 4, section 4.2.3.

The other structure enables the time offset (time zone) to be fixed or requested by means of the structure **timezone**:

type	*field*	*description*
int	**tz_tz_minuteswest**	Number of minutes offset west with respect to the Greenwich mean-time
int	**tz_dsttime**	Offset with respect to the time zone

Below is an example enabling the necessary information to be retrieved:

──────── gettimeofday.c ────────────────────────────

```
#include <sys/time.h>
#include <stdio.h>
#include <stdlib.h>
#include <unistd.h>

void main ()
{
    struct timeval tv;
    struct timezone tz;

    if (gettimeofday (&tv, NULL) == -1)  {
            perror ("gettimeofday");
            exit (-1);
    }
    printf ("Number of seconds : %d Number of microseconds : %d\n",
            tv.tv_sec, tv.tv_usec);

    if (gettimeofday (NULL, &tz) == -1)  {
            perror ("gettimeofday");
            exit (-1);
    }
    printf ("Number of minutes (West of Greenwich) : %d time zone :
%d\n",
            tv.tv_minuteswest, tv.tv_dsttime);
}
```

──────────────────────────────── gettimeofday.c   ────────

The execution of this program can give different information according to the configuration of the machine, and the time of year in which the program was run:

```
gandalf# ./gettimeofday
Number of seconds : 846708854 Number of microseconds : 626083
Number of minutes (West of Greenwich) : -60 time zone : 1
gandalf#
```

This example was run in France, at the end of October. At this time point, there is an offset of only a single hour, as indicated by the number –60. If the program had been run in summer, two hours of offset would have been indicated.

The errors which may arise from this call are the following:

error	meaning
EINVAL	Parameters not valid

The system call *settimeofday* may only be executed by the super-user. To fix the time or the time zone the reverse of the operation is carried out. The following errors may arise:

error	meaning
EPERM	May only be executed by the super-user
EINVAL	Parameters not valid

The calls *time* and *stime* have the following general forms:

```
#include <time.h>

time_t time(time_t *t);

int stime (time_t *t);
```

time gives the number of seconds elapsed since January 1st 1970, and *stime* fixes this duration, *stime* may only be executed by the super-user.

13.2.2.2 Display mode of kernel messages

The system call *syslog* should not be confused with the library function *syslog* which sends a message to the daemon *syslogd*. This system call enables the display mode of the message system to be configured and the message buffer to be handled. It is peculiar to Linux. Its general form is as follows:

```
#include <unistd.h>
#include <linux/unistd.h>

_syscall3 (int, syslog, int, type, char *, bufp, int, len);
int syslog (nt type, char *bufp, int len);
```

The first parameter enables the required command to be specified:

- 0: stop management of messages;
- 1: start management of messages;
- 2: copy the messages into the buffer **bufp** having size **len**;
- 3: copy recent messages up to a limit of 4 kbytes;
- 4: as above, but also delete read messages;
- 5: flush the message buffer;
- 6: de-activate the monitor display;
- 7: activate the monitor display;
- 8: sets the level of messages to be displayed.

It should be noted that the only call that a non-privileged user may carry out is No. 3. However, this call cannot be used directly, since the library function has priority when links are being edited. An example of this follows:

——————— demosyslog.c ———————————————

```
#include <stdio.h>
#include <stdlib.h>
#include <unistd.h>
#include <linux/unistd.h>

/* a system call is defined having the same number */
#define __NR_monsyslog __NR_syslog
static inline
    _syscall3 (int, monsyslog, int, type, char *, b, int, len);

void main ()
{
    char buf[4 * 1024];

    if (monsyslog (3, buf, 4 * 1024) ++ -1) {
            perror ("syslog");
            exit (-1);
    }
    printf ("%s \n", buf);
}
```

—————————————————————————— demosyslog.c ———————

The above example is equivalent to the command *dmesg* which displays all messages stored by the kernel. An extract of the result produced is now listed:

```
gandalf# ./demosyslog
<4>Monitor:  16 point font, 400 scans
<4>Monitor: colour VGA+ 80x25, 1 virtual  monitor (max 63)
<4>Calibrating delay loop.. ok -32.87 BogoMIPS
<4>Memory: 14680k/16384k available (796k kernel code,  384k  reserved,
524k)
>4>Linux version 1.3.100 (dumas@gandalf) (gcc version 2.7.2) #1 Sat May
11 15:08:56 MET DST 1996
>6>Serial driver version 4.12 with no serial options enabled
<6>tty00 at 0x03f8 (irq = 4) is a 16450
<6>tty01 at 0x02f8 (irq = 3) is a 16450
<6>lp1 at 0x0378, (polling)
<4>Sound initialisation started
<4>SoundBlaster 16 4.11> at 0x260 irq 5 dma 1,5
<7>Max size:314389  Log zone size:2048
<7>First datazone:68  Root inode number 139264
<4>ISO9660 Extensions: RRIP_1991A
```

The number between chevrons is the message level. It is this level which is used when calling the function *syslog* from the standard library:

constant	meaning
KERN_EMERG (0)	System unusable
KERN_ALERT(1)	Alert message
KERN_CRIT (2)	Critical message
KERN_ERR (3)	Error message
KERN_WARNING (4)	Warning
KERN_NOTICE (5)	Miscellaneous
KERN_DEBUG (6)	Debugging

This system call may generate the following messages:

error	meaning
EPERM	Use of syslog with a command which may only be used by a super-user
EINVAL	Bad parameter
EINTR	System call was interrupted. No data has been copied into the buffer

13.2.2.3 Machine status
The status of the machine is ascertained by using the system call *sysinfo*. This call is used by programs such as *uptime*.

Its general form is as follows:

```
#include <linux/kernel.h>
#include <linux/sys.h>


int sysinfo (struct sysinfo *info);
```

The structure **sysinfo** has the following fields:

type	*field*	*description*
long	**uptime**	Number of seconds elapsed since machine bootup
unsigned long [3]	**loads**	Load on the machine load during the previous minute, the previous 5 minutes, the previous 15 minutes
unsigned long	**totalram**	Usable memory
unsigned long	**freeram**	Free memory
unsigned long	**sharedram**	Shared memory
unsigned long	**bufferram**	Memory used by buffers
unsigned long	**totalswap**	Total size of swap
unsigned long	**freeswap**	Space available in the swap
unsigned short	**procs**	Current number of processes
char [22]	**_f**	Character alignment so that the structure fits 64 bytes

This system call may be used very simply:

———— demosysinfo.c ————

```
#include <linux/kernel.h>
#include <linux/sys.h>
#include <stdio.h>
#include <stdlib.h>

void main ()
{
    struct sysinfo si;

    if (sysinfo (&si) == -1) {
```

```
            perror ("sysinfo");
            exit (-1);
    }
    printf ("Result of the sysinfo call \n");
    printf ("Number of seconds since boot : ld \n",
            si.uptime);
    printf ("Uptime 1m (%ld) 5m (%ld) 15 (%ld) \n",
            si.loads[0], si.loads[1], si.loads[2]);
    printf ("memory (Kb) total %ld Free %ld Shared"
            "%ld Buffers %ld\n",
            si.totalram / 1024, si.freeram / 1024,
            si.sharedram / 1024, si.bufferram / 1024);
    printf ("Size of swap %ld free %ld \n",
            si.totalswap / 1024, si.freeswap / 1024);
    printf ("Process number %d \n", si.procs);
}
```

──────────────────────────────── demosysinfo.c ────────────

When run the format is represented in kbytes since this is more readable:

```
gandalf# demosysinfo
Result of the call to sys info
Number of seconds since bootup : 1512025
Load 1m (38752) 5m (30336) 15 (20224)
Total memory (in kbytes) 14680 Free 716 Shared 11624 Buffer 312
Swap size 34812 free 30116
Number of processes 49
```

The only error which this call may generate is **EFAULT** if the pointer passed as a parameter is not correct.

13.2.2.4 *Clock synchronisation*

The system call *adjtimex* is mainly used by the synchronisation system *xntp*. The aim of this call is to be able to alter the time on the machine by modifying the necessary kernel parameters. The general form is as follows:

```
#include <sys/timex.h>

int adjtimex (struct timex *buf);
```

This call takes the structure **timex** as a parameter, for which the complex declaration is found in the file **<linux/timex.h>**. The detail of this follows:

type	field	description
unsigned	**modes**	Mode selection
long	**offset**	Time to be added (microseconds)
long	**freq**	Frequency
long	**maxerror**	Maximum error (microseconds)
long	**esterror**	Estimated error (microseconds)
int	**status**	Clock status or command
long	**constant**	Constant
long	**precision**	Clock precision (microseconds) (read mode only)
long	**tolerance**	Frequency tolerance of the clock (read mode only)
struct timeval	**time**	Time (read only)
long	**tick**	Number of microseconds between two clock 'ticks'
long	**ppsfreq**	Frequency (read only)
long	**jitter**	
int	**shift**	Interval duration (read only)
long	**stabil**	Stability (read only)
long	**jitcnt**	offset limit (read only)
long	**calcnt**	Interval resolution (read only)
long	**errcnt**	Error resolution (read only)
long	**stbcnt**	Stability limit (read only)

This system call may generate the following errors:

error	meaning
EFAULT	The buffer points to a memory zone which cannot be written to
EPERM	The field mode is non-zero and the call has not been made by a super-user
EINVAL	The out of limits values have been assigned to **offset**, **status** or **tick**

13.2.3 Change of status of the kernel

The system call *reboot* enables a privileged process to control the re-starting of the kernel. The *reboot* syntax is as follows:

```
#include <unistd.h>


int reboot (int magic, int magic_too, int flag);
```

The first two parameters (**magic** and **magic_too**) should have the values 0xfee1dead and 672274793 in order for the call to be recognised. The parameter **flag** specifies the action to be taken according to its value:

- 0x01234567: immediate reboot of the system;
- 0xCDEF0123: immediate halt to all processes and to the system;
- 0x89ABCDEF: activation of workstation hardware reboot when the keys **CTRL ALT DEL** are pressed;
- 0: deactivation of workstation hardware reboot when the keys **CTRL ALT DEL** are pressed.

This call may generate the following errors:

error	*meaning*
EINVAL	Bad parameters
EPERM	Only super-users may use this system call

13.2.4 Dynamic system configuration

Linux allows super-users to change the response of the system without having to recompile the kernel or to reconfigure certain parts of the machine. This characteristic is specific to Linux, and should be used with caution since it affects the way the machine functions. The system call *sysctl* has the following general form:

```
#include <unistd.h>
#include <linux/unistd.h>
#include <linux/sysctl.h>


_syscall1 (int, _sysctl, struct __sysctl_args *, args);
int _sysctl (struct __sysctl_args *args);
```

It uses the structure **__sysctl_args** which is defined as follows:

type	*field*	*description*
int *	**name**	Table of integers describing the data to be read or changed
int	**nlen**	Size of the above table
void *	**oldval**	**NULL** or the address where the former values should be saved
size_t *	**oldlenp**	Available space for storing former values
void *	**newval**	**NULL** or the address for new values
size_t	**newlen**	Size of new values

The name of data to which access is required is expressed by constants. In the first instance, this amounts to designating the variable type:

constant	*meaning*
CTL_ANY	Any type
CTL_KERN	General information about the kernel and its operation
CTL_VM	Management of virtual memory
CTL_NET	Network
CTL_PROC	Information on processes
CTL_FS	File systems
CTL_DEBUG	Debugging
CTL_DEV	Devices
CTL_MAXID	Last identifier

Each category then has its own variables allowing different values to be accessed. **CTL_KERN** and **CTL_VM** are detailed here:

- **CTL_KERN:**

constant	meaning
KERN_OSTYPE	System name (string), Linux in this case
KERN_OSRELEASE	Version name (string)
KERN_OSREV	Version number (int)
KERN_VERSION	Kernel generation date (string)
KERN_SECUREMASK	Mask of maximum rights (structure)
KERN_PROF	Set-up information (table)
KERN_NODENAME	Machine name
KERN_DOMAINNAME	Domain name
KERN_NRINODE	Number of inodes allocated
KERN_MAXINODE	Maximum number of inodes
KERN_NRFILE	Number of file descriptors used
KERN_MAXFILE	Maximum number of files open
KERN_MAXID	
KERN_SECURELVL	Security level of the system
KERN_PANIC	Panic timeout (int)
KERN_REALROOTDEV	Real device to be mounted as a root after initrd
KERN_NFSRNAME	Name of NFS root
KERN_NFSRADDRS	Name of the machine having the NFS root

- **CTL_VM:**

constant	meaning
VM_SWAPCTL	Configure swap management (structure)
VM_KSWAPD	Configure the pagination system (structure)
VM_FREEPG	Set the threshold of free pages (structure)
VM_BDFLUSH	Control the management of cache buffers (structure)
VM_MAXID	

There now follows an example of usage providing the domain name of a machine:

```
————— demosysctl.c ————————————————————————

#include <linux/unistd.h>
#include <linux/types.h>
#include <linux/sysctl.h>
#include <stdio.h>
#include <stdlib.h>

#define DOMAINSIZE 50

_syscall1 (int, _sysctl, struct __sysctl_args *, args);

int sysctl (int *name, int nlen, void *oldval, size_t * oldlenp,
        void *newval, size_t newlen)
{
    struct __sysctl_args args =
    {
            name, nlen, oldval, oldlenp, newval, newlen};

    return _sysctl (&args);
{

void main ()
{
    int name[] =
    {CTL_KERN, KERN_DOMAINNAME};
    char mydomain [DOMAINSIZE];

    int mydomainlength = DOMAINSIZE;

    if (sysctl (name, sizeof (name), mydomain, &mydomainlength, 0,
0))
            perror ("sysctl");
    else
            printf ("domainname : %s \n", mydomain);
}
```

————————————————————————— demosysctl.c —————

The implementations of system calls are located in the following files:

- *kernel/sys.c* for *sethostname, gethostname, setdomainname, reboot* and *uname;*
- *kernel/pritnk.c* for *syslog;*
- *kernel/time.c* and *arch/i386/kernel/time.c* for *adjtimex, gettimeof day, settimeofday, time* and *stime;*
- *kernel/sysctl.c* for *sysctl.*

13.3.1 sethostname, gethostname, setdomain name and uname

These system calls manipulate the variable **system_name** and the **new_utsname** structure defines the type of this variable. The processing of these primitives consists of returning or modifying one or more of the fields of **system_utsname**.

For example, the code of the system call *gethostname* is as follows:

```
asmlinkage int sys_gethostname(char *name, int len)
{
        int 1;

        if (len < 0)
                return -EINVAL;
        if = verify_area(VERIFY_WRITE, name, len);
        if (i)
                return i;
        i = 1+strlen(system_utsname.nodename);
        if (i > len)
                i = len;
        memcpy_tofs(name, system_utsname.nodename, i);

        return 0;
}
```

After carrying out usage checks on the validity of the memory zone pointed to (**verify_area**), this system call boils down to performing a recopy of the filed **system_utsname.nodename** in the memory zone pointed to by **name**. In the case of the call *sethostname*, the inverse operation is carried out: a copy of the contents of the memory pointed to by **name** in **system_utsname.nodename**:

```
memcpy_fromfs(system_utsname.nodename, name, len);
```

13.3.2 reboot

As described above, the system call *reboot* allows the status of the kernel to be changed. In fact, this is composed of two operations: a complete halt of the machine, and restart.

Where it involves simply of stopping the machine (for example using the command *halt*), the operation is performed in two stages:

1. launch of **sys_kill(-1, SIGKILL)**, which has the effect of stopping all processes;
2. launch of **do_exit (0)**, which deletes all resources allocated, the kernel then returns under the control of the scheduler, which causes the machine to halt. In fact, this involves an infinite software loop since it is not possible to perform to hardware halt of the machine in software.

If the machine is to be re-started, *reboot* is actually assisted by calling the function **hard_reset_now** which effectively re-boots the machine. This function depends on the architecture of the machine it is acting on. In the case of the i386 architecture, it is situated in the file *arch/i386/kernel/process.c*.

13.3.3 syslog

The system call *syslog* is implemented in the module *kernel/printk.c*. The buffer containing system messages is a table of characters **log_buf** of size **LOG_BUF_LEN**. Two variables of type unsigned long enable this data table to be managed:

- **log_start**: marks the start of messages in the table;
- **logged_chars**: number of characters stored.

The call syslog next acts upon the buffer, either by duplicating it in the buffer passed as a parameter, or by changing its table indexes.

13.3.4 *gettimeofday, settimeofday, time and stime*

These system calls are responsible for setting or returning dates in the machine. They all use the global variable **xtime** of the type **timeval**.

13.3.4.1 time
This call uses the macro-instruction **CURRENT_TIME**, which returns the field **tv_sec** of the global variable **xtime**. The field registering the microseconds is always null.

13.3.4.2 stime
The system call *stime* just assigns the value passed as a parameter to the field **tv_sec** of **xtime**. It should be noted that is an uninterruptible operation, by virtue of the use of the functions **cli** and **sti**.

13.3.4.3 gettimeofday

In the first instance, this call retrieves data concerning the date and time if requested by the user. The operation is carried out by means of the function do_gettimeofday located in *arch/i386/kernel/time.c*.

This operation is necessary in order to have a precise time-stamp, including microsecond resolution. Linux provides two algorithms to perform this calculation: do_slow_gettimeoffset and do_fast_getttimeoffset. The first is used when these calls are made, and the second is reserved for initialising the operating system.

After carrying out the necessary calculation of the microseconds, the system call simply updates the timeval structure passed as a parameter. The whole of this operation is also uninterruptible.

Finally, the system call updates the global variable sys_tz of type timezone.

13.3.4.4 settimeofday

This operation is much simpler than the previous call. It is carried out in three stages and the parameters are copied into local variables new_tv and new_tz.

Once the variable sys_tz is updated, the time in the machine is recalculated in accordance with the new data for the time zone obtained via the function warp_clock.

Finally, the machine time is updated according to the new time passed as a parameter by means of the function do_settimeofday. This updates the variable **xtime**.

13.3.4.5 sysctl

Although the code for this call is located in the file *kernel/sysctl.c*, its operation is intimately linked to the virtual file system *proc,* which was described in chapter 6, section 6.6.6.

When the machine is initialised, the function sysctl_init creates the tree structure */proc/sys* if the file system */proc* is included in the kernel. This operation is carried out simply by the call register_proc_table. The latter generates the sub-directories *kernel, vm,* and *net.* In addition, the function unregister_proc_table is called when the file system is unmounted.

The creation of the tables needed to manage data is carried out by the function registersysctl_table. The inverse function is realised by carrying out a call to the function unregister_sysctl_table. These calls enable a file set to be added to the file system.

The system call *sysctl* is actually implemented by the function do_sysctl. Firstly, a check on the data passed as a parameter is performed. Then, by means of successive calls to the function parse_table, orders to search for data or to carry out modifications are triggered.

The function looks for the file system entry which corresponds to the data which it is desired to consult or to change. When the entry has been located, the call to the function do_sysctl_strategy carries out the required operations. However, in the case of the file *securelevel,* it is the function do_securelevel_strategy which is called. In fact, changes to the variable **securelevel** are subject to several restrictions, and it is necessary to use a particular function which performs the checks.

This module also monitors the management of inputs and outputs which can be directly carried out on files in the **/proc/sys** tree. These operations are achieved using functions **proc_readsys** and **proc_writesys**. The access rights are checked by means of the function **proc_sys_permission**. In fact, when an input/output on a file in the file system is performed, a call to the function **do_rw_proc** is carried out.

The files are managed in the form of character strings, integer tables, or structures. The functions **proc_dostring**, **proc_dointvec**, and **proc_dointvec_minmax** are responsible for the management of data at the file system level. However, the different types of data are above all managed by the generic functions **sysctl_string** and **sysctl_intvec** as well as by the more specific functions **do_string**, **do_int** and **do_struct**.

Although *sysctl* is linked to the file system *proc*, this call operates without the file system being mounted or compiled. However, the ease of handling data that a virtual file system offers greatly simplifies the process of the developer and user.

13.3.5 adjtimex

The system call *adjtime* is implemented in the file *kernel/time.c*. Detail of the algorithm which calculates the time from the time value contained in the global variable **xtime** as a function of the contents of the variable **timex** passed as a parameter will not be given here because this is outside the scope of the book.

However, the principle is to put into the variable **time_adjust** the time duration with which to readjust the machine clock. This value will be taken into account by the function **update_wall_time_one_tick** of the file *kernel/sched.c*.

This function will update the field **tv_usec** of the variable **xtime**. The regulation of the clock is performed successively in small increments. This call is used only by the daemon *xntpd*.

APPENDIX 1

Phases of a C compilation

In order to quickly present the different stages of a compilation of a C programme, an example programme (having limited use) will be shown undergoing the whole process of compilation:

——————— Exemple.c ————————————————————————————

```
#define MAXIMUM_VOLUME 10

void      main (int argc, char **argv)
{
    int    volume_total = 0;

    volume_total = MAXIMUM_VOLUME *2;
}
```

————————————————————————————————————— Exemple.c ———————

This programme performs a simple multiplication of a constant by two.

1
PRE-PROCESSOR

Running through the pre-processor may be performed in two ways:

- cpp example.c
- gcc -E example.c

The result is clearly the same: *gcc* simply launches the programme *cpp*! The resulting processed file is sent to the normal output.

```
gandalf# cpp example.c

# 1 "example.c"

void main(int argc, char ** argv)
{
        int volume _total = 0;

        volume_total = 10 * 2;
}
```

cpp has a number of interesting options:

- **-Wall**: flags all errors and warnings;
- **-IDIRECTORY**: flags a directory to search for header files;
- **-DMACRO**: defines a macro-instruction;
- **-DMACRO=value**: defines a macro-instruction and its value;
- **-M**: enables dependencies associated with files to be generated.

2
COMPILER

Compilation is a critical phase since it is at this time that the syntax of the code is checked, and the code is translated into assembly language. At this stage of the compilation process, certain optimisations can be realised. To transfer from C code to assembly code, two commands may be used:

- **gcc -S example.c**
- **cc1 example.c**

The assembly code generated will be located in the file *example.s:*

---------- Exemple.s ----------

```
.file "example.cpp"
.version "01.01"
gcc2_compiled.:
.text
.align 16
.globl main
.type main, @function
main:
pushl %ebp
movl %esp, %ebp
subl $4, %esp
movl %0, -4(%ebp)
movl %20, -4(%ebp)
.L1:
movl %ebp, %esp
popl %ebp
ret
.Lfe1:
.size main, .Lfe1-main
.ident "GCC: (GNU) 2.7.2"
```

----------------------------- Exemple.s -----------------------------

The options frequently utilised at this level of compilation are the following:

- **-On**: level of optimisation: from 0 (no optimisation) to 3 (maximum optimisation);
- **-g**: used for debugging: addition to the table of symbols;
- **-Wall**: indicates all errors or warnings.

The code may be recompiled using various optimisation and debugging options in order to observe the differences in the resulting assembler code.

3
ASSEMBLER

The assembly stage consists of transforming assembler code into binary code. This operation is carried out by the programme *as*. The list of different options may be obtained using the option **--help**. Execution proceeds straightforwardly:

```
gandalf as -o example.o example.s
```

4
LINKER

The final stage of the compilation process is the editing of links. This stage gathers together object files in order to generate an executable file, and the operation is performed using the command *ld*. This command is rarely carried out 'manually' since it requires quite a few parameters:

```
gandalf#ld    -m    elf_i386    -dynamic-linker    /lib/ld-linux.so.1    -s
/usr/lib/crt1.o
/usr/lib/crti.o /usr/lib/crtbegin.o -L/usr/lib/gcc-lib/i486-linux/2.7.2
-L/usr/i486-linux/lib example.o lgcc -lc lgcc /usr/lib/crtend.o
/usr/lib/crtn.o

gandalf# ls -al a.out
-rvxr-xr-x    1 dumas      users 2356 Apr 27 13:19 a.out

gandalf# file a.out
a.out: ELF 32-bit LSB executable i386 (386 and above) Version 1
```

The linker combines with the object file *example.o*, a header (*crt1.o, crti.o, crtbegin.o*), a trailer (*ctrend.o, crtn.o*) and the libraries by default (c and gcc) to create an executable file.

The option **-m format** represents the format that the developer wishes to generate. To call up the list of formats that the linker supports, the option -V should be used:

```
gandalf# ld -V
ld version cygnus-2.6 (with BFD 2.6.0.12)
    Supported emulations:
        elfi386
        i386 linux
        i386coff
        m68kelf
        m68klinux
        sun4
        elf32_sparc
        alpha
```

APPENDIX 2

Utilisation of *gdb*

A programme whose objective is to display two instances of a string passed as a parameter have been created to illustrate the functioning of *gdb*. The execution of this programme generates an error:

```
gandalf# occurrences ThisIsAProgrammeThatDoesNotWork
Segmentation fault
```

It is therefore necessary to look for the point which poses the problem. First, it is just necessary to launch *gdb*:

```
gandalf# gdb occurrences
GDB is free software and you are welcome to distribute copies of it
under certain conditions; type "show copying" to see the conditions.
There is absolutely no warranty for GDB; type "show warranty" for
details.
GDB 4.16 (i486-unknown-linux), Copyright 1996 Free Software Foundation,
Inc ..
(gdb)
```

The command interpreter for *gdb* is relatively powerful. For instance, it allows commands, filenames or expressions to be automatically completed after the first few characters have been typed, and allows a list of previous commands entered to be recalled, displayed, and modified or re-used. In addition, it is possible at any time to type the key word **help** to obtain help.

The first command to launch is **run**: this enables the programme to be executed. But this is of little use since it is given that the programme does not work! First, it is necessary to set the argument which will be passed to the programme by means of the key words **set args**. Next a stop point is put on the function **main**. To bring this about, the simplest action is to type **break main**.

Putting this stop point on the function **main** means that, at the time of programme execution, the debugger will stop at the function **main**:

```
(gdb) set args ThisIsAProgrammeThatDoesNotWork
(gdb) break main
Breakpoint 1 at 0x8048596: file coredumped.c, line 12.
(gdb) run
Starting        programme:        /home/dumas/10        à        Book/1        à
Eyrolles/Tools/sources/occurrences
ThisIsAProgrammeThatDoesNotWork

Breakpoint 1, main (argc=2, argv=0xbfffff828) at coredumped.c:12
12      char *new_str=NULL;
(gdb)
```

As anticipated, *gdb* stopped executing at the point in the programme defined by the stop point. The line marked (here line 12), corresponds to the line to be executed. At any time, it is possible to view the programme code by means of the command **list**:

```
(gdb) list
7       static char *doublestr(const char *str);
8       static void usage(const char *prg);
9
10      void main(int argc, char **argv)
11      {
12        char *new_str=NULL;
13
14        if (argc<2)
15           usage(argv[0]);
16
(gdb)
```

After this general overview of the debugger, the source of the problem will be sought. To continue execution, three commands are possible:

- **step**: step by step execution. The programme is executed one line at a time, and all functions met are examined;
- **next**: as above, except that the functions are not examined;
- **continue**: executes the programme until the end or until the next stop point.

By carrying out the operation **step** several times, the cursor arrives at the function
doublestr:

```
(gdb) step
14      if (argc<2)
(gdb) s
17      new_str = doublestr(argv[1]);
(gdb) s
doublestr (str=0xbffff947 "ThisIsAProgrammeThatDoesNotWork")
      at coredumped.c:27
27      char *ret_str = NULL;
(gdb) s
28      char *digit_str - NULL;
(gdb) s
32      if (str == NULL)
(gdb) s
35      if ((digit_str = malloc(sizeof(char)))==NULL)
(gdb) s
38      new-length = strlen(str)*2 + strlen(SEPARATOR);
(gdb) s
39      if ((ret_str = malloc(sizeof(char)*new_length))==NULL
(gdb) s
45      sprintf(digit_str,ö(%d)ö, new_length;
(gdb)
```

It is noteworthy that *gdb* indicates the parameters passed to the function.

The attentive reader has probably detected the error, in line 35. A memory zone
of the size of one character is allocated, but this zone is assigned to a character
string made up of a much larger number of characters. To correct this code, all
that is needed is to change the source code and to re-launch the compilation.

It is also possible to find out the value of a variable, the contents of structure
and the contents of a string based on its pointer. These operations can be
performed in a very simple way using the **print** command:

```
(gdb) print new-length
$1 = 68
(gdb) print str
$2 = 0xbffff947 "ThisIsAProgrammeThatDoesNotWork"
(gdb) print *str
$3 = 67 æCÆ
(gdb)
```

Finally, the last operation concerning the debugger consists of finding the point in the list where the function calls are located. This operation, is performed by the command **where**, or **backtrace**:

```
(gdb) where
#0    doublestr  (str=0xbfff947 ôThisIsAProgrammeThatDoesNotWorkö)
        at coredumped.c:46
#1    0x80485bf inmain (argc=2, argv=0xbffff828) at coredumped.c:17
#2    0x8048544 in _crt_dummy__ ()
(gdb) backtrace
#0    doublestr (str=0xbffff947 ôThisIsAProgrammeThatDoesNotWorkö)
        at coredumped.c:46
#1    0x80485bf inmain (argc=2, argv=0xbffff828) at coredumped.c:17
#2    0x8048544 in __crt_dummy__()
```

This command provides the list of different calls which have been carried out during the debugging, with, for each one, the name of the file in which the function, the line and the list of different parameters are located.

APPENDIX 3

Utilisation of *make*

When launched, *make* uses the file *makefile* or *Makefile* situated in the current directory. It analyses its contents and launches the commands indicated.

This tool is very useful since it enables, amongst other things, to avoid recompiling all but the necessary code.

The example which illustrates this section is also referred to in Appendix 4. It makes use of several files:

- *complex.c*: module implementing calculations on complex numbers;
- *complex.h*: interface to prototypes of module *complex.c*;
- *draw.c*: module representing complex numbers graphically;
- *draw.h*: interface to prototypes of module *draw.c*;
- *main.c*: principal file.

The associated file *Makefile* is then the following:

——————— Makefile ———————————

```
# Makefile for complex numbers
CC=gcc
RM=/bin/rm

# Compilation flags
CFLAGS=-g

# Files
```

```
SRC=complex.c draw.c main.c
OBJ=$(SRC:.c=.o)

PROG=complex
LIB=-lm
# Generation rules
$(PROG) : $(OBJ)
    $(CC) $(CFLAGS) $(OBJ) -o $(PROG) $(LIB)

# Let there be cleanliness!
clean:
    $(RM) -f $(OBJ) $(PROG)

# Dependencies
complex.0   : complex.c complex.h
draw.o      : draw.c draw.h complex.h
main.c      : main.c draw.h complex.h
```

——————————————————————————————————— Makefile ———————————————

The first part of this file is made up of various declarations lending a certain flexibility of use in the event, for example, of a need to change the compiler. Next, the options which will need to be used at compilation time are defined. Here, it involves the option **-g** which enables eventual errors to be debugged.

Next comes the enumeration of the different files needing to be compiled. The variable **OBJ** is based on a rule which avoids having to enumerate the set of object files on the assumption that it concerns the same names as for the source files except for the extensions.

The final part is the rule for creating executables. This rule is met only if all the object files have been generated. At the end of the file are located the dependencies which will enable *make* to only compile the modified files.

For example, suppose that all the object files have been generated, but that since the last compilation, a developer has modified the file *draw.h*. At the next compilation, only certain files will be recompiled:

```
gandalf# make
gcc -g -c draw.c -o draw.o
gcc -g -c main.c -o main.o
gcc -g complex.o draw.o main.o -o complex -lm
```

By virtue of the definition of dependencies, the file *complex.c* is not recompiled. In order to find out the dependencies of a programme, it is simply necessary to launch the **command gcc -MM draw.c**. This then produces a list of header files used by this module.

APPENDIX 4

Management of libraries

It may become necessary to look for a library: "Which library defines the function **sin**?" This question has been asked by all developers. One solution is to use the program *nm*. This program gives the list of symbols referred to in the library. This works whether the library is static or dynamic.

For example, a check should be made that **sin** is in the mathematical library:

```
gandalf# nm -P /lib/libm.so.5  |  grep sin
            U __isinf
            U __isinfl
00000000000016d0   T  asin
000000000000174c   T  asinh
0000000000001800   T  asinhl
00000000000018b4   T  asin
0000000000005354   T  sin
0000000000005378   T  sinh
00000000000053d8   T  sinhl
0000000000005438   T  sinl
```

The result is organised around three columns:

- The address at which the function in the library is located, if it is defined. In the case where it is merely a call, or a definition of an external function, no address is inserted. Address resolution is then performed dynamically at loading time.
- A letter indicating the type of symbol definition:

- **U**: undefined symbol;
- **W**: symbol defined, but which may be 'overloaded'. This allows it to define its own functions to replace those of the library;
- **T**: symbol defined normally.
- Name of a symbol.

2

STATIC LIBRARIES

The method of creating a static library is the same whether it is for ELF format or for a.out. It is necessary in the first instance to generate object files, and following this, the programs *ar* or *ranlib* do the rest! It should be noted that in certain systems (like Solaris), the command *ranlib* does not exist. In Linux, this command is equivalent to **as -s**.

There follows below an example of the creation of a library for handling complex numbers:

```
gandalf# gcc -c complex.c -o complex.o
gandalf# ar cru libcomplex.a complex.o
gandalf# ranlib libcomplex.a
```

ar possesses an impressive number of parameters, and the relevant section in the manual details each of these options well. The options used in this example enable the library having the name **libcomplex.a** to be created based on specified object files.

The command *runlib* which follows library generation enables the library index to be generated. To call up this index (which gathers together the functions and the variables exported), it is required to do the following:

```
gandalf# nm -s libcomplex.a

Archive index:
create_complex in complex.o
delete_complex in complex.o
sum_complex in complex.o
multiply_complex in complex.o
real_complex in complex.o
imaginary_complex in complex.o
sum_complex in complex.o
algebraic_complex in complex.o
conjugate_complex in complex.o
...
```

However, the prototype is not given, and it is therefore necessary to consult the header file to be able to develop this index.

The generation of shred libraries of the type a.out has always been a difficult operation. Since this format has been abandoned, a description of the format will not be given here, but all operations are described completely in [Engel and Youngdale, 1992].

The great advance brought by ELF libraries has been the ability to generate dynamic shared libraries. In order to create a dynamic library, it is necessary to compile different modules by adding the option **-fPIC**, and following this, the dynamic library is generated by means of link edits.

The following example shows the generation of a complex number library:

```
gandalf# gcc -c -fPIC complex.c -o complex.o
gandalf# gcc -shared -Wl, -soname, libcomplex.so.1-o libcomplex.so.1.0
complex.o
```

Each of the options is necessary and fulfils a particular role:

- **-shared**: specifies to the link editor that it should create a dynamic library;
- **-Wl**: enables particular parameters to be passed to the link editor;
- **-soname**: allows the 'proper' name of the library to be specified.

Dynamic libraries in fact have two names:

- the proper name: this is recorded in the library and is searched for by the dynamic loader when a program is run;
- the physical name: its use is limited to access paths.

This distinction may appear superfluous, but it allows the co-existence of several different versions of the same library on the same system.

The name of a dynamic library should conform to the form:

> lib*name*.**so**.*major.minor*

A supplementary number may be added later after the minor number.

In the previous example, the physical name of the library is **libcomplex.so.1.0**, and its proper name is **libcomplex.so.1**. If this library is added to a standard directory (for example in **/usr/lib**), the program *ldconfig* creates a symbolic link **libcomplex.so.1** → **libcomplex.so.1.0** in order that the appropriate image is found when the program is run. Finally, a link **libcomplex.so** needs to be created to the new version.

When a developer corrects errors in the library, or indeed when he adds new functions (for any modification which does not affect the execution of programs which already exist), it is necessary to reconstruct the library. It is sufficient to increment the minor number. When the developer carries out modifications which alter the course of existing programs, the major number of the library **libcomplex.so.1.0** must be incremented, and it must be given the proper name **libcomplex.so.2**. Finally, he must recreate the link **libcomplex.so** to the new version.

5
DYNAMIC LOADING OF LIBRARIES

One of the advantages which the ELF format brings is the ability to specify dynamic loading of libraries, and their unloading when the operation is terminated. Numerous programs such as *perl* and *Java* make active use of them.

This functionality necessitates the use of the library **libdl**, and the header file **<dlfcn.h>**. The whole principle of dynamic loading is detailed in [Lu, 1995].

The example below illustrates this characteristic:

──────── dltest.c ────────

```
#include <dlfcn.h>
#include <stdio.h>

#ifndef PI
#define PI        3.14159265358979323846
#endif

typedef  double  (*fun_t) (double);

void              main (int argc, char **argv)
{
    void          *ptr = NULL;
    char          *nombib = "libm.so";
    char          *function = "cos";
    fun_t         fun = NULL;
    double        result = 0;

/*  dynamic loading of the library */
if ((ptr = dlopen (nombib, RTLD_LAZY)) == NULL)  {
    fprintf (stderr, "dlopen(%s) -> %s \n", nombib, dlerror ());
    exit (1);
}
/* Retrieval of the function address */
if ((fun = (fun_t) dlsym (ptr, function))  == NULL)  {
    fprintf (stderr, "dlsym(%s) -> %s \n", function, dlerror ());
    exit (1);
}
printf (" Call of %s in %s \n", function, nombib);
```

```
    result = (*fun) (( double) PI / 4;

    dlclose (ptr);

    printf ("Result : %f \n", result);
    }
```

———————————————————————— dltest.c ————————

The compilation of this program, whose only aim is to carry out the operation $\cos \dfrac{\pi}{4}$, gives:

```
gandalf# gcc -c -g -Wall dltest.c -o dltest.o
gandalf# gcc -g dltest.o -o dltest -ldl
gandalf# ldd dltest
        libdl.so.1 => /lib/libdl.so.1.7.14
        libc.so.5 => /lib/libc.so.5.3.9
gandalf# ./dltest
  Call Cos in libm.so
  Result :  0.707107
```

The program is not linked to the mathematical library, but it is the function cos of the mathematical library that is called.

The prototypes of these functions are as follows:

```
#include <dlfcn.h>

void *dlopen (const char *filename, int flag);

const char *dlerror (void);

void *dlsym (void *handle, char *symbol);

int dlclose (void *handle(;
```

The function **dlopen** has as its second argument an option which specifies the resolution mode of the symbols. This option gives the three following choices:

- when loading, only the resolution of undefined symbols is carried out if possible (RTLD_LAZY), or;
- all of the symbols are resolved before the end of the call (**RTLD_NOW**), and;
- if one symbol is not resolved, the call fails.

The function **dlsym** enables a *handler* to be retrieved for the required function. Finally, the function **dlclose** enables a dynamic library to be unloaded, if no other application is using it. This means that, after **dlclose**, any call to a function from this library by a program will lead to the halting of that program.

REFERENCES

Aho A, Sethi R, Ullman, J. *Compilers,* Addison - Wesley, 1986.

Unix SYSTEM V – Reference Manual of the Management System, Masson – AT&T, 1989.

Bach M J. *The Design of the Unix Operating System*, Prentice Hall International, 1986.

Barlow, D. *GCC How to,* Technical Report, Linux Documentation Project, February 1996.

Beck M et al. *Linux Kernel Internals*, Addison-Wesley, 1996.

Card R, Ts'o T, Tweedie S. *Design and Implementation of the Second Extended Filesystem,* Proceedings of the Linux Dutch Symposium, December 1994, pp34–51.

Dijkstra E W. *Cooperating sequential processes*, Technical Report, EWD-123, Technological University, Eindhoven, The Netherlands, 1965.

Dumas E *et al, Guide du ROOTard pour Linux,* Technical Report, September 1997.
http://www.freenix.fr/linux/Guide
ftp.lip6.fr://pub/linux/french/docs/GRL

Ellis M, Stroustrup B. *The Annotated C++ Reference Manual*, Addison-Wesley, 1990.

Engel D, Youngdale E. *Using DLL Tools with Linux*, Technical Report, December 1992. [ftp://tsx-11.mit.edu/pub/linux/packages/GCC/src/toos-2.17.tar.gz]

Froidevaux C, Gaudel M-C, Soria M. *Types de données et algorithms (Data and algorithm types)*, Ediscience International, 1993.

Gallmeister B. *Posix 4: Programming for the real world*, O'Reilly & Associates, 1993.

Goodheart B, Cox J. *The Magic Garden Explained: The Internals of UNIX System V Release 4*, Prentice Hall, 1994.

Kernighan B W, Ritchie D M. *The C Programming Language, 2nd Edition*, Prentice Hall, 1988.

Kirch O. *Network Administration Guide*, O'Reilly & Associates, 1995.

Kleiman S *Vnodes: An architecture for Multiple File System Types in Sun UNIX*, Proc. Summer USENIX Conf, , June 1986, pp260–69

Knowlton K C. *A Fast Storage Allocator*, Communications of the ACM, 8(10), October 1965, pp623–5

Lewine D. *POSIX Programmer's Guide*, O'Reilly & Associates, 1991.

Lu X, *From the Programmer's Perspective*, Technical Report, Nynex Science and Technology, Inc, May 1995.

McKusick M, *et al, A Fast File System for UNIX*, ACM Transactions on Computer Systems, 2(3) pp181-197, Aug. 1984.

McKusick M, *et al, The Design and Implementation of the 4.4 BSD UNIX Operating System*, Addison Wesley, 1996.

Mills D. *RFC1305. Technical Report, Network Time Protocol (Version 3)– Specification, Implementation and Analysis*, University of Delaware, 1992.

Moreno J-M. *UNIX Administration*, Ediscience International, 1995.

Silberschatz A, Calvin P,. *Operating System Concepts* 4thEd, Addison–Wesley, , 1994.

Stallman R, McGrath R. *Gnu make*, Technical Report, Documentation GNU, April 1995.

Stallman R and Cygnus support, *Debugging with GDB*, Technical Report, Documentation GNU, January 1994.

Stallman R, *Using and Porting GNU CC*, Technical Report, Documentation GNU, November 1995.

Storner H. *Kerneld Mini-How to*, Technical Report, Linux Documentation, June 1996.

Tanenbaum A. *Operating Systems: Design and Implementation*, Prentice Hall, 1987.

TIS, *Executable and Linkable Format (ELF)*, Technical Report, 1993.
[ftp://ftp.ibp.fr/pub/linux/tsx-11/packages/GCC/ELF.doc.tar.gz]

Vahalia U. *Unix Internals: The New Frontiers*, Prentice Hall, 1996.

Welsh M, Kaufman L. *Le systeme Linux (The Linux system)* 1st ed, O'Reilly & Associates, 1995.

Welsh M, Kauffman L. *Running Linux, 2nd Edition*, O'Reilly & Associates, 1997.

INDEX

I

510   *Index*

kernel variables
continued
def_blk_fops, 257
def_chr_fops, 257
default_exec_
domain, 81
dev_tty_driver,
360
dma_chan_busy,
262
dqstats, 202, 204,
228
dquot_operations,
206
dquot_wait, 202,
204
event, 207
exec_domains, 81
ext2_sops, 236
file_lock_table,
209
file_private_mmap
319
file_shared_mmap
319
file_systems, 176,
196, 197
first_dquot, 202
first_file, 181, 200
first_inode, 179,
197, 198
free_area, 294
free_list, 211
fs_fops, 264
hash_table, 187,
197, 202, 206, 211
hung_up_tty_fops,
363
init_task, 74
initrd_end, 265
initrd_fops, 265

initrd_start, 264
inode_wait, 197,
199, 200
jiffies, 80, 85, 212,
217
keypres_wait, 363
last_pid, 85, 86
level1_cache, 187
level1_dcache,
206
level1_head, 187,
206
level2_cache, 187
level2_dcache,
206
level2_head, 187,
206
log_buf, 470
log_start, 470
logged_chars, 470
lp_fops, 268
lp_table, 266, 267
lru_list, 211
max_files, 200
max_inodes, 197
mem_map, 210,
306
module_list, 445,
446
mru_vfsmnt, 195
msgque, 424
need_resched,
266
nr_buffers, 211
nr_buffers_size,
211
nr_buffers_type,
211
nr_dquots, 203
nr_file, 200
nr_files, 201
nr_free_dquots,
203, 204

nr_free_inodes,
197, 198, 200
nr_free_quots,
202
nr_hash, 211
nr_inodes, 197,
198
nr_quots, 202
nr_running, 85
nr_tasks, 85
page_hash_table,
317
pipe_inode_
operations, 378
proc_root, 246
pty_state, 366
random_wait, 260
rd_blocksizes,
263, 265
rd_length, 263,
265
rdwr_fifo_fops,
378
reuse_list, 211-213
ROOT_DEV, 195
secure_level, 472
shm_segs, 430
super_blocks,
176, 196, 197, 224
swap_info, 320
swap_list, 320
symbol_table, 445
sys_call_table, 31
sys_tz, 471
system_utsname,
469
task, 74, 85, 86,
88, 245, 246
time_adjust, 472
timer_head, 80
total_forks, 85
tty_fops, 362
tty_ldisc_N_TTY,